ISBN 978-1-5282-6850-9
PIBN 10075386

c

THE
CELTIC REVIEW

II I

PUBLISHED QUARTERLY

CONSULTING EDITOR : PROFESSOR MACKINNON

ACTING EDITOR : MISS E. C. CARMICHAEL

VOLUME II

JULY 1905 TO APRIL 1906

EDINBURGH: NORMAN MACLEOD, 25 GEORGE IV. BRIDGE

LONDON: DAVID NUTT, 57-59 LONG ACRE, W.C.

DUBLIN: HODGES, FIGGIS & CO., LTD., 104 GRAFTON ST.

Edinburgh : T. and A. Constable, Printers to His Majesty

CONTENTS

CONTENTS

THE CELTIC REVIEW

JULY 15, 1905

THE FIONN SAGA

(Continued from vol. i. *p.* 366.)

GEORGE HENDERSON, M.A., B.Litt., PH.D.

THE CAMPBELL OF ISLAY RECENSION *(continued)*

The Origin of the Feinne

THERE was a great war between the Lochlanners (Scandinavians) and the Irish about Scotland, and the tribute which the Scandinavians had laid upon Ireland and Scotland. The cess was hard to bear, and grievous to the Irish king.

They were great strong men, and they used to come in summer and harvest, eating and spoiling all that the people of these lands were storing up for another year, and so they had great great wars.

There was a king in Ireland, and he sent for his adviser (*comhairliche*). In these times they had no Parliament as now, but counsellors who were wise men. 'I wish,' said the Irish king, 'to find a way to drive back these Scandinavians.' 'That,' said the counsellor, 'will not grow in a day, but take wise counsel and it will grow in time. Gather,' said he, the counsellor who was wise, 'the biggest men and the biggest women that you can find, in all Ireland, marry them to each other, and the seventh generation will settle the matter if you marry the offspring of these picked men and women.'

The counsel pleased the Irish king, whose name was not preserved, but as shown below, it probably was Art or another, the high king of Ireland.

So all Ireland was searched for big men and women, and a hundred of each were found and married.

The first race seemed to be too weak, so they married the biggest to each other without regard to kindred, only they did not marry brothers to sisters. The second race were not strong enough, so they chose the biggest and tried again.

The third race grew stronger, and the fourth stronger still. But when it came to the seventh generation, the men were so great and terrible, that they called them the *Fiantaichean*. They are called by some *daoine fiadhaich*, 'wild or terrible men.' They had yellow hair, as it is said in the lay of the *Muileartach* :—

> *Fuath na arrachd cha d' theid as*
> *Bho' n Fhéinn àluinn fhalt-bhuidhe.*
>
> Ghost nor bogle will not escape
> From the beauteous yellow-haired Feinne.

'I never heard of a minister or priest among them; they did nothing but hunt and fight' (W. Robertson of Tobermory).

There were 150 of that kind of people came to them from France and Spain and other realms. If they were strong, big, stout men, they took them under their flags, and the band was called ' An Fhéinn.' They were in Ireland and all about these islands. Here in S. Uist are places which we call ' *Sorrachd Choire Fhinn.*' Up yonder on the hillside are four great stones upon which they set their great kettle, and there are plenty of other places of the same kind.[1]

The standing stones which you may see in these islands we call *Ord Mhaoraich* or *Ord Bhārnaich*, bait hammers or limpet hammers. People say that they used these to knock off limpets and pound shells, as we use stones now ; but that I do not believe. They say that one of them threw one from the shore up to the hillside near the north end of South Uist, but that cannot be true. They were hunters only ; they went through moors and wastes with tents and booths to

---

[1] The square is made with four large flat stones on edge, the sides being set N.S.E.W., five feet by three, inside the oblong. Near this monument are several fallen *menhir*, tall standing stones.

sleep in, and they had great dogs. They killed deer and wild boars and lived upon them. When their great terrible stout warriors first came over to Alba from Ireland, the Scandinavians saw them and fled to their ships for fear. And that is the way in which the Fēinn [1] (Fayne) began.

'I,' said William Robertson at Tobermory, 16th September 1870, 'was in a place in this Island of Mull, below Cille Chonain, where I was working at making a road. I took out a man's bones. The cist in which the man lay was made of stones, and the bones were left there. The smith who was with us was a big man. He tried on the jaw bone, and it came down over his head. The bones of the legs and arms were as long as my stick. I saw them with my eyes. A dozen of men were there and saw them. No horse ever had such bones. My hand open would go into the bone. The smith was big, but the jawbone came down over his whole head, below his chin. The teeth were in. I am quite sure that these were the bones of a man.'

Tor Nam Fian is the name of a hill above the place where I found the bones : the Fian's mound. From that I am sure that such men were. There is a little of *Obair Na Feinne* the work of the Fēinn there, if one might believe that they did it. A stone is there called *an t-Ord Maoraich,* 'the bait hammer.' It is as broad as this table. But some say that it is the limpet hammer which the Feinne used, but that cannot be true. The bones which I found prove that. The men could not have worked such a stone as that; no, nor a man four times as big. They were strong men who guarded the realm. They were bred from big men and big women selected for the purpose. Their chief foes were '*Na Lochlannaich,*' the people of Lochlann, but people came upon them from many other places, as we learn from the lays. There were twelve *teaghlachs*, families in Fionn's household, and twelve rooms to each household, and a man and five score about each

---

[1] ['Fenians' is the form Campbell uses, but this term is not free from danger of confusion with a movement of our own times.]

fire (14,544). You might ask many, and few could tell where all are gone; none ever knew where they went. No one has any knowledge of their death, except of those who were slain in the battles, such as Goll, Oscar, Diarmaid, and others. Fionn was never slain; he is with the rest. Caoilte was not killed; Oisein (Ossian) was the last of the Feinne, and he it was who told Padruig (St. Patrick) about the Feinne long afterwards. They all went away in one day, as it is said by Oisein to Padruig in the Lay of the *Muileartach*.

> ‘Chunnacas sealladh nach fhacas riamh
> Bho bàs na Féinne ri aon latha :
> Rachadh thromh tholladh na sleagh
> Na corran thromh dhriom Osgair.’

That says that the Fēinne all died in one day.

> ‘A sight was seen that never was seen
> Since the death of the Feinne in one day :
> Through the spear wounds the quill-dressings [1] went
> Through the back of Osgar.’

They are *fo gheasaibh* under spells, undoubtedly. Did not a man see them in Dumbarton rock? He put his hand to a bell and they rose on their elbows. He said, ‘It is not time,’ and there he left them resting on their elbows.[2]

The Story of Cumal the Father of Fionn

Now the Feinne or Fian or Fiantaichean were all of one kindred and blood, and they did not know who was chief. So they sought amongst themselves for the man of the best head. Cumal was best at answering questions, and, as he had king's blood in his veins, they made him king of the Feinn. They came over here to Alba, and they drove out the Scandinavians, who fled to sea. When Alba was won, one said to the other, ‘Let us go back to Ireland.’

But Cumal said, ‘No. I say that if you reach Ireland

---

[1] [The point-dressings of the poisoned barbed arrow; the word occurs in :—

> ‘Eadar corran a gàine ’s an smeoirn.
> *Mairi nighean Alasdair Ruaidh.*’

[2] Many versions exist of this incident, which may be appropriately given later on.]

the king would rather see you burned on a hill than face you. He could not keep you there. Better keep the realm you have won; make your schemes and plans; make a king of the best man, and let us stay where we are.' Now Cumal was best and biggest, and had the best head, and so they chose him to be *Rìgh Na Fèinne*. They sent word (wrote a letter) to the King of Ireland, and told him that they meant to keep the realm. The king wished that no one had ever thought of them. He wrote a letter to the king of Lochlann, and he said: 'Come over and we will try if we cannot make some plan to get rid of Cumal and his warriors.' Cumal would let neither Irishman nor Scandinavian into Scotland, but himself only and his warriors.

There was a man in the Fèinn whose name was Arc[1] Dubh (*i.e.* Black-Black). He committed a grievous crime, and he was put out of the Fèinn. He went to the king in Ireland and sought service. 'What can you do?' said the Irish king. 'I can fight a hundred' (literally, the battle of a hundred is on my hand), said the warrior, 'for the least man in the Fèinn could fight a hundred, but I need food to match' (*i.e.* in proportion). 'I won't feed you,' said the king; 'I cannot afford it.'

Then they held a long argument.

'Do you know any way of keeping yourself?'

'I can fish,' said the black warrior.

'I,' said the king, 'have the best river in all these realms, Eas Ruadh (Assaroe, near Ballyshannon in Sligo): go and get married and be there. Two-thirds of the fish you catch shall be mine. One-third shall be yours and wages to boot, and so you may keep yourself. Will you take that offer?'

'I will take it,' said Arc Dubh, and so he was called the king's fisherman.

It is not told here, but elsewhere it is said that Arc Dubh was the fisher of Conn of the Hundred Fights.

[1] [*Cf.* Hagen who slew Siegfried; many reciters give the Gaelic form as Āchda Dubh, among whom was Robertson, Tobermory, one of Campbell's seanachies, and Āchda may be a folk-loan from Norse even if this character were not represented in their literature monuments.]

When the Irish king got Cumal's letter he wrote to the king of Lochlann, and he came in a long ship (long fhad), the king and his son, to Ireland. The Irish king had his hands spread to meet and welcome him because of the Fēinne. The two kings met and fell a-talking of the Fēinne.

'They say that none in this world are like them,' said the Scandinavian king. 'I should like to see them.'

'I have one of them here,' said the Irish king, 'and he will soon come with fish.'

Now all these Fēinne had secrets (*diamhaireachd*) that none could know but themselves. They were sworn not to reveal these secret powers. In the morning early came Arc Dubh to the palace before the Scandinavian king was up. As soon as he heard that the warrior had come he leaped up and came out half dressed. 'Is this a Fiantaiche?' said he.

'That style and title is lost,' said the fisher; 'perhaps it was my own fault, but I was in the Fēinn once.'

'If all the rest are like you,' said the king, 'they are a wonderful and a terrible people.'

'If you saw them,' said the fisher, 'you might well say that.'

'What tale can you tell of them?' said the king of Lochlann.

'I can tell this,' said the fisher. 'There is one amongst them, their king, who is called Cumal. If all there ever were or have come or that will come were to go against him, he would come out through them with his sword.'

'Will he be so till death comes to seek him?' said the king, 'or can he be slain?'

'I know how he can be slain,' said the fisher.

'Then tell me,' said the king.

'No,' said the fisher. 'I have sworn not to tell that secret.'

'If you will not tell,' said the king, 'I will slay you.'

'It is easier to tell than to die,' said Arc Dubh. 'Though I have sworn, I may break my oaths. His death is in his own sword, *Mac a Luinne*, and that will only slay him in the arms of his wife.'

Then said the king, 'I have the most beautiful daughter that ever the sun shone upon, the very finest drop-of-blood that ever trod on ground. I will send for her, and Cumal shall marry her, and then we may find means to slay him here.'

'That you shall do,' said the king of Ireland. 'Do you send your long ship for the girl, and I will invite (write to) Cumal, and we will make a wedding here and slay him.'

Then the traitor cherished a plan and told it to the king. So they wrote a treacherous letter to Cumal to come from Alba to Eirinn to a feast, and they sent a long ship to Lochlann for the king's daughter. The king of Lochlann was there and his son was with him, and another son of his was there also, and there too was the king of Ireland in the palace, and Cumal came, and there was feasting and joy.

The thing was so that the long ship arrived, and there was great joy in the palace about the king's daughter, and a great ball.

But when Cumal, who was as it were a king in Scotland, saw the king's daughter, he fell in heavy love with her. They danced and feasted for four or five nights, and because Cumal was a grand, tall, handsome, stately man, the king's daughter fell in love with him.

Then the king of Lochlann said to Cumal: 'Will you marry my daughter this very night?'

Cumal was willing and the king's daughter was overjoyed, and so they were married that very hour on the spot. Then all the company went to put the bride to bed, and they took the couple through seven doors and seven rooms and left them there. They went out and locked the seven doors as they went, but Arc Dubh was hid in the inner room under the floor, according to the scheme which he had made with the two kings. Cumal laid his sword on the board by the bedside. But when all was still the black traitor with his spear crept out from under the floor and took *Mac A Luinn*, the sword, from the table and laid it on Cumal's neck as he slept in the arms of his bride, and the weight of the sword, that never left a shred after a blow, took off the hero's head.

His bride did not know it, but when she awoke and found her husband dead in her arms she took to sorrow and woe and heartbreaking. She cried 'Murder!' and the traitor cried 'Murder!' and the company opened all the seven doors and came in and found Cumal slain and his bride lamenting and beating her palms. But the traitor took *Mac A Luinn*, the sword, and since he had the sword, Bran, Cumal's great hound, followed him. He went home to Eas Ruadh to his wife, and there he stayed as the king's fisherman, and that is the way in which Cumal was slain by one of his own men, Arc Dubh, the black-haired traitor who was turned out of the Fēinn for his crimes.

It is said Fionn's father was slain by his (Fionn's) grandfather, and so he was by the treacherous schemes of the kings of Lochlann and Eirinn.

It seems from old authorities that the place was in Munster of the Red Towers, or great red 'Mowin' (Dean of Lismore's Book, English 88, Gaelic 64, 65). Some of the slayers were of the Clanna Morna, and the first who struck a spear into Cumal was Garradh or Zarry Mac Morna. He told the tale to Fionn as a youth, at a hunting match in the days of Cuchulainn, in the presence of the character who speaks in the ballad. Garry says that Cumal oppressed his tribe, that he drove some to Scotland, some to Lochlann, some to White Greece. After sixteen years they came back to Eirinn, and there slew 1600 men in battle. They took their castles, and slew all that remained of the race of Cumal upon a hill. They surrounded a house in Munster where Cumal was. They all rushed in and struck spears into the body of Cumal,—Garry first. He says:—

16

'We made a rush that was not slow
To the house in which was Cumal;
We made deep wounds each one
With our spears in the body of Cumal.

17

'Although I was born
At the time when Cumal was slain, ·

For these deeds we 'll then
Avenge them.
We were a day
(A day that we were).'

In Irish history the fight is called the Battle of Cnucha.[1]

[1] *Fotha Catha Cnucha* = THE CAUSE OF THE BATTLE OF CNUCHA
(Hennessey's Trans. from LU.).

When Cathair Mōr, son of Fedelmith Fir-urglais, son of Cormac Gelta-gaith, was
in the kingship of Teamhair, and Conn Cēd-chathach in Cenandos in (the) rigdomna's
land (= in the land of the King of the World), Cathair had a celebrated druid, to wit,
Nuada, son of Achi, son of Dathi, son of Brocan, son of Fintan of Tuath-dathi in
Brega. The druid was soliciting land in Laigen from Cathair ; for he knew that it
was in Laigen his successorship would be.

Cathair gave him his choice of land. The land the druid chose was Almu.

She that was wife to Nuadha was Almu, daughter of Becan.

A *dūn* was built by the druid then in Almu, and *alamu* was rubbed to its wall,
until it was all white ; and perhaps it was from that (the name) 'Almu' was applied
to it ; of which was said :—

'All-white is the dūn of battle renown ;
As if it had received the lime of Ireland
From the *alamu* which he gave to the house ;
Hence it is that "Almu" is applied to Almu.'

Nuada's wife, Almu, was entreating that her name might be given to the hill, and
that request was granted to her, to wit, that her name should be upon the hill, for it
was in it that she was buried afterwards : of which was said :—

'Alm—beautiful was the woman !—
Wife of Nuadha the great, son of Achi.
She entreated—the division was just—
That her name (should be) on the perfect hill.'

Nuadha had a distinguished son, to wit, Tadhg, son of Nuadhu. Rāiriu, daughter
of Dond-duma, was his wife. A celebrated druid, also, was Tadg.

Death came to Nuada (= Nuada died), and he left his dūn, as it was, to his son ;
and it is Tadg that was druid to Cathair in the place of his father.

Rāiriu bore a daughter to Tadhg, *i.e.* Murni Muncaim (= Morneen of the fair
neck), her name.

This maiden grew up in great beauty, so that the sons of the kings and mighty
lords of Ireland were wont to be courting her.

Cumall, son of Trenmor, king-warrior of Ireland, was then in the service of Cond
(= Bōi dana cummal mac trenmóir rīg fennid herend fri lāimh cuind). He also, like
every other person, was demanding the maiden. Nuada gave him a refusal, for he
knew that it was on account of him (Cumall) he would have to leave Almu.

The same was mother to Cumall and to Cond's father, to wit, Fedelmid Rechtaide.

Cumall comes, however, and takes Murni by force, in elopement with him, since
she had not been given to him. Tadg comes to Cond, and relates to him his profana-
tion by Cumall, and he began to incite Cond and to reproach him.

About 1760 Fletcher got a version of the same ballad which is in the Advocates' Library.

'SAID FIONN TO GARRADH.

'Since I was not born at the time, how did you slay Cumal ?'

Cumal was the father of Fionn.

'SAID GARRA.

1

' It was Cumal who made our reproach,
'Twas he made our great hurting ;
[Far into exile Cumal hath set us
Out on the bounds of the [alien].

2

' A branch of us went to Albin,
And a branch to the Black Lochlann (*i.e.* Denmark),
And the third branch set out to Greece,
On the bounds of the Unknown.

Cond despatches messengers to Cumall, and ordered him to leave Ireland or to restore his daughter to Tadg. Cumall said he would not give her ; but everything he would give and not the woman (= he would give everything but not the woman). Cond sent his soldiers, and Urgrend, son of Lugaid Corr, king of Luagni, and Daire Dere, son of Eochaid, and his son Aed (who was afterwards called Goll), to attack Cumall. Cumall assembles his army against them, and the battle of Cnucha is fought between them, and Cumall is slain there, and a slaughter of his people is effected.

Cumall fell by Goll, son of Morna. Luchet wounded Goll in his eye, so that he destroyed his eye. And hence it is that the name 'Goll' attached to him ; whereof was said :—

' Aed was the name of Daire's son,
Until Luchet of fame wounded him ;
Since the heavy lance wounded him,
Therefore, he has been called Goll.'

Goll killed Luchet. It is for that reason, moreover, that a hereditary feud existed between the sons of Morna and Find.

Dairi had two names, to wit, Morna and Dairi.

Muirni went, after that, to Cond ; for her father rejected her, and did not let her (come) to him, because she was pregnant ; and he said to his people to burn her. And, nevertheless, he dared not compass her destruction against Cond

The girl was asking of Cond how she should act. Cond said : 'Go,' said he, 'to Fiacall, son of Concend, to Temhair-Mairci, and let thy delivery be effected there' (for a sister to Cumall was Fiacall's wife, Bodball Bendron).

Condla, Cond's servant, went with her, to escort her, until she came to Fiacall's house, to Tembair-Mairci. Welcome was given to the girl there ; and her arrival

3

'The first day that we were
On the turf of Erin of blue blades,
He slew of us and by our counting
Seventeen hundred on one small plain.

4

'There were slain of the tribe of Morna,
Of our Fianna and of our Lords;
And there he made a tower of our bones
In witness of the Feinne.

5

''Twas he who made our hearts heavy,
Our heads to be in the deepest glens.'

---

there was good. The girl was delivered afterwards, and bare a son ; and Demni was given as a name to him.

The boy is nursed by them, after that, until he was capable of committing plunder on every one who was an enemy to him. He then proclaims battle or single combat against Tadg, or else the full *eiric* of his father to be given to him. Tadg said he would give him judgment therein. The judgment was given ; and this is the judgment that was given to him, to wit, that Almu, as it was, should be ceded to him for ever, and Tadg to leave it (=and that Tadg should leave it). It was done so. Tadg abandoned Almu to Find, and came to Tuath-Dathi, to his own hereditary land ; and he abode in Cnoc-Rein, which is called Tulach-Taidg to-day; for it is from him it has been called Tulach-Taidg from that time to this. So that hence was said this :—

'Find demands from Tadg of the towers
For killing Cumall the great,
Battle, without respite, without delay,
Or that he should obtain single combat
Because Tadg was not able to sustain battle
Against the high prince,
He abandoned to him, it was for him enough,
Almu altogether, as it stood.'

Find went afterwards to Almu and abode in it. And it is it that was his principal residence whilst he lived.

Find and Goll concluded peace after that ; and the *eric* of his father was given by the Clann-Morna to Find. And they lived peacefully until (a quarrel) occurred between them in Temhair-Luachra, regarding the Slanga-pig, when Banb-Sinna, son of Maelenaig, was slain, of which was said :—

'Afterwards they made peace—
Find and Goll of mighty deeds—
Until Banb-Sinna was slain,
Regarding the pig in Temhair Luachra.'

Then when they noticed Cumal coming home after slaying this number of the Clanna Morna, Garradh knew that Cumal was a lover of fair women. Garradh sent his sister out to meet Cumal before he should come where they were.

This gift was Cumal's, whenever he met with a woman that he fell asleep, and as soon as he fell in with her he fell asleep. Then one in a frenzy came out and cried with a loud shout : 'If there be any alive of the tribe of Morna, let him avenge the nobles.'

6

'We made a rush that was not slow,
And reached the house in which was Cumal,
And made sore wounds each one
With his spear in the body of Cumal.

7

'He would bellow as though a cow were there,[1]
And he would roar as though a boar,
And though it was not a king's son's honour,
Cumal would kick like a *garron*.

8

'There thou hast, Fionn, Cumal's son,
A little of a tale about thy father ;
Without ill, without concealment, since then
Without esteem, without honour.

'THEN FIONN SAID :

9

'Though I was unborn in the time of Cumal of the keen blades, the deed that you did shamefully, I will avenge it in one day.

---

[1] Other variants in Gaelic are :—

 i. Dh' Eibheadh e mar mhuc, 's raoimhceadh e mar thorc s bhrammadh e mar ghearran s a shleagh fhein ma fheaman.

 ii. Dh' Eibheadh e mar thorc bhramadh e mar ghearan s a shleagh fhein na fheaman.

 iii. Leumadh e ri failgheas agus bhramadh e mar ghearran agus a shleagh fhein na fheaman.

'SAID GARRADH:

10

' Well wilt thou get that, thou man
To brandish the spear for thy father.
Put the kindred behind
And raise the common blood-feud.' [1]

How Cumal was slain

A prose story written by a schoolmaster in Mull about 1800 is in the Advocates' Library.

It begins by stating that Ireland was divided into five divisions. It goes on with part of the story of the Battle of Muchdraim,[2] which is not part of the Fenian story as I have learned it. He makes Cumal the smith's daughter, and then goes on with her, daughter and son, as in the true Fenian story. The son was taken by Luas Lurgann (nimble shanks), *nighean muime is oide 'n Righ dhleasanich*, sister of Coban Saor. They went to Coille Ultich. They made a bed in the middle of a great tree with a door to it, so that no one should know it. When he grew up she taught him to play at Clār-Tathlisc. She used to run races with him to the top of Beinn Eaduin. She ran behind and flogged him with blackthorn boughs. When he got but one blow at starting, he was taught that game. She taught him archery and

---

[1] The scribe here evidently spelt Gaelic according to his own system, by ear. The man who dictated to him had only got fragments of the lay; *e.g.*, verses 9, 10 have ceased to be verse at all, and after verse 5 is a bit of prose. After a hundred years or thereabouts the only bit of the ballad that survives out in the Long Island is verse 7.

With this compare Dean's Book, p. 65 of Gaelic, 88 of English, and notes. There seems to be no doubt about the fact that several bits are written together in the Dean's Book, but there is the story told in verse about 1520, 1760, and 1870.

Note.—According to note, page 89, Lismore Book, Cumal was killed at the battle of Cnucha. According to the ballad, pp. 75, 76, Zarri (or Garridh) tells Finn that he thrust the first dart into Cumal. Finn says that the news is rather too much to hear that Clanna Morna had slain his father. The other recites the evils done to his tribe by Cumal; how he had driven one branch to Albain, one to Lochlann, one to Greece. There was a great fight when they came back after sixteen years, and after the battle they all rushed to the house where Cumal still was and thrust spears into his body. This does not at all disagree with my story.

[2] [Battle of Moy Muchruime, A.D. 195, according to the *Annals of the Four Masters*; the tale concerning it is translated in O'Grady's *Silva Gadelica*.]

shinny. When taught she took him to the shinny match in the Royal Town, where he beat everybody. The king heard about *An gille luideagach bàn*, the tattered fair lad, and went to see him with the muime and named him as in other versions. She cried his name : 's tusa sin Fionn.

. . . .

After that he went off with the nurse and had but the legs when he got home.

Next day he went wandering and reached Eas Ruadh, where he met the fisher and begged a fish. The first was a salmon, a king's fish, and too good for him. So the tale goes on, as I have it, till the burnt finger gives him *fios an dā shaoghail* as they say, the knowledge of the two worlds. He got to know that the fisher's name was Forca Dubha, and that he had slain his father, and that his father's sword was near him. He beheaded the fisher and reached the house of a smith (*gobhin*), his grandfather.[1]

Here the story goes off to the sheep and the king's unjust decisions as in the story of the Battle of Muchdraim. Fionn got to be steward in the king's house.

[1] This is the Staffa version already translated. I do not accordingly expand Campbell's own condensed account, which in this section he meant to have done, but I add here several notes which he made on the back of several pages of his MSS. to the following effect :—

Fionn's wisdom tooth is mentioned in Lays, and is systematically ignored by people who wrote about Fenian matters as if they were grave history, *e.g.* the argument in Kennedy's MSS. finished before 1783, at p. 131 says Fingal discovered the fact by his magic art, which he performed, as traditionally related, by getting one of his fingers into his mouth and chewing to a joint.

> Chuir Fionn a mheur fui dheud fios
> Fhreagair càch am fios a fhuair.

i.e. Fionn put his finger under his knowledge tooth,
The rest replied to the knowledge he found.

As to Fionn's revenge, Campbell notes further on :—The first *fiosachd,* 'knowledge,' that Fionn got when he burned his finger and put it under his tooth, was that this fisherman was Arc Dubh, the Fenian traitor, who slew Cumal, his father; that his father's hound Bran, the son of Buidheag, and his father's sword, mac a Luinn, that never left shred after stroke, were at the fisher's house, and that the fisher would kill him unless he slew the fisher unawares. So he ate up all the salmon himself for he was tired and hungry.

3rd December 1871, Dublin.—In the Book of Leinster, Fionn's wisdom tooth,

Then Cairbre Ruadh and his people come in. They come to the King of Ulster, who joins with Fionn, who declares himself and is made King of Ireland.

> Seachd Bliadhna fiched gu fior
> Bha Ludhadh mac Con 'na Righ
> Gun bhàs gun ghàbhadh gun ghuin
> Fir, mnà, na gille bha n Eirinn.

So this is really two stories run together, but so that I can easily distinguish them by the aid of current traditions alone.

Fionn's Birth

When Cumal was slain the King of Lochlann came to Alba and took it and shared it with the King of Eirinn. They made slaves of the Fēinn, and made them hunt for them, and they fell to poverty and great straits, because they had no leader after they had lost Cumal. The king's [messenger] went back to Ireland, and there they found that the king's daughter was to bear a child, so they sent for the

---

'Det fiss,' is mentioned in a poem which begins 'Dām thrír tancatar illé' (Fol. 161 A 2).

At foot of p. 33 of his MS. he notes :—Cf. 1. The Volsung tale. 2. The wisdom of F., the swiftness of C., the cunning of Conan, and the sturdy strokes of Osgar were the public four that upheld the Feinn. But that was said long afterwards.

Fios Fhinn, luathas Chaoilte, fàthach Chonain, agus sàr (brath) bhuillean Osgair na Ceithir coiteacheann a cumail a suas an Fhéinn.

At foot of p. 37 he adds :—Robertson, Tobermory, said Cumal was killed by a fisherman. Fionn said to the fisherman : 'What death did Cumal meet?' The fisher said :—

> 'Tharnadh e mar mbuc agus
> Raibheadh e mar each,' etc.

'That will I do to you,' said Fionn, and he killed the fisher. That was his first exploit. He was very wise. He never went to battle that he did not know the result beforehand. I don't know how he got his wisdom. He was not so strong as many of his men. He was cunning and crafty.

According to a Macleod in South Uist he had no fuel, but *Broileagaig bheartan iarain agus dual na dhaghan a ghoisne*, which he explained to mean augur dust, and the hearts of feathers, and to be Irish Gaelic.

I wrote from ear, and do not know that I have written correctly. According to Robertson, Tobermory, September 16, 1870, *Beart do iarne guaine agus gual a dhathadh dhaoine.* The reciter was eighty-six and devoid of teeth, so I could but guess at unknown words.

fisher to ask his counsel. 'Wretched creature,' said the King of Lochlann, 'I will kill her, or rather I will leave her here in Eirinn, for it is my own fault. If she has a son slay him, if she has a daughter let her live.'

'Do this,' said Arc Dubh, 'swear twelve doctors and twelve midwives to watch her and wait upon her, and to tell when the child is born.'

That was his counsel to the king, and they took it. So. that was done. Twelve doctors and twelve midwives were got, and they were sworn, and all the household were sworn, for they feared that Cumal's son might do them harm if he lived and grew, so mighty was Cumal and so strong.

The king's daughter was left in the palace in Eirinn, and she fell to sorrowing and to woe. At the end of three-quarters and a year[1] about noon, as it might be now, the king's daughter fell ill, and about the gloaming at six or eight a girl was born. All were well pleased, and word was sent to the King of Eirinn. The doctors fell to drinking and merry-making, and the midwives fell asleep. But about midnight when all are asleep but one woman who was nursing a child by the fire, the king's daughter said—

'Is any one awake?'

'I am awake,' said the *bean-ghlùn* (knee-wife). 'What is it?'

'Come here,' said she softly.

The woman went to her, and she had a boy in her arms.

'I must wake the household,' said the midwife, whose name was Gumag.[2]

'Nay, nay,' said the king's daughter; 'don't do that, take him from my sight, throw him to the great hounds. It were better so than to see his father's son slain. But stop,' said

---

[1] Gaelic idiom for a year and nine months.

[2] Mòr, nighean Taoic.—Fletcher's Collection; it was the Clanna Morna who wanted to slay the child. [Others say]:—

It was his grandmother who stole him away to a distant wood and hid him in a hollow alder (*fearna*) tree, and fed him with fat. When he got strong enough to follow her she gave him a sword, and ran races. At last he cut off a cheek of hers and then it was time to get him christened.

she, 'if you will keep him alive I will pay you, and perhaps he will pay you himself if he grows to be a man. This is the one who will handle the realm.'

'But I have sworn to tell the king,' said Gumag; 'and how shall I nurse him, for I have no milk?'

'Open the press,' said the king's daughter, 'and there you will find food for Cumal's son. Set your oaths aside.'

So the woman pitied the babe, and his mother, the king's daughter. She opened the press and found flesh in it. She took a knife and cut a great strip of fat meat. That she thrust into the babe's mouth. She wrapped him in some clothes that were in the room, and then she stole out in the dark and thrust the child into a hole at the end of a byre, there to live or die amongst the cattle. Then she stole back and took her child upon her knee, and sat by the fire and nursed it till dawn.

When the others awoke she said to the lady: 'My head aches; you have no more need of me now, I will go and rest.' She was head nurse.

'Awake one of the others,' said the lady, 'and go, but come in the morning and see me again.'

Out she went, and in the byre she found the child with the meat in his mouth alive and well. She tucked him under her cloak, and off she went before the day had dawned through the big town of the Irish king and half a mile on the road to the hut of her brother, whose name was Art.

She went to Dubh Lochan Moine near a black peat pool. But the brother was not there. He had gone to help some builders to finish a great castle that was outside the town in a forest. She walked five miles through the forest with the child under her cloak sucking the fat meat.

The castle was nearly finished, and all were asleep when she got there. She cried aloud: 'Is Art awake? Tell him one has business with him here.' Art knew his sister's voice and her speech, and out he came in haste with nothing on but his shirt and drawers.

'What is the matter?' said Art.

'I have done an ill deed,' said she, 'and the following is upon me; take your axe and come with me to the black moss pool and help me to make a shelter there, and to hide.'

The wright was an old man with a white head. When he heard what his sister said he put on his clothes as fast as he could and shouldered his axe and set off, while she followed with the child, sucking the fat meat under her cloak. (*An am glōmadh an latha*) in the gloaming of the day the wright said : 'What have you under your cloak ?'

'That which belongs to me,' said she. 'Why should a man ask an old woman what she has under her cloak ? Though I had stolen something, my brother might help me in my need.'

Then they reached the place as the day broke, and the wright soon made a shelter of sticks and beams, and a hut by the black peat pool. Then he stopped.

'Not another turn will I do,' said he, 'till I know what you have got under your cloak.' Then he cast down his axe, and looked and saw the child.

'That,' said he, 'is the son of Cumal ; I will do to him as will do to this stake before I go hence.'

'Stop,' said Gumag, 'finish the bothy first for me.'

'It is done,' said Art.

'No,' said she, 'the doorway is not right.'

She thrust the child into some hole and got up and climbed on the wall of the hut.

'See,' said she, 'it wants a shaving off here. If you won't do it yourself hand me the axe and put your shoulder under the lintel.'

'I will slay that *isean na béisde*, whelp of the beast, Cumal,' said the wright, grumbling, and as he said it he stooped his head to go out of the hut. Then Gumag smote him with the axe, and chopped off his head.

'You are dead,' she said, 'and none shall know who killed you. You will tell no tales of me.'

Then she came down from the top of the bothy and

dragged the body of Art to some hole, and then she buried her brother.

Then she made a bed of leaves and branches and laid the child on it, while he kept sucking at the fat meat, and when that was done she went back to the palace to seek clothes, and to see the lady.

'What has happened,' said the king's daughter, 'and where is the child?'

Then Gumag told all that had happened from first to last.

'Perhaps, poor woman, the lad will repay you himself for all that you have done, even though you have killed your brother for his sake, for his hand will rule the realm yet.' So said the king's daughter.

Now, that is the way in which Fionn's grandfather, the King of Lochlann, managed to slay Fionn's father, Cumal, and that is how Fionn was saved. I never heard his sister's name, but she came to be the mother of Diarmad O'Duibhne, as it is said in the lay of Diarmad :—

> 'S olc a chomhairle chinn agam
> Aona mhac mo pheathar a mharbhadh.'

> 'Evil was the counsel that grew within me
> To slay the only son of my sister.'[1]

(as repeated in 1871 by W. Robertson, Tobermory, and frequently repeated by others elsewhere in 1860 and since. Not in Gillies, p. 287).

[1] [According to this *Duiben* was a sister of Fionn, for Diarmad's descent is traced from his mother.]

(*To be continued.*)

THE GLENMASAN MANUSCRIPT

PROFESSOR MACKINNON

GAELIC TEXT

'Do beirim-si brethir fir,' ar Bricne, 'gur bris Fergus triochat cath. B'a*nn* dib cath Inb(hir Tuaighe for) Niall Niamhglonnach[1] mac Rosa r*ua*id car .'. . . a n-dorchair Ruir . . . ruaid f*er*da an cathmil*idh*, agus *cath* . . . eile Cairn Eolairg a n-dorchair Camall*ichta* an ban gais*gedach*, agus cath mor Cairn Eolairg .dú a n-dorchair Bolg mac Builg mic Eolairg agus Eolarg mac Edh .. . . *da chaogat*, agus cath Inbir Loinne a torchair Finn mac Innadmair, rig Temra. Agus is e do bris cath Maistin ar clannaib Rosa co coitcenn; agus cath Mullach dub Rosa for clannaib Rosa fos; agus cath Mana for Conchobar agus for Ulltaib; agus cath cepcha for clannaib Durtacht ait atorchair Eogan mac Durtach't; agus cath Luachra for clannaib Deg*ad*; agus cath Duine da Beann; agus cath Boirche; agus moran eile nach airmighter ann so do cathaib, gurab do derbadh na cath sin agus na tuarasdal[2] adubairt an *senchaid* na raind-se :

> 'Fo fer Fergus fichtib tor,
> Do bris cath ar Conchobar;
> Ni fhaca laoch lith n-gaili,
> Do rois*ed* ó Rugraide.

> 'Mo na gach mac mac Rosa;
> Fo gach glac glac Fergusa;
> Fochla do rigaib mac Rosa,
> Ag fog*ail* airgid is óir.

---

[1] *The Martial Career of Conghal Cláringhneach* (quoted here as *Cc.*), recently published by the Irish Text Society (vol. v.), throws some light on this chapter in the early career of Fergus. Fergus attached himself to the party of Conghal in the year in which the former 'first took possession of his territory,' and shared in all his adventures until the latter was enthroned monarch of Ireland. Their people destroyed *Dun da Beann*, the seat of Niall Niamhghlonnach, in the absence of its lord, and took his wife Craobh, daughter of Durtacht, and sister of Eogan, prisoner. The lady, preferring death to captivity, threw herself into the Bann and was drowned. Afterwards they fought and slew Niall himself at *Aonach Tuaighe*, no doubt the Inb(er Tuaighe) of our MS. The name of the father of Finn, slain at Inver Loinne, is practically illegible. But there is enough to show that *Innadmar*, otherwise Findat-

(*Continued from vol.* i. *pp.* 314, 315)

ENGLISH TRANSLATION

I pledge my word, said Bricne, that Fergus fought and won thirty battles. One of these was the battle of Inver Tuagh against Niall Niamhglonnach (Bright-deeds), son of red Ros... where the manly prince and battle-warrior R. fell; another was the battle of Carn Eolarg, where the amazon Camallichta fell. There were also the great battle of Carn Eolarg where Bolg son of Bolg son of Eolarg and Eolarg son of E. (and) two fifties (besides) fell: and the battle of Inver Loinne, where fell Finn, son of Innadmar, King of Tara. He it was who won the battle of Maistiu against the whole of the clans of Ros; and the battle of Mullach dub (black-top) of Ros against the clans of Ros as well; and the battle of Mana against Conchobar and the Ultonians; and a stubborn fight against the clans of Durtacht, where Eogan the son of Durtacht was killed; and the battle of Luachra against the clans of Degad; and the battle of the Fort of two Peaks; and the battle of Boirche; and many other battles not here enumerated, in proof of which battles and exploits (?) the historian composed these quatrains :—

'A mighty man Fergus of the many towers,
Who conquered Conchobar in battle;
There has not been seen his equal in valour,
That issued from Rugraide.

'Greater than any son the son of Ros;
Mightier than any hand that of Fergus;
A model to kings is the son of Ros,
For acquiring silver and gold.

---

mar, monarch of Ireland in his day, and father of the reigning high king, Lughaidh Luaighne, is meant. *Cath Boirche* may be the battle fought against Boirche Casurlach (*Cc.* 168, 172) after the return of Fergus and Conghal from Norway. The Mourne Mountains were of old called *Beanna Boirche*. *Cath Mana* was fought against Conchobar at a later period, no doubt after Fergus's revolt in consequence of the murder of the sons of Uisnech. The 'stubborn fight' with Eogan son of Durtacht, where Eogan was slain, has already been described (v. *supra*, vol. i. p. 226). *Càrn Eolairg*, or *Carraig Eolairg*, is said to have been in the neighbourhood of Derry. *Maistiu* is now Mullaghmast, co. Kildare. [2] Cf. O'Don. Supp. *tuarastal*.

'Tri cet carpat do beir,
  Co n-armaib co n-ilsgiathaib,
  Co n-dei(g)-cealtaib .   .   .
  A tuarastlaib a oglach.

'Do berim da m-brethir fis (?),
  Agus ni ticfa tairis,
  Deich catha fichet .   .   .
  Gur bris Fergus a n-Eirinn.

'Cath Luachra for clannaib Degad,
  Sochaidi tuc fo mheabul ;
  Cath Maisdin for clannaib Rosa,
  Is cath mor Mullach dub Rosa.

'(Cath Boir)che an treas deroir ;
  Cath Inbir Loinne for Bre .   .   .;
  .   .   .   .   os aird,
  Agus cath Cairge Eolairg.

'.   .   .   san   .   .   .   mac Ro
  .   .   .   .   cet irna derg-oir ;
  Ni dar   .   .   .   .   .   gnath,
  Do mnaib amus is oglach.

'.   .   .   ar enech ni ar a gruaidh,
  Do tisad fo era uaid ;
  .   .   .   .   .   .   ni dubairt go,
  O'n lo   .   .   .   arm fen fo.'

                                        Fo.

'Is briathar damsa,' ar Bricne, 'nach b-fuil locht do . . .
Fergus . . . acht gan rige n-Ulad aigi agus gan rigain a
(din)gbala fos.' 'Is amlaid atu-sa, a Bricni,' ar Flidais, '. . .
for talmain oram acht gan oir(?) mo dingmala . . . agam.'
'Dar m-breithir am,' ar Bricne, 'ni fhaca . . . cele budh
ferr ina do cele (Oilill) Finn.' '(Dim)ain, a Bricne,' ar Flidais,
'ni gabthar uaidsi sin, oir tuca-sa grad dermar d'Fergus, agus
ar imtechta (imgesa ?) nach b-f. . . . ortsa acht mana chuirer
Fergus fo gesaib fa techt do m' breith-si leis o'n Gamanraid
d'ais no dligi.'

Ba fergach Bricne de sin agus is ed adubairt : 'Mor am-
rath an fhir d' a tucais an grad sin. Agus ni raibhe ben

'He gives three hundred chariots,
With weapons and many shields,
With suitable accoutrements . . .
In stipends to his warriors.

'I declare of certain knowledge,
And will not boast of it,
That Fergus won . . .
Thirty battles in Ireland.

'The battle of Luachra over the clans of Degad,
Multitudes he put to shame,
The battle of Maisdiu over the clans of Ros,
And the great battle of Mullach-dub-Ros.

'The battle of Boirche, the third I mention ;
The battle of Inver Loinne over Bre . . .;

. . . . . .

And the battle of Rock Eolarg.

' . . . . . .

. . (thirty) hundred *irnas* of red gold ;

. . . . .

To the wives of mercenaries and warriors.

' . . on his face nor on his cheek,
(No one) would have refusal from him ;
. . he never spoke falsely,
From the day (he became) a warrior.'   Mighty.

'I give my word,' said Bricne, 'that Fergus lacks in
nothing save that he is not king of Ulster, and that he has
not a queen worthy of him.' 'I am in similar plight, Bricne,'
said Flidais, '(I lack nothing) on earth except a suitable
husband' (?). 'By my word now,' replied Bricne, 'I never
met a more excellent spouse than (Oilill) the Fair, your
husband.' 'You speak foolishly, Bricne,' said Flidais, 'and I
will not hear such language from you. For I love Fergus
greatly, and when you depart (I ask nothing of you) save
to put Fergus under prohibitions as to his coming to carry
me away from the Gamhanraidh of consent or compulsion (?).'

Bricne was wroth when he heard this, and said : 'Sad is
the evil fate of the man to whom you have given your love.
For he never had a wife but eventually hated him. And he

riamh aigi nach tibr*ad* misgus dó.   Agus ni fuair ben a dingbala, acht cuidiugadh Medba re med a lathra ferrda.   Agus
red eile fos aidhblighes a anagh .i. tri coinnle gaisgid Gaidel
do marbadh ar a comairce an Emain Macha.   Agus ar na
righ*ibh* nochar eir*igh* grian t*ar* uillinn laoc(h)muir re rige.
Agus a rigan,' ar Bricne, 'do siresa an domun o cathair
Murni Molf*aige*[1] a tuaisc*irt* an domuin co ruigi so, agus ni
fhaca eturru sin fer budh ferr ina Oilill Finn.'

'Dímáin duitsi sin, a Bricni,' ar Flidais, 'agus ni gabthar
sin úaid.   Agus do gebair roighni shed Erenn do cinn mo
comarli-si do denam, a Bricni.   Agus oirdeochad-sa d'Fergus
mar do ghena, oir do chuala-sa go fuilid fir Eirenn ac dul ar
aon sluaiged ar cend tana bo Cuailgni an Ulltaib.   Agus
tiged-san d'iarradh faighdhe ech agus airm agus eididh ar an
n-Gamannraid, agus rachad-sa leis.   Agus gid tri deich cet
do deig feraib tig-se, ro-d-bia ainder a dingbala da gach ain fer
aca.   Agus berad-sa an m-boin maeil as ferr fuil an Eirinn ;
agus da roised mh' airgeda lim agus an Mael Flidaise, berad
as an galad[2] fir Eireñ gacha sechtmad aidche.'. Agus cuma
do bi 'g a radh, agus atbert an laid t-surgi[3]-si :

> 'A Bricni, eirigh uaim ar n-uair
> And sa rod go Cruachain cruaidh
> Cuir naoi n-gesa[4] for mac Roigh
> Mana ti let achetoir.

> 'Gid tri deich cet ro-d-fái i,le,
> *Fergus* úareid   .   .   .   rugraide (?)
> Ro-d-fia ainder gac(h) fer dib,
> Agus fáeifed   .   .   .   le a rig (?)

> 'Dá ría lim mo bo 's mo tain,
> Biathf   .   .   .   le Flidais
> Gid ar sluaiget beid coidche,
> Gacha sechtmad n-oidche.

---

[1] V. *supra*, vol. i. p. 14.   Later in the MS. Fergus refers to his adventures in
Uardha (the cold land), where this *cathair* was situated.   A detailed account of this
expedition is given in *Cc.* p. 112 *et seq.*

[2] The same phrase occurs later.   I have not seen the word *galad* elsewhere.   But
the meaning is evidently as I have ventured to render it.

has not had a spouse worthy of him, only the society of Meave because of his vigorous manhood. And besides there is another matter which affects his honour, the three torches of valour of the Gael have been slain in Emain Macha while under his safeguard. And during his reign the sun of prosperity did not shine upon the (subject) princes. Further, O queen, I have travelled the world from the city of Muirn Molfaig in the north to here, and in all my journeyings I have not seen a better man than Oilill the Fair,' added Bricne.

'Idle talk, Bricne, which I do not believe,' said Flidais. 'But you shall have your choice of the treasures of Ireland in return for carrying out my instructions, Bricne. I shall direct Fergus how to proceed, for I have heard that the men of Ireland are to go as one host to Ulster to carry away the cows of Cuailgne. Let him come for a subsidy of horses, weapons, and armour from the Gamhanraidh, and I shall go with him. And although three thousand stout men of you should come, a suitable wife will be provided for every man of them. And I shall bring with me my hummel cow, the best in Ireland. And if my herds and the Maol Flidais accompany me, they will amply supply the men of Ireland every seventh night.' And as she spoke she recited this love-song :—

> 'Bricne, leave me forthwith,
> And betake thee to sterile Cruachan;
> Lay nine prohibitions on the son of Roich,
> If he comes not instantly with you.

> 'Though three thousand should come thither,
> With Fergus (?)   .   .   .
> A wife for each man of them
> Shall wed with her lord (?)

> 'If I bring my cow and herds,
> Flidais shall feed the hosts
> Every seventh night,
> Should the campaign last for ever.

---

[3] Literally 'courting lay.' In modern S.G. *oran gaoil*, 'love-song,' would be the phrase used.

[4] In his report to Fergus (*infra*), Bricne mentions one or two of the nine taboos that Flidais laid upon him.

'An aos o thair, aidble main,
 A fil*eda* (?)   a samain (?)
 Dingebad dib, tólaib gal,
 Dithisd iš . . .

'A ingen as mór an gnim,
 Do bere do laim . . .
    . . . ríg . . . calma,
 Do treigen ar rid . . .

'Is e sin mo ceile cóir,
 An fer re n-abar[1] mac Roigh,
 A ben dingmala de,
 Nochar . . . nge, a Bricne.'

A B*ricne*.

Is ann sin do ghluais Bricne as an baile a mach(?) agus
ni ruc Ollam o banntracht riam ed*ail* . . ., ocus rainic roime
go dunadh Atha Fen.   Agus o d'conncatar lucht an baile h-e,
do eirghedar nile 'n a agaid, agus do fersad fir-cain failte fris,
agus do toirbretar poga imdha dó, agus do fiafraigedh de nar
buidech do Flidais é.   Adubairt Bricne gur buidech.   Agus
do bi an adaig sin an dunadh Atha Fen.   Agus do eirigh co
moch ar na marach agus do iarr a (th)idluc*tha* agus a el*mha*
leis.   Agus do seol*adh* tre caogait oglach leis .i. fer in gach
carpat finndruine da raib aigi, agus ba tanas de sluagh lan-
móir a linmarecht.   Agus tinmais celeabrad do maithib Oilella
Finn agus do fen.   Agus do innis d' Oilill co ticfa Fergus d'a
agallaim, agus d'iarraidh faigdhe ech agus eididh ar an
n-Gamannraid.

Is si so sligi do deochatar .i. tar cend Conlocha agus tar
sal Srotha Deirg agus a crich Breis mic Ealathan re raiter
tír Fiachrach Mide, agus tar traig Ruis airg*id* ris a raiter
traig Eothaile, agus tar Srath nan Druad ris a raiter Srath
an Fhérain, agus a magh Coraind ingine Fail mic Fidhga ris
in abartar Clar mic Aire an Choraind clann Uaine, agus laim
re maolan cinn t-Seinnsleibi ris in abartar Ceis caom alainn
Coraind, agus tar Sruth Fainglinn ris in abartar Buill.

---

[1] The usual phrases are *re n-abrar, ris a n-abartar, re ráiter, ris a ráiter*.   But
this form also occurs in this MS. and elsewhere.   Cf. *Cc.*, p. 30 n., *et aliis*.

'The folks of the East have vast wealth,
Their poets   .   .   .
I shall protect you, floods of valour
Two   .   .   .   .

'Lady, you have taken upon you
A great undertaking,
To forsake your brave king
For a   .   .   .'

'He is my rightful spouse,
The man called son of Roich,
His worthy wife I shall be,
(And do thou depart), Bricne.'

Bricne

Bricne thereupon left the stead, and never did Ollamh carry away (such) wealth from women before. He proceeded to the fort of Ath Fen. When the people saw him they all went forth to meet him. They gave him a warm welcome, kissed him often, and asked whether he was not well pleased with Flidais. Bricne said he was. He stayed that night in the palace of Ath Fen. He rose early on the morrow and asked for his presents and treasures. Thrice fifty warriors were sent with him, one in each chariot of white bronze which he possessed, and their number had the appearance of a large host. He bade farewell to Oilill the Fair and to his chiefs. And he told Oilill that Fergus would come to have parley with him, and to seek aid in horses and armour from the Gamhanraidh.

This is the road on which they travelled :—past the end of Dog-loch and the heel of Red-stream into the territory of Breas son of Ealathan, (now) called the land of Fiachra in Meath, and across the silver strand of Ros (now) called the Strand of Eothal, and over the Strath of the Druids (now) called the Strath of Feran, and into the plain of Corand, daughter of Fal son of Fidhga, (now) called the Plain of the son of Aire of Corand of the clans Uaine, and by the little round (or bare) of the head of Old Hill, (now) called the dear beautiful Ceis of Corand, and across the Stream of Fanglen (sloping-glen), (now) called Buill.

Is ann sin do impod*set* teglach Oilella uatha, agus tanic
Bricne roime go Cruachain.　Agus adconncadar an imirce
adbal mor ell*mha* d'á n-indsaige, agus ba h-ingnad mor leo
uile sin.　*Ocus* do t-shailedar gur b' é Cet no Conadar mac
Cecht agus crechi a h-Ulltaib aca bái and.　Tanic Bricne
roime a Cruachain a nonn, agus do feradh failti fris, agus do
fiafraigedh de cúich na crecha mora do bí aige.　'Ní h-ed
am,' ar Bricne, 'fuil agam acht m'edail-si o'n Gamanraid
sin .i. o Oilill Finn agus o na maithib ar chena.'

'Cindus tech tech Oilella Finn?' ar Medb re Bricni.　'Is
se tech as ferr gus a ranag-sa riam h-e.　Agus fos ni fhaca tech
b*a*d commaith ris,' ar Bricne, 'o'n lo do t-sires an doman ar
aon re Fergus.'　Agus ba fergach Medb de sin .i. fa tech sa
doman do chur tar a tech fein.　'Do neimdl*igis*,[1] a Bricni,'
bar Medb, 'imarbaidh do cur a m' cenn.'　'Ni cuirim-si ón
imarbaid a t' chenn,' ar Bricne.　'Acht aon ní: as é tech
Oilella Finn tech as lía ollamain agus anrath[2] agus oblóir[3]
agus eistrecht[4] mna agus macaim agus mindaéine;[5] curaidh
agus coraidh[6] agus cath-milidh agus cl*iath* bern*a*dha *catha*.[7]
Agus fledi feraind agus br*u*gaidh bailtead.[8]　Oir atáid an urdail-
si do churaidhibh comanmannaib ann .i. tri cet Ferdiad im
Ferdiadh mac Damhain, agus tri cet Fraech im Fraech mac
Fidaigh, agus tri cet Goll im Goll Oilech agus Acla, agus trí
cet Gamuin im Gamuin na Sidgaile, agus tri cet Duban im
Duban mac an gamna, agus trí cet Dartadh im Dartadh na

---

[1] I have not met with this compound elsewhere.　But it is evidently *dligim* with the
negative *neb-*, *neph-*, *nem-*, *neamh-*, S.G. *neo-*, prefixed.　The Dictionaries, Highland
Society's (H.S.D.), for example, give the adjective *neo-dhligheach*, 'unlawful,' but not
the verb.

[2] *anrath*, older *anruth*, the name of the bard next in rank to the *ollam* or *rig-bard*
who was the highest (*Ir. T.*, iii. (1), p. 5).　After the convention of *Druim Ceta*
(575 A.D.) the retinue (*cleir*) of the *anruth* was reduced to twelve.　Bricne, usually
described as *ollamh*, is, in this manuscript, also spoken of as *anrath*.

[3] *obloir*, 'a jester,' now in S.G. and I.G. *amhlair*, 'fool,' 'boor,' 'blockhead.'

[4] *eistrecht*: the exact meaning of the word is uncertain.　In *The Laws*, vol. i.
p. 138, *essrechta maccru*, 'toys of children,' include *camana*, 'hurley' or 'shinty'
sticks; *liathroiti*, 'balls'; and *luboca*, 'hoops.'　Perhaps here the word may be
translated 'playthings.'　Immediately below, the context would suggest 'dwarfs'
as the better rendering of the word.

[5] *min-daéine*: 'little folks,' 'children,' as distinct from *macaim*, 'youths,'

At this point Oilill's people turned back, and Bricne proceeded to Cruachan. And when the vast cavalcade was seen approaching them, all wondered greatly thereat. They thought it was Cet or Conodhar son of Cecht with plunder from Ulster. When Bricne arrived at Cruachan, he was welcomed, and people asked what this great booty was which he brought with him. 'None other,' said Bricne, 'than my presents from the Gamhanraidh, from Oilill the Fair and the nobles generally.'

'What sort of house is the house of Oilill the Fair?' asked Meave of Bricne. 'The best I ever visited,' said Bricne. 'And besides,' added he, 'I have not seen one to equal it, since I went to travel the globe along with Fergus.' Meave was wroth because any house in the world was named as superior to her own. 'You ought not to provoke me to a quarrel, Bricne,' said Meave. 'I do not,' said Bricne. 'And yet, in Oilill Finn's palace are to be found the greatest number of ollamhs and poets and jesters and women's playthings and boys and children; champions and warriors and battle-soldiers and valiant troops; country banquets, and town hospitallers. For this number of champions of like names are there, viz., Ferdia son of Daman with three hundred Ferdias in his train; Fraoch son of Fidach with three hundred Fraochs; three hundred Golls with Goll Oilech and Acla; three hundred Gamans with Gaman of Sidgal; three

---

'boys.' Cf. S.G. *meanbh-chrodh*, 'sheep,' 'goats,' in contrast with *crodh*, 'cows,' 'cattle.'

⁶ *coraidh*, preserved in I.G. as *coraidhe* (Din.); marked long (*córaidh*) in Dr. Kuno Meyer's *Contributions to Irish Lexicography* (K. M.). Here and elsewhere in this MS. the vowel is evidently short, suggestive of similar root with *curaidh*, if not indeed the same word with change of vowel.

⁷ *cliath bernadha catha*: an uncommon phrase. Cf. *in chliath-bern chét* LL. 61 a 22 (K. M.). *Cliath*, 'hurdle,' 'wattle,' is applied to men in close battle array; *be(a)rn* is 'gap,' 'breach.' The exact force of the phrase is doubtful, perhaps 'picked men to pierce the enemy's lines,' or 'to defend a pass,' 'fit to stand in battle's gap' (O'Gr. Cat., p. 408).

⁸ *fledi feraind agus brugaidh bailtead*: cf. *infra* (p. 32), the corresponding phrase, *m' istada agus m' adbara fleda a muigh*, used by Meave to magnify the resources of her own district. *Baile* is of the dental declension still—pl. *bailte(an)*. But I have not met the form *bailtead* (gen. pl.) elsewhere.

hundred Dubans with Duban son of Gaman ; three hundred
Dibeirge, agus tri cet Fosgamuin fa tri Fosgamnaib Irrais,
agus trí cet Breislend fa shecht m-Breislendaib Bhrefne.
Agus do berim-si do m' breithir, a Meadb, go fuilid an urdail
sin eile ann nocha d' inann anmanda doib.' Ba báidh le
Meidb, acht ger fuath le an Gamanraid, an moladh sin do
tabairt ar a h-oclachaib fein. Agus do gab Bricne ac tabairt
tesmolta tige Oilella Finn os aird, agus adbert in laid :—

'Lod-sa cuairt a Cruachain Aéi,
Indeosat daeib, ar áon caei :
Fó an *flaith* ranag ann *gan* fois ;
Fo an ceile d' an comadhus.

'Ranac go Dun Atha Fen,
Turchanas [1] ann ilar sgel,
Go h-Oilill Finn Íarrus cath,
Go mac rig nan Domnannach.

'Mó gach sluag sluag an duine
Aille a fir, aobdha a ruine ;
Fuiled tri cet fa ocht and
Do curadhaib comanmannaibh.

'Tri cet Ferdiad ann re h-ágh
Ima Ferdiad mac Damain ;
Tri cet Fraech fuiled a stigh
Far aon re Fraech mac Fidaigh.

'Tri cet Gamuin, gleo n-gaile,
Fa Gamuin na Sidgaile ;
Tri cet Duban, dreimne glac,
Fa Duban in a deg mac.

'Tri cet Fosgamuin, radh fhuis,
Fa trí Fosgamnaibh Irruis ;
Tri cet Goll go n-grinne n-ga,
Fa Gold Oilech is Acla.

'Tri cet Dartadh doib malle,
Fá Dartadh na Dibeirge ;
Tri cet Breislenn, baigh imné,
Fa t-secht Breslennaibh Brefni.

---

[1] *tair-chanim* and *ter-chanim*, ' I prophesy,' are common forms ; *tin-cantain* and *tin-chetal* in the sense of ' repetition,' ' incantation,' are also met with. Here this compound of *canim* evidently means simply to ' tell ' or ' repeat.'

Dartads with Dartad of Diberg; three hundred Fosgamuins with the three Fosgamuins of Erris; and three hundred Breslenns with the seven Breslenns of Brefne. And I declare on my honour, Meave, that there are as many again of different names.' Although Meave hated the Gamhanraidh, it pleased her to hear her own warriors' praises. And Bricne continued his laudation of the palace of Oilill the Fair, and recited the lay :—

> 'I fared forth on a visit from Cruachan Ai,
> I declare to you, on a certain road;
> Goodly the prince whose palace I quickly reached,
> Goodly his worthy spouse.

> 'I arrived at the castle of the ford of wagons,
> I told many a tale there,
> At Oilill the Fair's, warrior of Erris,
> Son of the king of the Domnanns.

> 'Taller than all others the people of that castle,
> Handsomer its men, pleasanter their disposition:
> Three hundred eight times told are there
> Of champions of like names.

> 'Three hundred valorous Ferdiads are there
> With Ferdiad son of Daman;
> Three hundred Fraochs abide there
> With Fraoch son of Fidach.

> 'Three hundred Gamans, bold in strife,
> With Gaman of Sidgal;
> Three hundred Dubans, of merciless grip,
> With Duban, that goodly youth.

> 'Three hundred Fosgamuins, a truthful statement,
> With the three Fosgamuins of Erris;
> Three hundred Golls with polished spears,
> With Goll Oilech and Acla.

> 'Three hundred Dartads , a loyal band,
> Around Dartad of Diberg;
> Three hundred Breslenns, of like devotion,
> With the seven Breslenns of Brefne.

'Mo gac(h) gair cloistecht re n-gair,
Lucht a teglaig *go* trom-grain ; [1]
Fuil a coimlin eile ann
Nocha d' inann a anmann.

'Ni fhaca an Eirinn, rádh fois,
Tegduis maith mar a tegduis,
Tec(h) Oilella co n-imat n-ga
Tec(h) linmar gus a lod-sa.'

Lod-sa.

'Is fir duitsi gurab maith tech Oilella Finn,' ar Meadb,
'agus gid edh as ferr mo tec(h)-sa go mór ana sé. Is ferr
gaisged mo laoch agus mo lath n-gaile. Is lia mh' urradha [2]
agus mo deóraid. Is lia mo macaim agus mo bandtracht. Is
lía mo t-sheóid agus mo maeine. Is lia mo chruid agus mo
c(h)etra. Is uaisli mo m(h)iledha agus as mó a feidm. Is
lia mh' aos ciuil agus oirfide agus eladha. Is lia m' ollamain
agus m' obloire agus mh' eistrechta.[3] Is lia mo mogaid agus
m' ec*hlach*a urlair.[4] Is lia mo banntracht agus mo bancuire.
Is ferr m' ist*ada*[5] agus m' adh*a*ra fleda a muigh, genmotha
ri-t(h)ech na Cruachna. Uair ní uil an Eirinn tech t-sam-
laiges na cudromaighes ris ar a med agus ar a caime agus ar
a cumdach ; ar imad a urrsgair[6] agus a imdadh agus a fhuin-
neóg ; ar imad a oir agus a indmais agus a leg logmar.

[1] *grain* in the old and modern usage carries the idea of 'horror,' 'disgust.' But
in this MS. the word is frequently used where such an idea cannot be intended.
Cf. *infra*, among many instances, *Do sgail do gnim is do gráin*, applied to Fergus,
where the idea conveyed must be complimentary. Cf. *Cc.*, p. 14, *úruath agus grain
Righ fair*, rendered, 'the fearfulness and majesty of a king are his.' In this particular
passage *ḡ* could stand for *gan*, 'without,' as well as for *go*, 'with,' and yield equally
good idiom. But to characterise a household as not in a special degree abominable
would surely be very faint praise.

[2] *mo*, 'my,' before vowels frequently, as here, becomes not *m'* but *mh*. So in the
old language *th' athir* for *t' athair*, 'thy father.' *Urradh*, 'man of substance,'
'guarantor,' as opposed to *deoraid*, 'dependent,' 'pilgrim,' 'weakling.' Later *urradha*
are linked with *uaisli* and *ard-fhlaithi*. Cf. S.G. *urra, urras, urrainn*, etc.

[3] *V. supra*, p. 28, note 4.

' Louder than all shouts the shout
    Of this household, of majestic mien ;
.   There are as many others again
    Whose tribe names are different.

' I have not seen in Ireland, I say it deliberately,
    A household to compare with this,
    The palace of Oilill with its many spears,
    The populous palace to which I fared.'

I fared.

' You are right in your praise of the palace of Oilill the Fair,' said Meave ; ' nevertheless mine is much the superior of the two.   The valour of my heroes and champions is greater. My chiefs and my dependents are more numerous.   Greater in number are my youths and women-folk ; my jewels and treasures ; my cows and cattle.   My soldiers are nobler born and more valiant.   My musicians, artists, and scientists are more numerous.   So are my ollamhs and jesters and dwarfs ; my slaves and my little children ; my women-folk and female attendants.   My resources and material for banquets are superior, apart from the (grandeur of the) palace of Cruachan.   For there is not in (all) Ireland a mansion that equals or compares with it in size and beauty and adornment ; in the number of its courts and rooms and windows ; in the amount of its gold and treasure and precious stones.

---

⁴ *echlach*, 'messenger,' is common, but *e. urlair*, 'floor messenger,' is not so. Finn's counsel to MacLugach (Ag. l. 586) has the line :—

Dá trian do mhíne re mnáibh is re h-echlachuib urlair,

which is translated : 'Two-thirds of thy gentleness be shown to women and to creepers on the floor' (*i.e.* children).   In our passage, where the term is coupled with *mogaid*, 'slaves,' the meaning may be, 'little ones who fetched and carried within the palace.'

⁵ *istada* : a rather uncommon word, preserved perhaps in I.G. *iosta*, 'apartment,' 'inn' (Din.).   Of old the word meant 'wealth' and the place where treasure was kept ; *i. flatha*, 'sway and soverance of a chief.'   Cf. *Ir. T.*, iii. (1), p. 280.   *V. supra*, p. 29, note 8.

⁶ Cf. *aurscor*, 'area,' 'yard,' O'Donovan's Supplement to O'Reilly's *Dictionary* (O'D. Sup.).

(To be continued.)

VARIATIONS OF GAELIC LOAN-WORDS

Charles M. Robertson

The Gaelic language, both in its literary form, and especially in its spoken dialects, possesses many illustrations of the truth that words taken from other languages conform, at best, only irregularly and uncertainly to the phonetic laws of the borrowing language. A borrowed word may on occasion conform in every particular to the laws in accordance with which the changes undergone by the native words of the adopting language have proceeded, but it is quite as likely to disregard and violate those laws. It may also appear in two or more different forms, and may conform to some phonetic law in one of the forms and violate it in another, or it may both observe and violate the law within the compass of the same form. The law of aspiration, for example, in Gaelic phonetics is that a single consonant standing originally between vowels has been aspirated. This happens to be observed in saighead, from Latin sagitta, where the single g is aspirated and the double t, though reduced to d, is not. So with the middle consonants in saoghal from saeculum, sabhal from stabulum, umhal from humilis, uibhir, Irish uimhir, early Irish numir from numerus. So also aoradh for adhradh from adoratio, iomhaigh from imago, and so on. In nollaig for nothlaig, Early Irish notlaic from natalicia, t has been aspirated and c, though standing alone, has not. So trionaid, Old Irish trindóit from trinitatem. It may be observed in passing that there has been somewhat of a tendency to preserve the last or stem consonant, case endings being dropped, and to slur, aspirate or drop middle consonants, and that in modern spelling in such cases final tenues are very generally replaced by the corresponding mediae. Examples not bearing upon our immediate purpose need not be multiplied as the words intended to be dealt with in their various forms provide a sufficiency of instances, but one may be noticed here. Patricius is found in modern Gaelic in four different forms. In Pàdruig *t* and *c* are unaspirated but reduced to the corresponding mediae. In Pàruig for Pàthruig *t* has been aspirated and lost and *c* made into *g*. Para, a curtailed form of the last, is used with a defining term following which carries the accent, and thus accounts for the shortening of the first vowel, as Para Mór, Big Peter or Patrick; Para Piobaire, Peter the Piper. In Arran, etc., the form is Pàdair, both in common use and in names like Kilpatrick, 'Cill-Phàdair.' The name has been confused in popular use with Peter and is usually so Englished. Peadair as a personal Gaelic name is hardly, if at all, known out of print.

Native words themselves, it is true, sometimes appear in more than one guise, but in their case differences of form exemplify with precision the laws and changes to which borrowed words run counter or conform at random. Piuthar, sister, for example is found in Irish as siur and in Early Irish as both siur and fiur, and in all its forms has come from a single original form svesòr, from which have come also Sanskrit svâsar, Russian sestra, Latin soror for sosor, and English sister. Till, return, appears also as pill, and in Irish as fill, and our Scottish fill, fold, may well be the same; the root is svelni, turn round, which has also given us the word seal, a while. The same root has given another group of variations in the case of its derivative seillean, a bee. This word is

seillean	in literature.
teillean	,, east Perthshire and in Lewis.
seinnlean	,, Kincardine on Oykel.
,,	,, Sutherlandshire, Creich.
seinnlear	,, ,, Rogart.
tainnleag	Helmsdale.
tuinnleag	Reay Country.

Nn is not pronounced, being assimilated to *l*, in those

forms in which it is written, but it has left its mark in a nasalisation and lengthening of the preceding vowels and a doubling of *l*, as seillean, tailleag with *ei* and *ai* as a diphthong and long.   In the Reay country form *ui*, as in many other instances in Sutherland *e.g.* uidh, ruighe, etc., has the sound of Gaelic *i* only, but *u* is necessary in spelling to show that *t* is sounded broad.   The Rogart form merely shows the characteristic change of *n* to *r* in the vicinity of other liquids in Sutherlandshire Gaelic.   All those seeming vagaries in respect to initial letter really exemplify the known fact that when a root began with *sv*, the Gaelic word derived from it may begin with *s*, with *t*, with *f*, or with *p*.

Variations of other but still native kinds are exemplified by the word for nettle which appears as neanntag, eanntag, ionntag, feanntag, and deanntag, and by that for a bat, ialtag, ioltag, eitleog, dialtag, mioltag, ealtag leathraich (Arran), dialtag anmoch (Perth), dealtag anmoch (Badenoch), and mioltag leathair (Irish).   Variations such as those, though they are extreme cases, do not violate but exemplify the phonetic laws of the language, and once a word is known to be native the limit of its variations is determined by those laws.

The vagaries of borrowed words, on the other hand, have an uncertainty about them that keeps the inquirer ever on the outlook for strange and unexpected forms.   Those forms are so numerous in some cases as to recall the proverb, ' Tha uiread de ainmean air ris an naosg,' (he has as many *aliases* as the snipe), and one of the many names of that bird is a case in point.   Budagoc or budagochd is sometimes heard as budragochd, budag, and in Mull even as gudabochd.   The word is from the English ' woodcock,' and though sometimes used rightly as designating that bird, is often misapplied to the snipe.   The Gaelic equivalent to ' Peter Piper picked a peck of pickled pepper,' etc., is :—

> ' Gob fad air a' bhudagochd
> 'S am budagochd gun ghob.'

The English ' warning,' in which also *w* becomes *b*, appears

in Gaelic in different districts as bàrnaig, bàirneigeadh, bar-
dainn, bardaig, bairlinn, or bàirleigeadh. 'Gardener' is
gairnlear, gairnear, and gairlear, as well as gairneilear. The
familiar 'gooseberry' is in Gaelic gròiseid, in East Perthshire
gròiseag, but in West Ross crobhsag, and in East Ross crobhr-
sag. The two first forms are based, of course, on the Scottish
which appears variously as grozet, grozer and grozel, and comes
from French grose, groseille. The English gooseberry is for
grooseberry and also comes from the French grose. German
has krausbeere and krauselbeere. Crobhsag, though it is not
directly, may be remotely connected with groiseid, grozet, and
groseille.

Diversities of form are not confined to such modern borrow-
ings as those, but are found in the older loan-words from Latin.
The extent to which variations, though of a subordinate kind,
may go, is well shown so far as number is concerned, in the
case of the Latin manicula, a sleeve. This word appears in
Gaelic in the following forms :—

muinchill	muilcheann	muinichill	muilicheann
muinchille	muilchinn	muinicheal	muilichinn
muincheall	muilchill	muinicheall	muinle

muilcheann   in Sutherland.
muilchceann ,, West Ross-shire.
muilchear   ,, East Perthshire.
muille   ,, Arran.

The word is munchille in Early Irish, and metathesis and
substitution of one liquid for another account for nearly all
the forms. The middle *i* in some of the forms is merely
the parasitic vowel heard in pronunciation between the
preceding liquid and *ch*. Muinle and muille arise from the
elision or silencing of slender *ch* that is characteristic of
the Gaelic of Arran, Islay, etc. The *c* which stands between
two vowels in the Latin word was aspirated in Gaelic and is
lost altogether in the Arran form. In the next case *c*, though

it did not stand between two vowels, was aspirated in the more usual form of the word. The Latin axilla—in Irish ascall, oscul, and ocsal, Middle Irish ochsal—is best known in Gaelic as achlais, but it also appears as asgall, in Arran asgaill, in Perthshire aslaic, or better, aslaig, and in dictionaries as aslaich and asgnail. Sasunn, Irish Sagsona, in Arran Sasgunn, England, from Saxon may be compared in passing.

Some of the oldest Latin loans ultimately associated with the early church show two or more substantially different forms. 'Officium,' which is not purely ecclesiastical, is in Gaelic oifig, with minor variations such as ofaig in Argyle, Sutherland, Lewis, etc., and afaig in Arran. A widely used, though rarely written, form of the word is ofhaich, with a derivative ofhaichear, an officer. Duncan Ban Macintyre has the latter written oighichearan, officers, in his 'Song to the Argyleshire Regiment.' Tigh-ofhaich, 'office,' is used for an outhouse. The special ecclesiastical meaning of officium, a formulary of devotion, etc., is recalled in one usage. 'Cha'n eil ofhaich ann,' There is nothing in it, literally, there is not an office in it, is said in Atholl of, for example, a disappointing book, and suggests a time when no value was set upon any books but those of devotion and religious exercise. If offic-ium had been a native word f, being double, would not aspirate, and c, being single, would, but both are aspirated in ofhaich and both unaspirated in oifig, etc. In 'apostolus,' Old Irish apstal, Gaelic abstol, p has remained unaspirated, perhaps in this case because pushed up against st, but in another form of the word it has been not only aspirated but lost entirely. In North Inverness and East Ross this word has become ostal, in Sutherland astal, and resembles the Manx form ostyl, older austyl. The Gaels, it would appear, were also under the necessity of borrowing the word infernum from Latin, but, whatever inference may be drawn from the fact, they were not content with having it one way, but must needs have it in two ways—ifrinn and iutharn. Ifrinn, Irish ifrionn, is the Old Irish ifurnn with a little shifting of letters. The Manx is iurin, which would very well represent the Perthshire pronunciation of iutharn. Diabolus appears as diabhol, which is appropriated to religious use, and diall, which is profane. The former is perhaps to be regarded as a purely literary form, and the latter as the form of common speech.

The diversities of many borrowed words centre round the letter *p*. This consonant seems to have been at all times a troublesome one to the Gaels, as to the Celts in general, and with its peculiarities and laws is of the first importance in Gaelic phonetics. In loan-words it often takes the place of, or is replaced by, *b* or *f.* An initial *b* is often made into *p* : ' blanket' is in Gaelic plangaid, and Bìobull, English ' Bible,' Latin 'Biblia,' is sometimes written and is usually pronounced Pìobull. A medial or final *p* on the other hand occasionally becomes *b*, as in òb from Norse ' hóp.' The interchange of *p* and *f* is found in several instances. ' Flower' and ' flour,' which are the same etymologically, both appear in Gaelic as flùr and also as plùr, with diminutives for the former meaning flùran, flùirein, plùran and plùirean. The same change of *f* into *p* is seen in plod, a fleet, raft, etc., from Norse ' floti,' while the allied Norse fljóta has given fleodradh, floating, and fleodruinn, a buoy ; and in punntainn and funntainn, benumbment by cold, from Scottish fundy, funny, to become stiff with cold. The converse is found in feòdar and peòdar, from ' pewter,' and also in fleòdar and pleòdar, whether these come from the same word or from ' spelter.' Flodach, lukewarm, and plod, scald, have both been referred to Scottish 'plot,' to scald. Fìreas in North Inverness and pìrcas in West Ross and in Sutherland apparently come from and mean ' appearance.' The Latin plecto has given fleachdail, flowing in ringlets, and in West Ross pleachd, a roll of wool ready for spinning. Gaelic fùdar and Irish pùdar, from ' powder,' may be noted. Feòcullan, a pole-cat, may be heard in East Perth as pòcullan. The Norse hjálm, helm, has given failm, falmadair, and palmair.

P, when aspirated *ph*, sounds *f*, and *f*, when aspirated *fh*, is silent, and often is lost. By a combination of those two processes we have in one instance *p* in different forms appearing as *p* and as *f*, and disappearing altogether. 'Peacock' is found in Gaelic as peucag, peuchdag, feucag, eucag, euchdag. The way the word has been dealt with in the language is interesting in several ways. Péabh-eun, péa-choileach or peubh-choileach, and péa-chearc or peubh-chearc, in which the specific 'pea' has been separated from the subjoined terms indicative of gender, do not call for remark except that péabh and peubh suggest a direct borrowing by Gaelic from the Latin pavo, a peacock, from which the English 'pea' has come through Anglo-Saxon 'pawa.' For the rest all the forms in Gaelic have been taken from 'peacock,' to the utter exclusion of the more homely hen. Not only so, but owing to the similarity in sound of the termination to the Gaelic feminine diminutive suffix -*ag*, the word has changed both its gender and its denotation. Peucag or peuchdag is, indeed, said by some authorities to be masculine and feminine, but by others it is set down as feminine only, and by all it is translated peahen, never peacock. The other forms are unhesitatingly dealt with as feminine. Popularly the word is feminine, so much so that when the male bird is meant coileach-peucaig is not infrequently used. With the change of gender the word readily lent itself to employment by bards and wooers as a poetic metaphor and an endearing term. Extensive use of the word as a term of endearment, when it is usually preceded by mo, my, thus : M' fheucag, meaning etymologically My peacock, and sounded M' eucag, or, in some dialects, M' euchdag, accounts both for the loss of the initial consonant and for a seeming change of signification in the case of the decapitated forms. So completely was the connection of eucag or euchdag with feucag and peucag forgotten that Gaelic lexicographers have recorded them with no other signification but 'a charmer, a fair or lovely female,' and our foremost authority on etymology has explained euchdag as 'featsome one' from euchd. The identification of euchdag

with peucag is easily confirmed.   The existence of the form
eucag is against a connection with euchd.   The renderings
given for peahen are eucag, feucag, peucag, etc., and for pea-
chick, isean na h- eucaig, and 'a beautiful woman' is given as
one of the meanings of peucag.   The hold that the word has
taken of the language is shown further by the adjectives
feucagach, peucagach, peuchdagach, peacock-like, beautiful as
a peacock, abounding in peacocks, and peucach, gaudy,
showy, and may justly be regarded as an index of the
susceptibility of the Gael to the impressions of resplen-
dent hues.

Two more words fall to be noticed as having *p* and *f*.
The first, bùlas, is from Scottish bools, a pot-hook, or rather
a separable pot-handle with a joint in the middle; pùlas is
given in dictionaries as a dialectic form.   The other, feursann,
a warble, a tumour in the hide of cattle, containing the
larvae of a fly, is, notwithstanding the difference of meaning,
clearly the Scottish fersie, English farcy, farcin, a disease
of horses.

bùlas	in literature.	feursann	in literature.
pùlas	dialectic.	féirseag	,, Arran.
buthal	in Arran.	peurtanan	,, Strathspey.
bùthals	,, East Perthshire.	fiartanan	,, N. Inverness.
bùlsg	,, Strathspey.	fòurtainean	,, Reay Country.
bùilisg	,, Skye.	fiarslanan	,, Lochcarron.
pùlais	,, South Sutherland.	fiaslanan	,, Gairloch.
fòlais	,, Reay Country.	féursnan	,, Skye.

All the dialectic forms of feursann, except the Arran one, are
plurals.

In one instance *p* and *g* are found in two different groups
of forms of the same word, but both represent an original *b*.
Pronnasg, brimstone, comes from the Scottish brunstane.
This word is derived from brun or bren, the old Scottish form
of burn, and means burning-stone or fire-stone.   The Norse
'brennisteinn,' and the English brimstone, old bremstone,

brenston, are similarly derived. In Gaelic it appears as —:

pronnasg	in literature.
pronastal	,, M'Eachen's Dictionary.
pronnastair	,, Arran.
proinistear, proinstear	,, Perth.
pronnastail	,, Badenoch.
pronnstail	,, Strathspey.
prunnastal	in Skye, Edinbane.
prunaistean	,, ,, Glendale.
pronastan	,, ,, Sleat, and in Lewis.
grumastal	,, Torridon.
grunnastal	,, Gairloch and Lochbroom.
grunastal	,, Sutherland, Helmsdale.
grunnastan	,, ,, Reay Country.
grunnasdan	,, MacLeod and Dewar's Dictionary.
gronnustal	,, vocabulary in Gaelic Bible, 1st edit.

In the one group of forms there is the ordinary change of b to p. In the other group the substitution of g for the original b is analogous to the long-standing substitution of c for p.

In early loans from Latin p was often replaced in Gaelic by c. Cailleach, an old wife, a nun, comes from the Latin pallium; Càisg, the Passover, Easter, from pascha; clòimh, wool, down, from pluma, and cuithe, a pit, a snow-wreath, etc., from puteus. The Latin presbyter appears in Old Irish both as prebiter and as crubthir. Patricius gave our Pàruig and Pàdruig, Old Irish Patricc, but it also gave Cothraige, one of the names by which St. Patrick was known, and which was neither more nor less than a Gaelicised form of Pathruig. In modern Gaelic there are a few instances of the correspondence of c to p. Padhal, a ewer, invites comparison with the obsolete cadhal, a basin, and clod, from English clod, with plod, from Scottish plod, ploud, a green sod; while cartan, which means a crab in Irish, is explained as a Gaelicised form of Gaelic and Scottish partan. Pràmh, a word of obscure derivation, is rendered a slumber, a doze, but requires the word for sleep expressed or understood, as pràmh-chadail. It is also rendered grief, dejection, gloom, when the phrase is fo phràmh, under a cloud, under heaviness of mind. The meaning would seem to be something like darkening, obscuration, cf. the use of teimheal, darkness, to mean a swoon. The different forms in which the word appears, prèamh or preumh (like freumh) in Atholl, and cnàmh and cnàimh—cnàmh-chadail—in West Ross suggest borrowing. Cape Wrath, which derives its name from the Norse hvarf, a turning, a shelter, appearing in English as wharf, is found in Gaelic in two forms. Generally it is Am Parbh, the turning or angle, but in Lewis Gaelic it is called An Carbh. Here the Norse hv, which in other place-names is met with as ch and as f, has become c in Lewis and p in the rest of Gaeldom, just as Indo-European qu became c in Gaelic and p in Welsh.

Two Latin loans show the change of p to c, and also appear in a variety of forms in modern Gaelic.[1]

Purpura, purple, appears in four guises.

Corcur, Old Irish corcur; here p has in both cases been changed into c.

Curpur, a form used in Lewis; here only initial p has been changed to c.

Purpur, Middle Irish purpuir; p has been kept in both positions.

Purpaidh, used in Lewis, Sutherland, etc., an adjective, influenced by the Gaelic adjectival suffix idh, as in diadhaidh.

Pulpitum, a pulpit, appears in six or seven forms.

Cùbaid; p has become c initially and b medially; t, though standing alone between vowels, has not been aspirated, but has sunk to d; the vowel u has become long, filling the blank left by the disappearance of l.

Cùbaidh, the form used in East Ross-shire and in Sutherlandshire; d or t—cùbaith ?—has been aspirated.

---

[1] Latin plecto has given not only pleachd and fleachdail, as noticed above, but also cleachd, a ringlet, fillet of wool; Early Irish clechtaim, I plait.

Cùbainn, the form found in Lewis; final slender *d* is changed into *nn*. So Sàbaid, Sabbath, in Lewis is Sàboinn and Sàboinnd.

Pulpaid, used in Tiree, and found in Shaw's Dictionary; *p* remains in both positions, *l* is retained, and consequently *u* is not lengthened.

Pùbaid, found in Kintyre and in Strathspey : *p* medially is *b*, *l* is gone, and *u* lengthened. A similar loss of *l*, but without a lengthening of the preceding vowel, is found in the Lowland Scottish form poopit.

Bùbaid, a dialectic form given by Dr. MacBain under cùbaid; *p* in both positions has become *b*.

Pumpaid, a form heard in Arran; it has come from pulpaid, which was doubtless Shaw's native Arran pronunciation at the time he wrote, not by change of *l* to *m*, but by loss of *l* through the form pùbaid, with intrusive *m* as. in tombaca, from tobacco. This same intrusion of a liquid is seen in buntàta, from potato, and in plang, from plack.

In the case of both those words it is clear that there has been reborrowing. Purpura was first borrowed as corcur in early times, and then borrowed again as purpur at some later period. Purpaidh is based of course on purpur. What the relation of curpur is to corcur and to purpur it is hard to say ; it may be based on neither, and may have been taken independently from purpura. Its agreement in form with cùbaid in having initial *p* changed into *c*, but not medial *p*, is in any case noteworthy. Cùbaidh and cùbainn go with cùbaid. Pulpaid and the remaining forms have been borrowed independently and quite possibly not from Latin pulpitum, but from English pulpit.

The change of *p* to *c* in loans from Latin is as old as the age of St. Patrick, and is attributed to British, that is, Welsh influence. The first missionaries to Ireland, it is maintained, went from Wales, and spoke the old Welsh or British language. In that language *p* often corresponds to *c* in Irish, as in Welsh penn, Gaelic ceann, head; W. plant, Gael. clann, Old Irish cland, children; Old W. map, Gael. mac, son. When Welsh met Irish this correspondence of Irish *c* to Welsh *p* was noticed; and as Latin, according to the theory, was first introduced to Irish speakers by Welshmen, it was supposed that the proper way to adapt Latin words to Irish use when they contained the letter *p* was to change that consonant into *c*. Examples like curpur and cùbaid, in which the change is only partly carried out, and others, like Parbh and Carbh, together with the analogous pronnastail and grunnastal, would, however, suggest rather that the change was not made deliberately, but took place naturally, and that it was the result of a native tendency of the language and not of extraneous influence or analogy. The theory of Welsh influence claims support from certain other peculiarities. One is the substitution of a Gaelic *s* for a Latin *f*, as in Gaelic srian, from Latin frênum. Here again Gaelic has *s* in certain cases, where Welsh has *f*; and on the theory in question it was supposed that it ought to have *s* also where Latin had *f*. One of the instances may be noticed. The Latin furnus, an oven, has given Gaelic sorn, a flue, vent; Early Irish sornn; Welsh ffwrn; Cornish forn. By a roundabout way through French fornaise, and English furnace, this same Latin word has reached Gaelic as fùirneis, foirneis, and ùirneis, a furnace; Irish uirnéis, fúirnéis; Middle Irish forneis. The principal difference of form in this case is analogous to that found in the cases of capella and cathedra, which have come into Gaelic direct from Latin respectively as caibeal and cathair, and roundabout through French and English as seipeal and seidhir, or seithir. The same word, that is to say, has been borrowed twice, first, straight from the original Latin, and then, after transmission through two intervening languages.

'THE RUIN OF BRITANNIA'

A CONTRIBUTION TOWARDS A RESTATEMENT OF EARLY SAXO-WELSH HISTORY

A. W. WADE-EVANS

[This paper attempts to show that the supposed homogeneous work attributed to Gildas before 547, really comprises two distinct books; the first called 'Excidium Britanniæ,' which includes chapters 1 to 26, and which was composed about 700; the second, from chapter 27 to the end, being the genuine 'Epistola Gildæ' written by Gildas before 502.]

PART I. *Chronological Argument.*

ANY one who desires to make original research into early Welsh history is bound to take as a fundamental document the chronicle which is now known as *Annales Cambriæ*, and especially the oldest of the three extant MSS. thereof, viz., that printed in *Y Cymmrodor*, vol. ix.

Now the reader must understand that the chronicler did not date events in our way; in other words, he did not compute from our A.D. 1. The *Annales* show that the ecclesiastics of ancient Wales were wont to take as their year 1 (which I will hereafter call Annus I) some important event in their own history; and the important event from which the *Annales Cambriæ* compute appears to be St. Germanus's 2nd Advent to Britannia, which it fixes in the year which would be in our reckoning A.D. 445. In other words, Annus I is 445, Annus II is 446, Annus LXXII is 516, Annus CCCLXIII is 807, and so on. Now supposing that a compiler had before him several chronicles, and supposing that in one case the Annus I was 445 (St. Germanus's 2nd Advent), and in a second case that Annus I was 429 (St. Germanus's 1st Advent), and in a third case Annus I was 400 (Stilicho's consulship), and in a fourth case Annus I was 449 (Bede's date of Invitation); and supposing also that he neglected this important fact, the result of course would be disastrous. If, for example, his own Annus I was 445, and he had an event before him placed opposite Annus CXXVI computing from 429, he would insert it as Annus CXXVI computing from 445, that is to say, he would insert as having occurred in 570 what took place in 554. This is precisely what the compiler of the *Annales* has done. He has inserted events as having happened in the era of 445 which really occurred, some in the era of 400, some in that of 429, some in that of 433 (St. Patrick as Bishop in Ireland), some in 449, and so on; and all this to such an extent that almost every single item in the first two centuries or so of his chronicle is demonstrably miscomputed, *and this is a chief cause of the chaotic state of early Welsh history.*

Before proceeding further, I will give three examples out of the many in order to make this all-important point quite clear :—

(*a*) It is universally admitted that St. Patrick died in 461. I make this statement on the strength of Dr. White's words,[1] which are as follows : 'The only date in St. Patrick's history about which there is ever likely to be a general agreement amongst scholars is the year in which he died.' After a reference to Professor Bury's investigations, he sums up :— 'This would make A.D. 461 the year of St. Patrick's death.' Now the *Annales Cambriæ* place it opposite Annus XIII, which in the era of 445 gives a wrong date, viz., $445 + 12 = 457$; but which in the era of 449 gives the right date, viz., $449 + 12 = 461$. Therefore this event was extracted from a chronicle which computed from 449.

(*b*) The date of the death of Cadwaladr, King of Gwynedd, has perplexed chroniclers and historians for centuries. We know from Nennius that he died in a pestilence during the reign of Oswy, King of Northumbria, that is between 642 and 670, and also that a great pestilence commenced in 664. It began, according to Bede, on the southern coast, and passed northwards into Northumbria and westwards into Ireland. The *Annales*, however, place both the pestilence and the king's death opposite Annus CCXXXVIII, which in

---

[1] White's *Latin Writings of St. Patrick* (1905), p. 230.

the era of 445 is $445 + 237 =$ A.D. 682. Notice what Rhŷs and Jones say in *The Welsh People* (127) : 'The *Brut* puts [the death of Cadwaladr] as taking place in 681, but the writer uses language which shows that for some reason he confounded Cadwaladr with Ceadwalla, King of Wessex, who did die in that year [Ceadwalla died really in 689]. If, from the few data we have to rely on, the matter is traced out, there can be no doubt that the year 681 is too late, and that in all probability it was in or very near to 664 Cadwaladr died.' The learned authors are undoubtedly right, although no explanation is given of the dates 681 and 682 of the *Brut* and *Annales* respectively. Now Annus CCXXXVIII in the true era of the Invitation is $428 + 237 =$ A.D. 665.[1]

(c) Opposite Annus CLXXXVI the *Annales* place this dark entry—'Guidgar comes and returns not' which Annus makes $445 + 185 = 630$. It obviously refers to some early well-known settlement whose best remembered leader was ' Guidgar.' The only known settlement of the kind of which we are reminded is that of Wihtgar and Stuf in the Isle of Wight in 514. A well-known place in the island called Wihtgaraburh was said to be called after Wihtgar, from whom also Alfred claimed descent through his mother. Wihtgar was no doubt regarded as the eponymous hero of Wight. But if ' Guidgar' came in 514, how was it placed in 630 ? Two mistakes were made. A scribe had before him the date ' A.D. DCXIV,' *i.e.* 514. The first mistake was to read DC as 600 instead of 500 (that being once a common way of writing 500). Having thus obtained the number 614, he proceeded to compute in the era of St. Germanus's 1st Advent, viz. 429. In other words, if 429 is made the Annus I, then 614 will be $614 - 428$, which is Annus CLXXXVI *as*

[1] As the *Brut* is undoubtedly based in its early events on the *Annales*, the pestilence of 664 was probably in an original text placed opposite Annus CCXXXVII, *i.e.* $445 + 236 = 681$ and $428 + 236 = 664$. Cadwaladr probably died in the year following that in which the plague commenced, for we must allow some time for it to have spread from the South to North Wales. This would explain the difference between the two chronicles.

above. Afterwards a second scribe, neglecting the era, inserted it without change in his own era of 445, so that the event was thrown 116 years out of its true date! Now I trust we may proceed.

1. The death of Maelgwn Gwynedd, whom Gildas rebukes in his *Epistola*, is placed opposite Annus CIII, which makes $445 + 102 = \text{A.D. } 547$. But now that we have seen good cause to doubt the accuracy of the early computations of the *Annales*, let us approach the matter from another side. Please compare the following genuine pedigrees :—

Cunedda Wledig.	Cunedda Wledig.
Einion.	Ceredig.
Cadwallon Llawhir.	Cedig.
Maelgwn (alleged date of death, 547 ; true date, 502).	Sant.
	St. David (born Annus XIV = in era of *Annales*, 456 ;
Rhun.	in Bedan era of Invitation,
Beli.	$449 + 13 = 462$).
Iacob (died 613).	
Cadfan.	
Cadwallon (died 633).	
Cadwaladr (died 665).	

The second of the above pedigrees proves that the birth of Cunedda has to be thrown back at least to the year 390. For if St. David was born in 462, his father must have been at least eighteen years old at the time, and so with Cedig when Sant was born. Hence Cunedda's birth at very latest cannot be after 390. But Cunedda's eldest son (who himself had a son) died before Cunedda left the north, so that his birth has to be assumed sometime about 370. Now notice in the first pedigree how crowded are the names between Maelgwn's supposed death in 547 and Iacob's death in 613, whereas how extended are the names between Maelgwn and Cunedda. These pedigrees, when carefully compared, prove conclusively that 547 is far too late for Maelgwn's death, and that therefore Annus CIII is to be computed in some much earlier era. Now fortunately the true era is not difficult to discover. If the first 110 years of the *Annales* (MS. A.) are carefully read, it will be noticed that eight ecclesiastical events are recorded and three military ones, which are as follows :—

Annus LXXII Victory of ' Badon' won by Arthur.
Annus XCIII Arthur's death at Camlan.
Annus CIII Death of Maelgwn Gwynedd.

Moreover, in the *Calculi* prefixed to the *Annales* two military events are distinctly computed from the consulship of Stilicho in 400. These are the words :—

'Item a Stillicione usque ad Ualentinianum filium Placide et regnum Guorthigirni, uiginti octo anni. Et a regno Guorthigirni usque ad discordiam Guitolini et Ambrosii anni sunt duodecim.'

'From Stillicho to Valentinianus and Vortigern's reign are 28 years; and from Vortigern's reign to the battle between Guitolinus and Ambrosius are 12 years.'

Now, by computing the victory at ' Badon' in the era of Stilicho, we get $400 + 71 = $ A.D. 471, which date is corroborated by the famous interpolation in the *Excidium Britanniæ* which computes ' Badon' as the Annus XLIV with one month gone [from Vortigern's Invitation], *i.e.* $428 + 43 = 471$. Again, as the annalistic year in the fifth century commenced on September 1 with the indiction, ' Badon' was won in October 470 of our reckoning, which is the fact underlying Geoffrey of Monmouth's absurd statement that Arthur slew with his own hand 470 men. Arthur fell at Camlan twenty-two years after ' Badon' *i.e.* 492, or Annus XCIII in the era of Stilicho. Maelgwn's death occurred ten years after Camlan, *i.e.* 502, or Annus CIII in the era of Stilicho. This calculation from ' Badon' to Maelgwn's death is made in a document which deserves greater attention than has hitherto been paid to it, viz., the tract called *O oes Gwrtheyrn* compiled in John's reign, and inserted in the Red Book of Hergest. \

, Now, as Maelgwn was alive when St. Gildas wrote his rebuke, the *Epistola Gildæ* was written before Maelgwn's death in Annus CIII a Stilichione consule, *i.e.* A.D. 502.

2. The *Calculi* prefixed to the *Annales* also contain the following :—' et in quarto anno regni sui Saxones ad Brittanniam venerunt, Felice et Tauro consulibus, quadringentesimo [vicesimo octavo] anno ab Incarnatione Domini nostri, and in the 4th year of Vortigern's reign the Saxons came to Britannia, Felix and Taurus being consuls, in the year of the Incarnation 428.'

How then is it that Bede places this event in 449 ?

In 532 Dionysius invented his system of Christian Chronology which we use to this day. After a while this system was criticised as follows :—If (it was argued) our Lord was born in A.D. I, then the day of the Crucifixion must be Nisan 15 and March 25, and a Friday, and the moon fifteen days old, and all in the year A.D. 34. But as a matter of fact it is not so, whereas these conditions are found in A.D. 12. Therefore, argued the critics, A.D. 12 according to Dionysius, must be A.D. 34 according to the truth of the Gospel. Consequently they introduced a new system of chronology, which they called that of Gospel Verity, against the system of Dionysius. Now we find that in Northumbria, in the middle of the seventh century, Vortigern's Invitation was fixed at 450, and this computation is quite right *if we only remember that it is according to Gospel Verity.* In other words, the date 450 is based on the date 428, because 428 according to Dionysius = 450 according to Gospel Verity. Bede's first mistake therefore was due to a confusion of the formulæ *secundum Dionysium* and *secundum Evangelicam Veritatem.* His second mistake (or at least that of one of his originals) is equally interesting. He says that the Invitation took place in the first year of Marcian, viz. in 449; but the first year of Marcian is 450. Why then did he say 449 ? There was a method of dating an event as having happened *when so many years were completed*, which method Bede neglected. The Invitation indeed was made when 449 years of our Lord according to Gospel Verity, were completed, which means 450. If the Welsh University came into existence when 1893 years of our Lord were completed, it signifies the year 1894.

Now if Dionysius invented his system in 532 a criticism of it was not possible till after that date. But the system of Dionysius was not introduced into Britain until St. Augustine brought it in 597, and therefore a criticism of it would be meaningless in Britain till after that date. In other words, the computation, according to Gospel Verity, was not possible in Britain till after 597. But the *Excidium Britanniæ* (said to have been written by St. Gildas who died in 554) computes the date of the Invitation, according to Gospel Verity, and therefore it could not have been written by Gildas nor before 597. For the *Excidium* places the Invitation after the third consulship of Aetius in 446 [and in 450].

Part II. *Nationality of Author.*

3. We have seen that St. Gildas wrote the *Epistola* before 502, the year of Maelgwn's death. The *Epistola* was addressed to the civil and ecclesiastical rulers of Britannia, so that we have here an opportunity of ascertaining what was meant by Britannia in Britain in 500. Gildas rebukes the five leading princes by name in the following order :—

> Constantine of Damnonia or 'Devon.'
> Aurelius Caninus.
> Vortiporius of Demetia (Pembrokeshire + West Carmarthenshire).
> Cuneglas or Cynlas.
> Maglocunus or Maelgwn Gwynedd (N.W. Wales) 'superior to almost all the kings of Britannia.'

As our author begins with Damnonia and ends with Gwynedd, and refers to Demetia midway, we are justified in locating Aurelius Caninus between 'Devon' and Carmarthen, and Cynlas in Mid or North Wales. The latter is almost certainly Maelgwn's cousin, as shown in this pedigree :—

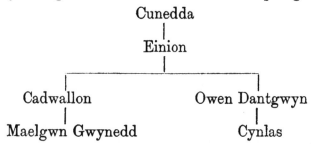

and Rhŷs is possibly right in locating the *arx* or stronghold of Cynlas at Dineirth (receptaculum ursi) near Llandudno. With regard to Aurelius Caninus (between Carmarthen and 'Devon'), compare the 'Roman' touch of *Aurelius* with the Ambrosius *Aurelianus* of 428, who is known from Nennius (c 41) to have been a native of *Campus Elleti* or *Electi* in the region called Glywyssing, between the river Usk and the river Llwchwr in S.E. Wales, and who is described as the last of the Romani in Britannia by the *Excidium*. The two were probably members of the same family, ruling somewhere due E. of Carmarthen and 'Devon.' In later times the eastern boundary of Demetia was roughly between Carmarthen town and Llandyssul. Add to this the fact that the Tombstone of this very Vortipore, whom Gildas addresses, ·was found a few years ago well within this boundary, near Haverfordwest, and we are led to conclude that even in 500 Demetia could not have been much more than it was in later times. Moreover, the patria known later as Ystrad Tywi, between Demetia and the river Neath, had been penetrated by the family of Cunedda, who expelled the Scotti from Kidwelly and Gower. East of this, barbarian reguli of the families of Vortigern, Brychan, and Glywys held from N. to S. as far as the lower Usk. We must therefore locate Aurelius Caninus between the river Usk and Poole Harbour. The determination of these boundaries must be settled in the future. The one point to lay stress on now is this, that the three rivers called Avon (Tewkesbury, Bristol, and Dorset) almost certainly represent

Britannic boundaries of the fifth and sixth centuries, Avon being the Britannic word for ' river.' In other words, the Dorsetshire Avon was probably the S.E. boundary of Britannia till some point on the Tewkesbury Avon in the north. Beyond this northwards, of course, were the Angles and Frisians. These together with the ' Brittones ' constituted the three nations who (as Procopius writing in 553-4 informs us) held the Roman province of Britannia in such great numbers that they over-flowed yearly into Gaul.[1] If we assume the Bristol Avon to have been the eastern boundary of Damnonia, then Aurelius Caninus must be given the patria of the three Avons, which was Romania *par excellence*. Without therefore determining at present the eastern boundary of Britannia, we are at once able to realise what was meant by that name in the year 500. But the *Excidium* tells us that for a hundred and fifty years from the Invitation of Vortigern the Saxons only made plundering raids into Britannia, that is from 428 to 577, in which last year occurred the crushing defeat at Deorham, when the Saxons acquired the three *caers* of Gloucester, Bath, and Cirencester, and thereby split Britannia into two fragments. Therefore the Britannia of St. Gildas in 500 was identical with that of Vortigern in 428. Be it remembered that 428 was as critical a date with the Roman Britanni as 1066 in English history, or 1536 in later Welsh history, because 428 is the year in which a king in Britannia joined the Saxon kindreds against the Roman Britanni. This king was the regulus of a little patria beyond Builth in Radnorshire, called after his name, viz. Gwrtheyrnion or ' Vortigernia.' He was not a Romanus, and probably not a Brython. The tradition is as follows :—' Guorthigirnus regnavit in Brittannia et dum ipse regnabat, urgebatur a metu Pictorum Scottorumque et a Romanico impetu necnon et a timore Ambrosii—Vortigern reigned in Britannia, and while he reigned he was in dread

---

[1] One must distinguish between Britannia as known to geographers and as known to officials of the Empire and as known to natives of the fifth century. In like manner Picti would have meant to Roman officials the people beyond the Wall, whether they were Picti properly so called or otherwise ; and so with the terms Scotti and Britanni. This is undoubtedly one great source of later confusion.

of Picts, Scots, and Roman aggression, and especially was he in fear of Ambrosius.' In other words, Picts from Scotland, that is the Cymry under Cunedda, and Scots from Ireland were pressing on his little patria beyond Builth.[1] Romani also were threatening him, and especially Ambrosius of S.E. Wales. All this occurred from 425, when he began to reign. Driven by necessity, he invited to his assistance the Saxon kindreds who dwelt beyond the Avons on either side of the lower Thames. Romania naturally resented this barbaric alliance and the independence of Vortigern, and execrated his memory accordingly. These traditions passing into the Church, whose stronghold lay in Romania, were accepted by later times without criticism.

Now if Britannia signified Wales + Cornish Peninsula as early as 425 and as late as 577, whatever genuine traditions underlie the Britannia of the *Excidium Britanniæ*, from the moment it depends on native accounts, must refer to it; and this is precisely the case when the early chapters based on continental writings are finished, and the invasions of Picts, Scots, and Saxons, based on native traditions, are commenced, as I have shown in my previous paper.

4. Inasmuch as the author of the *Excidium* is a Roman Britannus, whose patriotism is kindled by the memory of Ambrosius; and inasmuch as he refers familiarly to the topography of S.E. Wales (not to mention his reference to the Britanni of Armorica in a manner impossible to a Cymro or a Scottus, or a follower of Vortigern), it is clear he is a native either of S.E. Wales or of the Britannic territory between the Severn Sea and Poole Harbour. *In other words, he is not St. Gildas ap Caw o Priten*, who was neither a Roman Britannus nor a native of Romania at all. St. Gildas was the son of Caw o Priten, *i.e.* Caw of Pictland or Southern Scotland, a regulus 'beyond the mountain Bannawc' in Arecluta, which means 'on or opposite Clyde.' This Caw is also called Caw of Twrcelyn, which is a small commote or patria in Anglesey. People have often wondered why he was

---

[1] Vortigern was probably the head of a confederacy of reguli.

called by this name. The reason, however, will be found in the *Vita S. Cadoci,* where the twelfth century compiler has edited an important historical tradition almost out of recognition. In § 22 of the *Vita* he recounts a journey of St. Cadoc into Albania or Scotland where, in digging near a monastery or *llan* which he had founded, he discovered the collarbone of 'an old hero of immense size.' This hero or giant is made to return from hell, and, when questioned by St. Cadoc, replies, 'I reigned formerly for many years beyond the mountain Bannawc. It chanced that by the devil's instigation *I and all my raiders came to these coasts* for plunder and devastation. The king who reigned over the country pursued with his troops. A battle was fought and I and my army slain.' When asked who he was, he replied, 'Caw of Prydyn or Cawr [*i.e.* giant].' Caw is then converted, and the 'reguli Albanorum,' or kings of the Scots, give him twenty-four villæ or trevs. This extraordinary story is based on an account of St. Cadoc's journey amongst the Scotti—not of Albania or Scotland, but of Anglesey. Near Amlwch, in the old commote of Twrcelyn, is the extinct monastery of Cadog called Llangadog, the only one ascribed to him in the island. The twenty-four villæ are so many trevs in the commote of Twrcelyn, which the invader, Caw o Priten from Arecluta, was granted by his allies, the Scotti of Anglesey. In other words, Caw, father of St. Gildas, was one of those very Picti who came over the sea from the north in the fifth century, against whom the author of the *Excidium* rails so bitterly. If St. Gildas ab Caw had written the following from chapter 19 of the *Excidium* :—[The Picts and Scots are] alike in one and the same thirst for bloodshed, in a preference also for covering their villainous faces with hair rather than their nakedness of body with decent clothing—if, I say, St. Gildas the son of the Pictish raider who settled in Twrcelyn in Anglesey, had written this, he would have been attacking his own kin, his own father's *familia* who were wont to cover their faces with hair rather than their nakedness of body with clothing. Surely there is no lack of patriotism in the *Excidium*, but it is the patriotism of another patria, nay, of a patria which regarded that of Gildas as its bitterest foe. Note, moreover, the entire absence of all this in the genuine *Epistola* of St. Gildas, how in fact he makes us feel that Maelgwn Gwynedd, notwithstanding all his sins, was indeed the Island Dragon whom God had made chief over almost all the princes of Britannia even as He had made him taller in the stature of his person. No one can mistake the genuine affection of this monk for the head of the great Cymric house of Cunedda. He harks back with patriotic pride to the days of Maelgwn's young manhood, surrounded by gallant soldiers whose faces were like those of young lions. He is shocked that a king like this, so undoubtedly brave and splendid in his towering height, should have committed such crimes against Christ. There is too great a gulf between Gildas the Cymro to whom Latin was the *lingua Romana* and the Britannus of Romania to whom the Cymry were barbarians and Latin *lingua nostra*, for us to confound them.

5. Moreover, if the author of the *Excidium* had been Gildas ab Caw writing before 502, he could not possibly have made such a mistake as that in which he tells us that the Walls of Antonine and Hadrian were built after 388, and also the nine forts of the Saxon shore. For let it be remembered that the Roman occupation of Southern Britain was mainly military and that the bulk of the Roman Army was stationed for centuries on the Welsh border and in the north about this very wall of stone which would be known to every child from Cape Wrath to Land's End. Gildas, a native of Southern Scotland, writing before 502 of events of most significant import which were perfectly familiar to his father and grandfather who were actually on the spot, could not possibly have stated that Hadrian's Wall was built after the final withdrawal of the Roman legions by means of public and private subscriptions *and between cities which perhaps had been located there through fear of enemies*. This last sentence in itself betrays the late date of the work.

6. Nor could St. Gildas before 502 have made the sugges-

tion which the *Excidium* does in chapters 11 and 12, where it is assumed that the *merthyr* place names of South Wales are so called after supposed Diocletian martyrs. It is true that there are strong reasons for believing that St. Alban was an actual martyr in our sense of the word, of Britannic Romania. But inasmuch as these merthyrs (martyria), such as Merthyr Tydvil, etc., are all connected with localities where Irish influences are known to have prevailed and especially with the Irish family of Brychan of Brycheiniog or Brecon[shire], and inasmuch as the Irish are known to have used the word *martyres* in the sense of relics over which they were wont to build shrines which they called ' Houses of Relics,' it is practically certain that the merthyrs of South Wales are not built in honour of martyrs but are little shrines erected over the relics of saints. Now, as Brychan was the great-grandfather of St. David who was born in Annus XIV which in the Bedan era of the Invitation is 462, we are justified in dating the merthyr place names of South Wales, called mostly after Brychan's children and grandchildren, in the fifth century. As Irish influences decayed in Wales, this use of the word martyrium or merthyr decayed also. By the close of the seventh century the origin of these names was forgotten, especially amongst the Britanni living between the river Usk and Poole Harbour, so that the suggestion of the *Excidium* was quite natural in its own period and place, the word martyrium being taken in its Latin sense of a church ascribed to a martyr.

(To be continued.)

SLÀN LE DIÙRA CHREAGACH CHIAR

Domhnull MacEacharn

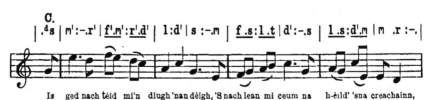

O, slàn le Diùra chreagach, chiar,
B'e m'aighear's m'iarrtas riamh bhi'd thaice,
A' sealg na h-èilde air an t-sliabh,
'S an làn-daimh chiar an riasg na glaice ;
Is ged nach tèid mi'n diugh 'n an dèigh,
'S nach lean mi ceum na h-èild' 's na creachainn,
'S tric thog mi fonn air lorg an fhèidh,
Le m'ghunna glèist' fo sgèith mo bhreacain.

O, slàn le d'bheanntan corrach, àrd',
Gach cnoc is càrn is àiridh fhasgach ;
Is ann fo'n sgàth bu mhiann leam tàmh,
Gu'n teid gu bràth fo'n chlàr mo thasgadh ;

O, soraidh leis gach srath is raon,
Gach coire fraoich, is caochan blasda ;
B'e fìon an fhuarain cuach mo ghaoil,
An iocshlaint shaor,—gach braon dhi
'nasgaidh.

Do choilltean dlùth, 's an ùr-mhìos Mhàigh
Bu chùbhraidh 'm fàs fo sgàil a bharraich,
'S a'gbrian a'sùghadh tùis nam blàth
A mhosgail nàdur tràth an Earraich ;
O, 's truagh nach d'fhuair mi fios 'na
thràth,
Nach robh e'n dàn domh àit eil' fhaicinn,
A choisinn cliù is mùirn a'bhàird,
Mar rinn an t'àit 's an d'fhàg mi'm breacan.

THE STUDY OF HIGHLAND PERSONAL NAMES

Alexander Macbain, LL.D.

In the first number of the *Celtic Review* Mr. Watson
dealt in a thoroughly scientific spirit with the ' Study
of Highland Place Names,' and I have felt ever since
that in the interests of ethnologic study the parallel
subject of ' Personal Names' should be considered.   The
more immediate reason for my undertaking this task
comes from some remarks in Sheriff Ferguson's excellent
articles in the last two numbers of the *Review* upon the
' Celtic Element in Lowland Scotland.'   He has expressed
the wish that for ethnological purposes as much were done
for the personal names as for the place names of modern
Scotland.   A good deal has been done since Professor Mackinnon set the example in his *Scotsman* articles on the ' Place
Names and Personal Names of Argyle' in 1887-8.   Nor has
the subject of ' Personal Names' been eschewed by Highland
writers, especially the clan historians; but the subject is
narrower in its limits and less objective than place names,
which, representing in large measure in words the physical
features of the country, invite the fancy of the amateur
philologist.   To him Donald appears to be undoubtedly
Donn-shuil or ' Brown-eyed,' and Maclaverty is still from
Fear-labhartach or ' spokesman,' or, better yet, as in the
latest clan history, from Fear Labhairt-an-righ, ' King's
Speaker'; while heads are sapiently shaken over the too
manifest explanation of Macrae as Mac-ratha, ' Son of Grace.'
And yet the etymologies recognised by Celtic scholars for
these names have been published in systematic and accessible
form within the last ten years.   We do not read one another's
works or articles, so that it may be quoted as true of us
what the poet says :

'Running with lampless hands,
No man takes light of his brother till blind at the goal he stands.'

The importance of the interpretation and history of personal names in the cases of ethnology and genealogy has been always recognised, but the Lowland writers who dealt with Highland subjects always fought shy of the subject; and indeed until a generation ago little good could be expected or received from the interpretations offered.   Philology as a science is quite recent, and its application to personal names is still more recent.   But now it is helping to solve some troublesome historic problems.   As an instance, the vexed question of Pictish origins has got—or is getting—its quietus from a study of the place and personal names of Pictavia.   After consideration of these elements of the Pictish problem, with one or two further facts, Dr. Whitley Stokes sums up the results in these sufficiently restrained terms :— 'The foregoing list of names and words contains much that is still obscure; but on the whole it shows that Pictish, as far as regards its vocabulary, is an Indo-European and especially Celtic speech.   Its phonetics, so far as we can ascertain them, resemble those of Welsh rather than of Irish.'   So Pictish, according to Dr. Stokes and other leading Celtists, was not Gaelic; it was a Brittonic language. Modern Celtic scholarship merely restores our confidence in the old chronicles of Scotland after the *douche* of scepticism thrown on them by Pinkerton and Skene.

On smaller points, too, light is reflected.   The names Macbeth and MacHeth puzzled Skene and his contemporaries; Dr. Skene regarded Beth as a personal name and refused to follow Robertson in elucidating the history of the MacHeths by acknowledging that Beth Comes was a transcriber's blunder.   Yet such is the case.   The 'shape-shifting' name of Eth, Ed, Head, Heth, Mac-Heth, Mac-Eghe comes after all—as it dawned on Mr. Lang—from Aed or Aodh, 'fire,' and is still found in the names of Mackay, Mackie, and Magee—in Sutherland, Galloway, and Ireland. And Macbeth proves to be no Pictish name either, as one eminent Celtic scholar thought and seems still to think. He regarded Macbeth as the enigmatic Karl Hundason of the Orkney saga, and jumped to the conclusion that Hundason or Dog-son was a translation of Mac-beth; therefore *beth* meant 'dog,' and it was Pictish, for no Aryan language has such a name for 'dog.' Although he knows of Maol-beathadh (servant-of-life), and he might know of Cu-beathadh (dog-of-life)—he is still unrepentant, though the early annals swarm with names such as these—abstract and material nouns going along with *cu, mac, maol*, and others. A study, therefore, of the formation, meaning, and history of Gaelic personal names is necessary for the ethnologist and historian of early Scotland.

Present-day personal names of the Highlands show specimens from all the strata—so to speak—of Gadelic history since Gadelic and its mother Celtic became independent languages. Donald or Domhnall, when restored to the pristine fulness of its form as Dumno-valos, is full brother to the princely name of Dumno-rix, the name of Cæsar's patriotic foe, and both have much the same proud meaning —'world-ruler,' 'world-king.' They represent, too, the Indo-European character of old Celtic names, which were formed from two stems welded together, as we see. The name Fergus—Ver-gustus or 'super-choice'—is common to Old Breton, Welsh, Pictish, and Gadelic, and indeed may thus be claimed as belonging to the period when all these languages were as yet one and undivided. A later stage is shown by a name like Cu-chulinn—'Dog of Culann'; the Gaels here seem to have adopted in Ireland the style of name-giving which belonged to the pre-Celtic inhabitants. The formula is no longer two welded stems, but the first element denotes servant, devotee, or son of some god or beast or object or idea, while the second element denoting this is, of course, in the genitive case. Hence come Macbeth and Macrae—'Son of Life, son of Grace'; and Mac-na-cearda, 'craftsman' (Sinclair from Tinkler); and hence, too, the numerous names with *maol* and *gille* prefixed to saints' names and otherwise, in the old annals, and still partially preserved: Maol-colum or Malcolm and Gillie-calum, for instance. Biblical names do not appear, curiously enough, earlier than the other foreign names which began to be adopted after the Norse invasions—in the tenth and eleventh centuries. Scotland was more exposed to foreign influences than Ireland, and the names in the Book of Deer (*circ.* 1100) contain nearly twenty per cent. of non-Celtic elements, while the corresponding entries of practically the same date in the Book of Kells in Ireland show only some twelve per cent. The Norman period coincident with the reigns of the immediate descendants of Ceannmor brought in a new system in state and church government, and also a new nomenclature; surnames began, and the old Gadelic Christian names gave way to such royal names as Alexander and William, or to such a favourite baptismal name as John—from John the Baptist. At the present time nearly forty per cent. of our Highland population bear one or other of these three names, but Donald holds the second place to John in the list of all Christian names. Of the individual ' Christian ' names in actual use only thirty per cent. are Gaelic names like Angus, Donald, or Duncan, and only thirty-seven per cent. of the population bear such Gaelic Christian names at all. The oldest Highland surnames Macdougall and Macdonald, which go back to the thirteenth century—to Dugall son of Somerled and to Donald Mor son of Reginald, son of Somerled. Donald's *floruit* is about 1250 and Dougall's about 1200. The rival Campbells, however, press hard on these dates, for the first recorded is Gillespic Cambell (1266), whom the genealogies represent as son of Dugall Cambel or ' wrye-mouth,' fifth in descent from Duibhne, from whom the family has the name O'Duibhne. Surnames were rare in the Highlands till the sixteenth and seventeenth centuries when the younger and minor clans escaped the tutelage of the Island lords and the 'lieutenancies' of Huntly and Argyll. Individuals were designated by a string of ancestors, ending usually with name of the croft or farm occupied, such as :— John MacHamish vic Aonas vic Allister Reoch *in* Ballachroan (1679). After the '45 matters rapidly changed; movements and expeditions to the Lowlands necessitated surnames; and these were adopted either from the clan to which the individual really belonged or to which he attached himself, or from the name of the district or place of his origin. It has been a common thing for the smaller septs to sink their real surname in the bigger tribal or clan name. Thus Rob Donn was really a Calder from the Oikel district, his family having in the eighteenth century registers the aliases of Mackay or Calder or Eckel; but the poet is now claimed as a 'real' Mackay. As in other parts of the kingdom, Highland surnames may be derived from other than patronymics. Epithets or Nicknames, such as Dow and Bane, form a large class; so do place names, such as Murray and Geddes, and names from rank, profession, or trade, have their clans and septs—Mackintosh (thane's son), Macpherson (the parson), and Macintyre (carpenter). As to the 'Celticity' of Highland surnames, the *mac* names account for close on half the population; but such a name as McAlister is only half Gaelic by etymology and forty per cent. of our *mac* patronymics are of this hybrid kind. On the other hand many English surnames, such as Brown, Morrison, Livingston, and Lindsay (Brehon's son, Mac-gillemhoire, Macleay and Maclintock), represent Gaelic originals, though in a census enumeration they must be reckoned English. The Celticity of the *individual* surnames in use amounts to sixty per cent. of the whole, while, as already stated, the Celticity of the Christian names is less than half that amount. The Celticity of the population as denoted by their surnames can only be guessed at roughly; it is about eighty per cent.

The Gaels by language are an Aryan or Indo-European people, and the parent people had a unique system of name-giving which the descendant nations have always preserved and presented. The Aryan name in full was a compound of two stems: Sanskrit Dêva-dattas, 'God-given'; Greek Diogenes, 'God's-bairn'; Slavonic Vladimir, 'famed-in-rule' (Gaelic, *flath-mór* by roots); and Teutonic Os-wald, 'ruler from the Anses or Gods.' Then in Celtic we have—Gaulish Devo-gnata, 'God's-bairn,' Argio-talus, 'silver-brow,' which

Pictish reverses in Tal-org and Talargan; Pictish Morcunn, now Morgan, Welsh Morgan, Old Breton Morcant, a Celtic Mori - cantos, 'sea-bright'; Ancient Welsh Maglo-cunus (Gildas, 550 A.D.), now Maelgwn, older Welsh Mailcun, Pictish Mailchon, 'high chief'; Pictish Congust, Old Welsh Cingust, Celtic Cuno-gustus, 'high choice'; Pictish Uven or Euganan, Welsh Ywein or Owein, Gaelic Eòghan or Eogan, 'well-born.' These 'double-barrelled' names characteristic of the Indo-European nations are usually epithets, drawn from the strenuous and warlike aspects of life—such as Alexander or Veremund, 'defender of men,' and William or Wilhelm, 'helm of resolution.' Animal names may form one of the elements, the wolf and the bear being prominent. Religion and kin naturally enter largely into the compounds; indeed, some nations, like the Greeks and Teutons, made the name show descent from either father or grandfather—such as *Dino*-krates, son of *Dino*-kles, or among the English lists of kings, *Ethel*-wulf (838-58), father of *Ethel*-bald, *Ethel*-bert, and *Ethel*-red. As a consequence of this genealogical practice, the meanings of these double-stemmed names are not always consistent, especially among the Teutons. The first element should qualify the second, but we meet with Theo-doros, 'Gift from God,' which is right, beside Doro-theos, which should mean 'Gift-god,' which is not so good, and is due to reasons of family descent. The Greeks were on the whole careful that the elements had a fair sense when combined; not so the Teutons, where we meet with names that mean 'Peace-war, War-peace, Peace-spear' (Fredegunde, Hildfrid, Fredegar). In fact, matters went so far that there were practically two lists of these stems, one for the first element of the compound, and the other for the second element. As the Teutonic names show the extreme development of this practice, the following short lists have been drawn up from Teuton names with the double purpose of showing how the system worked, and of giving the meaning of the most important Teutonic names borrowed into Gaelic. The first list, therefore, contains the element that

usually antecedes in the double-barrelled name, and the
second list gives the element that generally comes last :—

Gud, god, god.
Os, As, An, gods, Anses.
Rógn, regin, gods, counsel.
Thor, god Thor.
Hug, hu, thought.
Ercan, archi, pure.
Her, har, army.
Sig, victory.
Ead, éd, possessions.
Uodal, ul, patrimony.
Heim, hen, home.
Wil, will.
Ethel, al, noble.
Hrod, rod, ro, famed.
Hlod, lud, famous.

frid, fred, urd, peace.
mund, protection.
win, friend.
red, counsel.
bert, bright.
ward, warden.
ketill, kell, kettle.
helm, helmet.
ric, rich, ruler.
leif, láf, heritage.
trygg, tric, true.
wald, old, wielder.
bald, bold.
wulf, olf, wolf.
bern, burn, bear.

Our best known names will be found by combining these
elements : God-fred, ' God's peace,' becomes in Gaelic Goraidh,
older Gofraidh, whence the patronymic M'Gorry. The name
is still common among the Macdonalds. An-láf, ' heir of the
Anses,' gives the name Olave, Gaelic Amhlaibh, whence the
sept name Mac-aulay. Regin-ald, ' Gods' ruler,' is known in
Gaelic as Raonull, English Ronald ; M'Ranald, M'Crindle,
Clan-ranald. Reynold is the best English form. The god
Thor gives many names : Thor-mund gives G. Tormod, or, in
some dialects, Tormailt (cf. *iarmailt* from *firmamentum*), and
is Englished as Norman or ' North-man,' simply because of
the like sound. Thor-ketill or Thor-kell, ' Thor's sacred
vessel,' gives the names M'Corquodal and M'Corkle, as well
as the Christian name Torcail or Torquil. Of a similar origin
and force is Askell, ' kettle of the Anses,' found in M'Askill.
Hugh means ' thought,' and does duty now for the old Gaelic
name of Aodh, which latterly became a mere grunt (Y M'Ay
of Strathnaver) and sadly required the strengthening it got
from the diminutive of Hugh, namely Hucheon or G. Hùis-
dean, which properly in Gaelic ought to be Aoidhean or
' little Aodh '—still found in the Skye name of Macquien,

sometimes wrongly rendered as Macqueen. The Clann Huis-
dean of Sleat are now the leading branch of the Macdonalds,
and, in the person of Lord Macdonald, lay claim to the chiefship.
The name Arcen-bald or Archibald, ' pure and brave,' is the
favourite translation of Gaelic Gilleasbuig or Gillespic, 'bishop's
serf,' though the connection is not clear either by form or meaning.   Harold or Herald appears now only in the Gaelic surname of M'Raild ; and the elements of the name are reversed
in Walter, whence Watt, and the old northern (Moray and
Black Isle) sept of M'Watt, M'Wattie, and Watson. The
M'Watties were also a sept of the Buchanans. The name
Sigfrid or Sigurd appears now only in the obscure Skye sept
name of M'Siridh, who, of course, like all minor septs, try to
hide themselves as Macdonalds and sometimes as Mackinnons.
Sigtrygg or Sitric gives the Galwegian name of M'Kittrick
or M'Ketterick.   Edward is in G. confused with the famous
Norse name Iomhar or Iver, Norse Ivarr or Ingvarr, ' youth,'
which gives M'Iver, M'Eur, M'Cure—the latter two names
in Galloway.   Ul-rick or ' patrimonially rich ' was in Galloway and Carrick confused with the old Gaelic name of
Ualgarg, 'high temper,' appearing as Ulgric, the name
of one of the leaders of the wild Galwegians in 1138 at the
Battle of the Standard. This name was brought north by
the Kennedys of Lochaber, who are known in Gaelic as
M'Ualraig or M'Uaraig.   Henry means ' home-ruler,' and in
Gaelic becomes Eanraig, whence M'Kendrick and Henderson.
M'William is still a sept name.   Robert means 'gloriously
bright' (Hrod-bert) and gives G. Rob, and sept names like
M'Robbie and M'Robin. The name Lud-wig, 'famed warrior,'
now Lewis, is a favourite among the Grants, and among them
—and elsewhere — translates the Gaelic Maol-domhnaich,
' servus dominicus,' on principles none too clear. The southern
M'Burney is all that remains of the common Norse name
Bjarni or Bear, represented in Gaelic by M'Mhathain or
Matheson of English.

    These Indo-European double-stemmed names also under-
went a process of compression ; ' pet ' forms were developed,

wherein the second element suffered condensation, or was
entirely dropped, leaving a diminutive in its stead, or even
leaving no trace of its former existence at all. Ordinary
'pet' forms are Maggie for Margarita and Biddy for Bridget.
In Greek Demo-sthas stood for Demo-sthenes; and in Old
German Sicco acted as 'pet' form for Sige-rich, Sig-bert,
and, indeed, for all names beginning with *sig*. So Hugo
was a diminutive for Hubert and such names; and even the
simple Hugh, without diminutive suffix, was and is used.
The strengthening of the *g* of *sig* to *cc* shows that there was
a second part—that the name was a compound. Similarly
in Old Gaelic the adjective *find*, now *fionn*, white, ended in
d, and this was hardened to *t* where a name like Find-barr or
Find-chath (fair-head, fair-warrior) was curtailed with the
diminutives -*án* or -*óc*, resulting in Fintán, Fintóc, now Fionndan, Fionndag, whence M'Gille-Fhionndaig or M'Lintock—St.
Findan's devotee. And, further, the adjective *fionn* itself was
used as the final pet name. The diminutives in Gaelic were
mainly -*án*, -*óc*, and -*e*, with other side forms in -*ine*, -*éne*, -*in*,
and combinations like -*óc-án* (-*ucán* -*agan*, as in Fionnlagan
from Fionnlugh-oc-an or Maol-agan 'shaveling,' whence Milli-
gan). The English diminutive in -*ie* or -*y* appears in Norse
and German as *i*—Gunni (now Gaelic Guinne, Clan *Gunn*),
for Gunn-arr or Gunnbjorn (war-bear), and German Willi for
Wilhelm, our Willie. In the case of adjectives, the pet
name may be the adjective simply: as Norse Ljótr or Ljót,
'ugly,' perhaps for Ljót-ulf, 'ugly wolf,' from which comes
the Gaelic Leòd, MacLeòid. In old Gaelic, adjectives of
colour especially were used as names, such as *dubh* in Mac-
duff and the king's name of Duff, Latinised as Niger or
Nigellus. The favourite name Aed or Aodh simply means
'fire' and is declined as a *u*-stem; it is also a diminutive,
with fuller forms, Aedan or Aodhan; Aed-uc-án or Aodhagan,
whence comes the Irish name of Egan.

As in the case of Teutonic names, Gaelic names may be
presented in two lists, the first of which forms the first
element in the double-stemmed name, the second list con-

taining elements usually terminal. In the following lists, the old names, with unaspirated medial consonants, are in italics :—

Aed, Aodh, 'fire.'	-*aed*.
Aen, aon, 'one, unique.'	-all (=*valo-s*), 'wielding.'
Ail, 'rock.'	-barr, 'head.'
Cath, 'battle.'	-beartach, 'powerful.'
Car, 'dear.'	-bhne, 'being, going.'
Cell, 'war.'	-car, 'dear.'
Comh-, *com-*, 'with.'	-cath, 'warrior'
Con-, 'high.'	-ceartach, 'director.'
Domn-, Dombn-, 'world.'	-*cobar*, 'help.'
Dun-, 'strong.'	-donn, 'lord, brown.'
Each, 'horse.'	-*gart*, 'head.'
Eo-, 'good.'	-gal, 'valour.'
Fael, Faol, 'wolf.'	-*gel*, 'white.'
Fer-, 'super, man.'	-gan, -guin, 'kin.'
Find, Fionn, 'whyte.'	-*gus*, 'choice.'
Flaith-, 'dominion.'	-*lug*, lach, 'winner.'
Lug, god 'Luga, winner.'	-*laech*, lagh, 'hero.'
Muir, 'sea.'	-*ri*, -raigh, 'king.'
Niall, 'champion.'	-thach, '-ious.'
So-, su-, 'good.'	-tighearn, 'lord.'

From *aodh* terminal, we have Cin-aed, 'fire-sprung,' the well-known name of Kenneth, now ousted in Gaelic by Cainnech or Coinneach, 'fair one,' whence the clan name Mackenzie; Irish M'Kenna and Galwegian M'Kinnie are from Cion-aodh or Kenneth. Aon-ghus or Angus means 'unique choice'; hence M'Innes, M'Ainsh, and M'Nish. Allan comes from two sources—Old Gaelic Ailene or Ailin (*ail*, 'rock'), the name of the old earls of Lennox, or from Norman Alan, an Allemann or German (*all* and *man*), to which we may compare Norman, Dugall or Dubh-ghall (Black foreigner or Dane), Fingal (Norse-man), Frank, etc. Cath gives Cathal (* *Catu-valo-s*), whence M'Kail, Call; Fer-char is for 'very dear,' whence M'Erchar, Farquharson; Cellach, 'warlike,' gives the surname Kelly and M'Kelly, and after being borrowed by the Norse as Kjalakr it becomes M'Killaig. Com-gan, 'Con-genial,' was a famous saint, and M'Gillechomhghain became M'Cowan and Cowan. Con-chobhar denotes 'high help,' and is the famous name Connor. There is a sept of M'Conchers still in Lorn. Domhn-all, as already said, means 'world-lord,' and Domhnaghart appears in the sept name Clann 'Ille-Dhonaghart at Benderloch, who claim to be Macdonalds in 'English.' The name Duncan is in Celtic Duno-catus, 'strong warrior' or 'burgher,' whence M'Connachie and Clan Duncan or Robertson. Each, 'horse,' gives Each-thighearn, 'horse-lord,' whence M'Echern, M'Kechnie; and Eachdhonn, 'horse-lord,' is the old form of Eachunn, which is Englished as Hector (Greek, 'holder'); it gives the sept name of M'Echan. Eoghan or Ewen practically means the same as Latin Eugenius, 'well-born,' whence M'Ewen. Faolan denotes 'little wolf,' and in the compound Gill'Fhaolain or Gillfillan, gives M'Lellan, and, further, M'Killigan (M'Gill'Fhaolagain). Fergus is 'super-choice,' and gives M'Kerras and Fergus-son. Fionn or Fionndan is a diminutive for St. Find-barr, and we have the sept names of M'Lennan (Gill'Fhinnein), M'Lintock, and M'Clinton. Fingon or Finguine, 'Fair-bairn,' gives the sur-name Mackinnon. The Scotch name Finlay is a late form— Finnlaech, 'fair hero'—for the old name Find-lug; Lulach seems for Lug-laech, 'Luga's hero,' and anyway still remains in the sept name M'Lullich (M'Lulli in fourteenth century). Fionnaghal is a female name denoting 'fair shoulder,' rendered into English rather curiously as Flora. The name M'La(ve)rty has already been referred to; it comes from Flaithbheartach, 'dominion-holding.' The sea gives several names: Mur-chadh, 'sea-warrior,' * Mori-catus; Muircheartach, 'sea-director,' whence M'Urardaigh, M'Kirdie, M'Mu(r)trie, and Irish Moriarty; perhaps Muireach or Muireadhach (* Mori-tāco-s?), though this is explained as denoting 'lord,' *muire* being a shorter form meaning 'steward.' Hence Murdoch, M'Vurich, Currie; but Murcheson is from Murchadh. Muriel, the female name, comes from * Mori-gela, 'sea-white.' Niall, with *gus* added thereto, gives Niallghus, which appears in the form of M'Neilage, from M'Nelis, as

M'Fetridge comes from M'Petrus, and M'Cambridge from M'Ambrose. Ruadhraigh is for 'red prince,' whence M'Rory; but there is no connection between this name initially and the Teutonic Roderick, 'famed prince.' Mac-queen comes from Suibhne, 'good-going,' the opposing name being Duibhne.

A feature of Gaelic names is the frequency of animal names. Professor Zimmer explains these names as the first portion of the ordinary double-stemmed name; in fact, the animal name is a reduced or pet form. This may be, but there are several cases where the name has been directly assumed from the animal. 'The Fox' was the official title of The O'Caharny, Prince of Teffia, for some three hundred years, even as late as 1526, when M'Eochagan and 'The Fox' made a contract in Gaelic, which is still extant. The dog was first favourite; Bran-chu (raven-dog), Faol-chu (wolf-dog), Mil-chu (greyhound); then the mastiff or *Madadh* gave the names Maddeth and Madan or Modan. St. Catan, or 'little cat,' gave the name Gille-catan as the eponymus of Clan Chattan; Mac-Mahon means 'son of the bear'; Math-ghamhaim (bear) was a favourite name, just as Björn was among the Norse. The wolf was known as Sitheach, whence M'Ithich, M'Ithichean (M'Keith, M'Kichan), and Shaw; another name for the wolf was Mac-tire, 'son of the soil'; while Faolan, really a diminutive of Faol-chu, has already been noticed. The famed poet Ossian gets his name from the diminutive of *os*, 'a deer'; and the borrowed *Columba* gave the saint's name first, and from it come Callum and Malcolm. M'Culloch no doubt means 'son of the boar'; and pig names are common—M'Cráin, Banbán, Orcán, M'Turk (Galwegian). The Gaelic name Cailean, which appears in English as Colin, is really a native name denoting 'whelp.' A Scottish king bore the name in the form of Culen, which is the usual form of the word *cuilean*; the Irish shows *coileán*; the root is so far *cul*, and Cailean must be a dialect form, such as we have in the case of *dail*, 'a plain,' which appears in its proper root form as *dul*, with a genitive *dalach* (cf. *lathach*, 'mud,' old Irish *loth*, root *lut*).

A certain class of names in Old Gaelic depart in a remarkable manner from the Indo-European system of double-stemmed names, and 'pet,' or reduced forms of the same. This consists in a name where two nouns are brought together, the one of which governs the second in the genitive. The heroic name Cu-chulinn is a good example; the name means 'Culann's hound.' Other names are Mog-néit, 'slave of Néit,' the war goddess; Nia-Corb, 'champion of Corb'; and Fer-Corb, 'Corb's man.' These names remind us of some Bible names: Obed-Edom, 'servant of the god Edom'; Gabriel, 'hero of El (God)'; Absalom, 'father of peace.' Professor Rhŷs is probably right in explaining these combinations as due to the influence of the previous non-Celtic population. Under Christianity the system came into great vogue; the saints took the place of the old Gadelic deities and totems. The term *mug*, 'slave,' was replaced by *mael* or *maol*, 'bald,' that is, 'tonsured one' or 'devotee' of the saint mentioned. Thus Mail-Patraic means 'devotee of St. Patrick'—under the saint's charge or born on his day, or some other connection. In Scotland *gille* (servant) was after a time a greater favourite than *maol*; and *maol* itself got confused with *mál*, 'prince.' For instance, Máil-dúin, now Muldoon, is really 'prince of the fort,' not 'slave of the fort.' Besides *maol* and *gille*, other initial terms were *cu* (as Cu-mara, 'dog of the sea,' whence Mac-namara); *mac*, 'son'; *fer*, 'man'; and *der*, 'daughter.' The governed nouns may be persons, places, abstract ideas, and material nouns. Thus, *cu*: Cu-Corb, Cu-Ulad, 'Ulster's hound'; Cu-Breatan (Britons'), Cu-sléibhe (dog-of-the-hill), Cu-cuimhne (memory's dog), Cu-catha (battle), Cu-sìthe (peace), and Cu-dúiligh (keen-ness?), which last three appear in the old Maclean genealogy, and Cu-duiligh or Conduiligh is still known as a Maclean name—the Maclean pipers, known as Rankins, being Clan Duly. *Mac* shows much the same sequences: Mac-Talla, 'echo' (son of the rock); Mac-na-braiche, 'son of the malt' (whisky); Mac-na-maoile, 'son of the baldness,' a side form for Mac-Millan (Mac-na-mil).   Macbeth and Macrae we have discussed.   Columba's grandfather is called by Adamnan Filius Navis, which is Mac-luing (Galwegian M'Lung) or Mac-naue.   Mac-coise, 'footman,' gives M'Cosh, M'Lave is Englished as 'hand'; and, doubtless, the Galwegian M'Lurg is for 'footman.'

Maol is used similarly, though its chief use is with saints' names : Maoldúin ('fort,' confused with mál), Maol-rubha ('promontory,' not 'peace,' as it is usually explained) ; Maol-umha (bronze) ; Maol-snechte (snow); Maol-bethadh (life), Maol-onfhaidh (storm)—Millony of the Cameron genea-logies.   With adjectives it is doubtless *mál*, 'prince,' that is originally meant : Maol-odhar, Maol-dubh (but there was a Scotch St. Duff), Maol-mordha (great).   The word *gille* is confined to saints' names, though we meet with Gill'onfhaidh beside Maol-onfhaidh and the unique Gille-bhràtha, 'servant of doom,' doubtless for Maol-brátha (M'Gillivray).   One or two interesting saints' names may be noticed.   Maol-Brighde and Gille-Brighde are 'St. Bridget's devotee.'   These names have a diminutive or pet form in *n* : Bridein, whence M'Bride. Similarly Macbeth or Maol-beth has Beathan or Bean, whence M'Bean ;   Gille-maol, 'bald lad' has Maolan, whence M'Millan ;   Gille-naomh has Naomhan or Niven ;   Gille-glas has Glaisean, whence M'Glashan.   Adamnan's name appears in Gilleownan (1427), but the sept name M'Lagan shows an interesting double diminutive form of the name as Adhamh-agan, Gill'A'agan.   The saints present their names often in diminutive form with terminal -óc or -og, and prefixed *mo*, my.   St. Ernan appears as Mo-ern-oc or Mernoc, as in Gille-mhernog, M'Gillemhearnaig, which is Englished as Graham —being originally a sept name in the Graham country. Maclehose appears to be from St. Thomas.   *Gille* is widely used with adjectives : Gille-riabhach (brindled)—M'Ilwrath ; Gille-odhar, M'Ill'uidhir (dun), that is, M'Lure ; and M'Ghille-dhuibh (black) becomes M'Gillewie.

An extraordinary development of this name system occurs

with the adjectives *dubh* and *donn* (dun). They are used in much the same way as *maol*, especially with local names or nouns. Thus—Dubh-dothra 'Black of Dodder' (738) ; Dubh-droma 'Black of the ridge'; Dubh-da-locha, 'B. of two lochs,' and there is a number of names made with *da* (two) prefixed. With abstract nouns we have Dubh-sìthe, 'Black of peace,' which degenerates into Du-sìth, Duffie, and M'Phee. The adjective *donn*, dun, also means, 'lord' in the old language (*dun-no-s, root *dun*, strong), but its use with genitives may not arise from its meaning of 'lord.' We have Donn-boo, brown or lord of cows; Donn-cuan (harbours); and Donn-sléibhe (of hill), whence Donleavy, and Gaelic Mac-Dhunleibh or M'An-lei, which becomes Mac-leay, and is Englished as Livingstone.

Surnames from personal names are either in patronymic form, as M'Cormick, son of Cormac (Corb-mac, 'charioteer'), or in genitive regimen Iain Dhughaill—John Dugald's (like English John Williams), or with an adjective form of the patronymic, as Iain Domhnullach, John Macdonald. The surnames Donald, Duncan, and Donaldson are English in form and creation; but Tyre for M'Intyre and Clean for Maclean (Gill'Sheathain or John's Gille) are from Gaelic Taor and Cle'an, forms already 'reduced' in the original language. Patronymics from official or trade names are common in Gaelic; Iain Tàillear and Iain Mac-an-Tàilleir stand side by side in Gaelic, but the English in this case is only Taylor, for the word is a borrowed one. Gow (Smith) is commoner than M'Gown in the English form. Dewar (pilgrim) has still the side forms of M'Indeòir, M'George (Galloway), and M'Leòra or M'Lure (Mac-Gille-dheòradha). Most of these professional and trade names have long ago been translated into English. A common name in the Black Book of Tay-mouth is M'In-esker or 'Fisher's son,' but it is now known only as Fisher. The greatest source of surnames next to patronymics is place names. Nearly every prominent High-land place name has been so utilised. Urquhart, Brodie, Buchanan, Murray, Sutherland, Drummond, Dallas, Logan, and others claim to be clans.   Surnames from Gaelic epithets are fairly common.   The two great clans of Campbell and Cameron derive their names from 'crooked' mouths and noses ; this admits of little doubt.   But in the case of the Camerons it is equally undoubted · that the place names Cameron or Cambrun gave rise to the Lowland Camerons and the De Cambruns of the fourteenth century.   Other Gaelic epithets giving English forms are Bain (fair), Begg (little), Moir (big—for vowels compare Baird and Caird), Keir (dun), Duff or Dow (black), Glass (grey), Garrow (rough), Galt (Lowland), and others.

It is not until the facts and principles of Gaelic and Irish personal nomenclature are mastered that investigation can be extended into the old Celtic districts between the Solway and the Clyde.   Galloway still, according to Mr. Dudgeon ('*Macs* in Galloway'), has twenty per cent. of its names beginning with Mac ; and Celtic names are strongly in evidence in the early charters and other historical documents.   Irish influence is shown in the old A' (*i.e.* O') forms in A'Carson, A'Cultan, A'Costduff, A'Hannay, A'Shenan (found in Kintyre beside O'Senog), A'Sloan (Sluaghadhan), A'Sloss, possibly also Agnew (O'Gnimh), and Adair (O'Daire, and M'Dair, Galloway, 1622).   The British of Strathclyde have left many evidences of their former existence in place names, and we have, in regard to personal names, their equivalent of Gaelic *gille* with saint names in Gos-patrick, Guostuff or Cos-duff, Quos-cuthbert, Cos-oswald, and Cos-mungo (Welsh *gwas* = Gaelic *gille*).   While Ulgric has been claimed as Teutonic Ulric, a mistake on the other side is made in claiming Uchtred as Gaelic (Ochtraigh).   It is Teutonic, as forms like Uctebrand and Hutting or Ucting show.   Owing to the disappearance of Gaelic in the seventeenth century Galloway personal names present the same difficulties as the place names.

'NEVER WAS PIPING SO SAD, AND NEVER WAS PIPING SO GAY'

E. C. CARMICHAEL

THE 'people of peace' have ever been held to be gifted with music. When their green hillocks are open, music and song may be heard so sweet and alluring that the incautious mortal, unable to resist their charm, goes into the bower to join in the merriment and remains a half willing if sometimes unwitting prisoner, till some accident or a friend releases him. Then he finds that he has been a year and a day, seven, nine, or even twenty years in the fairy knoll, while he thought 'twas but an hour or a night, so beguiling were the music and the dance and the little folks themselves! Many instruments the fairies have too—pipes and harps and other wind and stringed instruments, and all so greatly superior to those of human make that a fairy instrument is a coveted treasure among the people of earth. But not many of these have been bestowed on the children of men, and the few seem all to have been given by the women of faery. Here are some stories of fairy pipes which I have heard in the Hebrides, and now translate from Gaelic.

The famous Maccrimmons, pipers to the Macleods of Macleod, owed their renown in music to a fairy. When the Macleod of the day returned from one of the Crusades, he brought with him from Cremona a servant who, quite according to Highland usage, became known by the name of his home. Cremon married in Skye, and when his son was old enough he sent him to the school or college of music at Boreraig, in Glendale, to learn pipe music. This school was celebrated throughout Alban and Erin and Sasunn and the divisions of Europe, and had many pupils, especially for the bagpipes. Cremon wished his son to be a good piper, that he might obtain the honourable position of piper to Macleod of Macleod, for musicians were highly esteemed among the ancient Gaels, and the office of musician to a great chief was one of much honour and dignity, conferring on its holder many valued privileges and possessions.

But 'Mac Cremmain,' or MacCrimmon, as he was called —the son of Cremon—had no aptitude for the Highland pipes, they were foreign to his race and nature, and his fellow-pupils held rather aloof from the strange lad whose ways were more of his father's land than of his mother's. So the lad was sorrowful and miserable, and he often went out with his sorrow and his misery to the lee of a green knoll at a little distance from the college, to brood and to wish that he could play the pipes like his fellow-students.

One day the 'Piobaire mor'—great Piper, as the head of the college was called—got an invitation to the marriage of a great Chief, and he was asked to bring some of his pupils to help to entertain the guests. There was much excitement in the college, and much speculating and rivalry among the lads as to who would be thought worthy to go. When the 'Piobaire mor' announced his choice of pupils, MacCrimmon's name was not among them, and though he had not really expected to be among those chosen, he was heavy and sad with disappointment. After the others had set out for the Chie f' dun MacCrimmon could not longer restrain his feelings, and he threw himself down in his lonely haunt on the green hillock and wept the tears—the bitter tears—of disappointed hope. While he was dead to all around, he was startled by the sound of a voice asking why he grieved so greatly. Looking up he saw a woman, small indeed, but of beautiful face and form, dressed in a soft green gown, gazing at him with pity shining in her eyes, and peace and love in her face. He knew she was one of the 'sithe' or fairies, and he was afraid. But she looked at him so tenderly and spoke to him so kindly that he poured out before her all his heart's heavy sorrow. He told her that he could not master the bagpipes, and that he played so badly that he had not been taken to the wedding, that the other pupils were not friendly, and that he was altogether miserable. The kind little fairy put her slender hand on the lad's dark head and comforted him, and she told him he would play better than any of the other students some day. She then gave him a chanter, the like of which had never been seen before by mortal eyes. She told him that the possessor of that chanter would carry with him ' Buaidh na Piobaireachd '—the championship of piping. But should a word ever be said in disparagement of the chanter she would instantly take it back, with all the skill it conferred. Then the lovely green-robed fairy disappeared as mysteriously as she had come, leaving the lad too much lost in surprise to think of thanking her.

MacCrimmon hurried back to the college, put the chanter in the pipes and blew it. To his delight he found he could play, and not merely the tunes he had tried so unsuccessfully to learn but tunes he had never tried before, and even new tunes that no one had ever heard ; and he could play them, too, better than any one he had ever listened to—better than the ' Piobaire mor ' himself ! His happiness was now as great as his grief had been before, and he could hardly sleep or eat, he only wished to play his wonderful chanter night and day. When his teacher and fellow-pupils returned after a few weeks' absence—for the festivities connected with the marriage of a great Chief were somewhat prolonged—they could scarcely believe their eyes and ears. The stupid foreign lad who could not play when they left, could now play better than the great Piper of the famous college of Boreraig ! Quick questions were asked and the lad told his tale. All knew of the music of the ' sithean ' or fairy bower, and all knew that he to whom a ' sithe ' gave the gift of music was indeed endowed beyond all hope of rivalry. The wonderful chanter was examined and commented upon, but no one could make out of what material it was made. It did not seem to be made of metal, of wood, or of stone.

Those who had formerly jeered at MacCrimmon now envied him and vainly tried to imitate his playing. But it was useless. MacCrimmon could make his pipe move the hearts of his hearers so that they had no will but as it impelled them. Did he play 'Geantraighe' they danced and sang for joy and pure happiness of mind and body. Did he play 'Suaintraighe' they slumbered peacefully and with a happy smile dreamt of their dear ones and of pleasant days with their comrades. Did he play 'Gultraighe' a wild passionate longing and a great sorrowful lamenting came into every heart. Never was such music heard before. From far and near people came to hear it and to wonder at it, and MacCrimmon's music played with their souls as the north wind plays with the leaves of the birch tree on the brown mountain side.

MacCrimmon became piper to Macleod of Macleod, and his son, and his son's sons succeeded him for many generations, and the fairy chanter descended as the most valued possession of the family. Their fame was known wherever music was loved. The college at Boreraig, where the first Maccrimmon had been so backward a learner, was under their teaching, and people came from Erin and from Sasunn and from all the divisions of Europe to learn music in Skye.

Before students were considered fit to leave the college—and the several courses lasted from four to ten years—they had to be able to play one hundred and ninety-nine tunes, some of them very intricate, besides exercises, and to be masters of theory and composition. It is said that in later days the Maccrimmons gave diplomas to successful graduates. These diplomas had on them pictures of Dunvegan Castle, of the galley of Macleod, and of various musical instruments, a seal, and the name of the holder, with the dates of entrance to and departure from the college.[1] Two of the Macintyres of South Uist, hereditary musicians to Clanranald, were among the last students at this school—about the beginning of 'the '45.' Four cows are said to have been paid for their education there.

A Skye tradition says that it was practically the last of the Maccrimmon pipers who composed the beautiful and

[1] A family of the name of Robertson in Inverness—whether town or county I do not know—is said to possess one of these certificates.

pathetic 'cumha' or lament known by his name, and that it
has a double prophetic meaning in that it was a lament for
himself, for he foresaw that he would be one of the many to
give up life in the ill-fortuned Stuart wars, and also for
the fairy's gift. This Maccrimmon was the only man killed
at the Moy Rout, and after his death his son inherited the
chanter and the office. On one occasion Macleod of Dunvegan and Macleod of Raasay were returning in the Dunvegan galley after visiting the chief of Abercrossain, now
Applecross. Maccrimmon, as usual, was with his master and
was asked to 'seid suas'—blow up. He sat on the prow, the
piper's seat, and began playing. But the wind was so strong
and the sea so rough in the Sound, that his fingers kept
slipping off the chanter with the rolling of the galley. At
last it got so bad that MacCrimmon threw down his pipes
in anger, and began abusing the chanter because he could not
keep his fingers on it. While he was speaking the chanter
gave a leap over the side of the vessel into the sea. Mac-
Crimmon remembered, too late, the command handed down
by his fathers, for the chanter had gone as the fairy giver had
said, so many generations before, that it would. And with
the chanter went the championship of piping ; and the home
of the Maccrimmons is desolate, and their hereditary office
unfilled. The set of pipes, called 'an oiseach' (oinseach?)
with which the fairy chanter was used, is carefully kept at
Dunvegan. Will the green-robed lady ever relent and return
the chanter, and with it the championship of piping ?—though
indeed there are now no Maccrimmons in Skye to hold them.

Another legend is somewhat different. There was on a
time a great gathering of pipers to be at Dunvegan, and there
was no piper better than another far or near, on mainland or
island, who did not take the road for the Dun. When the
day came, there surely was the multitude of people—Macleods and strangers. It happened that Macleod of Dunvegan
had a herd boy who was very wild to see the heros of the
drones and to hear them for himself, and he asked Macleod
if he might stay at home that day. 'Thou little rascal that

thou art,' said Macleod, 'thy work is tending the cattle; and good as piping is, it cannot keep the bulls from fighting, nor the calves from falling into the ditches. Away, boy, and do not return here till the black herdsman night brings thyself and the cattle home together.' The lad went away downcast and disappointed, and drove the cattle to the shieling. He sat down on a fairy knoll and put the black chanter of the pipes in his mouth. But he had a scarf round his neck and his emotion was so great that his breath came in sudden jumps and leaps, and the chanter was but a bad stepmother to the pipes. At last he threw it away and hid his head in a heather tuft for fear the dogs and the calves would see and mock at him. He had hardly put his head down when the 'sithean' opened and the pretty little lady of melody came out. She put her white hand on the boy's head, 'Bonnie lad,' she said, 'what has put against thee, and what harm has the black chanter of the pipe done thee?' He told her everything as it was, and how he himself wished things were. The lovely fairy then gave him his choice of three championships —the championship of sailing, so that his boat of spotted yew would cut a slender oaten straw, so good her steering, and that her keel would scrape as with sharp knives the limpets from the tops of the hidden rocks; or the championship of battle, so that the raven of the Dun would be satiated with the blood of his enemies every day on which the sun rose or darkness lay; or the championship of piping, so that he would bring the birds from the trees and that he would give peace and relief to wounded men and pain-worn women. The boy did not doubt nor delay in deciding which was better, the championships of sailing or of fighting, but without a word backward or forward he chose the championship of piping. Then the beautiful little fairy said, 'Thou hast thy wish from this time,' and she went back into the bower, and the knoll was as it had been before. The boy stared at the place where she had been, but there was nothing to see—only soft green grass and flowers. He took up his pipes and played. But there was the wonderful thing! The music that was

there!   He had never known that there could be such music.
And as he played the cattle and the dogs, and the deer of the
hill, and the birds of the air, and the creeping things of the
earth came round him to listen.   After he had played for
a long time he thought he would go away back to Dunvegan,
for he felt he must tell everybody about the wonderful fairy
and show them the gift she had given him.   It was there the
great piping was, on the green sward, and the many pipers
from all places, and it was there the people were, gentle and
simple in their crowds listening to them.   When Macleod
saw the herd lad with his pipes under his arm listening with
the others he was angry, and he asked him why he had left
the cattle and come to the castle when he had given him
fast orders to stay at the shieling.   The lad answered that
he could not keep away from the piping any longer, and that
he felt sure he could play as well as the best piper there.
Macleod laughed at the boy's presumption, but to punish
him, told him to blow up, adding that if he failed to make
good his boast he would get a hard thrashing.   The boy blew
up, and he played, and *that* was the playing and *that* was the
music!   At first the other pipers laughed, then they stared,
then a great silence fell over them.   When he had finished
they all admitted that the herd lad had indeed 'buaidh na
piobaireachd' the championship of piping, and they eagerly
crowded round him with questions.   He told his tale, and then
all said that he to whom the fairy queen of melody gave her
gifts was indeed a musician, and they piped no more that day,
for they said, 'This young lad shames us all.'   The lad was
taken from herding the cattle and made piper to Macleod of
Dunvegan, and a good farm with its share of cattle and horses
and sheep and goats was given to him and to his heirs so
long as they should continue pipers to Dunvegan and follow
its chief in war and in peace.

The hereditary musicians to the Macdonalds of Clanranald
were Macintyres, and they too, got a gift of music from a
fairy.   This is how it was.   A son of the musician—for the
Macintyres were musicians before they got the fairy gift—had

a sweetheart of the little people. She was a very beautiful
lady with a skin like the fair breast of the kittiwake and
cheeks like the wild red rose by the mountain stream. Her
eyes were of the deep blue of the juniper-berry, and her long
hair was the colour of soft, pale, unwrought gold, that glim-
mered in the sun and fell about her like golden mist. Her
voice was like sweet mellow music. The gown she had was
of soft trailing stuff of the pure colour of the green sea
when it lies over white sand, and as she walked it was
like the moving light on a sloping field of long, green grass
when the low wind blows over it and the sun's brightness
is gently veiled. 'Her steps were the music of song,' and
her fingers were so deft and quick that she could prepare a
fleece of wool, pick it, and card it, and spin it, and dye it,
and weave it into a big tartan plaid all in an hour by the sun;
and her head and mind were so clever that she knew even
what was happening far off. One evening when the fairy and
young Macintyre were walking on the green flowery machair
near to the farm of Smearclaid in South Uist that his father
held as Clanranald's musician, she told him that strangers
from Erin over the sea were coming to his father's house to
hear if the Macintyres were indeed as good musicians as was
reported. 'But,' the fairy said, 'I will give you this reed, and
you must go home and put it in your father's pipes and play
to the strangers. Then they shall see that report said not
enough of the music of the Macintyres.' For the pretty little
lady was jealous for the fame of her lover's family.

The young man did as she told him. He went home, and
there, sure enough, were the strangers being hospitably
entertained with food and drink after their journey from far
lands. After they had eaten, and while they were resting,
the lad said to his father that he would now take the pipes
and amuse the strangers who had come home to them from
over the waves. 'You play!' said the father; 'you could
never play anything in your life—you will just cause us to
be laughed at.' The young man however prepared the pipes
and put in the fairy reed, and he played the music that

astonished every one. His family listened with surprise and delight, and the strangers were without speech. They had never heard or dreamt of such nobly sweet music—music which spoke to their souls and told them good and great things that they had never felt before in the world. It seemed not of earth, so sweet and strange it was. And the lad did it so simply—he just blew as usual, and he moved his fingers with no more trouble than any one else, yet he played fast, loud, joyful music, and slow, solemn, sorrowful music. It was like the music of 'Tir nan Og'—the Land of the Ever-young.

After he stopped playing his listeners sat silent for a long space, for they could not speak. But when the spell left them and the strangers' speech came back, they whispered to each other that none dared compete against that, and that they themselves must not touch the pipes. So, as it was the mannerly custom among the Gaels to invite strangers to show their skill, they soon took leave of Macintyre and his family, for it was considered rude to refuse to play when asked. After they had, with much pretended hurry, bid good health be with their entertainers, they hastened to their coracle and sailed away out of that, saying to each other, 'If that is what the lad does who, they say, cannot play, what can the old man's music be?' and they returned no more to South Uist, for they themselves were known musicians—but they had no fairy reed or chanter!

BOOK REVIEWS

Higher Grade Readings in Gaelic, with Outlines of Grammar. Edited by ALEXANDER MACBAIN, LL.D. Northern Counties Publishing Office, Inverness: 1905. 1s. 6d. net.

Boys and girls in Highland schools speak Gaelic fluently, in pronounced dialect form for the most part. How best to utilise this acquirement of theirs in order to further their mental training and general culture is a vital question in the education of these children. Hitherto it has been practically ignored. But the Scottish Education Department has, by a recent Minute, offered a Leaving Certificate in Gaelic, and Dr. Macbain, a foremost Gaelic scholar and an experienced teacher of eminence, has printed this booklet for the use of pupils qualifying for this certificate.

To meet the case of such pupils fully, it will be found that not one but two books are required. First and foremost there is urgently needed an outline of Gaelic Grammar, such as is provided here, but with a graduated course of exercises for translation and retranslation, with examples here and there showing how such exercises ought to be done, especially in the rendering of idioms and figures of speech. Such a volume would usefully provide in an appendix specimens of such examination papers in Gaelic as have hitherto appeared. A separate volume would be required for general reading. The Reading Book should contain carefully selected specimens in prose and verse from the best modern Gaelic authors, with a short note giving the principal facts in each author's life, and a sentence indicating the special feature of his genius. Meanwhile, aspirants for the Gaelic Leaving Certificate will find Dr. Macbain's little volume most valuable. For a first edition it is very accurately printed. Of the section on Grammar it may be said that it would be difficult to pack into twenty-six pages of print a greater amount of sound and accurate knowledge of the Grammar of Scottish Gaelic than is found here. There is, considering the space, nothing left out that ought to be in, and hardly anything in that were better out. In the tables of sounds both the *mediae* (*b*, *d*, *g*,) and the *tenues* (*p*, *t*, *c*,) are equated with the English *tenues* (*p*, *t*, *c*). This is somewhat confusing. It is the case, as our caricaturists have noted, that Highlanders and Welshmen, when speaking English, are apt to sound the *mediae* with a force half-way between the *mediae* and *tenues*. But in speaking their own tongue they differentiate their *b*'s and *p*'s, *d*'s and *t*'s, *g*'s and *c*'s as successfully as Englishmen. In actual practice, however, a confusion in the equation of sounds in a grammatical treatise does no harm. Highland boys and girls acquire their knowledge of Gaelic sounds elsewhere. The grouping of Nouns in the various declensions is the most scientific hitherto printed. But it will always be a question whether the Scheme of Declension favoured by the philologist is the best suited for the schoolboy. The old-fashioned Five Declensions of Latin Grammar, having no philological basis, will maintain their place in our grammars for beginners for some time to come. It is somewhat difficult to see how Dr. Macbain could give in the Verb such a form as *tha mi air bhith a' bualadh*. The selections for Reading and Recitation are chosen, it need hardly be said, with judgment. They are all of high literary excellence, and that is the chief thing to be aimed at. But it must be said that they lack variety. This is especially the case in prose. All the selections are from one author—Dr. Macleod. Now, while it will be at once admitted that no educated man of our time has written Scottish Gaelic prose with such charm as Dr. Macleod, it still remains true that there are several other writers of conspicuous merit, and that, to be truly educative, the reading of Gaelic-speaking boys and girls should not be restricted to one author, however excellent. And even in verse, most readers will miss extracts from such well-known poets as Mary Macleod, Alexander Macdonald, Duncan M'Intyre, and Rob Donn. The mode of writing followed will, as a whole, commend itself to all Gaelic scholars. The traditional orthography is adhered to except upon cause shown. Such words as *déidh* and *déigh*, *éirich*, *éirigh*, and *éiridh*, with several others, are distinguished, and the correct form used in the proper place. Many apostrophes are removed, and a still greater number could be dispensed with. An apostrophe properly represents a suppressed letter. We speak in groups of words which we weld into one continuous sound, and in consequence we shall always have a good many apostrophes. In many cases it is a matter of indifference which vowel is suppressed. The utmost one can do is to endeavour to be somewhat uniform : e.g. *mise 'm aonar*, *mis' an nochd*. In some cases the clashing sounds are of different quality, and then the stronger survives : e.g. *do an tigh* becomes *do'n tigh*, 'to the house,' or *d'an tigh*, 'to their house,' the *o* of the preposition being stronger than the *a* of the article, but weaker than the *a* of the possessive pronoun. Our Gaelic writers have, unfortunately, extended the scope of the apostrophe. They have made it to stand not merely for a suppressed letter, but occasionally for suppressed words, such as *a* the possessive pronoun, *a* the so-called relative, *ag* of the present participle, and *do* of the infinitive. In such cases the practice ought to be in Gaelic as in other languages to use the apostrophe only when ambiguity may arise. Thus one writes *'athair*, 'his father,' to distinguish from *athair*, 'a father,' but no apostrophe is needed in the case of *athair-san* and *athair fhein*, the emphatic forms sufficing to prevent ambiguity. The aspiration of a word does away with the need for an apostrophe in the same way : *Tha fhuil dearg*, 'his blood is red.' Similarly, when the *g* of *ag* is suppressed we write *a'* : *a' toirt da*, 'giving him.' But when *ag* is suppressed the apostrophe is not required : *Tha mi toirt da*, 'I am giving him.' Two words, *cha'n* or *cha n-*, *gu'n* or *gu n-*, Dr. Macbain has treated in strange fashion,—he writes *chan*, *gun*. Our ancestors who fixed our Gaelic orthography found certain fluctuating sounds which they attached by a hyphen to the succeeding, although they formed an essential part of the preceding, word : *an t-athair*, *ar n-eun*, *gu h-àrd*. Irish scholars wrote also, consistently, *cha n-òl*, *gu n-iarr* ; but, somehow, our Scottish authorities wrote *cha'n ol*, *gu'n iarr*. The late Dr. Clerk and some others sought to remove this anomaly, but unfortunately they placed the hyphen upon the wrong side of the nasal, and wrote *cha-n òl*, *gu-n iarr*. Now comes Dr. Macbain and writes the only other possible variant—*chan òl*, *gun iarr*, without hyphen or apostrophe. Surely in this case it were better to let even ill alone, unless one was prepared to write such forms as *ant athair* for *an t-athair*, *arn aran* for *ar n-aran*, *nah eòin* for *na h-eòin*, *guh àrd* for *gu h-àrd*. One might also suggest that in a subsequent edition such double forms as *toir* and *tabhair*, *bhi* and *bhith*, with others, should be differentiated in actual use : *An toir thu leat e ? Cha tabhair. 'S eudar dhomh bhi falbh ; faodaidh sin a bhith.* So also *agus* and *is*, which are not only different words, but of different construction. Dialectal words and forms are more difficult to handle. When illustrating dialect, local sounds and forms cannot be too closely reproduced; in writing verse, the ring of the line must be preserved at all hazards; while in presenting the various stages of the language historically for the benefit of advanced students, the varying practice of different writers must needs be reproduced to a large extent. But when one writes the language for the use of boys and girls, one ought surely to write even local diction and idiom in the established orthography. We in Scotland write *cas* and *clach* instead of the older *cos* and *cloch* for the very good reason that we pronounce the words invariably with the *a* sound instead of that of *o*. When we differ among ourselves the matter is not so clear. But surely when the historic sound or form is still in use, respect for the past ought to give it the preference. If you insist on writing: *Thoir sin dha na h-eich*, because *do* has become *dha* in your local usage, I have an equal right to reply in my dialect: *Na do'air, horrósa*. But between us we would thus make the Gaelic page repellent, unintelligible, and Gaelic literature impossible. Could we not agree, when writing plain prose, to reproduce our local sounds and forms in historical literary form *when these are still in living use among us*? If we could bring ourselves to do so, we would have a fairly uniform standard to go by, and we would hope to attract rather than repel our few readers. By following such a rule one would write *maith* not *math*, *t'athair* not *d'athair*, *duit* not *dut*, *fallan* not *fallain*, *gnothach* not *gnothaich*, and scores of other such forms which appear in Gaelic books otherwise well written, and, from their contents, deserving of study.   DON. MACKINNON.

William Butler Yeats and the Irish Literary Revival. By HORATIO SHEAFE
     KRANS. London: Heinemann. 1s. 6d. net.

Mr. Krans's book on the Irish Literary Revival has little interest for students of the movement. It is mainly taken up with an analysis of Mr. Yeats's poetry and philosophy, and deals only in a slight, and not always well-informed, way with the Irish Literary Movement as a whole. Whatever may be said of Mr. Krans's knowledge of Mr. Yeats's work, his book, which professes to deal with the whole literary movement, shows an amazing want of knowledge. Mr. Krans is an American, and manifests the worst faults of American literary appreciation. It is hard to take his rather fulsome praise of Mr. Yeats seriously. We feel sure that Mr. Yeats himself would be the first to resent an attempt to place him on a pedestal which he has never shown a desire to occupy. Mr. Yeats's poetry is in need of no boom. Genuine lovers of poetry recognise him as a leading poet, if not the leading poet of the day. But that is quite a different thing from being head and front and mainstay of the Irish Literary Revival. Mr. Yeats's best work is in his English verse, verse that has in it much of Mr. Yeats's Celtic spirit and charm. He has attempted, not in vain, to reproduce the spirit of the art of Ireland in English. But the Irish Literary Revival aims at more than this. It hopes to take up the tradition of Irish literature at the point where it had almost flickered out, revive a literature in the Irish language rich with the inspiration of the new time, voicing the hope of a national life full of promise. This must be the work of other hands than Mr. Yeats. But towards its realisation he has done much. He has directed attention to the great sources of Irish poetry and romance. He has, especially in the last number of *Samhain*, laid down excellent rules for the guidance of workers in the purely Irish field of poetry and the drama. In reaction against the modern theatre of commerce he has been mainly instrumental in establishing in Dublin a theatre where literary drama flourishes. Better than all, he has given the Irish poets and dramatists the example of his own highly finished work.

Both the Irish Literary Movement and Mr. Yeats are worthier of better treatment than they have received at the hands of Mr. Krans. Is there no one who will give us an adequate book on the subject which is of interest not to Celts only, but to all lovers of literature throughout the world?   SEATHAN MACDHONAIN.

Uirsgeulan Gaidhealach. Stirling: Eneas Mackay. 6d.

Uirsgeulan Gaidhealach is a choice little book containing four Gaelic stories. Three authors are represented in the little collection of modern tales. We have already an indication of their merit in the fact that they won prizes at the Mòd, and they are now published in this form under the imprimatur of the Comunn Gaidhealach. It is a modest beginning in what should prove a fruitful and a useful line of work, and it is to be hoped that the Comunn will receive such encouragement in it as will warrant it in undertaking the issuing of works of even larger compass.

There is a story of two Highland *cailleachs* who were, on one occasion, passing some criticisms on a sermon they had just heard, and this is how one of them put it. 'The sermon had three faults: (1) It was read; (2) it was not well read; and (3) it was not worth reading.' If this story is reversed it will apply to the brochure under review. It has three excellencies: (1) It is all written in Gaelic; (2) it is well written; and (3) it was well worth being written.

Of course it is possible to point to an occasional slip in diction or idiom. *Thoir t' uan geal dhachaidh as a' nead glan* is a little mixed. If the expression, '*chaidh na beannachdan 's na guidheachan matha fhagail air gach taobh,*' were used in Skye or in the Outer Isles, or in many other parts of the Highlands, it would convey a very different idea from that intended by this writer. In those parts *guidheachan* means profane swearing.

Such points, however, are neither numerous nor serious, nor do they by any means detract aught from the general excellence of the book. We hope to hear that the first edition is exhausted, and a second in demand, by the time the Mòd meets in the autumn.   M. M.

Ballads of a Country Boy. By SEUMAS McMANUS.
Dublin : Gill and Son. 1*s.* 6*d.*

One of the leaders of young Ireland said, 'Come and let us make national songs to warm the hearts of our people,' and truly to-day Ireland is a nest of singing birds.   This neat little volume of poems gives fresh justification to the statement.   There is achievement and genuine promise in the Country Boy's work.   The ballads are, however, of unequal merit, and there is sometimes a lack of artistic finish which perhaps shows that some of them may be juvenile.   Though the poems can hardly be said to strike a new note, they are full of Celtic atmosphere and genuine feeling.   There is no affectation, all is simple and sincere, as befits the Country Boy. There is also the cry of the city dweller for nature, for the heath-clad hills of Ireland, and a yearning, touched with exquisite regret for the fresh young days that are past.

Perhaps Mr. McManus is most universally successful in his love-songs. Yet humour and pathos are not awanting.   'Father Phil' and the poem describing the old schoolmaster are gems in their way, and 'The Mountain Waterfall' is a fine piece of descriptive work that reminds one of 'Coire Cheathaich.'   Many of the ballads are full of rousing patriotic enthusiasm and of that love which all her true children feel for Eire.   From one such poem come the following lines :—

'There's not a little bell that blows in Ireland's dewy glens,
There's not a sagan waves a spear above her many fens,
There's not a tiny blade of grass on all her thousand hills
But this fond breast with tender love to overflowing fills.
O, Ireland for your holy sake I'll joyful bear all pain,
To your high cause I'll consecrate my heart, my hand, my brain.'

Beautiful as some of Mr. McManus's poems are, however, his reputation will probably continue to rest on his prose work, which has many keen admirers.   M. N. MUNRO.

[*A number of Reviews are held over.*]

NOTES

Notes on the Study of Gaelic

INTRODUCTORY

These Notes, attempted at the suggestion of the Editor of the *Celtic Review*, are intended to help in some degree those who possess a conversational knowledge of the Gaelic language, and desire to speak and write it with accuracy.   There are, it is believed, many such.   Gaelic is still vernacular in most parts of our Highland counties, and there are abundant indications that the Scottish Gael are awakening to a consciousness of the loss they would sustain by the death of their language.   In the meantime teacher and pupil have to face difficulties not only in the matter of suitable text-books, but also in the lack of any definite tradition. In the teaching of Latin or English every one knows fairly well what course to follow. New and improved methods, it is true, are being adopted, to the saving of time and effort; but after all the old tradition has produced good scholars, and may do so still. The case of Gaelic is different. Here there can hardly be said to be any *via trita* : each goes his own way according to his lights. If the study of Gaelic goes on, as we hope it will, we may expect in the course of some years to see an evolution of method which, with suitable text-books, will at once facilitate the labours of teacher and pupil, and raise the standard of the work. Just at present it ought to be useful to outline a plan of study such as might be sufficient to cover the ground of the leaving certificate in Gaelic. It need hardly be said that the scheme is tentative, and subject to improvement in the light of further experience. The style and scope of the papers set for the certificate will necessarily exert a powerful influence ; so far we know these only in a general way.

In an introductory paper such as this, it is pertinent to ask what are the objects to be attained by a study of Gaelic. What is the good of it ? By this is not meant its immediate utility from a commercial point of view, a test which, strictly applied, would, I fear, make short work of most of the subjects in our ordinary school curriculum, but rather whether it serves any serious purpose of educational value or of practical importance. Something may be urged on both these sides. So long as Gaelic is vernacular, we shall require ministers and schoolmasters with a scholarly knowledge of the language. This surely need not be insisted on, and there is at the present moment a very real need of both. From an educational point of view, it must be admitted that in Gaelic we in Scotland possess an instrument of culture which has never been properly utilised, because we have not been taught its value. Others—Germans, Frenchmen, and Englishmen—have found the study of Gaelic to be the ' open sesame ' to the understanding of certain facts and conditions of primitive Aryan civilisation. Mr. Alfred Nutt's study of Cuchulainn, the Irish Achilles,[1] may be cited in illustration. The ' sea-divided Gael,' Scottish and Irish, possess an inheritance, traditional and linguistic, closely akin to that of the Greeks and Romans, yet different and complementary. The key to all this is a knowledge of the language. Coming to more recent things, we may say that a knowledge of Gaelic is essential to the right understanding of the history of Scotland. Scotland, most of it, was Gaelic speaking up to the time of the Reformation. Its church and its institutions were thoroughly Celtic up to Malcolm Canmore. Scotland north of the Grampians was opened to Saxon influence only after the rising of 1745. The Highland boy who reads Latin should know that Calgacus is Calgach, that Dumnorix is Righ an Domhain, and that Caractacus is, etymologically, the ancestor of MacCarthy. Our Duncans and Donalds

---

[1] David Nutt. 6d.

should have added respect for their name and race from learning that they represent the old Gaulish Dunocatos, Fort-warrior, and Dumnovalos, World-chief. Modern Scottish Gaelic literature, from the Dean of Lismore down-wards, even including the forgeries of Macpherson—which after all are not wholly forgeries—is valuable both on account of its form and of its matter. It possesses qualities of its own, distinctively Celtic, which have been frequently insisted on, and come as a revelation to the less imaginative, but still appreciative Teuton. In point of form, no language, not even excepting ancient Greek and modern French, is richer in idiomatic and felicitous terms of expression. Shrewd, racy, and pungent, with proverb or apothegm to illustrate and enliven every turn, Gaelic is an ideal language for narrative or argument. Differing *toto caelo* from English in its idiom and its manner of thinking, it affords a discipline in translation closely analogous to that given by Latin. Above all, it is *our own* tongue.

In all teaching of language, and certainly not least in the case of Gaelic, the first essential is correct pronunciation. Clearness and distinctness of enunciation must be insisted on from the beginning and right through. For this, a necessary preliminary is a thorough drill in the sounds of the Gaelic alphabet, vowels and consonants. It is unnecessary at this stage to go into details; we shall see hereafter how essential this is for the sake of spelling. Once the values of vowels and consonants are understood, Gaelic spelling loses most of its terrors, and indeed is seen to be highly serviceable and very fairly consistent in representing the spoken word.

Spelling, writing, and dictation should be practised from the start. It is a sound principle that we should enlist the services of the ear, the eye, the hand, and the tongue, and exercise in the written forms of words should not be deferred to a late stage.

With regard to grammar, it sometimes seems to be implied that it should be left over for the advanced stages. This may be partly true of a language such as English, which has practically lost its inflections, and therefore can hardly be said to have a grammar. It would certainly be a serious error to teach an inflected language like Gaelic on such a principle. In Gaelic one is brought up against grammatical facts from the very first, and these have to be understood and put in practice. What is of import-ance, however, is that the learner should not be burdened with facts of grammar for which he has no immediate use. Grammar is after all not an end in itself, and it should be introduced regularly, gradually, tactfully, with care that the pupil is not at any one time introduced to more gram-matical facts than can be fully exemplified in composition. Strictly speak-ing, of course, matters should be so arranged that the grammar arises naturally and consecutively from the reading, both being combined with practice in speaking and in writing. This is a counsel of perfection.

In the notes which follow I shall attempt to outline a first year's course suitable to children of thirteen to fourteen, as a basis of two hours per week, or eighty lessons in the school year. W. J. WATSON.

The paper set for the LEAVING CERTIFICATE Examination (Gaelic, 29th June, 2-5 P.M.) is printed here by permission of the Controller of H.M. Stationery Office.

I. Translate into English the following extract :—

Long mhòr nan Eilthireach.[1]

'N am measg chunnaic mi aon long mhòr a thug bàrr orra air fad ; bha iomadh bàta beag a' gabhail d' a h-ionnsuidh, agus thug mi fainear gu robh iad a' deanamh deas gu a cur fa sgaoil. Bha duine leinn as gann a thog a cheann fad an latha, 's a bha a nis ag amharc gu geur air an luing. ' An aithne dhuit,' thuirt mi ris, ' ciod i an long mhòr so ?' ' Mo thruaighe !' ars' esan, "'s ann domb as aithne ; is duilich leam gu bheil barrachd 's a b' àill leam de m' luchd-eòlais innte ; innte tha mo bhràithrean is moran de m' chàirdean a' dol thairis air imrich fhada do America mu Thuath ; agus is bochd nach robh agamsa na bheireadh air falbh mi cuideachd.' Tharruing sinn a nunn d' an ionnsuidh ; oir tha mi ag aideachadh gu robh toil agam na daoine so fhaicinn a bha an diugh a' dol a ghabhail an cead deireannach a dh' Albainn, air tòir dùthcha far am faigheadh iad dachaidh dhaibh fhéin 's d' an teaghlaichean. Cha'n 'eil e comasach a thoirt air aon duine nach robb 's an làthair an sealladh a chunnaic mi a thuigsinn. Cha tig an latha a théid e as mo chuimhne. Bha iad an so eadar bheag agus mhòr, o'n naoidhean nach robh ach seachdain a dh' aois gus an seann duine liath a bha tri fichead bliadhna 's a deich.

II. Translate into English *one* of the following :—

(a) *Badan fraoich.*

Ceud failt' ort fhéin, a bhadain fhraoich,
    Bho thìr nan aonach àrd,
An tìr a dh' àraich iomadh laoch,
    Ge sgaoilt' an diugh an àl ;
Tha snuadh mo dhùthcha air do ghruaidh,
    Seasaidh tu fuachd is blàths :
'S e mheudaich dhomh cho mòr do luach
    Gu'n d' fhuair mi thu bho'n Bhàrd.

(b) *Ealadhna*[2] *Dhonnachaidh Bhàin, am Bàrd.*

Dheanainn duit ceann[3] is crann[4] 's an Earrach
    An àm chur ghearran an éill ;
Is dheanainn mar chàch air tràigh na mara
    Cur àird air mealladh an éisg ;
Mharbhainn duit geòidh is ròin is eala,
    'S na h-eòin air bharra nan geug ;
'S cha bhi thu ri d' bheò gun seòl air t' aran
    'S mi chòmhnuidh far am bi féidh.

III. Reproduce, in Gaelic, and, as far as possible, in your own diction and idiom, the passage read out. (*See* p. 93.)

---

[1] Emigrant.
[2] Accomplishments.
[3] He who leads the horses.
[4] The man who guides the plough.

IV. Translate into Gaelic *one* of the following passages :—

(a) Shinty.

The games of the boys were all athletic,[1]—throwing the hammer, putting the stone, leaping, wrestling, and the like. But the favourite game was 'shinty,' called *hockey*, I believe, in England. This is played by any number of persons, as many as a hundred often engaging in it. Each has a club, or stick bent at the end, and made short or long, according as it has to be used by one or both hands. The largest and smoothest field that can be found is selected for the game. The combat lies in the attempt of each party to knock a ball beyond a certain boundary in the opponents' ground. The ball is struck by any one on either side who can get at it. Few games are more exciting, or demand greater physical exertion, than a good shinty match.

(b) About Seals.

Very well, then. It is now May, about the 20th, and we are at the other side of the world, in the Island of St. Paul. It is cool and misty ; but there are few warm or clear days in this quarter, even in summer. We can see a few large seals on the rocks, seven feet long every one of them. The nearest one shows no fear of us, and we need not fear him. He is very fat, and it is well for him that he is so. When he has his family gathered round him on that rock, he will stay there to defend them against all comers for the next three or four months, and during that time he will neither eat nor drink. Young ones are there also. When these are about three months old, they venture into the water ; but at first they soon scramble out again, spitting and crying as loud as they can. In a few days, however, they learn to swim perfectly.

V. Answer any *two* (not more) of the following four questions :—

1. Give the genitive singular and nominative plural of *bean, bò, caora, cù, long, sliabh.*

2. Give, with examples, three cases in which the Article is used differently in Gaelic and English.

3. Translate the following sentences into idiomatic Gaelic :—

> Both are equally good. He gave thirty shillings each for the sheep. I shall
> be back before Monday. He will be twelve years of age a month hence.

4. Express in English the meaning of these sentences and phrases :—

> Olc air mhaith le càch e. Tha mi sgìth, 's mi leam fhìn. Cha b' fhearr a
> nasgaidh e. Cha bu ruith leis ach leum.

(III. *See* p. 92.) *This paper must not be seen by any Candidate.*

To be read out twice, slowly and in an accent with which the Candidates are familiar, by the Supervising Officer (or the Teacher) at 2.45 P.M. *The substance of this story is to be reproduced by the Candidates in Gaelic. No notes may be made while it is being read.*

Before commencing to read it, the Supervising Officer or the Teacher must write upon the blackboard the title of the story as follows: 'Bàthadh a' Chuilein.' *He should also warn the Candidates that they are not to aim at reproducing the passage in all its details, and in the same words or order of words as the*

---

[1] Fearail.

original. What is desired is that they should attempt to ,relate¯ the story 'in Gaelic, in their own diction and idiom. Great importance is attached to grammatical correctness, and full credit will be given for idiomatic phraseology.

Bàthadh a' Chuilein.

Chaidh binn a' chuilein a thoirt a mach air ball, 's b'e sin a bhàthadh ; agus air son mo chuid-sa de'n ghnothach, 's ann orm a thainig a' bhinn a thoirt gu buil, 's e sin ri ràdh, 's ann domb a b' éigin mo chompanach beag, bòidheach a chur gu bàs. Thog mi leam e ann am bhroilleach, 's mo chridhe an impis sgàineadh ; agus o'n a bha'n t-uisge a' sileadh gu trom chomhdaich mi e le sgiath mo pheiteige gu a chumail tioram. 'Nuair a ràinig mi an linne dhubh 's am biodh iad a' bàthadh chon is chat, bha i ag amharc cho dorcha 's nach robh de chruas cridhe agam na leigeadh dhomh a thilgeil innte. Thill mi ceum air m'ais o bhruaich na h-aibhne 's chaidh mi stigh fo phreas beag seilich, agus chrùbain mi an sin gus an robh mi cho fliuch 's ged a bhithinn air mo thumadh 's an abhainn. Cia fhad a dh' fhanainn mar sin na maireadh solus latha cha'n fhios domb, ach bha e nis a' fas dorcha, 's b'eudar an tigh a thoirt orm. Fliuch gus an craiceann, air chrith leis an fhuachd, 's ach beag as mo chiall leis an eagal, leum mi air mo bhonn 's ghabh mi roid chum bruaïch na h-aibhne 's thilg mi an dùile bhochd 's an linne. Thug e aon sgal as. Cha d' éisd mi ri tuillidh ; ghlaodh is chaoin mi, 's theich mi cho luath 's a bheireadh mo chasan mi. 'Nuair a rainig mi an tigh, thilg mi dhiom m' aodach 's leum mi do m' leabaidh. Cha bu luaithe thigeadh neul cadail orm na bha sgal a' chuilein 'n am chluais. Mhair an gnothach mar sin fad na h-oidhche. 'S a' mhaduinn bha mise cho tinn 's nach b' urrainn domh mo cheann a thogail bhàrr mo chluasaig. Bha dithis 's an tigh an latha sin aig an robh ionndrainn glé ghoirt. B'iad sin màthair agus companach a' chuilein, 's bha iomadh latha 'n a dhéigh sin mu'n deachaidh sgal a' chreutair bhig as mo chluais.

[*Readers of the Magazine will be interested to notice that the above piece is taken from Mr. Donald Mackechnie's excellent contribution to the first number (July 1904) of the* CELTIC REVIEW.]

Celt and Semite and the Determination of our Origins

If philology may afford a precious contribution to the determination of our racial origins, no light can be thrown upon the darkness of that distant past without a combined exegesis of the notions we derive from Geology, Palæontology, Anthropology, Ethnography, Epigraphy, and even Astronomy.

A priori, the racial formation of the Celtic group succeeding in the West, on its habitat, to the *Race of the Dolmens* was probably anterior to the development of Aryan or Semitic civilisations in the East. Most probably, according to the hypothesis of M. André de Panaguia, the Celtic Race proceeded, at the Stone Age, from the invasion of the habitat of the *Race of the Dolmens* by tribes of the Eastern Black Race, by a mixture of those invaders with that *Race of the Dolmens*.

If the climates of the North have lightened the complexion of the original specimens of the Celtic Race, our relationship with the Dravidian remainder of the Black Race in the south of India seems most probable. And that opinion can be defended with the arguments presented by R. P. Van den Cheyn, the learned Indianist, in his Mémoires on *The European Origin of the Aryas* and the *Asiatic Origin of the Black Race*. Most probably, also, the early language of the Celts derived from a mixture of the Asiatic dialect of the invaders of the Black Race with the language of the *Race of the Dolmens*. What was that language? A rudimentary tongue, probably still monosyllabic, corresponding to the rudimentary civilisation of the *Race of the Dolmens*. If the migrations of the *Race of the Dolmens* reached the North of Africa, on what ground can the hypothesis be formed of a non-Aryan migration proceeding, in the inverse direction, from Syriac or Egyptian lands towards the future habitat of the Celts?

From analogies between the radicals in the Celtic and the Semitic tongues, and, perhaps, from the similitudes in some of the religious rites!

But what more possible than that the earliest Semites, like the earliest Celts, should have received their polysyllabic form of language and their common religious myths from the anterior civilisation of the Eastern Black Race?

But, according to a chronology based upon induction, whereas the earliest racial, linguistic, and religious civilisation of the Celts was *pre-Ramaganic* and Lunar, the racial, linguistic, and religious civilisation of the Semites was *post-Ramaganic* and Solar, and the ancestors of the Semites could not have brought from Egypt, *via* North Africa and Spain, to the earliest Celts what they had not yet received themselves.

It is certain that, without mingling and without contact, the earliest Touranian Tribes derived from the anterior civilisation of the Eastern Black Race much more certain linguistic and religious analogies with the Celto-Aryan group of the habitat of the ancient *Race of the Dolmens*, and certain, too, that the Far-Eastern Touranians, the Chinese (although their original monosyllabic tongue developed unvaryingly true to its own genius) were not without points of contact with the earliest Celts as to the notion of the *Art of Analogy* which combined music and poetry, art of which the rules or *canons* had been consigned in the *Yo King*. In fact, it was the earliest Bardic Science common to the Celts, to the Touranians, and even to the Chinese. LIONEL ORADIGUET, D.D., LL.OO.V.

The Bagpipes in the Bible

From *The Expository Times* of January 1905 :—

'What was it that the elder son heard when he returned from the field? It was the bagpipes. So says Mr. Phillips Barry in the second part for 1904 of that most scholarly annual, the *Journal of Biblical Literature*. And it seems impossible to doubt that he is right.

'The Greek word is συμφωνία. Now, συμφωνία in Greek, perhaps as early as the time of Aristotle, means some musical instrument. It appears as an Aramaic loan-word in Daniel iii. 5, and is translated "bagpipe" by every competent translator. Again, it occurs in Roman writers in the Latinised form *symphonia*, and that in Latin it means "bagpipe" is proved, not only by the passages in which it occurs (Mr. Barry quotes very many of them), but also by the fact that with the meaning of "bagpipe" it passed into all Romance languages.

'Turn to the word as it occurs in Luke xv. 25. How has it been rendered in the Church? The Syriac palimpsest, found in the Convent of St. Catherine on Mount Sinai by Mrs. Lewis, has "sephûnyō," clearly a loan-word from the Greek again, and taken in the Greek meaning. In the Western Church "bagpipe" was the prevalent translation as late as the fifth century, when Jerome set it aside for the more general sense of the antiphony. The Vulgate chose "symphonia," and Wiclif followed with "a symphony," undoubtedly in the sense of bagpipe. Ulfilas alone of the early translators chose the sense of "singing" (saggwins). There can be no reasonable doubt that the verse ought to be translated : "Now his elder son was in the field, and as he came and drew nigh to the house, he heard bagpipe and dancing."'

REPLY

St. Mulvay

The church of 'St. Mulvay' in the parish of Barvas, Lewis, so named by Martin in his *Western Islands*, is known in Gaelic as *an Teampull Mór*, the great temple ; *Teampull Eòrabaidh*, the temple of Eoropy ; and *Teampull Mo-Luaidh*. This last would be written phonetically *Teampull Moluay* or *Muluay*, and I suggest that Martin's form, as printed, is due to his having written his *u* as *v*, as he might very well have done, or to his MS. having been misread to that extent. Sir Arthur Mitchell's 'St. Molonah' is surely a misprint for *Molouah*. The dedication was certainly not to St. Molios (*Molaisi*), but in all probability to Moluag of Lismore, whose name, though it is found with the affectionate diminutive in several place-names, appears in the *Four Masters* as *Lughaidh*, which with the honorific *mo* would give Mo-Lu'aidh in modern Gaelic. The remains of the old church which still exist indicate, as I am informed on good authority, that the building was of a style and construction superior to the ordinary *Cill*.　　　**W. J. W.**

TRANSLATIONS FROM DAFYDD AB GWILYM

By Mrs. Cecil Popham

The Burial of the Poet dead from Love

A MAIDEN brightly fair art thou, whose brow is as a lily 'neath a golden web. I loved thee with a worthy, an infinite love. Blessed Mary! is there deliverance for me? Keep thyself well for fear of thy kin avenging thy honour; I have not paid the price. There is with me, O my beloved, heavy sighing for the want of thee, from the deeps of my unfeigned madness. Because of this, fair and beautiful jewel, guilty wilt thou be—by the relics of grace—of my murder.

In a grave amidst leaves in the sappy greenwood shall I be buried. Funeral canopies of green birch shall I have to-morrow 'neath the branches of the ash, a surplice shroud about me, and linen bright as the summer clover. And the green leaves of high dignity with soft cries shall implore grace for me. Flowers of the grove will curtain me, on a bier of eight rods shall I lie, and the sea-gulls will come in thousands to carry it. And a host of mice with eyes like sparkling jewels will come from the fair woods to join my funeral train.

Let my church be a summer glade at the foot of a steep hillside, O dearest friend, and the two priests to minister there two nightingales of the bower, chosen by thee.

And there in a wheat-field shall be altars of wood, with motley floors, and a choir; no door shall be there to close in anger, for none will covet a bower of flowers. Brethren skilled in bardic lore shall be there, and grey priests knowing the Latin tongue, whose knowledge has been learnt from the books—the green books of the forest. The note of an organ of splendid covering shall mingle with the sound of monastery bells. And there, amid the birches of Gwynedd, is my grave in readiness.

A fair, green spot, a wooden bed, the church of the cuckoo and nightingale, amid young woods. And the cuckoo perched upon the green trees shall pray for my soul like an organ, chanting paternosters, orisons, and psalms in another voice. Yea, in the summer months masses and sweet supplications shall be offered for me, in memory of love. And may God at the appointed day be there to comfort the Poet in Paradise!

The Wind a Messenger to Morfudd

The Sky-Wind of dexterous kind and mighty sound walks yonder; a chill being art thou, O wind, rough of voice, a hero of the world, without foot, without wing. How strange is it! how marvellous! that to thee it is given to come from the heights of the Heavens without ever a foot; how swift was thy coming this moment over yonder hill-slope!

Say unto me an earnest chaunt, thy course whither is it, north wind of the glen? O friend, go for me from Uwch Aeron, brightly fairly, clear of tone, sparing not thyself, neither fearing the Little Hunchback.

. . . .

By thee the bushes are made bare, as by thee leaves are winnowed; none shall question thee, none stay thee, nor a mighty host, nor the hand of authority, nor blue blade, nor flood, nor rain. No mother's son can kill thee in a moment of frenzy, fire cannot burn nor guile betray thee, thou canst not drown, thou canst not be stayed,[1] cornerless art thou; there is no need of a swift horse under thee, nor bridge over stream, nor boat; from thee springs neither office nor family.[2] The blessing of God art thou upon the earth, a mighty roaring that strikes upon the oak-tops; grasshopper of the firmament, of a swift nature, a proper leaper art thou over wooded Nature.

. . A quick creature of dry nature, a starry firmament, a journey passing great; archer of the dawn above.

. . . .

Maker of bad weather on the seashore, wanton of the sea sand-banks, an eloquent and alluring thief art thou!

Thou strewest the ground with leaves and teasest them thereon; a sprightly carouser art thou, an assaulter of the hills, the sail-yard goblin of the white-breasted brine; to the ends of the earth thou wilt fly and rage to-night, O wind of the hills. Woe is me! that I put my love so deeply on Morfudd, my golden maid! A fair lady has made of me a captive slave. Fly on high! fly to the house of her father, strike the door, cause it to be opened to my messenger before the day. And seek a way unto her, oh! wail and sing unto her the sound of my sighing. Speak of my not unworthy attractions. . . . Speak to my unfailing faith; long though I have been in this world, a true lover am I. Sad is my countenance without her, if true not untrue she; go up towards the bed of Gwen (Venus), go down, O wizard of the firmament, go unto Morfudd the honey-sweet, go in peace, a good wind art thou!

[1] Alternative rendering: Nor go astray.
[2] Alternative rendering: Thou art subject neither to potentate nor fairy.

THE GLENMASAN MANUSCRIPT

Professor Mackinnon

GAELIC TEXT .

Uair is ann sein atáid tri caogait prim-imdadh fa m' imdaid caim, cruth-alainn, cumdach-ghloin-si fodeisin, con a ceitheora uaithne orda, co n-geim. do lícc loinnerda logmair a cenn gacha h-uaithni dib sein, go n-ceit(h)ri cumdaightib egsamlaib
3. impa o maidin go fesgar.   Agus an tan bertar a cumdaighte do cennaib na n-uaithne soillsighit co coitcenn do cach.   In a tuillim-si fein caoga curad maille frim im Fergus agus im Cormac Conloinges[1] mac Conchobair.   Agus in a fuilleann Finnabair agus Cainner derg con a caogait *ingen* maille ríu, a n-egmais ar n-ollamhan agus ar n-eices.'

' Noc(h)a gellaim-si am,' ar Bricne, 'imarbáidh do dhenam ritsa.   Acht aon ni chena : Is se tech Oilella aon tech as ferr an Eirinn.   Is si so tuarascbail an tighe sin : tri caogait primh-imdaidh and, agus tri caogait fo-lepa fa 'n prim-leab-áidh, agus urlar alainn umhaidhe co nach roicheann sal na sir-otrach.   (C)eithri cathaire[2] deg im a doirsib.   Imdaid an Oilella sin : tri caogait oclach innte fa m-bi cathbharr ordha, agus tri caogait ri-*ingen* innte fa m-bí cumdach oir, agus tri caogait rí-macam, a fegmais fhiled agus ollaman.   Caoga en a timchell na lepta sin, go cennaib airgid en-gil uile, agus co [3] cluim [4] alaind orda ar a cend, go slabradaib sreth-geala solus-gembna iter gach da en dib acht éin.   Uball cairche[5] orda ar cenn gacha slabr*aid* dib sin, co m-ba binnigter re tedaib menn-chrot[6] a lamaib suadh ac a sír-sinm binn-fogur na n-uball coirc (h)i[5] sin an tan co n-fagluaisenn gaoth tar feige

---

[1] MS. *Conloigges*.

[2] In I.G. the native word *cath(a)ir* (Welsh *caer*), 'city,' 'stronghold,' 'capital,' and the borrowed word *cathair* (=cathedra), 'chair,' are distinguished, the latter being written *cathaoir* (Din.). In S.G. both words, although distinct in usage, are written and declined in the same way. *Cathedra*, through French, has become in English *chair*, and this again has been borrowed in the North Highlands as *seidhir*.

[3] MS. *coo*.

(*Continued from pp.* 32, 33.)

ENGLISH TRANSLATION.

For there are to be seen thrice fifty principal rooms sur-
rounding my own fair, beautifully-shaped, crystal-adorned
room, with its four golden pillars, the top of each mounted
with gems of flashing precious stones, which are covered
with four diverse coverlets from morn till eve. And
when these coverings are removed from the pillars they
gleam in the face of all beholders. In addition to this,
fifty champions of mine are in attendance upon Fergus
and Cormac Conloinges son of Conchobar. And there
are, besides, Finnabair and red Cainner with their fifty
attendant maidens, not to speak of our ollamhs and men
of learning.'

' I do not profess to dispute with you,' said Bricne. 'And
yet, the palace of Oilill is the grandest in Ireland. This is
the description of that mansion. There are thrice fifty
principal rooms, and thrice fifty inferior couches around the
principal couch, on a polished floor of copper, without a speck
of dust or permanent blotch. Fourteen chairs are round its
doors. As to Oilill's room : thrice fifty warriors wearing golden
helmets attend there, with thrice fifty royal maidens dressed
in gold, and thrice fifty royal pages, besides poets and ollamhs.
Fifty birds are round that bed, with heads all silver-white,
with beautiful golden plumage on the head of each, and with
white chains flashing with gems between each two birds save
one. A musical ball of gold on the end of each of these chains.
And when wind blows gently over roof or skylight or window

---

⁴ *cluim* (Welsh *pluf*) from Latin *pluma*. In the North Highlands *clòimh* is the
common word for *olann*, 'wool.' In I.G. *clúmh*, with derivatives, survives in the
original sense of 'feathers,' 'down,' 'plumage' (Din.). So in S.G. (*v.* H.S.D.) *clòimh*,
clòimhteach, etc.

⁵ *cairche, coirchi* : more commonly *cairche ciúil*, 'a musical instrument of some
kind.' Cf. Ag. 6592-4 *et aliis*; *Ir. T.*, iv. p. 328. But the word is also used in the
sense of melody, *e.g:* *grith cairchi na cathbarr ic a crothad* (K. M.).

⁶ *menn-chrot*, lit. 'kid-harp.' The simile was common in describing sweet
sounds. Cf. *Ir. T.*, iv. p. 330 : ' *ocus binnithir re tétaib menncrott il-lámaib súadh
oc a sirseinm bindfogur gotha in macaim ocus a irlabra.*

no tar forles[1] no tar fuinneog*a* an tighi sin. Clar[2] d' airged agus d' finndruine re druim Oilella gurab é is fege do 'n bruigin sin ar n-dol trithi suas. Caoga cathbharr óir im á aindrib agus im á ingen*aib*. Tri caogait cat(h)bharr rig ann fós a timchell Oilella Finn.' Agus is cuma ro bui ac a radh, agus atbert an laid ann :—

'Amra an tech tech Oilella,
Tangamar as co buidech,
A b-fuil imad fian iar fír,
Imath rig, imat ruírech.

'Tri caogait and d' imdaidibh
Co m-benait re fraigh fithe,
An gach imdaid dib fo leth,
Caoga gan cle*it*h adchithe.

'Imdaidh alainn Oilella,
Aibind feis in a fachraibh,
Go[3] fraighidh caim credumha,
Co n-uaithnib óir deirg dath caéin.

'A h-ichtar na h-imdaide
D' airget ro gheal fa 'n ruire,
A medbon do chreduma,
A h-uachtar do 'n ór buide.

'Imtighid fa 'n imdaid sin
A h-eoin tre bithe betha ;
Binne gach ceol chanaid slogh
Eistecht re glor a n-greatha.

'Cristal agus carrmhogal,
Na ceithri uaithnib orda ;
Is caoga shudrall n-gloine
Im an imdaid suairc slogda.

'Caoga slabrad sainighthe
D' ór tire sicir salmda,[4]

---

[1] *forles* = *air* + *leus*. The word has survived in S.G. meaning 'chimney,' and especially the smoke-hole in the roof of a thatched cottage.

[2] In the form *clàraidh* the word survives in S.G. meaning 'wooden partition.' *ùrlar clàraidh* again is 'a deal floor.' In the sense of 'board,' 'table,' 'lid,' 'level surface,' *clàr* is in common use. In dialect *clàr* is met with as a verb : *chlàr e orm e,* 'he persisted in attributing it to me.'

of that mansion, the melody of these musical balls is as sweet
as that of the strings of a lyre touched by the fingers of
a sage.   At Oilill's back is a partition of silver and white
bronze which, proceeding upwards through the building,
forms the ridge of the palace.   Fifty golden helmets protect
the girls and maidens.   There are, moreover, thrice fifty
kings' helmets around Oilill the Fair himself.'   And while
saying this he repeated the lay :—

> ' A wonderful palace the palace of Oilill,
> I have come away from it well pleased ;
> Many a champion is there, in truth,
> Many a king, many a lord.

> ' Thrice fifty rooms are there,
> With lofty walls reaching to the roof ;
> In each individual room of them
> Fifty (warriors) are conspicuously seen.

> ' The beautiful room of Oilill,
> Delightful a feast within it ;
> With its gleaming walls of brass,
> Its beautiful pillars of red gold.

> ' The bottom of that couch
> Of pure white silver for its lord to rest upon,
> Its middle of brass,
> Its upper part of yellow gold.

> ' There move round that couch
> Its birds never ceasing,
> Sweeter than human music
> To listen to their warble.

> ' (Decked with) crystal and carbuncle,
> The four golden pillars ;
> Fifty crystal lamps
> Are a-light in the pleasant, peopled room.

> ' Fifty chains of special pattern
> Of the gold of the peaceful holy land,

---

³ MS. *cco.*

⁴ The gold of Ophir, no doubt. *Sicir* usually means ' wise,' ' sure,' and connects
with, if not a loan from, the Scottish *siccar,* itself probably from L. *securus.*   *Salmda*
is an adjective from *salm,* the Gaelic form of *psalmus,* ' psalm.'

Nocha breg ader mo bel,
Ar gach dá en san adbha.

'Urlar alainn umaide
Impe as gach aird do thegaim;
Secht fichit fer fri comlonn
Fa 'n righ as lucht do leabaidh.

'Clár d' airged as d' findruine
Re druim Oilella atmeide,
Is an imdaid a cath colg,
Co m-benadar re fraig feige.

'Trí caogait coradh comola,
O rig-damnaib co flaithib;
Tri caogait coradh frith dala,
O macamaib co maithib.

'Caoga bleidi [1] bán-airgid
Re comol medha mescda;
Caoga niam-lann [2] umaidhe,
Caoga cúach, caoga easgra.

'Tri caogait cathbarr órdaide
Im aindrib is an adba,
Is tri caogait cat(h)barr righ,
Is e a fhir gurab amra.'

Amra.

Adubhradar maithe fer n-Erenn uile nach cualadar riam
tuaruscbail tighe bud f herr [3] in a sin. Do leigedar secha iar
sin an imarbaid. Ba h-ait(h)rech le Meidb imarbaidh do
dhenam re Bricni. Uair do bí d' á neimnighe agus d' a
dálaighe [4] fuair sí imarbaidh úada gur fer si failte fri Bricni.
'Moide do bearmáis edail duit,' bar isi, 'a fheabus adeire
maith.'

Do coraigeadh teach mór na Cruachna iar sin, agus do
t-shuidh Meadb agus Ailill agus Fergus agus Cormac agus na
maithe ar chena. Do t-shuidedar na h-ollamain, agus do

---

[1] Cf. Ag. 122 : bleidhidha búis 7 bánóir : 'goblets of crystal and pale gold.'
[2] From the context lann must mean some kind of vessel. O'R. gives 'gridiron'
as one of the many meanings of the word. Cf. Wind. Wört. s. v.

My mouth does not utter a lie,
Upon each two birds in the dwelling.

' A polished floor of copper
In whatever direction I approach it;
Seven score men, fit warriors,
Are the guardians of the king's bed.

' A partition of silver and white bronze
To the back of the incomparable (?) Oilill,
In the room of many swords,
Which joins to the wall of the roof.

' Thrice fifty champions carousing
Of princes and nobles;
Thrice fifty champions in waiting
Of youths and gentlemen.

' Fifty goblets of white silver,
For drinking intoxicating mead;
Fifty polished trenchers of copper;
Fifty cups, fifty beakers.

' Thrice fifty golden helmets,
Around the maidens in the abode;
And thrice fifty kings' helmets;
Truly, a wonderful palace.'

                   Wonderful.

All the chiefs of the men of Ireland said they never heard a nobler description of a mansion. Thereupon the disputation ceased. Meave was sorry that she entered upon a dispute with Bricne. Still, because it was on account of her own virulence and combativeness that he debated with her, she made Bricne welcome. 'We will reward you all the more,' said she, ' that you have spoken so well.'

The great palace of Cruachan was thereupon prepared, and Meave and Ailill and Fergus and Cormac and all the chiefs sat down (to the banquet). The ollamhs were seated,

---

[3] MS. *b^d fherr b-fherr.*
[4] *dálaighe.* The offered rendering is suggested by the context.

t-shuid Bricne ar belaib Fergusa. Agus an uair do batar cach co subhach, adubairt Bricne : 'Ac súd, a Fhergais, na tri caogait carpat co n-echaib agus co sciathaib, agus tri cet brat cumdaigh, agus na tri deich cet irna derg óir do ghellais do mnaib do theglaig do chum cumdaich ecsamla edaich na cath-miled.' 'Ro-t-fhia buaid agus bennacht, a Bricni,' bar Fergus ; 'as mor an tidhlacadh sin agus as adbal an tigernus.' Et tucadar tres eile oil agus aibnesa, agus tarrla coir comraid ider Bricni agus Fergus agus Cormac agus Dubthach agus Aongus mac Aonlaime Gaibe. 'Ba beg a fis duitsi, a mo popa[1] a Ferguis, mesi ac suirgi duit,' ar Bricni. 'Ga baegal[2] fuarais dam a nosa, a Bricni?' bar Fergus. Cuma do bí 'g a rádh, agus adubhradar na roind etarra and sin :—

'Beg a fis duit a nosa,
    A Ferguis móir mic Rosa,
    Misi ac denam do dala
    Ris na rignaib roc go málla.[3]

'Ader rit, a mic Cairbri,
    Ge tagraisi co h-arnaidh,
    Robsat badhaig na tirte,[4]
    Gid at garb na fíadnaisi.

'Dano pill ar do gnuis gloin,
    Geis ort is troig mná troguin ;[5]
    Mana thuga let o a tigh
    Rigain Oilella echtaigh.'

'Na h-abair,. a fhir dana,
    An t-aithesg nach inrádha ;
    Ní fúi(gh)mís de re 'r linn lá
    Ar n-inadh a Conachta.'

---

[1] *popa* : Used very frequently, expressive of affection and familiarity. In the North Highlands (N. H.) *bòbag, boban, bobaidh* are used as familiar and affectionate terms to boys, step-fathers and fathers. Cf. Macdonald's well-known chorus :—

Ho-ro mo bhobug an dram.

[2] *baegal, baoghal,* common as noun and verb : 'danger,' 'hazard'; 'to endanger,' 'belie.'

[3] I take *málla* to be the S.G. *màlda.*

[4] *badhaig* might stand for *baghaig (bágach)*, 'warlike.' But *gid* in the next line suggests an antithesis between *badhaig* and *garb*. I take the word to be formed from

and Bricne sat opposite Fergus. When the others were
making merry, Bricne said : 'Yonder, Fergus, are the hundred
and fifty chariots with their horses and shields, and the three
hundred mantles, and the three thousand *irnca* of red gold
which you promised to the women of your household, in order
to provide armour of diverse pattern for your warriors.'
'The luck and the blessing are yours, Bricne,' said Fergus ;
'the wealth is great and the ownership (thereof) vast.'
Another while was passed in drinking and enjoyment, when
Fergus and Cormac and Dubthach and Angus son of One-
hand Gaba came to have talk with Bricne. 'Little did you
know, my dear Fergus, that I have been a-courting for you,'
said Bricne. 'What scrape have you got me into now,
Bricne?' said Fergus. As they spoke thus, the following
staves were repeated between them :—

'Little have you thought now,
  Great Fergus, son of Ros,
  That I was making a tryst for you,
  With ladies of gentle bearing.

'I say to you, son of Cairbre,
  Though you debate the matter hard,
  The lands are kindly,
  However rough the witnesses.'

'Now, withdraw your words,
  A taboo is upon you, and the pangs of a woman,
  If you do not carry away from her home
  The queen of featful Oilill.'

'Do not say, shameless one,
  What is unseemly,
  We shall not get in our day (elsewhere),
  Our position in Connaught.'

---

báid, in S.G. *bàidh*, 'affection,' 'kindliness.' The pl. *tirts* is not common ; but cf.
Bid terc flaithi na thirthe, 'the nobles of these lands are few.'

  [5] Among the *geasa* which Beiuda, daughter of the King of Lochlann, imposed on
Conghal Clairingnech and his followers was *troigh mhna troghuin* which is rendered,
'pangs of a woman in childbirth,' a reference, no doubt, to the *nóinden* or 'couvade'
of the Ulstermen ; *v. Cc.* pp. 112-13 note 6. In the MS. *troguin* joins to the next line.

'Do chuir[1] do gaisged ar cul
On ló tangais o d' dun;
Do sgail do gnim is do gráin,[2]
Do chuaid do brig acht becán.'[3]

Beg.

Ac a cloistecht sin do dubairt mac Carbri Ceinnléith, tuc (Dubthach[4]) cuinnscleo d' á cois uad am Bricni go tarla druim an ollaman can airisim sa rí-theinid ro moir, gur bo tenn-obair d' aos fedma an tighe a thárrachtain gan a dhódh agus a drum-losgadh.

Ro eirich geoin mór sa m-bruighin de sin. Agus tarradar moran do na h-Ulltachaib an arma, agus do regradar Túatha Táiden an t-uatbas. Do thogaib Medb a cend iar sin, agus do fhiafraigh co[5] h-obann: 'Cred fa rababhair[6] do'n ollaman, a Ullta?' ar sí. 'An ní as minic tanic ris,' ar Dubthach, 'a thenga luath labhar fein.' Ba h-olc mor le Fergus an ni sin .i. Bricne d' esonorugadh 'n a fhiadhnaisi. Agus ro t-shainn[7] Dubthach d' indsaigid, agus nir léigedar an Dubloinges dó. Ro ghabustar Meadb agus Oilill a coir-iugadh caich co coitcenn fá Bricne d' esonorughadh 'n a fiadnaisi. Ro ba maith le mnaib agus le macamhuib na Cruachna[8] nile an esonoir adbal sin d' fhaghail do Bricni, agus as ed adubradar nách fuair olc riam bel bud oirchisi d' a fhaghail ana in bel sin; nair ni raibe a Cruachain, do med an grada d' aroile, dias nach cuired run marbtha agus mí-chóraigte a ceile etarra.

Do leicetar secha sin an oidce sin. Agus o tainic an maiden ar na marach do eirich Fergus agus an Dubloinges agus do goiredar Bricne cuca ar fód foleith, agus do fiafraig-edar de: 'cinnus ata an dail-si re ceile?' 'Ader-sa rit,' ar Bricne, 'amail adubairt Flidhais fritsa .i. dul d' íarraidh

---

[1] or, chuaid.　　　　　　　　　　　　　　　　[2] Cf. p. 32 note 1.

[3] becán : beagan like mòran is, in S.G., now construed as a noun governing the gen. I should write : Chaidh do bhrigh ach beag as. But for this usage of the word, cf. Silva Gadelica (Sil. Gad.), p. 248: do bi Iubdán i n-Emain co cenn bliadna acht becan : 'I. was almost a whole year in Emain.'

[4] I infer that it was Dubthach who kicked Bricne from his quarrelsome disposi-tion, and from the fact that it was he who immediately afterwards explained to Meave the cause of Bricne's disgrace.

[5] MS. cco.

'You have cast your valour aside,
Since you have left your castle,
Your prowess and dread have taken wings, ;
Your vigour has all but vanished.'

Little.

Upon hearing what the son of greyheaded Cairbre said, (Dubthach) gave a violent kick to Bricne, so that the back of the ollamh was forthwith in the great blazing fire, and it was all the attendants could do to save him from being singed and his back burned.

There was great confusion in the hostel because of this. Many of the Ultonians drew their weapons, and the tribes of Taidiu responded to the uproar. Meave raised her head and suddenly asked: 'What have you done to the ollamh, Ulstermen?' said she. 'What has often hurt him,' replied Dubthach, 'that sharp loud tongue of his.' Fergus resented greatly this public insult to Bricne. He longed to attack Dubthach, but the Dubloinges prevented him. Meave and Oilill blamed all and sundry for dishonouring Bricne in their presence. The women and youths of Cruachan were all pleased at the great insult which Bricne received, and they said that no tongue ever deserved punishment more than his; for there were not 'in Cruachan (even) two who loved each other ever so much, but Bricne managed to put deadly and irreconcilable enmity between them.

The matter passed for that night. When the morrow's morning came Fergus and the Dubloinges summoned Bricne to a place apart, and inquired of him : 'How does this tryst hang together?' 'I (only) tell you,' said Bricne, 'what Flidais asked you to do, viz., to go to the Gamhan-

---

[6] For the form and idiom cf. *Cc.* 114. *Cred fa rabhabhair do bhar n-ollamh?* 'Why were you angry with your O.?' In this usage, the substantive verb construes in I.G. with the preps. *do* and *le*, in S.G. with *ri*, e.g. *cia bhi leat?* 'Who was annoying you?' Cf. S.G. *cò bha riut? Bheir mise air*, 'Who annoyed you? I will make him.'

[7] In two other passages later the same form occurs, and in the same sense : 'he strongly desired.' From this verb comes *saint, sant,* S.G. *sannt* 'greed,' 'covetousness,' whence the denominative *santaigim,* S.G. *sanntaich* 'covet.'

[8] MS. *na Cruachan.*

fhaigde[1] ech agus arm agus eidedh ar an n-Gamannraid, agus co ticf*a* sisi let con a h-airgedaib agus gus an m-buin mail as dech fuil an Eirinn, agus do bera deich cet ar fhichit cet ban dingbalaib rig agus ruirech a coinni do teglaig-si .i. ben a coinne gach aein fir dib ; agus da tora lib, beraid as a n-gal*ad*[2] fir Erenn gacha sechtmad oidchi, iter feraib agus mnaib agus macámaib agus min-dáinib gach n-oidche. Agus denaid bar comarle uime sin,' bar Bricne. 'Agus da n-dechthai ann bid mana mor-gliad agus bid adbar urbadha é. Agus do gebtái imghuin urlam agus imbualadh aithes*ech* o curadaib clisde[3] coimdeasa agus o greidib gadhamla gaisgid na Gamannraidi.' 'Ni b-fuil ann sin,' ar Fergus, 'acht mar nach bethea-sa fen itir a Gamannraid, a Bricni.' 'Ni biú, a ard-fhlaith,' ar Bricne, 'nair ni h-insib*air* me; agus is cora midluc*a* co h-Emain.' 'Ni ba fír sin, a Bricni,' ar Fergus, 'uair mana tí tu do t' deoin linn ticfair do t' ainndeoin, a los t' fuilt agus t' finnf*aid*.'[4] 'Rachat-sa ann,' ar Bricne, 'agus bit aithrec(h) lim.' Agus is cuma do bui ag a radh, agus ro can in laid agus do fregair Fergus:—

'Sgel agam duit, a Fhergais fhéil,
A m(h)ic reid Roigh, nocha sgél reidh,
Tuc Elidais duit, bid mana n-glonn,
Is aidbs*ech* lim, gradh taibs*ech* trom.

'Da n-ana a bus do cu(i)r si ort,
Mad mesa let, nai n-gesa a nocht.'
'Rac(h)at-sa siar, do berí lém,
Beg a thor lem dol ar a ceand.'

'Mad slan an fer atconnarc thiar,
Da n-eirge a ferg, b*ad* derg an sliabh.
"Do bér-sa *test*," ar Oilill Finn,
"Nar curta ar lear[5] fer ós a cinn."'

---

[1] *faighde*, *foighde*, 'aid,' 'subsidy.' The word survives in S.G. *faoighe* (*fo* + *guidhe*), and until quite recently the practice,—a genteel sort of begging. The word was also used for the present received: *a dol air f.*, 'going round for contributions'; *f. chlóimh*, *eórna*, etc., 'the contribution received, in wool, barley,' etc. The practice gave rise to many familiar sayings. Cf. the Scottish *thigging* (Jamieson's *Scot. Dict.* s.v. *thig*).

[2] Cf. *supra*, p. 26 note 2.

[3] *clisde* from *cle*(*a*)*s* 'feat,' now, in S.G. more commonly 'trick,' 'prank.' In I.G.

raidh for a subsidy of horses and weapons and armour, and
that she would come away with you with her herds and her
hummel cow, the best in Ireland, and would bring along with
her three thousand women fit to mate with kings and lords
to meet your people, *i.e.* a wife for every man of them; and
should you carry these away, they will sustain the men of
Ireland every seventh night, both men and women, youths
and children, each night.   Do you deliberate upon that pro-
posal.' added Bricne.   'And if you go on that expedition, it
will be an omen of great contests and the cause of disaster.
For you will have instant combat and vigorous fighting from
the featful dexterous champions and the nimble battalions
of the warriors of the Gamhanraidh.'   'That means,' said
Fergus, 'that you do not (intend to) accompany us to the
(country of the) Gamhanraidh, Bricne.'   'I do not, great
prince,' said Bricne, 'for you will not miss me; and (moreover) the feeble's proper (home) is in Emain.'   'That will
not be so, Bricne,' said Fergus, 'if you come not with us
willingly, you will come in spite of you, to save your hair and
pile.'   'I shall go,' said Bricne, 'and I shall rue it.'   And
while talking thus, he chanted this lay, Fergus replying :—

> 'Tidings for you, generous Fergus,
>   Mild son of Roigh, not peaceful tidings,
>   Flidais has bestowed upon you, omen of greed deeds,
>   I know it well, great manifest love.

> 'Should you abide here, she has laid upon you,
>   If to your sorrow, nine taboos this night.'
>   'I shall go west, and carry her away with me,
>   A lightsome task to go in quest of her.'

> 'If him I saw in the west be hale and well,
>   Should his ire arise, the slope will be red;
>   "I give my word," said Oilill the Fair,
>   "He shall be the first to be sent adrift on sea." '

---

clis is a noun meaning 'a start,' 'a surprise.'   In S.G. *clis* is an adj., 'active,'
'quick'; *na fir chlise*, 'aurora borealis.'   ·

[4] In the mod. language *folt, falt* is the hair of the head; *fionnadh* (*finnfad*), hair
on the body, and especially the hair and fur of animals.

[5] To be sent adrift on the sea was a not uncommon punishment, *v.* Trip, *Life*
(W. S.) pp. clxxiv, 222, 288 ; Cáin Adamnain (K. M.) p. 43.

'Sluag Cruachna atcim, gid imdha dib,
  Bid beg bar grain dar láim an righ ;
  A lucht-sa a nall, da n-dechtaéi síar
  Do ficfa rib clesa fir.[1]

'A lucht-sa a nall, gid dimbaig lim,
  Ruaicfedid coinbruin [2] os bar cinn ;
  Beid lama an uir ; bed bana beoil ;
  Iarrfaigter áir ; biathfaidter eoin.

'Domnall sa sloigh, da m-beri oirb,
  Fuicfide faidb, nocha b' asbrainn [3] soirb ;
  Da ti Fermenn mac Dara Deirg,
  Do bera asbrainn ; mairb ar in leirg.

'Goll Acla a n-íar, da tis a slógh,
  Seolfaid a airm, bed mairb co leor ;
  Ni rac(h)-sa lib, ni biú-sa treas ;
  Anfad a bus, bad é mo les.'

' A Bricni baeith, do ficfa leam,
  Ar sgáth mo sgeith, a cleith ced rend.'
' Atu-sa a nois a n-galar trom
  Adlaic mé, a fhir, do m' tig a nunn.

'Tair lim do d' deoin, a Bricni binn,
  No ticfa a nos, a los do cinn.'
' Rac(h)at-sa let, bud mana der ;
  Bud olc mo diol, bud fir an sgel.'

                                    Sgel agam duit.

Is i comarle ar ar h-oirised aca techt ris na tosgaib sin.
Agus tangatur a Cruachain a nunn as a h-aitle, agus do suidh
Oilill agus Dubthach do chum na fichle agus do batar ac a
h-imirt re h-athaid.   Is sí sin úair agus aimser tanic Fergus
d' agallaim Oilella agus Medha.   Agus do gab cet acu fa
imtecht d'iarraidh faigdhi airm agus eididh ar an n-Gamannraid.   Agus fuaratar ced ré thinech o Oilill agus o Meidb.
Agus do fiafraigetar do Dubthach nar mithigh leis imthecht
leo.   'Tigid romainn,' ar Dubthach, 'agus innisid damsa gá
h-inad a m-beithi a nocht.'   'Ata a fhis sin agam sa,' bar

---

[1] MS. adds .d.
[2] The word may read *combrain*. Is the meaning 'dog-ravens'? A proper name
Conbran is met with.

'I see the hosts of Cruachan, numerous though you be,
Your strength will be of small account in opposing the king:
You folks here, should you go west,
Will encounter genuine feats of arms.

'You people here, though distressful to me,
Birds of prey will wheel over your heads;
Hands will be in mould; lips will be pale;
Slaughter will be rife; birds (of prey) will be gorged.

'Should Donald and his hosts attack you,
They will obtain booty, it will not be a slight encounter;
Should Fermenn son of Daire the Red be there,
He will make a charge; the dead on the field (will be many)

'Should the host of Goll Acla from the west come,
His force will be well led, the dead will be numerous;
I will not accompany you, I am not over strong,
I will stay here, that is best for me.'

'Foolish Bricne, you shall come with me,
In the shelter of my shield, protection from a hundred lances.'
'I am now labouring under heavy sickness,
Restore me, O hero, to my home.'

'Come with me, willingly, sweet-voiced Bricne,
Or you will come instantly to save your head.'
'I shall accompany you, an omen of tears;
My lot is hard, true the tale.'
                                        Tidings for you.

They resolved to go on that quest. And thereafter they
went over to Cruachan, and Oilill and Dubthach sat down to
play chess for a while. That was the very time when Fergus
went to have parley with Oilill and Meave. He sought permission to go to the Gamhanraidh for a subsidy of weapons
and armour; and he received leave readily from Oilill and
Meave. Dubthach was asked whether he was not ready to
accompany them. 'You go forward,' said Dubthach, 'and
tell me where you mean to stay this night.' 'I know,' said

---

[3] *asbrainn* I have not met with, unless the word equates with the modern
spàirn, uspàirn 'great effort.'

114

THE CELTIC REVIEW

Medb, 'a tig Modho Minadhmad*adh* m'oll*aman* cerda-sa[1] an dúnad Atha Deirg ar dub-abainn Brea, re raiter Ath s̄ mŏ ar Suca.'[2]

Do gluaisetar rompa an Dubloinges agus Fergus no co rangatar co dúnad Atha Deirg. Agus do eirigh Moda Minadmad*adh* in a coinne, agus do toirb*ir* póca d' Fergus agus do Cormac Conloinges, agus do fer failti re maithibh an Dubloinges o sin a mach. Do fresl*ad* agus do frit(h)eol*ad* iad as a h-aitle, uair do bui fl*ed* mór urlam incaithmi aige do Oilill agus do Meidb. Uair ba rath mor in righ-bruiden[3] sin, agus fa h-e prim-c*erd* an cuigid é fós. Agus do batar ann fós treidhe ar a n-eimig*ter* cerd .i. foridhi renn, agus cáor comraic, agus feth tar faobar; agus[4] do batar aige *tr*eigi ar a n-imig*ter* brug*aid* .i. coire ansgoich, agus mo c(h)en re gach n-daim, agus gan diultadh ré nech. Agus do batar ann co trath fuin*idh* do ló. A n-imthús co n-nigi sin.

Imthusa Dubthaich do berar os aird. Tanic an trath nóna cuige a Cruachain, agus rug*ad* an cluithi fair agus do leig*ed* gair mór fanamait nime. Agus do eirigh co deinm-nedac(h), agus do fiarfaig d'a gilla a n-geibti na h-eic(h) no i n-innilti an carpad. 'Is ed á meig*in*,' ar in gilla. Agus tug*ad* na h-eich do chum Dubthaich. Agus do luid in a

---

[1] *cerd*, now *ceard*, cognate with Latin *cerdo*, 'craftsman.' In older Gaelic literature, the general meaning is 'artist,' 'artificer,' and especially a worker in metals, 'brazier,' 'jeweller,' although the term is not infrequently applied to a poet and musician. It is in the latter sense chiefly that the term is used in Welsh: *cerdd*, 'an artist'; *pen-cerdd*, 'the chief performer,' *e.g.* on the harp. On Gaelic ground the former idea was always predominant; and in process of time, through the decay of native industries in metals, the *ceard* became the patcher of pots and pans, 'a tinker.' The word was borrowed into Lowland Scotch, and has yielded the surname 'Caird.' Here Moda Minadhmadadh is described as *ollamh cerda* or 'head of the guild,' and *prim-cerd* or chief *cerd* of the whole province. He is also a *brugaid* or 'hospitaller.' Perhaps *maer*, *maor*, 'steward,' might cover his various offices.

[2] The *Suca* or 'Suck' is a river in co. Roscommon, *v. O'Grady's Catalogue of Irish MSS.* (*O'Gr. Cat.*), p. 367.

[3] In this MS., as elsewhere, *bruiden*, *bruigen* frequently means 'a mansion,' 'a castle,' as well as 'a hostel' or public place of entertainment. The old writers mention six *rig-bruidens* or royal hostels as existing in Ireland at this time. These were *Bruiden dá Choca*, 'in a district which belongs to Meave and Ailill'; *Bruiden dá Ger*, or *Bruiden mic Cecht da reu*, in Connaught (Brefny); *Bruiden Brúadaig*, in Ulster; *Bruiden Forgaill Manach* (whose daughter, Eimhir, was the wife of Cuchulainn), beside Lusk; *Bruiden dá Derga* (*Berga*) in the east of Leinster; and

Meave, 'in the house of Moda Minadhmadadh, my chief steward, in the fort of Red-ford on the black river of Brea, called the Ford of . . . on the (river) Suck.

The Dubloinges and Fergus fared forth and arrived at the fort of Red-ford. Moda Minadhmadadh rose to meet them, and kissed Fergus and Cormac Conloinges, and welcomed all the chiefs of the Dubloinges. They were served and ministered to thereafter, for he (Moda) had a great and excellent banquet ready for Oilill and Meave. For that royal hostel was a great Rath, and he (Moda) was moreover the principal steward of the province. Besides there were there a triad (of rules) which a *cerd* observed, viz., point thrusts (?), and furious combat, and respite in fighting; and a triad which an hospitaller observed, viz., the ever full caldron, and welcome to every company, and refusal to none. And they were there until close of day. Their proceedings thus far.

With respect to Dubthach: the afternoon found him still in Cruachan; he lost the game, and he was loudly and derisively laughed at. He rose up angrily and asked his servant whether the horses had been caught, or the chariot yoked. 'There they stand,' said the lad. The horses were brought to Dubthach. He stepped into his chariot and drove

---

Bruiden mic dá thó, also in Leinster. The definite number six may have been fixed upon, as W. S. suggests, to correspond with the six cities of refuge of the Hebrews, to which the *bruidens* of the Gael bore some analogy. All the *bruidens*, we are told, were asylums of the 'red hand'—(*Ba coimeirque laime deirce nach bruiden* (Rc. xxi. 314). The writer of this MS. would uphold the importance of the *bruiden* of Moda Minadhmadadh, and he gives details which add somewhat to our knowledge of the old Gaelic life. Two of the rules of the road which the *brugaid* or hospitaller observed, —'welcome to all,' 'refusal to none,'—need no explanation; they are in vogue now. *Coire ansgoich*, as here written, *coire ansguith* elsewhere, 'the irremovable caldron,' is no doubt the *caire ainsic*, 'the never dry' or 'ever full caldron' of *The Laws*. In each *bruiden* a caldron (or caldrons) stood which was never empty. Every guest, as he entered, had the privilege of thrusting a flesh fork into this caldron once. What he took up he might eat. But if he took nothing, he had not a second chance: *In fer do theiged iar sin t-shligi, do bered in n-ael is in coire, ocus na tabrad do'n chét gabhail, iss ed no ithed. Mani thucad ní do'n chét tadall, ni bered a n-aill.* (Ir. T. i. 96). The function of the *cerd* in Moda's hostelry is new to me. He deals not with feasting, but with fighting. But the rendering I give of the *cerd's* triad is largely conjectural. The phrases were evidently technical and of definite meaning.

⁴ MS. *agus agus*.

carbad, agus tanic roime co dúnad Atha Deirg. Agus o
t' conncatar gillannrad an Dubloingis Dubthach do mallaiget-
ar ḍo. Toirrlingis Dubthach as a .carbad, agus tanic a
sdec(h) a raibi Fergus. Agus atrachtatar cach roime.

Imthusa ghilla Dubthaich. Do dech in a timchell, agus
do batar eich na Dubloingsi ar sgor, agus eich Fergusa ar
sgor, agus eich an cerdha ar sgor eile. Agus tug gilli
Dubthaich a agaid ar gillaib na Dubloingsi agus do gairetar
na gillai dó, agus nir leigetar é fén ina a eich cuca. Tug a
agaid ar gillaib Fergusa, agus nír leigset cuca é. Agus tuc
a agaid ar gillaib an cerda fos. 'Fort do choll dúabais,'[1] ar
siat, 'da n-gabtái an doman uile frit mar do gab(a)d so, ni
fuigbidtea inad do cinn ann.' Agus do sir in gilli an baile fo
tri, agus ni fúair inadh a sgu(i)rfe a eich na tech leptha na
biadh na tomaltus. Agus o nach b-fuair, tanic ar agaid a
tigerna a muigh,[2] agus is ed isbert : 'Is gilli droch tigerna
ata mar atu-sa a nocht, gan biadh, gan dig, gan leabaid.'

Do eirigh Dubthach in a shuide o t' cúala an comrad sin
agus atbert : 'Cidh duitse, a Moda,' ar sé, 'gan biadh gan
digh gan tech leptha do tabairt do m' gilla.' 'Na tigbi
leptha,' bar Moda, 'ni fhuil aen tech agamsa dib ach an t-aon
tech a sa m-bíatar cach co coitcenn, agus ni bia do gilla-sa na
gilla oglaeich eile do tig(h) leptha ann. Dala an bidh,' bar
Modha, 'mad beg ré d' gilla-sa saith ein fhir, do geba saith
náonmar.' Ro ba lonn le Dubthach an freagra sin, agus tarla
corruighi etarra. Agus do sa(i)nn[3] Dubthach eirghe, agus
nír leiged do. O do cúaidh aire caich do Dubthach do eirigh
agus tuc béim cloidme do Modha co n-derna da ordain[4] de.

Do eirigh Fergus fái sin, agus do eirgetar an Dubloinges
d'indsaige Fergusa, agus do congbatar h-é. Agus ni fúair
Fergus riám ni do cuirfe a cend Modha do marbadh do
Dubthach. Agus rugatar as an oidchi sin co h-anbúainech
co tanic an maiden ar na márach cuca. Agus ro eirigh Fergus

---

[1] duabais : the opposing word suabais is oftener met with, whereas in
adjective form duaibsech is much more common than suaibsech. Cf. Fair a chol ocus
a dhuabais, 'upon itself be the evil that it brings' (S. G., p. 242); ort do choll
duaphis, a Chonghail, 'on yourself be your dire ruin, Congal' (Cc. p. 242). Also, ort
do choll uathbháis, a Chonghail, 'on you is your dire destruction' (Cc. p. 96).

to the castle of Red-ford. And when the attendants of the Dubloinges saw Dubthach (approaching) they cursed him. Dubthach alighted from his chariot and proceeded to Fergus's quarters. Every one made way for him.

As to Dubthach's servant, he looked round and found the horses of the Dubloinges, the horses of Fergus, as likewise those of Moda, each in a paddock apart. He approached the stable boys of the Dubloinges, and they laughed at him, and would not permit him or his horses to find room with them. He went to Fergus's men and they repulsed him. He then approached the landlord's servants. 'Death and destruction to you!' said they, 'if the whole world were to receive you as we do, you would get no resting-place in it.' The lad scoured the stead three times, and he could find no place for his horses, nor bed nor food nor fare (for himself). When everything failed him he came to where his master was, and this is what he said : 'The servant of a bad master I must be, seeing that I am this night without food or drink or bed.'

Dubthach sat up when he heard this, and said : 'How is it, Moda,' said he, 'that you do not provide food and drink and a sleeping-place for my servant?' 'With respect to sleeping-houses,' said Moda, 'I have not a single one save that which is common to all the company, and neither your servant nor that of any other warrior shall find room therein. As to food,' added Moda, 'if one man's surfeit does not satisfy your servant, he will get the surfeit of nine.' Dubthach was furious at that answer, and the two quarrelled. And Dubthach was eager to rise, but was not permitted. However, when he ceased to be observed Dubthach rose up and gave a sword blow to Moda, which cut him in two.

Fergus rose up thereupon, but the Dubloinges rose also and held him back. And Fergus never after met with anything to compare with the slaughter of Moda by Dubthach. And they passed that night anxiously until the morrow's morning came. And Fergus rose up and approached

---

² MS. *muich*.   ³ *v. supra*, p. 109 note 6.
⁴ *ordu*, now in I.G. *orda*, disused in S.G., 'a piece,' 'a fragment.'

ann sin agus tanic ós cinn Modha Minadhmadadh agus ro gab ag á égaine go h-adbal, agus is ed isbert : ' Is truagh an gnim do rinnis, a Dubthaich,' ar se, ' agus is olc do gnim an Emain dár marbuis Fiacha mac Concobair agus Daire mac Feidlimthi. Agus olc na h-echta eile do rónus .i. Laidis agus Lennabair da ingin Eogain mic Durtacht, agus Moirenn muingheal ben Munnremair mic Eirginn,[1] agus Eitni Cinn-fhinn ben Eirrgi Echbeóil.[2] Agus ni h-engnam tuc ort in gním sin do denam.' Agus is cuma ro bui ag á rad(h), agus atbert an laid ann :—

' A Dubthaich, do fheallais oirn,
Cian do raduis fo meabal ;
Acht gid olc do gním a nocht,
Ro b' olc do gním an Emain.

' Fiacha Finn mac Conchobair,
Is re d' laim-si do rochair ;
Bás Daire mic Feidhlimthi,
Ger b'eiséin, nír gním sochar.

' Moirenn moingeal marbaisi,
Ben Muinremair gan mebal ;
Eitne ceinnfinn crechtnaigis,
Ben Eirrgi, fa cruaidh debaid.

' Láighis agus Lennabair,
As i do lámh ro-t-cirre ;
Edain fhinn a Berramain,
As tusa fos ro-s-mille.

' Taet let Moda Minadhmad,
Mór-cerd Medba gan bine
Ge do (gh)ne-se echta uill,
Ni h-e cruaidhe do craide.

' Dít tánic ar n-indarbadh,
Gen co tic dit ar furthain ;
Do millis flaithes Ferguis,[3]
Tren a n-dernais, a Dubthaich.'   A Dubthaich.

---

[1] Elsewhere Munremar is described as son of *Gerrchend.* Cf. *Rc.* xxii. 196.
[2] Cf. *supra*, vol. i. pp. 214, 216.

Moda Minadhmadadh's body, and was greatly lamenting him, and spoke thus : 'Woeful is the deed which you have done, Dubthach,' said he, 'and evil was your deed in Emain, when you slew Fiacha son of Conchobar and Daire son of Fedelmid. And cruel were the other murders you have done, viz., the murder of Laidis and Lennabair, the two daughters of Eogan son of Durtacht, and Moirenn of the white neck, the wife of Fatneck son of Eirgiu, and Ethne of the fair head, wife of Errge Horse-mouth. And it is not (desire of) renown that caused you to do this deed.' And as he spoke thus he recited the lay :—

'O Dubthach, thou hast betrayed us,
  For long thou hast brought shame to us;
  Though thy deed this night is evil,
  So were thy doings in Emain.

'Fiacha the Fair, son of Conchobar,
  By thine hand he fell;
  The death of Daire son of Fedelmid,
  Though it was he, was not a deed to benefit.

'Moirenn white-neck thou hast slain,
  Wife of Fat-neck, without shame,
  Ethne fair-head thou hast wounded,
  Wife of Errge, a cruel quarrel.

'Laidis and Lennabair,
  'Tis thine hand that mangled them;
  The fair Edain from Berramain,
  Thou hast destroyed her also.

'Moda Minadhmad has fallen by thine hand,
  Meave's great artificer who committed no crime;
  Although thou doest savage deeds,
  It is not from the hardness of thine heart.

'Thou hast been the cause of our exile,
  Although thou canst not aid us now;
  Thou hast ruined the sway of Fergus,
  A wild deed thou hast done, O Dubthach.'

O *Dubthach.*

---

[3] *Ferguis* for *Fergusa* to suit the metre. In the modern language the name, like several others, has changed from the *u* to the *o* declension.

Robatar amlaid sin an oidhche sin. Agus ro eirgetar is in maidin ar ná marach co h-imsnimach egaintech. Agus atra*cht* Fergus fén co dobrónach, agus ro gab ac aithb*ir* imaithbh*ir*[1] co mór ar a maithib, agus atbert : 'Ni fhuigem inadh no onóir a Connachtaib d' eis an gnima-sa do rónamar.'

Rangatar na sgela sin co Cruachain. Do h-iachtadh agus do h-eigmed acu ac á cloistecht sin. Do eirigh Medb agus do tinoil a teglach. Agus ro greis na Mainedha co mór, agus do cuir techta ar cenn Ceit agus clainni Mágach, agus adubairt friu eirge agus an Dubloinges do lenmain co digháir agus a dígail forro an t-ain[2] echt do rónsat. Eirgis Oilill agus gabais ag á fasdód, agus is ed adubairt : 'Ní dingentar an comarli sin itir agamsa,' bar Oilill. 'Ní muirbfidter ar n-deoraid 'n a n-ain[2] echtaib ; agus ni thuitfid ar comaigthig 'n a cintaib ; agus ní mo ath-chuirfimid tigerna foghla agus e*cht*ráinn Eorpa ré aimsir in ar n-agaid.' Do sguir*edh* do lean-main Fergusa acu íar sin.

---

[1] *aithbir*, occasionally written *aithfir*, 'reproach.' The phrase *ac aithbir imaithbir* was not uncommon, the meaning being strengthened, 'greatly reproaching.'

[2] This idiomatic use of *aon* is not unknown in S.G. *B' esan an t-aon duine* means not that he was the only man, but that he was the one beyond all others. Cf. *Rinn iad aon duine de Chumhal,* 'They made one man of Cumhal, *i.e.* they made him king' (Dr. Henderson's edition of *Fled Bricrend*, p. 148). Cf. also MS. v. 10*a*, Advocates' Library, Edinburgh, where in a hymn attributed in the Brussels copy to St Columba, Holy Scripture is spoken of as *aen na leabar*, 'the one, (*i.e.* the best) of the books.'

Thus was that night passed. They rose on the morrow anxiously and sorrowfully. Fergus moved about mournfully; and, severely reproaching his chiefs, said : 'we shall no longer have place or power in Connaught after this deed which we have done.'

These tidings reached Cruachan, and the people yelled and roared when they heard them. Meave rose and gathered her household together. She greatly pressed the Maines, and sent messengers for Cet and the sons of Magach, urging them to pursue the Dubloinges closely and avenge the terrible murder which they committed. But Oilill was restraining her, and said : 'I shall have no part in these proceedings,' said Oilill. 'Our dependants shall not be put to death for their violent deeds ; nor shall our allies fall for their crimes ; and neither shall we make an enemy for a season of the greatest riever and raider in Europe.' The pursuit of Fergus thereupon ceased.

(To be continued.)

NOTE

The Battle of Plorait

In the very interesting collection of Gaelic songs published by D. Macpherson (Dòmhnull MacMhuirich) under the title of 'An Duanaire,' there is an elegy on the famous Captain Macpherson, whose accidental death in the forest of Gaick in the year 1800 gave rise to some strange tales. In this lament the following lines occur :—

'Caiptein thu air sliochd Ghilliosa,
'Choisinn am blàr a bha 'm Plorait,
A leag an trup Gallda gu h' ìseal.'

The name *Plorait* has probably been unfamiliar to most readers of the poem, and remained a mystery to me until I happened to discover, while reading some specimens of Westmoreland dialect, that *Peerith* is the local pronunciation of *Penrith*. This makes the matter quite clear : the poet's reference is to the skirmish fought at that place in December 1745 (during the retreat of Prince Charles's army from England), in which the Macphersons played a leading part. The local pronunciation of the name was evidently picked up by the Highlanders at the time, and retained in tradition as late as 1800.   W. A. CRAIGIE.

O, 'S TU 'S GURA TU TH' AIR M' AIRE

Malcolm Macfarlane

At last year's Mod, I was introduced to a gentleman, John
Reilly by name, who was anxious to interest some Gaelic
person in a tune which he had noted down in Eriskay, one of
the islands of the Outer Hebrides, during a term which he
had spent there as teacher. Mr. Reilly told me that he was
much impressed by the melody when first he heard it, and
was at pains to make the best record of it in his power,
selecting from the variants of several singers what appeared
to him to be the best rendering, and writing the music in the
style in which it was sung by the old people. Having no
Gaelic he was unable to give me the words. In the course
of time, Father Allan MacDonald of Eriskay kindly sent on,
at Mr. Reilly's request, the following stanzas. One of the
verses does duty in the well-known popular song 'Faill
ill ó agus hóro éile.' I have fitted the words to the notes
according to what I conceive to be the proper way. But,
never having heard the words sung, I cannot be positive as
to its being the customary way.

Gleus B♭

| m₁,s₁,d:m,s,m | f.m:r,s,d | s₁:- | m₁,d₁:: :- | m₁,s₁,d:m,s,m | f.m:r,s,m | d:- | -,m,s:l₁-,s |

O, 's tu 's gura tu th' air m' air...e; O, 's tu 's gura tu th' air m' air..e; 'S tu féin, a

| s:-,m | f.m:r,s,d | s₁:- | m₁ :d₁ | m₁,s₁,d :m,s,m | f.r :m.d | l₁:- | s₁:- ||

rùin, tha tighinn dlùth fain-ear dhomh; Gu'n d'fhalbh mo shùgradh o'n dh'fhàg thu'm bail - e.

Feasgar foghair air an achadh bhuana,
Saoil sibh féin nach mi fbéin bha truagh
dheth :
H-uile té 's a fear fhéin ri gualainn,
'S mo leannan falaich, gur fada bhuams' e.

Innsidh mis' mar tha gaol nan gillean :
Tha e tòiseachadh anns a' chridhe,
Cheart cho beag ris a ghràinnean chruith-
neachd,
'S e fàs cho mòr 's nach eil seòl air thil-
leadh.

Innsidh mise mar tha gaol nan gruagach :
Far an cuir iad an snaim, cha 'n fhuasgail ;
Bheir e 'n fheòil leis bhàrr nan gruaidhean
Mar shneachdadh bàn bhios air bhàrr nam
bruachan.

A phiuthar chridhe, nach cum thu chòir
rium ?
Na leig le griasaiche dubh nam bròg mi ;
No gu tàillear a dh' fhuaigheas clòimhn-
tean ;
Ach balach riomhach a dhìreas ròpa.

SEA-STORIES OF IAR-CONNACHT

Úna ni Ógáin

It is early morning, some miles out from the Connemara coast, and we are sailing with a light breeze among the outer islands and long, dark reefs, the weed turning golden under a low July sun, which is just high enough to touch the great Cruacha inland with rose-colour, and give the clear shallows above the rocks and shell-sand those dark purples and shining greens which are the glory of these western seas.

There are four of us in the pookawn (or open fishing-boat), sharing the delight of the music of the sea against her bows, and the colour and radiance of the morning. My friends, honest, kindly, brave, are familiar with every foot of the wild and intricate though lovely coast which lies near Ceann Léime; they know their wide island-strewn bay 'like their own house-floor,' as they say. Not a change of the precious weed-growth, not a stray piece of flotsam, escapes their trained observation. They know the wild lives out here well, too, and can tell the larger seals, who lie here undisturbed, one from another. And herein lies at least part of the interest of the following stories, told me 'in friendship,' for they do not readily speak of these things.

We are talking, part Irish, part English. 'You must see strange things at times, by day and night,' I said. ''Tis true for you,' says Martin. 'Only yesterday we were far out, and came among a pack of big fish, the "wild fish" of the great sea. They are not good for a small boat, and they hunting.[1] And there are strange things by night. But the queerest *we* saw was in the day. Pat and I were out in this boat one morning bringing in weed, and all of a sudden a very big man rose out of the sea quite near us, about thirty

[1] The larger porpoise are said by the fishermen on the West Coast to hunt in packs after the 'bradán-stáirne,' or sturgeon, 'like hounds after a fox,' some on the surface, some deeper down; and the sturgeon often takes refuge close alongside or under a sailing-boat.

yards from the boat, and stood up in the sea from his waist up. When he first came up his arms were spread out from him, very long arms, like an oar; and big, long hands, and fingers on him near a foot long, and his height from his waist up about my own height [5 ft. 9 ins. or so]. He stayed looking at us about a minute, and then he brought the hands up above his head, and then down flat on the water before him, and he hit a shower of sea-spray up that near covered him, and it went as high as our mast. He went down into the water then again, under the cover of the spray. He had no dress on him, but his skin was very black-looking and shining. He had not the eyes or skin of a dead man; he was not dead, but had the face of a man in full strength. Both I and Pat saw him plain, in full day. We were too surprised to speak to him. A sea-man he must have been.[1]

'I knew a man well too, a near neighbour (God be with him, he's dead now), he went out fishing with the lines one Saturday night. 'Tis not held good to go out that time. The men here stay in Saturday night, go to mass on Sunday morning, and out Sunday night. Well, this man was a great sailor, and a strong man, and he went out a long way, by himself. He got a good take of bream and cod; and just as the day was breaking, he saw a man's head come up from the sea at the bow of the boat. And the strange man took hold of the ropes, and came in over the bow of the boat, and he walked up along her to the second thwart. And he stooped and took up a good cod by the gills, and he spoke no word, and did no harm, but went out quiet and easy over the side of the boat, with the fish in his hand, and down into the sea again. The boatman was left speechless for a good while, and when he came in, he said no matter what length he lived he would never go out of a Saturday night again.

'There do be mermaids (*maighdini mara*) many a time out on the rocks here, in the deep sea. And there is one point

---

[1] Corroborated in every point by Pat, his brother.

of rock, within in the bay, where one does be seen at times, before a storm. She was there two years ago. But there are two of the neighbours (and yourself knows them both well), Pàt and Shawn, saw one very close. They were out towards Ceann Léime, lifting the lobster pots; and all of a sudden, about two o'clock of the day, they saw a woman out before them in the deep, quite near the boat. Very fair she was, and reddy-gold hair on her head, and down over her. She saw them before they saw her, and was watching them. When Pat saw her he was so frightened the oar dropped from his hands. He stooped for it, and he and Shawn looked at each other, and when they looked her way again she was gone. They both saw her quite plain.'

Then follows an interesting discussion between the elders and the young man as to the form of the *maighdini mara*. The elders are sure the sea-maids and sea-men are shaped just like those of earth. The young man had 'seen a picture of them one time in a book, and they were shaped like a salmon from the waist down, and wouldn't those that could make the book and draw the picture be right?' But the older men are certain that the western sea-maids and sea-people are made just 'like Christians,' only finer—and I, having heard older tales, from other neighbours, know they must be right. Is not their speech full of the quiet assurance of eye-witness? And who, listening to the mysterious talk of such fisher-friends, and surrounded by the sea-lights and wave music, can venture to set limit to the magic of the Fairge Mhór?

'THE RUIN OF BRITANNIA'

A CONTRIBUTION TOWARDS A RESTATEMENT OF EARLY
SAXO-WELSH HISTORY

A. W. WADE-EVANS

[This paper attempts to show that the supposed homogeneous work attributed to Gildas before 547 really comprises two distinct books; the first called 'Excidium Britanniæ,' which includes chapters 1 to 26, and which was composed about 700; the second, from chapter 27 to the end, being the genuine 'Epistola Gildæ' written by Gildas before 502.]

(Continued from page 58.)

PART III. *Date of Composition.*

7. The alliance which Vortigern, from beyond the Wye in modern Radnorshire, made with the Saxons, exposed Romania to the marauding expeditions of the latter. In order to check these, the *Excidium* tells us that the Britanni after suffering considerably, made a rally under the Roman Ambrosius and won a signal victory. Our author continues as follows :—

'From that time [*i.e.* Ambrosius' victory] our fellow citizens were sometimes victorious, sometimes the enemy, in order that the Lord according to His wont might try in this nation, the Israel of to-day whether it loves Him or not. This continued up to the year of the siege of *Badon Hill*, and of almost the last great slaughter inflicted upon the rascally crew. *And this commences as I know the 44th year with one month now elapsed; it is also the year of my birth.* But not even at the present day are the cities of our patria inhabited as formerly; deserted and dismantled, they lie neglected until now, because although foreign wars have ceased, civil wars continue. The recollection of so hopeless a ruin of the island *and of the unlooked-for help* (insperatum auxilium) has been fixed in the memory of those who have survived as witnesses of both marvels. Owing to this (unlooked for help), kings, magistrates, private persons, priests, ecclesiastics, severally preserved their own rank. *As they died away when an age had succeeded ignorant of that storm and having experience only of the present quiet,* all the controlling influences of truth, etc. were overturned.'

BRITAN
IN
BRIT
A.D.428-
by
A.W. Wade-

Dun of the Frisians

Wall of Hadrian

CYMRIC
PICTS

FRISIAN SEA

Loidis

Elmet

SCOTTI
SCOTTI
TWRCELYN
Llangadog

R. Dee

CYMRIC PICTS

A N G L

SCOTTI

R. Teify

SCOTTI

DEMETIA

Vortipore's
Tomb   Allt Cunedda

SCOTTI

Vortigern

Brychan

R. Avon

M A N I A

Gloucester

St Albans
Glywys

CAERLLEON

Cirencester

Deorham
577

SEVERN SEA

R. Avon   Bath

R C

JUTES

SAXO

DAMNONIA

Porchester

R. Avon

Now it has been long supposed that this battle of Badon Hill refers to the twelfth great victory of Arthur in October 470. *Arthur, however, never fought a battle at Badon Hill.* In the genuine list of Arthur's victories, Badon Hill is an interpolation from this very document. At least five MSS. of the Arthurian Tractate give thirteen battles, four MSS. omit one of the names in order to make up the twelve, whilst others jumble up two names for the same purpose. Why is this? Because Badon Hill *had* to be inserted owing to the supposed evidence of the *Excidium*. The following is the genuine list:—

I. Estuary of River Glein.	VII. Forest of Celidon.
II. River Dubglas.	VIII. Castellum Guinnion.
III. River Dubglas.	IX. Caerlleon.
IV. River Dubglas.	X. Traeth or Traetheu Roit.
V. River Dubglas.	XI. Bregomion.
VI. River Bassas.	XII. Mons Agned.

The Mons Badonicus of the *Excidium* was confused with the Mons Agned which is the genuine victory of October 470, and as this was also the year of St. Gildas's birth, the following words were inserted—'And this commences, as I know, the 44th year with one month now elapsed; it is also the year of my birth.' Annus XLIV in era of Invitation is $428 + 43 = 471$, which agrees with the *Annales* and Geoffrey's number 470 as I have shown above.

Moreover, Badon Hill is described lower down as an *auxilium insperatum*, an unlooked-for help. A victory of Arthur, a chosen dux bellorum of Britannic princes could not possibly be called an unexpected help. When the military forces of Britannia combined under this chosen general who had already won eleven victories, there was nothing of the nature of unexpectedness or of help in his victory at Mons Agned in 470.

Now there is only one Bellum Badonis known in Welsh history, and it is to this the *Excidium* refers. It is placed opposite Annus CCXX[X]I in the *Annales* MS. A. as 'Bellum

Badonis secundo.' The last word, of course, is inserted under the influence of the misunderstanding of the *Excidium*. It is the battle known to the English as *Bedan-* or *Biedan-heafod*, won in the year 675 by Wulfhere, King of Mercia, over Wessex. It was a victory which kept Wessex in a state of chaos for years, during which time the Britanni between Severn and Poole Harbour obtained respite from Saxon aggression. It will now be seen how a Britannus of this quarter could call Badon Hill 'an unexpected help.'[1]

8. We have still to allow for an age to succeed ignorant of the storm which culminated at Badon Hill. If the reader will look carefully through the *Excidium* he will notice that the author is continually carping against the Britanni in a manner and on grounds quite foreign to the *Epistola Gildæ*. In chapter I he says he will not attack the brave soldiers, for his words are directed against the 'dangers caused by indolent men,' that is the hierarchy. He proceeds as follows :—

'I saw that in our time even, as Jeremiah wept, "The widowed city sat solitary, heretofore filled with people, ruler of the Gentiles, princes of provinces, and had become tributary." *By this is meant the Church.* "The gold hath become dim, its best colour changed," *which means the excellency of God's word.* "The sons of Zion," *that is of the holy mother the Church,* "famous and clothed with best gold have embraced ordure." . . . To this age of ours has been added besides those impious and monstrous sins which it commits in common with all the iniquitous ones of the world, *that thing which is as if inborn with it, an irremovable and inextricable weight of unwisdom and fickleness.* . . . In my zeal therefore for the holy law of the Lord's house, constrained by the reasons of my own meditation or overcome by the pious entreaties of brethren, I am now paying the debt exacted long ago. The work is in fact poor but I believe faithful and friendly to all noble soldiers of Christ; *but severe and hard to bear to foolish* APOSTATES.'

---

[1] It may be well to remind the reader at this point that the only foes of the Roman province mentioned in the *Excidium* are Picts from beyond the Wall, Scots from Ireland, and Saxons from the Saxon shore between Essex and Wight. The Angles and Frisians are not referred to. Such of these as lived south of the Wall would be Britanni to a Roman. The absence of any special reference to them by our author, seems to indicate that in the traditions which he follows, they are regarded as friendly.

He explains the ready entrance of heresies into Britain on the ground that it was *a country always wishful to hear something new and at all events desiring nothing steadfastly* (ch. 12). He explains the 'Ruin of Britannia' as being due to certain vices and

'Especially the vice which to-day also overthrows the place which pertains to all good in the island, *i.e.* hatred of truth together with those who defend it, love of falsehood together with its fabricators, undertaking evil for good, respect for wickedness rather than kindness, desire of darkness in preference to the sun, the welcoming of Satan as an angel of light.'

No one can doubt but that these passages refer to something special, some falling away towards novelties on the part of the Church. There are *apostates* whom the Britanni are inclined to follow. The reference of course is to what Bede describes thus (v. 18) :—

'Aldhelm, when he was only a priest and abbot of the monastery of Malmesbury, by order of a synod of his own nation, wrote a notable book against the error of the Britons in not celebrating Easter at the proper time, and in doing several other things not consonant to the purity and the peace of the Church; and by the reading of this book *he persuaded many of them who were subject to the West Saxons to adopt the Catholic celebration of our Lord's resurrection.*'

In other words, the Britanni between Severn and Poole Harbour were the first to surrender the Celtic Easter for that of the Latin Church. This they did whilst Aldhelm was Abbot of Malmesbury in their borders, that is to say, between 675 and 705. Now inasmuch as Bede had the *Excidium* in his hands by the year 725, it must have been compiled between some date after 675, not far from 705, when the author could reasonably speak of an age new to that which finished with 675, and on the other hand the year when Bede is known to have had the book, viz. 725.

9. Our author was writing during a period of peace from external foes, and although reference is made to civil strife he yet speaks of his age as *præsens serenitas* or the present quiet. Now Bede says (iv. 12) :—

'When Koenwalh [King of Wessex] died [in 672] his under rulers

took upon them the kingdom of the people and dividing it among themselves held it ten years . . . Ceadwalla having subdued and removed
these rulers, took upon him the government. When he had reigned two
years . . . he quitted his sovereignty for the love of the heavenly
kingdom and, going to Rome, ended his days there.'

The Saxon Chronicle states :—

'685. This year Ceadwalla began to contend for the kingdom.

688. This year Ine succeeded to the kingdom of the West Saxons
and held it 37 years; and he built the minster at Glastonbury . . .
and the same year Ceadwalla went to Rome.'

The aggression of Mercia, and perhaps the restlessness of the
Britanni had thrown Wessex into confusion. Out of this
tumult rose Ceadwalla and Ine of the royal race of Wessex,
and perhaps of Britannic blood as well. At least they were
both regarded as Britannic in those Britannic traditions upon
which Geoffrey of Monmouth founded his famous book. A
period of interblending seems now to have taken place
between the Saxons and subject Britanni, and Celtic Christianity is seen to be giving way to the Latin form of Wessex.
This appears to me to be the age of the *præsens serenitas* of
the *Excidium*.

10. When Bede received the *Excidium*, the famous interpolation dating Badon as Annus XLIV etc., had already been
inserted, and the little book could not but have undergone
slight modifications when transcribed by an 'intelligent'
editor labouring under this delusion. Bede gives no indication that he knows the *Epistola Gildæ*, so that we are justified
in assuming that when he received the *Excidium* it had not
as yet been prefixed to the former. One of the modifications
which it underwent before Bede received a copy, was in
reference to the site of St. Alban's martyrdom. In recounting supposed Diocletian martyrdoms in Britannia he mentions
'St. Alban of Verulam, Aaron and Iulius, citizens of Caerlleon, and
the rest of both sexes in different places who stood firm with lofty
nobleness of mind in Christ's battle' (ch. 10).

This sentence, with what follows, places us at once in S.E.
Wales among the *martyria* or *merthyrs*, as they are now
called, which commemorate individuals of both sexes. St.

Alban of course ought to be amongst them, that is, in Britannia, so that 'Alban of Verulam' must be a mistake.[1] Now
notice that the martyr is made to cross the river Thames to the
site of his sufferings, which river is impossible, as it is much
too far away from the city of St. Albans. Bede, although he
insists on Verulam, yet carefully avoids mentioning the name
of the river. Bede also follows an independent authority in
recounting this martyrdom, and it is significant that the
crucial passage which locates the site in relation to the river,
is corrupt (*i.e.* tampered with) in all the MSS. He tells us
enough, however, to show us that Alban suffered on the side
of the river opposite to the city, some distance from the city,
and on a hill 500 paces from the [river]. This proves that
the river referred to is the Usk in Monmouthshire, and the
city is Caerlleon itself; for two miles away from the city on
the opposite side of the river, and five hundred paces from
it, is Mount St. Albans with the ruins of Alban's shrine
thereon. This point is of vital importance, because it is one
of the localities which we are certain St. Germanus visited
when he came to Britannia in the fifth century. The shrines
of Aaron and Julius are also in the immediate neighbourhood.

PART IV. *Sources.*

11. Our author refers to his authorities in these terms :—

'Not so much by the aid of native writings or records of authors,
inasmuch as these (if they ever existed) have been burnt by the fires of
enemies or carried far away in the ships which exiled my countrymen
and so are not at hand, but shall follow the account of foreign writers
which because broken by many gaps is far from clear.'

He distinctly refers to Rufinus's *Ecclesiastical History.*
He is also acquainted with some of Jerome's writings, and
perhaps Salvian and Orosius. He also quotes Virgil (which
St. Gildas does not do, and would not do, if one may judge

---

[1] I would suggest that *verolamiensem* was an Anglian or Saxon guess or misreading for some form of the Welsh name Caerlleon written in the margin or between
the lines. The scribe who added the name of the Thames could not possibly have
known the neighbourhood of our modern St. Albans near London.

from his words in chapter 66 of the *Epistola*). Notice, however, that the above words do not exclude native writings,
and distinctly suggest that he had at least thought of
possible Britannic traditions in Armorica. If among the
insular writings before him there are also those of Armorican
origin, he is clearly unable to distinguish between them.
There was frequent communication from the fifth century
between the Britannia of Britain and that of France. Saints
moved to and fro between them, and St. Gildas himself died
in Brittany in 554. In this very year Procopius was writing
of the three great nations of Roman Britain, viz. Frisians,
Angles and 'Brettones' who were annually migrating to Gaul
in vast numbers. The earliest settlements of 'Brettones'
seem to have taken place in the days of Maximus, and since
that time a stream of them had flowed apparently from
Cornwall, 'Devon,' and Monmouth. The Armorican peninsula,
from its western point, gradually became a new Britannia,
with Romania to the east and even in its midst; in short,
a land of 'Brettones' and Romani, like what Britannia from
Usk to Dorset Avon must largely have been. If, therefore,
amongst the *insular* Roman Britannic traditions which our
author had before him, there were also Roman-Britannic
traditions *of Armorica*, he would possibly have had some
difficulty in differentiating between them. Our author's
sympathies are constantly with 'Roman' as against 'anti-
Roman' opinion. He says:—

'Only those evils will I attempt to make public which Britannia
has both suffered and inflicted upon other and distant citizens in the
times of the Roman Emperors.'

Any attempt on the part of the Britanni to act independently of the Romani, is an evil in his sight which merited an
excidium Britanniæ. He even sympathises with the Romani
in the opprobrious epithets they hurl against the Britanni—
'crafty foxes,' 'cowards' and the like. It is hard to explain
so intense a Roman partisanship on the part of so late a
writer who tells us distinctly that the last of the Romans in
Britannia was Ambrosius, who was a contemporary of Vortigern in 428. We are driven to conclude that he is incor-

porating sentences and affecting attitudes from 'Roman' traditions, and especially from that Britannia across the Channel where Romania was so much more significant than it was in Britain. We are confirmed in this opinion by several little points, particularly the following.

12. Far and away the most celebrated passage in the *Excidium* is that which gives part of the letter to Aetius in 446, called the 'Groans of the Britons.' The following is the whole of it :—

'The miserable remnant therefore sent a letter to Agitius, a man holding high office at Rome ; they speak as follows :—*To Agitius in his third consulship, come the groans of the Britanni;* a little further in their request: *the barbarians drive us to the sea, the sea drives us upon the barbarians ; by one or other of these two modes of death we are either killed or drowned ;* and for these they have no aid.'

This is all, so that if we lifted the passage from the context it would cause no break in the reading. The extremely fragmentary and isolated character of so important a document and event, immediately suggests that our author is not very sure of the material he has before him. The letter is undoubtedly genuine, and is undoubtedly inserted here because of the supposed chronological coincidence. For mark that the barbarians referred to are not Saxons but Picts and Scots. The Saxons are to appear at the false date, 450 A.D., and Aetius was third time consul in 446. The letter is therefore inserted as leading up to the climax of his sermon. .

Now it so happens that shortly before the year 446, the cities of Armorica had revolted, and the Patrician Aetius (who had had to deal severely with them previously) had sent against them an army of barbarians under Eocarich the Alan king. The Armoricans in terror appealed to St. Germanus of Auxerre *who had just returned from his second visit to Britain in* 445. The saint succeeded in persuading Eocarich to desist from devastating Armorica and to give a most faithful promise of peace on condition that the pardon which Eocarich had bestowed should be sought by Germanus from the Emperor *and from Aetius.*[1] The saint in con-

---

[1] See Constantius' *Life of St. Germanus* (Bk. II. ch. i. § 62).

sequence went to Ravenna to intercede for the peace of
Armorica, carrying the celebrated 'Groans of the Britons'
with him.　Our author had this document before him which
he ignorantly applied to the Britanni of the island, who, as all
the evidence shows, were well able to take care of themselves.

Three things in conclusion:—

(a) I most earnestly commend to my countrymen, the
Britanni of to-day, the study of the *Excidium,* for it is the
one great impediment which has hitherto prevented the
history of Wales (and of England too) from being based on
a sound scientific foundation.　When the origin and nature
of the *Excidium* are understood, Wales, in her beginnings in
the fifth century, will be seen in proper perspective.

(b) This paper would not be (at least in its present form),
were it not for the minute researches and great conquests of
my friend Mr. Alfred Anscombe in the field of chronology,
and especially of early British and Irish chronology.　Ten
years ago Mr. Anscombe, owing to his solution of the
difficulties connected with the dates 428, 449, 450, etc.,
had come to the main conclusion which I have here
attempted in my own way to elucidate, viz., that the
Excidium is a non-Gildasian work of the seventh century.
His letters will be found in the *Academy* (Sept., etc., 1895),
and masterly articles from his pen will also be found in
various numbers of the Celtic *Zeitschrift* and *Archiv,* the
Athenæum, the *English Historical Review,* and in two Chronological Tracts published some years ago.　All the chronological
arguments in the first part of this paper are based on his
researches, although of course he must not be held responsible
for the way in which I state them, or for any deductions of
my own.

(c) With reference to the so-called Teutonic school of
English historians, headed by Stubbs, Freeman, Guest, and
Green, followed by scores of imitators, it must not be forgotten that these leaders were intense English nationalists
whose predispositions very naturally led them to perceive

only those facts or supposed facts and incidents which served to exalt their own nationality. When evidence was wanting (as in the case of the origin of the Angles), they sought to build up theories based on no scientific grounds, but only on what they felt as patriotic Englishmen *must* have taken place. The most conspicuous example of this is the well-known book called *The Making of England* by John Richard Green. This writer could be called not inaptly the nineteenth century Geoffrey of Monmouth, were it not that Geoffrey built up his romance on genuine traditions, whereas Green erected his on his own patriotic intuitions. In saying this, however, I am anxious not to be regarded as reflecting on these well-known writers for being such ardent nationalists (I am a nationalist myself), for it is good that he who writes on a subject should be in love with it; indeed, it is the lover who always understands best the object of his heart's affections. Moreover, I am deeply and patriotically grateful to the Teutonic school for having laid so much emphasis on the acknowledged fact that Englishmen are not Welshmen; for, in perpetually insisting on that, they also insisted on what is to me equally as satisfactory, viz., that Welshmen are not Englishmen.

THE FIONN SAGA

(Continued from p. 19.)

GEORGE HENDERSON, M.A., B.Litt., PH.D.

THE CAMPBELL OF ISLAY RECENSION (*continued*)

Fionn's Youth—First Exploit[1]

To put the tale on the short cut, my dear Company, as an old man said when telling this in Uist, Gumag was seven years in that hut by the black peat pool in the forest, and every day she went to the palace in the big town to seek

[1] [An old version of Boyish Exploits of Fionn is translated by Dr. Meyer in *Ériu* vol. i. 1904.]

food and clothes and all that she needed. All knew her, and none knew her secret but the king's daughter. All that she asked or wished was given her and done, and the child grew strong and stout.

On a day of these days she went on an errand when the child was three-quarters of a year old. There was a great greyhound bitch (*saighead mialchoin*) in the palace, and she had followed Gumag to the hut. She was afraid that this great hound would harm the child. She used to give the child a bit of food, and stuff a faggot of birch into the door-way when she went to the town. She never ate her break-fast till she went to the palace. On one of these days the greyhound got out the birch faggot and took the food out of the child's hands. But when the child could not get the food he took the hound by the snout and tore her in two down the back. When the *muime* came back the hound was dead, and that was a grand tale for the lad's mother.

' How does the child get on ? ' she said.

' None would believe the tale that I have to tell,' said the *muime*, but thus it happened, and then she told how Fionn, who was but three-quarters of a year old, had slain the hound.[1]

Now the child never saw any one but his foster mother, Gumag, and she taught him all that she knew. She taught him to swim. She used to put one hand under his chin and the other at the back of his head and duck him in the black moss pool, and make him dive to the other end under water.

She taught him sword play with sticks and branches from the forest. He never saw any one but her. He learned what others learn from his *muime*.

He was so swift that he caught the birds on the trees while she was gone to the town.

Fionn's First Race

Now the people began to talk about the nurse. Those

[1] I suspect that more belongs to this. The hound ought to be mythological like the snakes of Hercules. Meantime I have it thus. Oct. 1871.

that did not see her about the palace to-day might chance to see her to-morrow or next night, and so the talk began.

At seven years old the lad had grown great and strong, and the king's daughter began to ask if he were like his father.

'Like him?' said the nurse; 'that he is. He is not a whit below his father in size and strength and swiftness and beauty and seeming.'

'Could he keep his life from the Irish if I were to see him here?' said she.

'None could catch him,' said the nurse, 'in the five-fifths of Eirinn. Though all in the realm should come he could keep his life.'

'Bring him here,' said the king's daughter, 'and let me see my son.'

Some say that he was seven, some twelve years old at this time. All agree that he was a child.

So the nurse went home to fetch the son of Cumal.

'Can you run fast?' said the *muime*.

'I can,' said the lad.

'Come,' said she, 'run off to that hill-top and let me see how many blows I can give you with this birch besom before you get there.' She struck him a blow and out he went and off to the hill, and never another blow could she get at his back till he reached the top of the hill.

'Now,' said she, 'take the birch besom and see how many blows you can lay on my back before I get to the hut again.'

Off she set as fast as she could run, and he followed and laid on all the way till her back was sore and the besom worn.

'You can run,' said she.

'Would you like to go to the town and see the lads play at shinny?'

But he did not know what that was, for he had never seen a human being but Gumag his nurse.[1]

---

[1] This incident occurs in many stories as part of the training of a soldier. It needs to be placed amongst the others, and meantime it seems to fit here, where it was placed by MacNeill in Barra.

. To the hut the nurse brought her son whose name was Domhnull.[1]

On a day when she was at the town seeking food, the lads were hungry, and they saw three deer coming towards the hut.

'What creatures are these?' said the son of Cumal.

' 'Creatures on which are food and clothing,' said the other.

'If we were better for that, I could catch them,' said the son of Cumal.

He ran after them and caught them, and they were ready for the nurse when she came back from the town. She flayed them, and they ate the venison, and she made him a dress of the deer's hides.

Fionn's First Ride[2]

When the deer were eaten she went again to the town. When she was gone there came a great wild horse that belonged to the king.

'What creature is that?' said Mac Cumal.

'A creature on which pastime is taken. Men ride upon him,' said the lad.

'If we were the better for him, I would catch him.'

'You ill-conditioned ragged lout, you catch that creature!' said the other; 'it would beat the best man in the realm to catch him.'

He could not stand this chatter, so he struck Domhnull a box on the ear and brained him.

'Be there, you two score and ten over (beyond) the worst,' said he.

---

[1] This is to be extended from the versions in London, and if possible from the version known to a tinker near Oban, by name MacArthur, whom I have been hunting for several years without success. I think that this slain son ought to be the son of the Irish king, or of the Norwegian, or of some foe to the Fenians, but this bit needs clearing up. Cf. *West Highland Tales*, iii. 147, where it occurs as incident in prologue to 'Lay of the Great Fool.'

[2] [Cf. *West Highland Tales*, iii. 178, where Gaelic is given, as an incident in prologue to 'Lay of the Great Fool.']

He stuck an oaken skewer through his ear and hung him behind the door of the hut. Then he stretched his legs after the horse, and the tattering hides of the deer fluttered and streamed behind him. He caught the horse and mounted him, and the horse that never had suffered to see a man betook himself to the stable for fear.

Fionn's shinny

Now when he got near the big town, he had never seen men, and he saw a lot of scholars, great college lads and the king's son, and the king's son coming out of school to play. So he went to play with them. When the game began, the lads were divided into even hands, and the ball was let out. The lad in the deer's hides got the ball and he struck it a blow with his palm, and a kick with his foot, and a stroke of his club, and drove it home.

'Let us divide again,' said the king's son, 'for the game is not even.'

'I would rather have this one than the lot of you,' said one of the leaders. He got his choice, and the king's son got all the rest on his side. The ball was let out. But the lad in the deer's hides got hold of it again and struck it a blow with (bit of) his palm, and a kick with (of) his foot, and a stroke with his club, and none could catch him, so that end was won.

He was put on one side, and all the college lads and the king's son at their head went against him, and the ball was thrown out the third time. But the lad of the hides got the ball as before and drove it home, and won the third time, and they were furious. They would play no more, but they would bathe.

Fionn Slays the King's Son

His nurse had never called him anything but *an t-amadan mor*, the great fool, and '*creid orm*,' i.e. 'believe in me,' was what she used to say to him, and he used to repeat.

When the king's son had lost three games he was furious, and came swaggering up to the lad with the hides. 'And who are you?' said he, 'of the gentle or simple of Ireland, who hast that strange jargon?'

'I,' said he, 'am the great fool, the son of the warrior's wife, the foster son of my nurse, and the foster brother of Domhnull, the nurse's son, going to commit folly, and if need were I could make a fool of you.'

'You! you ragged wretch,' said the king's son, 'you make a fool of me?'

'Believe me,' said the great fool, and then he gave him a box on the ear and brained him. 'Be there,' said he, 'two score and ten over the worst, as is Domhnull the nurse's son, with the oaken skewer in his ear behind the door of the hut.'

So he killed the son of the king of Lochlann, whom he brought in the long ship when he came to Ireland, and sent for his daughter to slay Cumal.

Fionn's Baptism

The lads used to bathe in a great fresh-water loch that was beside the palace, and they had gone out to swim. When the great fool saw them he went out amongst them, and he thought of the plan that his nurse had of ducking him in the black peat pool. So he took the lads by the chin and the back of the head and ducked them to teach them how to dive. But those that he ducked he drowned, and those that he did not drown he brained upon the stones at the bottom of the lake.

'*Co leis an gille maol fionn*?' said his grandfather, the king of Lochlann, who was looking out of a window. 'Who is that bluff *Fair* lad with a king's eye in his head, who is drowning the schoolboys?'[1]

'Water is about him,' shouted the nurse. 'He has gotten his name from his grandfather, Fionn son of Cumal son of

---

[1] *Co am fear fada Fionn agus rosg righ na cheann?* according to another version; *co e am Fionn anain*(?) *duine?* according to another.

Trathal son of Treunmor son of Luthan son of Aodh son of Aidh son of Art son of the High King of Ireland.'[1]

Then the king came to the water side.

'And who are you?' said the king.

'Believe me,' said Fionn, 'I am the great fool, the son of the warrior's wife, the foster son of the nurse, and the foster brother of the nurse's son Donald, going about committing folly for myself, and if need were I could make a fool of you too.'

'Well, then,' said the king, 'it was not you that made me a fool but my counsellor on the day that I slew your father and did not kill your mother.'

'Seize him and slay him,' shouted the king. But none would wet his shoe.

Then troops were got, and armies and horses and men to catch him, but he came out of the water and ran for his life.

After that he never was called anything but Fionn mac Cumail.[2]

The Beast of Loch Lurgann

When he came out of the water all that could stand under arms about the place had gathered. When he ran off his nurse ran after him for fear of her life, and all that had gathered with the king at their head ran after them.

O mo ghràidh, 'Oh, my love!' shouted the nurse, 'will you leave me behind after all that I have done for you ever since you were born for all these years, will you leave me here with the following upon me?'

---

[1] This pedigree, made up from various incomplete versions of it, gives the mythical seventh generation after Art or Arthur, son of the High King of Ireland. That would make Art the king who began to improve the breed of warriors who were to conquer the Norsemen in the seventh generation.

[2] September 16, 1870 : Robertson, Tobermory (p. 139), told this story of the birth and youth of Fionn, his naming by a Bishop, his pedigree, his escape to Coille Ualtair, the wild wood : the death of the nurse and the growth of the monster of Loch Lurgann in Eirinn, his journey to Eas Ruadh, his meeting with the fisher, the fish myth, the roasting of the salmon, the death of *Achda Dubh*, and the wisdom tooth. With his wisdom he (Fionn) came to be over the Fiantan, and after that he was ever with them. The dragon myth was not in this.

The lad stopped and seized the nurse, and in his haste he took the first hold that came handy. He caught her by the two ankles and slung her on his shoulders, and off he set for the wilds with the following at his heels. He ran fast and into a big wood that was called *A choille Bhliadhnach*, 'the yearly wood,' where the Norsemen could not follow, and so he ran for seven miles and never stopped to think of' the nurse. But that wood was thick and thorny, and in his haste Fionn, the great fool with the deer's hides, knocked the nurse against the trees, and tore her through the brambles and thorns, so that she was torn to shreds and killed.

When he stopped to breathe he looked, and behold he had nothing in his hands but the two shanks—*an dà luirgeann*.

He had no time to wait for lamentations, so he threw the shanks into the loch. 'You are Loch na Lurgann,' said he, and that loch is called Loch Luirgeann to this day, and it is in Ireland.

They say that a monster or two monsters grew from the shanks of Gumag, and we have a common proverb amongst us—'What kindred had Fionn mac Cumail to the monster of Loch Lurgann?'

I don't know what that kindred was unless he was foster son. They say the monster cried out from the loch: 'I will hold battle against you on the day that you do not expect it,' *i.e. Cumaidh mise cath riut an latha nach saoil thu.*

Fionn in the Wilds

When the traitor was slain and Cumal avenged, Fionn took the sword and went on his way through the forest, and because he had the sword Bran followed him.

He went on through the woods, and as he went he was ordering men and drilling armies. He smote at the trees as if they were foes, though there was no man there. At every blow he smote off the top of a tree; at every thrust the sword was up to the hilt in a tree root (*barr agus bun*).

But he had none to help or fight him, he had need of food,

and he lacked shelter, and his dress of hides was tattered and
torn, and so he wandered in the forest with his sword and his
hound, and lived on wild creatures which he hunted and slew.
So he wandered on far and long till he came to a great glen
near the sea at the end of Eirinn, and there he was as it were
a herd on the hillside. There he fell to prayers and to wish-
ing and longing [for adventures].

The Giant Sailors

On a day of these days he saw a ship on the ocean (*hamh*,
from Norse *haf*) coming into the strand.[1]

When Fionn saw this ship, he fell to praying and longing
till she came to port. In her were three men whose like he
had never seen for size and seeming, and they had tarry
canvas jackets and trousers on as one old man informed me.

'God of grace,' said Fionn, 'this is terrible. My head
would hardly reach their knees. Shall I hide or shall I
flee?'

But so it was that he walked down the glen to meet them
with his sword and his hound and his tattered hides. They
fell to walking to meet him, and he stood upon a hillock to
make himself tall.

'What news, my little lad?' said the first of these big
seamen. 'Are you often here or hereabouts, and what do
you here?'

'I am the king's herd,' said Fionn.

'Do you often go to the town where men are?' said the
sea-giant.

'Sometimes,' said the herd.

'I should be much your debtor if you would tell me if you
have any news of Fionn mac Cumail?' said the sailor. 'I
have heard that the chase was upon him and that he fled to
this glen.'

'I have no news to give,' said the herd. 'Are you on the
track of Fionn the son of Cumal?'

[1] Runs *re* sailing, but not put in here.—J. F. C.

'We are,' said the sailor; 'we have come here in pursuit of him.'

'And whence came you ?' said the herd.

'*A rìgheachd nam fear mór*,' *i.e.* 'from the realm of giants,' said he.

'But why have you come, and what do you want with Fionn ?' said the herd.

'I will tell that when you tell me where Fionn is,' said the giant.

'I will tell that if you will let me give you a tap with this little sword,' said the herd.

'Done !' said the giant. 'I am not afraid of such a *bead-agan*, "impudent fellow," as you.'

'Well, but come behind this hill,' said the herd, 'for fear the others should mock us.'

They went, and when they were out of sight Fionn said, 'Here is Fionn mac Cumail.'

'Where ?' said the giant sailor, looking all round about him. 'Where is he ?'

'Here !' said the other. 'I am Fionn mac Cumail mhic Trathail mhic Treunmhoir mhic Luaithe mhic Aodh mhic Aidh mhic Art mhic Ardrigh Eirinn, and this is Bran, and here is Mac A Luinn, the sword of Cumal that never left shred after a stroke.'

'You ridiculous little imp, you *beadagan*,' said the giant, 'not you nor your like of a poor ragged wretch do I want, but Fionn.'

Then Fionn got angry and with one blow he smote off the giant's head as he smote off the tree-tops in the forest.

'Take that for mocking me,' said Fionn.

The second giant came round the hill to see what had kept his comrade.

'Where is my comrade ?' said he.

'I slew him because he mocked me,' said Fionn.

'You ridiculous little imp,' said the giant. 'Where is he ?'

Then Fionn's rage increased. He could hardly reach the

man's knees, so he hewed at his legs, and down he fell like one of the great trees in the forest. When he was down Fionn smote off the giant's head.

'Take that,' he said, 'for mocking me and for doubting my word.'

The third giant came after the rest, and he said: 'Well, little man, have you told your tale to my comrades? and where is Fionn?'

'I am Fionn,' said the other, 'and I have slain your comrades because they mocked me and doubted my word.'

The big sailor laughed, and Fionn grew wild with rage, and flew at the giant. The giant went at him to crush him.[1]

The Sea-Giants' Second Adventure

But the lad with the sword smote him about the waist and cut him in two. So Fionn killed the three big sailors who came in the big ship because they mocked him and would not tell their errand or believe him.

When the giants were slain, Fionn went to the strand and swam to the ship, and there he staid all alone, praying and longing as before. There he used to sleep. At the end of a while, after that, he saw another ship sailing into the port from the western ocean ('hav'), and if he had not seen the first crew he had never seen the likes of the crew of that long ship. They drew their ship into the port and anchored close to the first ship and waded on shore. If they were no bigger than the first crew, they were no less. Fionn was on shore, and he thought of fleeing or hiding. But so it was that he

---

[1] According to other reciters, each of these giants came alone in a big ship which he managed like a boat alone. Each in turn held parley with Fionn and laughed at him and lost his life. Fionn took the ships and slept in them, and owned all the riches and cargo. Their story was that the daughter of the king of An Domhain Mhoir (the great deep, or the wide world, or the whole universe, or the emperor of Rome according to some) had come to Eirinn with the chase after her, and whoever could turn the chase was to have her to wife, half the realm, and all when the king is dead. It was written in books and prophecies that none could turn that chase but Fionn with Bran and the sword. This I take to be a bit of another adventure misplaced. The rest follows and fits in with the story told here.

walked down to meet the giants as he did before. They met and saluted each other, and after a long talk one said—

'Have you ever seen or heard on sea or land anything of Fionn mac Cumail, or of those who came here to seek him?'

'They came here and Fionn slew them,' said the lad.

'Nay,' said the giant.

'I will swear on this sword if you like,' said the other.

'If that be so,' said the giant, 'we may as well be gone.'

'Why did you come?' said Fionn.

'I won't tell you that, you little creature,' said the giant.

'I told you the truth,' said the lad.

Fionn killed these three giants because they mocked him and would not believe him.

'Well, then,' said the giant, 'I will tell you the story.'

The Dragon Myth [1]

'There is a monster in a loch in the realm of great men, and there she has been these two hundred years and more, and every day a living person has to be put out to the monster to be eaten on the shore. It was in the prophecies that Fionn mac Cumail should come and slay the monster, and when the king of the realm of giants heard that Fionn had come he sent the three best warriors in his realm to seek him. If he has killed them we may as well go home. It is better to die there than here. Thrice has the law come round that the king was to send his own son out to the monster, thrice has he got the sons of poor men sent out instead, and now the law has come round so that next time the king's own son must be sent out to the monster unless he gets Fionn to fight and slay her. He is afraid for his son's sake, and he wants Fionn.'

'Will you take me for Fionn?' said the lad.

[1] That the association of Fionn with the Dragon Myth is of old date, 1250 to 1530, appears from a passage in the Dean of Lismore's book, p. 18 (original Gaelic), which may be thus translated :—

> ne'er left monster in loch
> nor venomous snakes
> in Erin of Saints
> the great hero slew them.

'I will take you at all events,' said the giant; and so he did. He put Fionn into one pocket and Bran into the other.

'If the other three had been as civil they might have been alive,' said Fionn; 'but they are dead.'

'The Lord be praised that I have got even you,' said the giant.

They sailed (and the man who told this story in Barra here said for the fifth time):—

[The Sailing Passage]

They hoisted the speckled flapping sails up against the tall rough wooden masts. The ropes that were loose they tied, and the ropes that were fast they loosed. They set a pilot on the prow, and a helm in the stern, the broad sea, the blue sea, the slasher, the waves were beating hither and thither about her planks. Their music was the blowing of whales and the snorting of sea-hogs, the biggest beast eating the least and the least doing as best he might; the bent whorled whelk that was at the bottom of the ocean played crack on her great gunwale and smack on her floor, and she would have split a slender grain of oats, so well did they steer her.

They had a gentle little breeze, such as they might choose, a breeze to uproot willows and tear heather from hills, that drove the ridges with the furrows, and so they were till they reached the realm of great men and the port and anchorage where they wished to be. Then they drew the ship to shore and dragged her seven times her own length upon green grass, where the schoolboys and blackguards of the great town could play her no tricks nor pranks.

When they got there they had a tale to tell, as I have after a while.

When they got to land the big sailors let Fionn and Bran loose on the shore, and all the people ran to see the little wonder. They were like to drown themselves and each other in the sea with their haste to catch them. But the king's daughter was there, and a woman caught him up in her skirt and gave him to the Princess for a pet. She put him in her bosom and nursed him and called him a baby.

She called him *Seudag*, 'little jewel,' but most people called him *An troich*, 'the dwarf,' but that affronted him. He slept with the king's daughter, and the king was rather ashamed that his daughter made so much of this little Troich that the sailors had brought. But Fionn put his finger under his wisdom-tooth and found out that they were people under glamour (*sgleo*), that they were not really bigger than other people, and that he could kill them all if he tried. So he lived as he was, content to be the little jewel of the king's daughter for about a year.

The king could not abide the sight of him, but Fionn did not mind, because he knew by his wisdom-tooth that he could beat the king and all his men, and he had the beast to slay.[1]

One of these nights the king's daughter began to weep and to wail, and Fionn awoke.

'What is wrong?' said the Troich.

'My third brother! alas! my third brother! I shall see him no more,' said she.

'Where is he going?' said the Troich.

Then the king's daughter fell to telling all that has been told here about the books and prophecies, and the beast in the loch, and the people that she had eaten, and the people who had gone to seek Fionn son of Cumal, and how they had brought her little pet the Troich, and how she said at last the turn has come round to my youngest brother, and he is to be put out on the loch to the monster, and I shall never see him more. 'Alas! alas!' and then she fell to crying and beating her palms.

Fionn was silent a while and still.

'What would you give to a man who would save your brother?' said he. 'Send me in his stead,' said the dwarf.

'That will not help,' said she. 'That will not be of any use. And I like you better than my brother,' said the king's daughter.

---

[1] In this it is easy to trace Thor [as] in the Edda and Gulliver's Adventures in Brobdignag, which were suggested to the author [of *Gulliver's Travels*] by an Irish popular tale, as it is said.—J. F. C.

'I will go to the beast,' said Fionn, 'nevertheless.'

Then she cried worse than ever. Early in the morning Fionn went out and put his finger under his wisdom-tooth, and because of his gift (*a thaobh 'fhios*) he found out all that ought to be done. If he got first to the beast he would kill her; if Bran got first she would kill both; that he found out.

So he made a plan and went to the king.

'What does that Troich want here?' said the king.

'I want to go to fight the monster,' said Fionn, 'and I want my hound to be tied up so that I may get first to the beast with my sword.'

'That will do no good,' said the king; 'and what is the use of binding that dirty little cur that the least man in the realm could hold with his little finger?'

'Unless you do as I wish,' said the Troich, 'the highest stone in your castle shall be lowest, and I will ruin your realm.' But they laughed at the little man.

But the king's adviser was wiser than he, and he said: 'It is best to try what he wants.'

So against the king's will they began the work. They went to the smithy and forged three chains and three iron bands and three hooks, and these they fastened to three logs of oak. They clasped the bands about the neck of Bran and hooked the chains to them, 'and now,' said Fionn, 'let the best three men in this realm of giants try to hold my dog.'

He put an iron belt round his own waist and an iron belt to that, 'and now,' said he, 'let the best eight men in the realm try to hold me.'

Then he shouted: 'The beast is coming,' and he cut a caper and broke from the eight and out he went. He whistled, and Bran broke a chain.

'Set sixteen men to hold me,' said the Troich.

So sixteen of the stoutest amongst the giants held the chain, and Fionn sprang out and broke from them and whistled, and Bran broke a second chain.

'Set twenty-four men to hold me now, if they can,' said the Troich.

So that was done, and Fionn sprang out in spite of the twenty-four giants, who fell sprawling on the ground, and he whistled, and Bran broke the third chain.

'Will you do what I wish now?' said the Troich.

That they would all gladly do, for they saw that they had a valiant champion to deal with, and they were afraid. So they went to the smithy again and forged three greater iron chains, and three greater iron bands, and three greater hooks, and they made the chains fast to three greater beams of oak, and these they built into a great strong stone wall, and so they fastened up Bran in the way that the Troich had found out from his wisdom.

After that the king took the Troich out to the hills to hunt, and Bran was left at home.

When the chase was done, the king said: 'You will be tired walking home, for the way is long.'

'The way is short by the loch-side,' said Fionn.

'But there is the beast,' said the king, 'and she will suck you in with her breath and swallow you.'

'No matter,' said Fionn, 'I will take the short cut and fight the beast.'

All the people who had heard of this came flocking to see the dwarf go to the beast, and they cried to him from the loch-shore: 'Why do you not go to meet the beast, she is coming to spoil the realm?'

'When my foe comes to me on green grass I will go to meet her,' said Fionn.

The monster was coming, and she smelt him and she sucked in her breath. She sucked so hard that Fionn fell to earth head foremost. He whistled, and Bran heard him and sprang and broke a chain.

Twelve over a score (i.e. thirty-two) giants fell upon the dog to hold him.

The beast came nearer and landed and sucked in her breath and Fionn fell, but as he fell he whistled as loud as he could, and Bran broke a second chain, and all the giants in the place fell upon him to hold him fast. Then the beast came to grass and sucked again, and this time Fionn blew a loud shrill whistle as he was sucked in.   Bran heard the whistle and broke the last chain, and broke loose and ran and sprang after Fionn down the monster's throat in a storm of wind.

Bran had a claw on his foot that was poisoned ; that was his gift.   Now Fionn began at one side with *Mac-A-Luinn* (his magical sword), and Bran began at the other with the teeth and nails inside the monster, and so they worked till they made their way out, one on each side, through maw and hide.   And so died the monster by the hand of Fionn as had been foretold in the books and prophecies long before he was born.

When the king's daughter came to know what was going on she was as one that is crazed, and down she ran to the shore.   But when she got there the little jewel was alive and the monster was *duisd*, a great lump on the strand.

There was a great soldier in the realm looking on from a high tower, and when he saw that the beast was still, with three small creatures moving beside her, he said to the king's son that he should go down and cut off the head and say that he had done the deed.   He had *claidheamh caol cinn airgead*, a slender silver-hilted sword, in his hand, and he went down to slay Fionn and take the head.

But Fionn met him and said—

'I will kill you as I killed the monster.   You would be some time before you killed her, and I have saved you.   No head or tail shall you have.   Behold I am Fionn, and I have slain the monster, and I could slay you all if I chose, as I killed the best three of you in Eirinn.'

When they heard that, all the big men ran for their lives, and the king fell upon his knees, with his hat in his hand, and begged merely for his son and pardon for himself humbly.

But Fionn had lost all his clothes, and all that was left of his skin was red as blood with the venom.   Bran had lost his hair and most of his hide and the shoe that guarded the *cruth nimh*, the venomous claw, and Fionn said to the king—

'The highest stone in your castle shall be the lowest

unless you heal me and my hound and make us whole as we were before.'

So doctors were got at once, and Fionn was healed and clad; but Bran was not made the same as before, for he was now a white mixture after he was healed, and they could not make a shoe like the old one.

'What colour was Bran?' said the king.'

Then Fionn looked at Bran and he said this lay—

> [a goodly shape my hound had had
> its neck-joint from its head a length;
> its middle broad with burly side,
> its chest as garron's, its claws hooked:
> yellow paws there were on Bran,
> its sides were black, its belly white,
> its back green to lay to the chase
> with two pricked ears blood-red.]

When the king heard that, he sent for people who dyed Bran as he was before; and because they could not make a shoe to fit the claw, they made a golden shoe for it. Then Fionn was well pleased.

Fionn stayed for a long time as one of the family in the realm of the big men, and he was worthy of that, for he was of noble race himself. They wanted him to marry the king's daughter and stay there, but he said: 'I have much to do in this dirty world, and first I must go to Alba and see my father's people there.'

This he had found out by putting his finger under the tooth.

'That is bad,' said the king, 'to part so soon after all that you have done for us.'

'Send a ship with me to Alba,' said Fionn, 'and that is all I ask in return.'

'That I will do,' said the king; 'to any port in Alba, and I will load her with much gold and treasure.'

So that was done. And that is how Fionn got all the gold which he paid to foes, for you know that it is said in the lays how he paid much gold :—

> ['mac Chumhail nan cuach (cōrn) ōr
> the son of Cumal of the golden cups (or horns).']

Here too he got his cup about which so much is said in lays and stories.

It was made of gold or silver, and it was good for healing. *Cuach Fhinn*, ' Fionn's Cup,' we call it.

So after Fionn had been with the king of the giants for a long time, a long ship was got and loaded with gold, and he sailed to Glen Eilg. There a boat was sent ashore with the gold, and it was hidden in a cave. He had never been to Alba or to any other realm but Ireland till then, and when he landed he did not know where to go.

(*To be continued.*)

THE REV. DR. BLAIR'S MSS.

Rev. A. MACLEAN SINCLAIR

THE Rev. Duncan Black Blair, D.D., was born at Strachur, in Cowal, Scotland, July 1, 1815. He began going to school at Inverscadle, in Ardgour, in 1823, and studied under John Finlayson, at Shiramore, in Badenoch, from 1828 to 1833. He entered the University of Edinburgh in 1834, but was laid up with influenza in Edinburgh for a few weeks in January 1837. In April 1838 he went to the Isle of Skye to act as tutor to the children of Malcolm Nicolson, in Ullinish. Through the summer he was attacked by typhus fever and confined to his bed for ten weeks. On September 13 we find him writing a song of praise for his recovery. On the 20th of the same month his sister Anna, who had been waiting on him in his sickness, died of the fever. He composed a very touching elegy about her on the 28th of the month. Owing to the debilitating effect of the fever on his constitution he had to remain at home with his father at Lublia, in Badenoch, for two years. He spent a good deal of this time studying and writing Gaelic poetry. Entering the Divinity Hall in Edinburgh in November 1840, he was licensed to preach on May 1, 1844. He spent the greater part of 1845 in the Isle of Mull. He came to Pictou in May 1846, removed to Ontario in May 1847, and returned to Pictou in October 1848. In August 1850 he went to Scotland, and remained during the year. He married Mary, daughter of Captain Hector MacLean, of the 93rd Regiment, in August 1851, and came back to Pictou. His wife died June 6, 1882. She was a good-looking, sensible, and pious woman.

Dr. Blair had charge of the congregation of Barney's River and Blue Mountain, in the county of Pictou. He lived at Barney's River—*Abhainn Bhàrnaidh*—about five miles from the spot at which John Maclean, the Gaelic bard, composed his *Coille Ghruamach* in 1819. He could not, however, sing from his own experience the following lines:—

> Cha 'n ioghnadh dhòmhsa ged tha mi brònach,
> 'S ann tha mo chòmhnuidh air cùl nam beann,
> Am meadhon fàsaich air Abhainn Bhàrnaidh,
> Gun dad a's fèarr na buntàta lom.

Dr. Blair died on the 4th of June 1893. He had lived in comfortable circumstances, was an excellent linguist, a good poet, and a devout man. As an accurate writer of Gaelic he had no superior. The Gaelic poems written by him—the titles of which I give in English—were as follows:—

In 1833.

		LINES
The vanity of earthly things .	. .	124

In 1837.

A song of praise after sickness .	. . .	200
The Martyrs . .	. . .	308
The Last Judgment .	. . .	512
A prayer to the Holy Spirit .	. . .	108
A poem composed at Loch Laggan	. . .	40

In 1838.

A song of praise after a fever .	. . .	90
A lament for his sister .	. . .	184

LINES

Death and the grave	72
Another lament for his sister	120
David's lament for Saul and Jonathan . . .	72
A lament for Charles Urchart	240
The Dead in Sin	72
The Refuge for Sinners	112
A song of praise	108
Immanuel	1962

In 1839.

On Death	44
The Court of Death	270
The Believer's Song of Love	2096
Lament for Pliny Fisk	440
The Old Man and the Young Man . . .	1200
A lament for John M'Master	184
Lines on Mrs. E. Rowe	208
Spiritual Meditation	1960
The Desires of the Soul after Christ . . .	200
A journey to Arisaig	376
Lament of the Mull Women	2254

In 1842.

Lament for Rev. John Kennedy . . .	666
Signs of the Times	189
The Foxes	780

In 1844.

Through Brae Laggan	80
Lament for Rev. John Finlayson . . .	420

In 1848.

The Falls of Niagara	152

In 1849.

Lament for Macdonald of Ferintosh . . .	100

In 1851.

Lines on Rev. Alexander M'Intyre . . .	32
Farewell to Sutherlandshire	48
A love-song on Mary Maclean	40

In 1873.

LINES

A lament for the old elders 52

From June 1882 *to July* 1887.

A lament for his wife 104
A song for a marriage 32
A lament for his daughter 72
Four songs in favour of the Crofters . . . 200
A song on the Queen's Jubilee 80

D. B. Blair composed his first poem on January 11, 1833. It is on the vanity of earthly things, and contains one hundred and twenty-four lines. It shows that the author of it was a youth of serious thoughts and good sense, that he had a thorough knowledge of the nature of rhyme and the mode of constructing poems, and that he could write Gaelic with perfect accuracy. He composed his next poem— a song of praise for his recovery from sickness—on January 13, 1837. It was written in Edinburgh, and contains two hundred lines. This song, or hymn of thankfulness, shows beyond all doubt that the author of it was a true poet. It was really the beginning of his life as a man of song. The poet was at Iona, July 29, 1851, and wrote, not a poem in praise of Columba, but a love-song addressed to Mary Maclean, who became his wife about a month afterwards. This was the first secular poem ever written by him.

Dr. Blair's poems may be divided into sacred poems, laments, and secular poems or songs. There are seventeen sacred poems, eleven laments, and ten songs. The whole of the poems contain 16,650 lines. The most of the long sacred poems and several of the short ones are excellent productions, and should be published. Two of the elegies are also of a high order. The songs are all very good. The poems that are really valuable would make a volume of about four hundred pages.

Dr. Blair translated into Gaelic an Anti-Patronage Catechism in 1842, and a Church Catechism by Dr. M'Leod, of New York, in 1843. He translated the following compositions into Gaelic verse :—

Habakkuk's prayer, in 1837; Moses' hymn in the 15th chapter of Exodus, in 1837; the *Believer's Riddle* by Ralph Erskine, in 1839; the first three books of *Paradise Lost*, the Book of Psalms in long metre, a number of popular English hymns, in 1881; Clement of Alexandria's hymn in 1885; and the Book of Psalms in short metre. He began his translation of the Psalms into long metre about the beginning of October 1876, and finished it about the end of April 1878. He revised and rewrote it between July 27 and October 25, 1878. He began his translation of the Psalms into short metre in October 1889, and finished it on May 19, 1890. He read the Hebrew Bible almost as easily as he read the Gaelic or English Bible. His versions of the Psalms are probably as literal and smooth as any version can be.

Dr. Blair translated some of his own poems and the most of Dr. M'Gregor's hymns into English. He also wrote several poems in English. But by far the most valuable of his English writings is his *Grammar of the Gaelic Language*. This is an excellent work and should be published.

The following is Dr. Blair's translation of Clement of Alexandria's Hymn :—

LAOIDH

Le Clement Alexandria

Thus' a ghlacas lothan fiadhaich,
'Chuireas srian 'nam beul,
Is tu Sgiath 'nan eun neo-fhaondrach
Nach téid claon 'nan réis.

Is tu Falmadair na h-òigridh
Gus an seòladh ceart ;
Buachaille nan uan geal, fior-ghlan,
Caoirich Righ nam feart.

Do chlann ionmhuinn shimplidh tionail,
Bheir iad moladh naomh
Do Chriosd le bilibh neo-chealgach,
Righ nan leanaban maoth.

A Righ nan naomh, Fhocail neartmhoir,
Mac an Athar Aird,
Thus', a Riaghlair gliocais shiorruidh,
'S tu 'm Fear-dion o chràdh:

Tha thu sona feadh nan saoghal,
Shaor thu 'n cinne daonn';
Iosa, Buachaille na greadhainn,
'S tu 'm Fear-treabhaidh caomh.

Is tu Stiuir gach luinge 'shèolas,
Srian na h-òigridh fhaoin;
Sgiath nan calman naomh a thriallas
Anns an iarmailt chaoin.

Is tu Iasgair chlann nan daoine,
'Rinneadh saor leat féin;
Glacaidh tu na h-iasga geamnuidh
As an fhairge bhréin,

A mhuir bhuaireasach ro shalach
'Bhios ag at le tuinn;
Le biadh glan na beatha blasda
Ni thu 'n tional cruinn.

Aodhaire nan caorach reusant',
A Righ threin 'tha naomh,
Stiuir do chlann gun chron 'nan gluasad,
Cuairtich iad gach taobh.

A cheum Chriosd, a shlìghe neamhaidh,
'Fhocail threin, bhith-bhuain,
Aois nach tomhais linnean siorruidh,
'Sholuis fhior nach truaill;

'Thobair trocair o 'n tig feartan,
'Bheir dhuinn neart gu feum,
Iosa, Chriosd, thoir beatha dhoibh-san,
A ta seinn cliu Dhé.

Bainne neamhaidh, milis, blasda,
Chiochan glan nan gràs
Thig à broilleach bean-na-bainnse,
Gliocas naomh o 'n àird.

Beathaichear le sin na ciochrain,
Lionaidh iad am beul
Le lòn spioradail ro chùbhraidh,
'Bhios mar dhrùchd nan speur.

A nis thigeamaid mar òg chlann
'Thabhairt gloir do'n Triath;
D' ar Righ, Iosa, seinnear cliu leinn,
Iobairt chubhraidh fhial.

Iocamaid cis naomh gun ghearan
Do'n Fhear-theagaisg mhor,
Gun cheilg molamaid le chéile
Leanabh treun na glòir.

A chòisir na sìthe mairinn,
Sibhse ghineil Chriosd,
A naomh shluaigh le chéile seinnibh
Molaibh Dia na sith.

The following literal translation of the hymn I copy from Coxe's edition of the Ante-Nicene Fathers, vol. ii. p. 296 :—
'Bridle of untamed colts, Wing of unwandering birds, sure Helm of babes, Shepherd of royal lambs, assemble thy simple children to praise holily, to hymn guilelessly with innocent mouths, Christ the Guide of children. O King of saints, all-subduing Word of the most high Father, Ruler of wisdom, Support of sorrows, that rejoicest in the ages, Jesus, Saviour of the human race, Shepherd, Husbandman, Helm, Bridle, Heavenly Wing of the all-holy flock, Fisher of men who are saved, catching the chaste fishes with sweet life from the hateful wave of a sea of vices. Guide us, Shepherd of rational sheep, guide unharmed children, O Holy King, O footsteps of Christ, O heavenly Way, perennial Word, immeasurable Age, Eternal Light, Fount of Mercy, Performer of virtue; noble is the life of those who hymn God, O Christ Jesus, heavenly milk of the sweet breasts of the graces of the Bride, pressed out of thy wisdom. Babes nourished with tender mouths, filled with the dewy spirit of the rational pap, let us sing together simple praises, true hymns to Christ our King, holy fee for the teaching of life; let us sing in

simplicity the powerful child. O choir of peace, the Christ-begotten, O chaste people, let us sing together the God of peace.'

The measure used by Dr. Blair runs as follows in English :—

> Pass me not, O gentle Saviour,
>> Hear my humble cry ;
> While on others Thou are calling,
>> Do not pass me by ;
>
> Let me at a throne of mercy
>> Find a sweet relief ;
> Kneeling there in deep contrition,
>> Help my unbelief.

Clement of Alexandria composed his hymn about A.D. 200.

As an example of Dr. Blair's rhymed version of the Psalms, Ps. cxxvii. in long metre is here given :—

> 1. 'N luchd-togail saothraichidh gun fheum
>> Mur tog Iehobhah féin an tigh ;
>> 'S faoin obair an luchd-faire fòs,
>> Mur gleidh Iehobhah 'm baile stigh.
> 2. Is dìomhain duibh bhi 'g éirigh moch,
>> Us anmoch bhi ri caithris bhuain,
>> Ag itheadh aran bròin us airc ;
>> Mar sin da sheircein bheir e suain.
>
> 3. 'S e Dia bheir toradh bronn mar dhuais,
>> Mar oighreachd luachmhoir bheir e clann.
> 4. Bidh mic na h-òig' mar shaighdibh geur
>> An làmhan gaisgich thréin gach am.
> 5. Is sona 'n duine sin gu bràth
>> A lionas làn a dhòrlach dhuibh ;
>> Sa gheata labhraidh iad gun sgàth
>> R' an naimhdibh dh'easbhuidh nàire gnùis.

Dr. Blair always writes, not 'us, a's, or even is, but us.

ANNA MHÌN, MHEALL-SHUILEACH

Domhnull MacEacharn

SEISD—
Mo chailin mhìn, mheall-shuileach,
'S cianail mi o 'n dhealaich sinn ;
Mo nigh'n donn nam meall-shuilean,
O, Anna, thug mi spéis duit.

A bhean, nam beusan stòlda,
De 'n chinneadh a bha mòrail,
Ged 's fbad o cheil' a sheòl sinn,
Gu 'm b' òg a thug mi spéis duit.
    Mo chailin mhìn, etc.

Gun chaochladh no gun mhùchadh,
Tha 'n gaol a thug mi 'n tùs duit,
Ged rinn an saoghal mùileach
Ar stiùradh fad o cheile.
    Mo chailin mhìn, etc.

Ged tha mo cheann air liathadh,
'S mo là a nis air ciaradh,
'S i t' ìomhaigh ghaoil bha riamh leam,
O 'n chiad là thug mi géill duit.
    Mo chailin mhìn, etc.

Is cuimhne leam nuair bhà sinn
'N ar cloinn a' ruith mu 'n àirigh,
'S do chuailein donn bu tlàithe,
A' snàmh 's an oiteig Chéitein.
    Mo chailin mhìn, etc.

Gur tric gun fhios do chàch mi,
'N uair 's àirde 'n guth 's an gàire,
A' cuimhneachadh nan là sin,
Ged 's fhada dh' fhàg mi 'm dhéigh iad.
    Mo chailin mhìn, etc.

Ar leam gu bheil an saoghal
'S gach nì a th' ann air claonadh,
Tha ceòl a mhàin gun chaochladh,
'S an gaol a tha 'ga ghleusadh.
    Mo chailin mhìn, etc.

Mo shoraidh bhuan a rùin leat,
Tha 'n tim a' ruith gu siùbhlach,
Is sinne, mar is dùth dhuinn,
'Tigh'n dlùth air ceann ar réise.
    Mo chailin mhìn, etc.

THE GREY WIND

L. McManus

From the east comes the crimson wind, from the south the white, from the north the black, from the west the grey.—SEANCHUS MÓR.

I

IN A CORNER OF CONNACHT

I LIVE in the midst of bogs, brown, black, heather-clad. My bogs lie in a corner of the barony of Gallen in Connacht, the name Gallen linking us with the days of Cormac son of Art the Lonely, who was High King of Ireland two centuries before the coming of Saint Patrick. It is called after Gaileng of the dishonoured spear, who having made an oath upon the weapon, broke it, violating the spear, and was banished by his father westward across the Shannon. Three clans of the Gaels of Scotland took the heather for their badge, and the cross-leaved variety has a connection with Red Hugh O'Donnell, chief of Tirconnel in the sixteenth century, the young, valiant hero of the red-gold hair famous in Irish history, whose story is told so eloquently in *The Flight of the Eagle*, by Standish O'Grady. It was the badge of the Macdonalds, and his mother was An Nighean Dubh (*Ineen Du*), the Dark Daughter of the Lord of the Isles, a woman of an imperious will, who ruled Tirconnel for her son, while he, a boy of sixteen, lay a prisoner in Dublin Castle. The white bog-cotton makes silvery patches here and there, and in this wild garden of our bog we find the yellow star-like asphodel, and the round leaf sundew with its red hairs and white flower-tufted stalk. Orchis in numbers and the pink red battle grow in the yellow mossy ground, while the bracken and bramble hold that corner of the bog by the alder and birch plantation, where earlier in the year the fox-gloves and emerald green ferns make a thicket for themselves. Over there in that piece of waste land near where the Scotch firs rise among the bracken, there are dark patches of mud, and long, coarse grasses mingling with the mosses,—the *curragh* it is called, upon which, if the cattle tread, they are sucked down into the treacherous ground, for there is death as well as beauty in our bogs.

Following the road called *Bother-na-Teampuill*,[1] when we speak in Irish, we see on the right a hill overlooking that swelling bog which a spade has not touched for over a hundred years. Some day the heather-clad expanse may feel the impulse to move, given by its black hidden waters. The hill is called *Cnoc-na-Fuileach*, the Hill of Blood, and no man now knows the origin of the name. Once a battle was fought upon its slope, leaving a slaughter so terrible that even after all tale of its happening and the names of those who met in conflict had long faded from the minds of the people, it is still remembered as a place of carnage. Standing on the summit, I seem to catch echoes of the tumult, and see the dim forms of the hostings meeting in the shock of battle. The shadowy figures carry battle-axe and spear, the 'sword of light' (of steel) or the sword of bronze, great shields hang on their arms of yew, or of hammered bronze, and I know the captains and heroes by the splendour of their weapons, gold and silver hilted and embossed. It may have been that the High King of Ireland met the Danes here—'the foreigners of the armour,' as they are called in the *Wars of the Gael with the Gaill*—for five miles away stands a round tower, the stone guardian once of the monks, their books, and sacred vessels when the Northman appeared across the Moy ; or the battle may have broken between the King of Connacht and some rival prince, when the O'Conors in the eleventh century were first rising into power ; or later still, William Fitz-Adhelm, the Norman and first of the Burkes, may have enforced his claim to Connacht on that hill.

Looking from its summit towards the north, you see the wooded crown of the fairy-rath, *Lis Ard*, the rath that Raftery, the blind peasant poet, sang of in the Irish, 'the little sharp hill,' on the slope of which, when a wanderer in Galway, he longed to lie ; and to the south are fields dotted with

[1] The church road, lit. the temple road.

cattle and bordered by bogs, and beyond again, across the straight, white road that leads to the railway and the outer world, the Red Field (*Parc Ruadh*), rath-marked, ending in a hill the name of whose *lis* preserves that of some ancient chief; while, in the west, rises the mountain, Sliebh Carn, on whose height in ages past was reared a cairn above a hero's grave.

But the Hill of Blood has an older interest than that long-forgotten battle. In some dateless time men stood there and laid their leader to rest in the round crest of the hill, burying him sitting upright, his face to the west, a vessel with food by his side, that his spirit might be sustained in its passage to the other world. There he sat through three thousand years or more, indifferent to the step of the Gael, and the Dane, and the Norman above his head, deaf to the fury of the battle that rang one day along the slopes. Then a nineteenth century ploughshare struck the flag that covered the grave, and the secret the hill had kept so long was revealed.

Visible from this hill is a field bordered eastward by the river Geisthan, known as *Trian-na-Croise*, the Third of the Cross. In old divisions of land in Ireland, we find the terms of second and third, and fourth and fifth and sixth often used in the place-names, and the reason is usually clear, but here imagination has room to weave its own explanation. The name is centuries old, and perhaps may be coeval with the saint who, fifteen hundred years ago, came hither to preach the Faith to our pagan forefathers. Not far off are the remains of his church, and it may have been that he made a cross and placed it there on the high land above the river for the people to see, which later became a mark in the division of the land. As you descend the slope towards the river, three unhewn stones of immense size attract your attention. They lie not far from the bank, and the man looking for fish will tell you that they are called *Cloc-na-Diarmid*, the Stone of Diarmid, but why he does not know. His grandfather could have explained the meaning of the name, and told the story of the flight of Diarmid with Gráine of the golden hair, the King of Ireland's daughter. But with the establishment of the national schools, the old romances ceased to be repeated before the children, and a generation grew up ignorant of the tales in which their forefathers had delighted. These stones of Diarmid are to be found all over Ireland, and are cromlechs, though tradition has connected them for some centuries with the Fianna. Reared in the dim past, many are older than the first of the tales told of Finn mac Cumhal, or of Ossian, or Diarmid; older, too, than the Red Branch cycle of romance; tombs raised over heroes, or men and women great in their day. The one we look at has been overthrown, and the huge upper slab is broken. Some antique king sleeps there, and the hurrying river keeps the secret of his name.

II

The Franciscans have left their mark in my corner of Gallen; the old ruin in the churchyard was their friary. Passing under the crumbling arch of the church, we see the carved stone pedestals of their altar by the ivy-clad wall, though the altar stone itself is missing. It may be that flag over a neighbouring tomb, for the body of the church is full of graves, two trees disputing possession of the ground with the dead. Mass was celebrated here in the ruins when the penal laws were relaxed. The church was built in the first years of the fourteenth century; and the fishing weir of the friars over the river that flows close by remained till about a few years ago when it was replaced by a bridge. Old men can show us where their mill stood, and a man clearing out the old lime-kiln yonder found an ancient bronze crucifix, probably part of the sacred furniture. The Franciscans became a wealthy order in Ireland. In an inventory of one of their houses there is mention of forty suits of vestments made of cloth of gold and silver and silk brocade, as well as of a number of gold and silver chalices inlaid with precious stones. In the southern window of the church there are two skulls upon the sill, which have lain there so long that no one now knows out of what grave they came. An old man of eighty told me that they had been there in his grandfather's time, and a special reverence is attached to them. Once a man came into the churchyard, and, laying his hands upon them, cursed his enemy, deeming the curse would be more deadly recorded thus. The lintel and sides of the window protect them in a measure from the weather, and for two or three hundred years, or more perhaps, their identity lost, their hollow sockets have watched each century's procession of mourners as the dead were brought hither. They may have been men alert, strong, full of life and fire when Patrick Sarsfield held Connacht for King James, or have seen the Ironsides cross the barony when Ireton led them hither. Some chance has selected them from the countless dead around to keep watch and ward upon the churchyard.

Standing a few yards nearer to the river, but within the consecrated enclosure, is a small dome-shaped building. It is the *cill*, the original church, and is probably fifteen hundred years old. The door is towards the west, and the Franciscans when they came faced it with dressed stone, for behind these stones is the old rough frontage with the sloping jambs of the fifth or sixth century. The stone roof overlaps, but on the western wall there are traces of the Franciscan masons. If you stoop—and you must bend low, for the centuries have raised the ground before the doorway, half filling the opening—and enter the church, you find yourself in a dimly-lighted room with a small window in the eastern wall and a grave in the corner. The church is oblong, as were the Patrician churches, about ten feet in length and six in width. When prayer was first offered within it, the people around had probably been just converted from paganism, and the old gods, though in the process of being obscured, were not yet fully dethroned. Men still saw Lugh of the Long-Hand, the Sun-god, coming up out of the east with the white hound by his side, and had dreams of the magic birds of Angus Óg, the god of youth and love, or desired a gift from the cauldron of the Daghda, the good god from whose golden harp, as he played, the seasons sprang. In one of the famine years of the

forties in the last century, the *cill* had an occupant for a time,
a woman crazed from hunger and misery, who had wandered
into our parish.   For some months she made her home in
the little church, feeding on nettles and such food as she
could find, till in the end her people found her and carried
her away.

Returning from the churchyard, we pass into a road on
the right, bordered on one side by a bog and on the other by
meadow and wood.   Not many years ago there was no road
here, only a track.   Then the road was made, and in the
making a number of silver coins were found.   They were discovered under an old thorn tree, planted perhaps to mark
the site of the treasure.   I have one before me now as I write ;
the face is full on the obverse, the hair is puffed yet flowing
round the cheeks, and the head is crowned.   It is the face
of the Plantagenet king, Edward iii.   The silver piece is
crossed on the reverse, a groat of his reign.   About two
hundred coins were in the hoard, and all with the exception
of ten are of that period.   Some were minted in London,
others at Waterford and Canterbury.   The oldest piece is a
coin with the head of one of the Alexanders of Scotland.
The last Scottish king of that name died in 1285.   The Stuarts
were then uncrowned, their dynasty not yet established.   Not
till nearly one hundred years later (1371) did the first Stuart
reign.   The little coin was minted so long ago that those who
first held it in their hands would have thought it incredible
if told that the descendants of the King's High Stewards
should wear the crown of Scotland and later that of England.
It may have been brought into Ireland with the soldiers of
Edward Bruce, and passed into the possession of one who lived
here in our barony in the fourteenth century.   The Norman
families of Burke, Barrett, and d'Exeter Jordan had by that
century planted themselves firmly in this and the neighbouring counties.   There was a circulation of English money, and
the silver pieces probably belonged to one of these lords.   Did
a servant steal them, or a friend tempted by some need ?
Spoil they may have been taken in a raid, or perhaps a

faithful messenger, carrying the dues to his lord, seeing foes
approach, buried them in the ground. Quite certain it is
that he who put them there never returned to recover the
treasure. Over five hundred years have passed since then
with their checkered chapters of Irish history. The Norman
lords had forgotten their Norman French, and had adopted
the Irish language, laws, dress, and customs, keeping great
state, large households, bodyguards, brehons, just as their
Gaelic rivals did when the clay fell on these coins; when the
spade flung them up to the light of day again, the castles of
the lords were in ruins, and their descendants scattered. On
the coin I hold, the king's eyes are as freshly marked as when
it came from the mint. Rounded, shining, without lids, they
give a queer look of life to the silver face, a look of amazement. 'By the splendour of God!' he seems to exclaim in
his Norman French. 'Into what strange world have I come.'
And from the Scottish coin one may fancy that a voice that
should speak in Gaelic but which instead utters its words
in mingled Norman French and Anglo-Saxon asks, too,
bewildered questions. 'Who speaks of my High Stewards?
Kings? who called them royal? I am Alexander of the race
of Fergus of Erin, King of Alba, I alone am king. What
names are these I hear? James? Charles? Who are they?
And of what battles do you speak and name the Boyne
and Aughrim?'

History and folk-lore meet in my corner as indeed they
meet everywhere all over Ireland. The kingdom of the
Sidhe, too, is powerful. Irish fairy-lore has a distinction
of its own, echoes from pagan Ireland, of its myths and
rites. From the point where the coins were found we look
directly on *Lis Ard*, the tree-covered rath on the summit
of a hill. As you stand there among the ash and beech, if
your eyes travel west the bright gleam of water—should the
day be clear or the sun shining—that meets your gaze, are
the two loughs, Cullin and Conn, lakes whose shores and
islands are connected with tales of magic and romance. They
lie at the foot of Ben Nephin, the cone-shaped mountain that

reveals or hides itself to us as the clouds will, clothed sometimes in a garment of the deepest blue, or again so pale and vague that it seems dissolving into the ether. It is well known the Sidhe inhabit *Lis Ard*. The old man Tadhg told me he saw them once on the rath, the elemental life revealing itself to his mortal eyes. It was sunset, and he was digging at the foot of the hill, and looking up the slope saw a number of men and women among the trees. All their faces were turned upon him, but none spoke, the figures watching from the verge of the trees, motionless, silent. And Tadhg knew that those who dwelt in the fairy palace within the mound had taken off the cloak of invisibility, and that their presence was a signal for him to go. So with a greeting to the watchers, he took up his spade and went away before the twilight fell.

III

Caves have a mystery and romance about them. In fairy tales all over Europe, the giant, if he does not live in a castle, makes a cave his habitation. Dragons, too, and superhuman creatures dwell within them. Through caves the popular imagination found entrance to the hidden and marvellous, into the kingdoms of the beings of magic and faery. In them, or in underground chambers, the hero whom his people expect to return, lies in an enchanted slumber. The legend of the heroes who thus sleep, and who at some national crisis shall awake and come to the help of their people, is common to Europe. Charlemagne, Frederick Barbarossa, Arthur of Britain are said not to be dead, but lying each asleep, and shall return. Deep under the castle of Kronberg in Denmark, Olger Danske, the Danish king, awaits the call to arms: at Denmark's need he shall awake. Clothed in armour, he sits before a marble table, his head on his outspread arms. So long has he been held by that strange sleep, that his beard has grown through the marble to the floor, and when he springs to his feet the marble shall break. There is a story told of Olger Danske and his enchanted sleep that may be compared to a story told of the Fianna. And as Irish influence can be traced in the Norse sagas, the tale perhaps is Celtic, borrowed by the Norsemen, and connected with their national hero.

Once Olger Danske was disturbed in his underground chamber. A peasant found the door by chance and knocked upon it. The door opened, and a voice within said, 'Is it time?' Entering the cavern, the peasant saw the kingly sleeper, a great, shining sword across his knee. 'Is it time?' the voice asked again. The peasant, astonished and afraid, replied, 'It is not.' 'Give me your hand,' the king said. The peasant thrust forward an iron bar. Olger Danske grasped it, and left the mark of his fingers upon the iron. 'There are men still in Denmark!' he said. 'I need not yet awake.'

Compare this tale with the Irish legend. It is the heroes of the Fianna who are asleep within a rath, their swords lie by each man's hand, their horses are stabled near; thus they await the call which shall send them to their feet. Then the Fianna shall leap on their horses and outward from the dark cave, and onward to save Ireland in her hour of need. But the call has not yet come, and the heroes still sleep. One day a peasant found the door in the rath, and, going in, followed a passage till he reached the cave. The sight he saw there filled him with amazement. Squadrons of horses, bridled, bitted, accoutred, stood motionless in their stalls. By each horse a soldier slept, his weapons by his side. The peasant, in his hurry to retreat, stumbled, and touched one of the men. The hero sprang to his feet and drew his sword. 'An bhfuil an t'àm ann?' he asked (Is it time?). The peasant answered, 'Ni'l; go codlidh aris' (No; sleep again), on hearing which the soldier sank backward again. Another version tells how the Fianna will not awake till a great trumpet that hangs at the mouth of the cave is blown thrice. Once a man had the courage to blow it twice, but, terrified at the sight of the awakening heroes, dropped it and fled.

All over Ireland there are artificial caves, many of which are believed to be the habitations of the Sidhe, a belief that is a survival from the thought of pagan Ireland. *Tir na n-óg*, the Land of Youth, was to be found beneath these mounds. Free from care, pain, death, a land against which laughter peals, a land of lasting weather, a 'lovely land throughout the world's age on which many blossoms drop.' *Tir na n-óg* was the paradise of the Gael. Its mystery and beauty linger round the raths. Within them are houses of crystal, golden fruit-bearing trees, blue, shining seas, the singing of birds, and marvellous and delightful sights and sounds. Yet flesh and blood shrinks from entering the unknown hidden world. I heard a story here of a woman who was carried away by the Sidhe. By some means, before the seven years had passed after which rescue would have been impossible, she managed to be snatched out of their power. She told her friends that while away she had been taken to the heart of every rath in Ireland, to kingly halls and blossoming meadows, to every palace of fairy delight, but in no rath of all those she had entered had she found beauty and marvels equal to what she had seen in the rath *Lis Ard*. Here is a touch of local pride which makes the chief rath in this parish the most beautiful palace of the Sidhe in Ireland. A woman who had travelled so far in the hidden world, and who had seen so much would have been an interesting person to have met. 'Is she living now?' I asked. 'She died some time back,' I was answered. 'It was the other side of the river, back there at Treenkeel, she died.' And at the answer I knew that the woman was old, very old, and that she would be heard of again and again up each century of our history, and beyond history, into the mist of the Tuatha de Danaan —the people of the goddess Dana.

There are several artificial caves in this corner of Gallen. Some of the old men say they were built by the Danes. That, of course, is not true; the mistake arose through their confusion of the name Danaan with that of Dane. When the Tuatha de Danaan ceased to be regarded as gods, they were supposed to live on in the Other World, entrance to which might be found in mounds and caves as well as in loughs and rivers and the sea. As the people gradually lost memory of their history, a process which occurred slowly within recent times, the two names were confused when explaining the origin of the caves. It is, however, a fact to note that the Danish invasions are stamped into the memory of the Irish-speaking peasant, while those who have lost their native language have no knowledge of that page of Irish history. The Irish speaker, who knew a vast amount of mingled legend, history, and folk-lore, sent down to him through the medium of the language in which all relating to his past had been enshrined, told and retold for generations, knew very well that the Danes had once harried his country. Old Tadhg Brennan, of whom I have spoken, used to point to a heather-clad hill beyond the river Geisthan, and say that the last Dane in Ireland—and the last man also who knew the secret of making ale from heather—had been killed there. He was well aware of the connection of the Danes with his country, through oral tradition, while his grand-children who have lost their native language, and have not been taught Irish history at the National School, know nothing about those marauders and sea-kings.

There is a cave here in a rath known as *Lis-Dubh*, which had a series of passages and chambers. The entrance is in the side of the mound, half hidden by bramble and thorn. A good many Irish ancient romance-tales centre round caves. Great adventures occur in them—sieges, plunders, marvellous happenings. At the *Lis-Dubh* cave you feel you are near a story which the years have veiled. You cannot lift the veil, but you see phantom shapes and shadows thrown upon it from the other side. *Lis-Dubh*, the Black-Fort, our fore-fathers called it, and one wonders why. Standing on the *lis*, on the roof of the caves, the undulating land spreads for miles before you. The pale, blue mountains rise in the west, and two shining lines of water cross the plain, the rivers Geisthan and Gilore. Three centuries ago, when woods grew in this

part of the parish, it must have been a beautiful scene.
Now, in its nakedness, as you gaze along the horizon to the
north and north-west, you receive the impression that the
innumerable little hills are a succession of waves, each one of
which seeks to reach the encircling goal of the sky. Nothing
in the scene explains the reason of the name. It and the
cave keep their own secret.

On the crest of a low hill near *Lis Ard*, there are, or were,
two artificial caves. Many years ago part of the hill was
enclosed, and planted as an orchard. Hoary apple-trees shake
their white and pink blossoms in spring over what remains of
the caves. The man who had made the orchard broke into
and partly destroyed them. The Sidhe did not avenge themselves, and probably retired to the finer halls of *Lis Ard*.
When Tadhg Brennan was a little boy he saw the caves in
good condition. He entered one, and stood upright, under
a flagged roof. There he saw, or thought he saw, the traces
of a fire and pipes. These orchard caves have a story attached
to them. Years ago a man named Goulding—(it is interesting to note how local names are always given by the narrators
of these stories)—who lived on the mountain Slieve Carn,
had a son who every morning went to school. Before long
the boy showed such remarkable knowledge, that his father,
in an excess of gratitude, went to the hedge-school to thank
the teacher. But the teacher said he had neither seen nor
taught the boy; the father then found that his son went to
school at the orchard caves, and that his teachers were
the Sidhe. Among the things that he learnt to make were
the pipes of the bagpipe. Now, the Tuatha de Danaan, we
remember, were clever artificers, and the Sidhe are but the
dethroned Tuatha de Danaan, the gigantic figures of Irish
mythology. Thus in this story there is a stroke given
straight out of the dim, ancient world of the Gael, a fragment
from that mythology, the door to which has been thrown open
by such scholars as St. Zimmer, de Jubainville, and others.
Under the instruction of the Sidhe, at the orchard caves, the
boy, when a man, became so famous an artificer that he had

not his equal in Ireland. He taught the art of working in-
metals to a family named Egan ; and here we pass from
legend to fact. Such a family existed, who were all clever
artificers. The mythical boy is the link with the metal-
workers of mythological Ireland and a real family in modern
and Christian Ireland. The fairy character of the boy is
further shown in the story, and not only is he the pupil of
the Sidhe, but visits them at *Lis Ard*, and, with the cap of
darkness on his head, rides with them on the wind towards
the sea. In short, though called Goulding, he is himself one
of the Sidhe. The ruined caves in the orchard have thus an
interest to the mythologist ; in them the forge of the Tuatha
de Danaan has been kindled, and the legend casts a glow
over the spot.

IV

With the superhuman and spiritual world so near us, but
little of the materialism of other countries has touched our
thought. Deep down we keep the same conception of the
visible and invisible world. We still stand at the point
towards which the pendulum of thought in other lands is
swinging back from the dogmatism of the materialist through
the results of psychical research.

The belief in the mysterious inherent power in the element
of water goes back beyond written history into the twilight
of the earliest ages. It appears in the first myths of the
world, in the religions of highly developed races, in Judaism
and the Christian Faith. A belief so universal, so old, has
some deep root in the spiritual part of man himself. It is
true, awed by the forces of nature, primitive man made gods of
the elements. The sun, under whose rays the earth blossomed,
the fruits ripened, and the seed yielded their grain, was a
power before whom he bent the knee, it mattered not what
name he called it—Apollo, Lu-lam-fada—to him it was a god.
In the healing spring and stream he saw beneficent forces ;
and sacred wells and rivers arose. Ireland has a number of

such wells, the sanctity of which can be traced back to pre-Christian days. There are others again that received their sacred character after the coming of the Faith. Many of these are called by the names of the saints who built their cells beside the spring, and who, consecrating the waters, there baptized their converts. Those that had been held in reverence in pagan Ireland with wise tolerance were blessed by St. Patrick and the early saints, and thenceforth were connected with the new religion. Thus the Holy Well of Ballintober in this county was called *Slan* or Health when Dana was still worshipped as the mother of the gods, and Crom Cruaich, the King Idol of Erinn, still stood on the Plain of Adoration. St. Patrick built a church beside it and blessed the well.

There is a holy well not far from us, surrounded by a wall, with an old white thorn close by, to which votive rags are attached. A story is told about the well which, even in its modernised form, shows its antiquity. Every one in the parish knows that the well is no longer in the spot where ages ago it first welled up. It has moved within the memory of man—so the people will tell you—from the little hill Cilleen, which is about half a mile away, to its present site. The cause of its flight was a woman. A 'station' was held at her house, and, in her anxiety to get the priest's dinner ready quickly, she went to the nearest well, which was that of Cilleen, and drew water from it. But the water refused to boil, refused indeed to be anything but icy cold, though the fire burned fiercely beneath the pot. The priest on hearing what she had done bade her throw the water back into the holy well. The woman obeyed, but the spirit of the well was not appeased, and that night the well moved from the hill of Cilleen to gush forth clear and sparkling in its present position. In spite of the 'priest' and the 'station' the ancient character of the tale appears through its modern dress. Further proof is given in the stories told of Cilleen itself. It is impossible, or useless, to till the ground upon which the well once stood, for neither oats nor potatoes nor

any other crop will grow there. Once a man, despite this
fact, tried to dig the soil, but the spade was thrown out of his
hand, and a white bird flew up from the ground. A thorn
bush grows upon Cilleen; if struck with a hatchet an animal
will come out.

Here we pass into folk-lore, one of the doors through which
we can gather some of the thoughts of primitive man. The
legend of the flight of the well, the stories told of Cilleen, are
but echoes from an older belief. Especially interesting is that
reference to the white bird. In *The Happy Other World*,
Mr. Alfred Nutt quotes a translation from an early Irish
manuscript, in which it is told that once, in the form of white
birds, some of the denizens of the raths and the fairy palaces
of the loughs—the Sidhe in short—approached St. Patrick.
Flying to a lough, with flapping wings, they appeal to him to
make them Christians. 'O help of the Gael,' they cry, 'come,
and come hither!' Commenting on this legend, Mr. Nutt
remarks that it took the peculiar genius of the Celt to conceive this appeal, and to extend to the creatures of the
elements, and the dethroned divinities, the blessings of the
Faith. The white bird of Cilleen is akin to the birds of faery,
is, in fact, one of them. Note, too, the tale of the thorn tree.
Struck with iron its geni appears. Iron, in the conception of
the early northern races, had latent in it the power of magic.
The smith could cast spells. The steel sword as it superseded
the one of bronze was the 'sword of light.' Songs were made
to the weapon, and the swords of heroes had magical properties. The woman stolen by the Sidhe in the Irish song,
who, as she hushes the fairy child to sleep, appeals between
the refrain of the lullaby to a friend, requests that her husband
will bring a black-hafted knife when he comes to rescue her.
A steel needle stuck in the cap of a baby, in a tale told me by
an old woman, prevented the Sidhe from stealing the child.
Only to the stroke of the steel would the spirit respond who
inhabited the bush. All these tales are the dim echoes of a
forgotten mythology, interesting for that reason, throwing a
little light upon what the far-off, pagan forefathers of the

Gael believed. The breaking forth of a river where no river had been before, or of a lake or well, is also a very ancient conception. The Four Masters, copying from very ancient records, mention such occurrences. And these eruptions are not all legendary tales, for there is evidence of lakes having been formed near the historic period, Lough Neagh probably being made by some vast flood.

In nearly every holy well there is a sacred trout. It is immortal, or supposed to be such. In a way it is immortal, for the idea takes us far back, up twenty centuries and more, to the mystic salmon of Connla's Well. There by that Well grew nine hazel-trees whose crimson nuts were the nuts of knowledge. The bright hued shells held the visions of poets, the inspired thoughts of the world, the completed dream of the artificer. And as they dropped into the water, bubbles of brilliant red colour followed, and the salmon hearing the sound swam forward and ate them, acquiring thus all knowledge and wisdom, and perception of beauty, and creative power in literature and art. Then leaving the well, with the rich red spots of knowledge on their side, they went down the river; and to any man who could capture one was given of the divine gifts hidden within the nuts of the nine hazel-trees.

The presence of fish in the sacred wells of pre-Christian Ireland, the myth of the salmon of knowledge, must have been turned to account by the early saints. Our Lord, Tertullian says, was the heavenly ichthus, or fish, and we, His disciples, are the smaller fishes, who are born in the waters of baptism. 'The Irish saints,' writes Archbishop Healy in his sympathetic tract on the Holy Wells of Ireland, 'were no strangers to this beautiful symbolism.' And thus it may have seemed to many a missionary, as he penetrated into the centres of paganism, that the Lord's hand had been before him, and that in the fish to which mysterious powers were attributed, and in the wells sacred to some god of healing, he had symbols by which he could explain the inner truths of the Faith he had come to preach.

THE BUTTERFLY'S WEDDING

[A fairy phantasy, translated from *Uirsgeulan Gaidhealach* (Mackay, Stirling), a collection of Mòd prize compositions.]

LONG, long before your grandfather's time, when the world was young and the cocks spoke Greek, the butterfly thought that he would marry a wife. She must be fair as the primrose in the glens; stately as the fairy lady of the hills, and good at housewifery as the ant of the feal-dyke.

He told the fly; but she only crooked her nose and laughed. 'I'll walk up and down, I'll walk here and there,' said the butterfly, 'till I find my heart's desire.' 'The prayer of the seven grey goats go with you,' said the fly; 'the meeting of the seven foxes, and the blessing of the seven fairies be with you, till you find your heart's desire; I will take a little wink of sleep in a daisy's breast for a year and a day, and then I will expect to hear news of your wedding.'

So it was. The butterfly bound a circlet of gold on his left foot; he put three shining cowrie shells in the hollow of his thigh; he spread his speckled wings to the soft, warm wind of evening, and he set out. He set his back to the north and his face to the south, and for seven summer weeks he went without resting, over rivers, over fields, over ridges, over bens and glens and seas, till he came to the green isle, where sun does not set and moon rises not, and where never sound was heard but the sound of the sea and the note of the white swan that sits on a green hillock in its very centre. Seven weeks this swan sleeps without waking; but on the seventh Sabbath Day she wakes, and she utters three notes so sweet that the round world listens and the harper of the hills gives three groans of sorrow for envy. The butterfly reached the hill; he flew three times round the swan; he leaned against a grass blade; he put a cowrie under his head and slept. He dreamed that he was in a king's castle, where the house beams were of silk thread; the king's daughters danced on them, each with a tuft of sweet herbs in her bosom. He heard the sweetest music that ever ear heard or heart inspired, music to wake love, and banish fear; music that would wile milk from the yeld cattle. What was this but the song of the awakening swan. The swan raised a silver stalk in her beak, and at once a black cloud came over the face of the sun, and every grass blade on the island began to quiver. This was a flight of seashore birds, answering the note of the swan, and coming with food and drink to entertain the butterfly.

'Drink seven celled cups of honey; eat seven fat baps of bread; then tell the cause of your journey,' said the swan. The butterfly sneezed, and the swan frowned. 'If it please you, the oyster-catcher put snuff in the honey,' said the butterfly. The swan whistled and the oyster-catcher fell cold and dead. The meal ended, and talk began.

Said the butterfly: 'I am the bright son of the sky, and I go from the north lands to the south, seeking my heart's desire. She must be fair as the primrose in the glens; good at housewifery as the ant of the feal-dyke.' The swan said that she would sleep for the seven weeks till she should get the knowledge of the three worlds: the world whose beginning is memory, the world whose mid part is memory, and the world whose end is memory; then she would give him three signs whereby he would find his heart's desire.

So it was. The butterfly passed the time in bathing, and insulting the rainbow for that it had fewer colours than his wings. On the seventh Sabbath Day the swan awoke, and she uttered her cry ere a juggler could perform a feat. The butterfly was there, and he stood on one foot and made obeisance. The swan whistled. Instantly a stonechat came where they were. 'Here,' said the swan, 'you have the bird of sharpest eye and keenest ear in the bird world. He has got lore of the weather from the old man of the moon; knowledge of the earth from the old woman of night (the owl), and skill of the ocean from the maiden of the sea. He comes and none knows whence; he goes, and no man knows whither; he will be to you a guide to your heart's desire. You will fold your wings and sit on the stonechat's back till he lights on a bare grey flag that is before the cottage where lives your heart's desire. Three autumn weeks the stonechat will go in the nostril of the wind, over rivers, over fields, over ridges, over glens and bens and seas, till he comes to the bounds of the Land of Calm. The first Saturday thereafter you shall see five wonders, and then you will know that you are near to the flagstone that lies before the cottage where lives your heart's desire.'

Thus it was. The butterfly folded his glittering wings; he put three shining cowries of the shore in the hollow of his thigh; he sat on the stone-chat's back, and that bird flew away. The butterfly's head grew dizzy with the speed of the going. It was as swift as the hunter's arrow; swifter than the spring wind; nimble as the lightning. The stonechat sped eastwards. Three autumn weeks they spent so, without food or drink or weariness; and then they came to a loch of spring water in the midst of a wood. Such peace and quiet were over that loch that the bees that live in the stars could see their shadows in it. The butterfly knew that this was the Land of Calm. They alighted on a creek in the middle of the loch; they drank their fill of dew, and slept.

They awoke on the morning of the first Saturday, and no sooner were they awake than they saw a beetle making for the creek, sailing on a cabbage leaf, and steering with his foot. 'Do you see that?' said the stonechat. 'I see what I never saw before,' said the butterfly, 'one of the five wonders of the Land of Calm.' They went then to the wood, and, at a tree's root, they saw a cat shaving a calf-herd with a woollen thread. 'See you that?' said the stonechat. 'I see what I never saw: one of the five wonders of the Land of Calm,' said the butterfly. They climbed a tree, and they faced eastwards. 'What see you?' said the stonechat. 'I see two suns and two moons dancing a reel, and the stars clapping their hands,' said the butterfly. They descended, and they went on till they came to a green hill. When they came to it, the top rose off the hill, and there were gulls in grey breeches and tartan bonnets, schooling red bees. 'Another of the wonders of the Land of Calm,' said the butterfly. They were coming back to the creek when they saw a little deserted house at a rock's foot. They set an eye to the window, and *there* was a cock plaiting a straw rope with the spurs of one foot and playing a whistle with the other foot. He invited them in; he would play them the *Chickens' Lament* till food was ready. So it was. The cock gave them food and drink, music and conversation, and at the dusk of evening they left.

The stonechat set his face to the east and flew; with the speed of his going he would leave the swift spring wind far behind. In the mouth of lateness, he alighted on a smooth grey flag before a cottage, and the butterfly knew that this was the end of his journey. A fence of trees was round the house, with apples of gold growing on them; dew milk on the head of each small blade of grass. The windows of the cottage were like a mirror, and thrushes sang music on every bush. They went in; and sitting in a room they saw the maiden of golden-yellow locks, a maid mild as night, beautiful as the sun, faithful as the echo of the rocks.

'Welcome to the butterfly,' said the maiden; 'great is your travel, long your journey. I dreamed last night that you would come to-day.' The golden circlet that was on the butterfly's foot leaped on the maiden's arm; the cowries leaped and settled themselves in her bosom; and the butterfly knew that she was his heart's desire: he stood on one foot and saluted her and kissed her. The stonechat drank his fill of the breath of the skies; he set his back to the east and his face to the west; he left wind and storm-rain behind, and he sped over rivers, over fields, over bens and glens, to the green isle, to tell the swan of the butterfly's journey. The butterfly folded the maiden in his wings, and set his face for the daisy where he had left the fly asleep. The fly awoke; she looked on the maid of golden-yellow locks, and she crooked her nose again at the marvel of her beauty.

A wedding was made on a ragweed's top that lasted for a day and a year; every insect of the plain and every bird of the air was invited. The oyster-catcher got drunk and attacked the gulls; they screamed at the curlews. The peewit got drunk on snuff and assaulted the sea-swallows. The coots piped and the ants danced. When the wedding was over, the butterfly raised his wings, and he and his wife left for the cottage at the bounds of the Land of Calm. And if no lie was told me, they are there still.

BOOK REVIEWS

Clan Donald. By the Rev. A. MacDonald, Minister of Killearnan, and the Rev. A. MacDonald, Minister of Kiltarlity. Inverness: Northern Counties Publishing Co. 21s. *net.*

After the lapse of a long interval since the publication of volume ii., we are now able to welcome the appearance of the third volume of the history of Clan Donald. It is printed and bound in style uniform with the two preceding volumes.

This third book contains the history of the Sleat family, and that fittingly enough, when we consider the authors' theory of the chiefship set forth at length in their third chapter. There are many clansmen who will dissent from the view taken in this work as to the rightful chief of the Clan. Since the Clan has been divided, no chief of the name has led the whole Clan, and the question must therefore be settled on different premises from those admitted and approved by the authors of *Clan Donald*.

Without doubt this volume is the most interesting and the best of the three from an antiquarian point of view. It is the result of much and painstaking labour, and, as we know on good authority, years have been passed in collecting and arranging details of genealogies. The collection too is a successful one and many of the pedigrees contained therein appear in print for the first time. It is to be regretted that the authors had not at hand a more plentiful supply of dates; readers interested would moreover be glad to know the names of the wives of many of the individuals figuring in the genealogies.

One point that has struck us forcibly is what we may call the authors' penchant towards legitimating individuals who are generally considered not to have been born in wedlock. A case in point is that of Black John of Bohuntin. We are told (vol. iii. p. 425) that in the Charter Chest of Lord MacDonald there is an original document in which it is expressly stated that John was the 'third lawful son of Ranald MacDonald Glass of Keppoch.'

The authors preface the above by a statement, which, if correct, very materially detracts from the value of their work—'tradition has been found to have been invariably very wide of the mark when looked at in the light of authentic documentary evidence.' Had the reverend gentlemen kept this statement 'invariably' before their minds during the course of their work, much that is interesting would have had to be discarded, and we have no doubt that much that is authentic history, resting solely on tradition, would have had to be rejected, and as a natural consequence the three volumes would have been of considerably less bulky proportions. In the present case they have neglected to inform us as to the authority of this original document in Lord MacDonald's Charter Chest, neither have they given its date, and we may be excused if meanwhile we believe in the tradition which is still unquestioned in Lochaber and amongst all his descendants there, that Black John of Bohuntin was not only an illegitimate but also an adulterous son of Ranald Mor of Keppoch.

Again, in the instance of Donald Gallach, we are told on page 9, vol iii., that 'our entire information regarding him is based upon tradition,' but the bias in favour of legitimacy so characteristic of our authors has led them to write that Donald's father 'formed a matrimonial alliance' with the daughter of the Crowner of Caithness whilst on his return from a raiding expedition to the Orkneys. The authority for this statement, historical or traditionary, is the following : ' Austine (*i.e.* Hugh of Sleat) having halted at Caithness, he got a son by the Crowner of Caithness' daughter, of the name of Emma. . . . This son was called Donald Gallich, being brought up in that country in his younger years.'—*Collectanea de Rebus Alban.*, p. 307. The impartial reader may judge of the nature of that 'matrimonial alliance' in which the lady and son are not for years taken to the home of the child's father. The bearing of Hugh's only legitimate son towards his brothers is intelligible only when viewed in the light of his knowledge of their illegitimacy.

In their chapter on the Chiefship we consider that the authors of *Clan Donald* have slipped into a serious error on this same subject of legitimacy and its bearing on handfast marriages.

We are referred to vol. i. (p. 432). In that volume and in the present they appear to us to have misunderstood the relation of the Canon Law to the Civil Law of the time. Before the Reformation, as regards marriage, the Canon Law was the law of the land, and it is therefore absurd to say, as in vol. i., that a 'marriage became good in law without the imprimatur of the Church.' It is more so to assert, as in present volume (p. 163), that 'these marriages were not solemnised by the Church,' and yet that 'their offspring was regarded as legitimate by the Canon Law of the Church.' As Canon Law this is startling—the statements are self-contradictory. The Church never recognised handfast marriages, neither did she consider their offspring as legitimate.

We might point out that the fourth degree of kindred in the phraseology of Canonists is not fourth but third cousinship.

In a work which not only aims at being the last word on the subject but advances several novel theories the least one would look for would be a complete and careful reference to authorities that the student might be able to satisfy himself by referring to the works cited.

This blemish, whilst rendering disproof impossible, prevents the work becoming a standard authority. To cite merely one instance, in vol. ii. (p. 18), the authors congratulate themselves on discovering that Christina Nic Ruari was Countess of Mar and mother-in-law of Bruce. No authority of any kind is quoted in support of this statement. Something more than the mere dictum of the reverend authors is required to convince the sceptic.

The historical argument is also seriously impaired for the general reader by the neglect to render into English, Gaelic quotations, many of which are beyond the ability of all but accomplished Gaelic scholars to translate : *e.g.* vol. iii., p. 572—

> 'Bha mi eolach a' d' thalla
> 'S bha mi steach ann a' d' sheomar.'

conveys nothing to the mere English reader.

In the matter of indices our authors seem to be of one mind with Dean

Swift who regarded them as an Hebraical method of reading books, beginning where others usually leave off—a compendious way of coming to an
acquaintance with an author—in which the writer is used like a lobster, the
best meat being looked for in the tail and the body placed on the dish. But
the twentieth century student will have his way, and the lack of a good
index is a serious defect.

In conclusion we may congratulate our learned authors on the valuable
material they have brought together, more particularly for the wealth
of genealogical information in the third volume, and whilst thanking them
for their efforts, we trust that the day is not far distant when a new edition
will have discarded these, and other defects.   'CREAG AN FHITHICH.'

Y Cymmrodor, Vol. xviii.   London, 1905.

The valuable Magazine of the Honourable Society of Cymmrodorion has
printed many able and learned papers illustrative of the History, Literature,
and Antiquities of Wales.   This latest volume of the Society consists of
nearly two hundred pages, and is wholly taken up with one article, than
which none of its predecessors is more interesting to Welsh, and especially
to Gaelic, scholars.   It is a searching inquiry by Principal Rhŷs into the
origin of the Welsh Englyn and kindred metres, among which the *Retoric* or
'Run' of Old Gaelic Tales is included.   Some seventy years ago a Welsh
scholar, the Rev. Rice Rees, observed that an old Latin inscription found in
Carmarthenshire was in verse, and could, without much difficulty, be written
out in two hexameters.   The inscription reads :—

Seruatur fidæi	His faith he kept,
Patrieq(ue) semper	He loved his country well—
Amator hic Paulin	Here, mindful of the right,
us jacit cultor pienti	Does Paulinus dwell.
Simus æqui	

In literary Latin, the inscription would run :—

Servator fidei, patriæque semper amator,
Hic Paulinus jacet, cultor pie(n)tissimus æqui.

And keeping in view the Celt's substitution of stress for quantity in verse,
the lines would scan as follows :—

Servátor | fídei | patri | æque | sémper a | mátor
Híc Pau | línus | jacet | cúltor p(i)en | tíssimus | æqui

Principal Rhŷs has examined the old inscriptions of South Britain, and
has found a large number of them capable of being read in lines of verse-
hexameters, full or curtailed, pentameters, etc.   The South Britains, by
long contact with Roman civilisation, acquired a knowledge of Latin verse-
structure.   They assimilated the knowledge, and adapted it to suit the
genius of their own tongue.   Roman verse, borrowed from the Greeks, was
based upon the *quantity* of the syllable, long or short.   To what extent it

preserved the purity of classical times by the time it passed to the Celt is a
moot point. But by the latter it was modified in an essential degree. The
Celt made the stress of the syllable, not the quantity of it, the dominating
feature of the line. The Gael, who did not come directly in contact with
the Roman, probably acquired his knowledge of Latin verse from the
Briton. Anyhow, he modified it in the same way. Accordingly, we find
the old hymns written in Latin by the Gaelic missionaries abounding in
what, from a classical standpoint, would be a great disregard of quantity.
Principal Rhŷs's view is that both Briton and Gael adopted the Latin
metres, thus modified, and wrote their early poetry which now survives in
Englyn and *Retoric* upon this model. In adjusting the inscription, or the
old stanza, so as to make it read as a modified hexameter or pentameter
line, a considerable amount of manipulating and conjecture is necessary.
The writings are very old, and the readings too frequently very uncertain.
But there is a sufficient body of fairly reliable material to make the theory,
if not mathematically demonstrable, as probable as it is undoubtedly
original. Here, for example, is a specimen of how a Gaelic *retoric* is
treated. Professor Windisch printed from *The Book of the Dun* (Cow) a
short fairy tale as a suitable reading lesson in his *Kurzgefasste Irische
Grammatik* (Leipzig, 1879). It is entitled *Ectra Condla Chaim maic Chuind
Chetchathaig.* Condla was one day with his father Conn, from whom the
Macdonalds claim descent, in Upper Uisnech, when a brilliant lady from
Faëry appeared and invited Condla to Mag Mell, 'plain of delight.' No
one saw the lady but Condla. His father asks whom he is speaking to,
and the lady replies as follows:—*Adgladadar mnái n-óic n-álaind socheneóil,
nad fresci bas na sentaid. Ro charus Condla Ruád, cotngairim do Maig Mell,
inid rí Boadag bidsuthain, rí cen gol cen mairg inna thír ó gabais flaith.* 'He
speaks to a young woman, fair, of high descent, who is not subject to death
or old age. I have loved Condla the Red; I invite you to Fairyland, where
reigns Boadach the ever-living, a King without wail or woe in his land, since
he began to rule.' Professor Windisch, more than twenty years ago, saw
that the above and similar passages in this tale and elsewhere were constructed in some kind of verse, and wrote out one or two of them in two
contributions to the *Revue Celtique* (vol. v. pp. 389-91 ; 478-9). Here is the
arrangement of this *Retoric* by Principal Rhŷs :—

Adglad | adar | mnái n-óic | n-alaind | socheneóil ||	11 syllables.
nad fresci | bás na sent | aid ||	7 ,,
Ro charus | Condla | Ruád cot | ngairim do | Maig Mell ||	12 ,,
Inid rí | Bóadag bid | suthain rí | cen gol | cen mairg ||	13 ,,
inna thír | ó gabais | flaith ||	7 ,,

that is to say, the 'strophe consists of three curtailed hexameters and two
half-pentameters.' It would be a most interesting study to examine St.
Patrick's Hymn and the principal *Retorics* or 'Runs' of Gaelic Sagas as
preserved in the old MSS. and recovered from reciters, with the view to
ascertain how far they could be written out in lines modelled upon Latin

versification.   In any view of it, Principal Rhŷs's contribution to the elucidation of an obscure subject is of the utmost importance.

DON. MACKINNON.

The Mabinogion : Mediæval Welsh Romances.   Translated by LADY CHARLOTTE GUEST. With Notes by ALFRED NUTT. London: David Nutt, 1904. *Fcap. 8vo*, pp. xi, 384. *Price 2s. 6d. cloth*; *3s. 6d. leather*.

We are delighted that the enterprise of Mr. Nutt in issuing at a low price a convenient and handsome thin-paper edition of the *Mabinogion*, has been so far appreciated that a new edition has been called for within two years and a half.   Lady Guest's translation is too well established to need any introduction; and this reissue is substantially her rendering with the necessary minimal alterations merely, and the addition of learned notes by Mr. Alfred Nutt, and, now, of a list of some of the personal and place names with English meanings—occasionally more ingenious than successful, but that only where success seems barely possible—and elucidations by Mr. Ivor B. John.   The little volume makes delightful reading, even for those who cannot read the original; but however great its charm may be, that of the original Welsh is far greater.   The language of the original is terse, and each word seems to have a living sense of responsibility for its own being in entire harmony with all its comrades; and the story is in every case compressed into the smallest possible number of words, throbbing with a latent rhythm as they march on, while its colloquies are the most idiomatic conceivable.   Far more terse is the Welsh of the *Mabinogion* than that which, under the influence of Welsh *littérateurs* and the more recent recrudescence of pre-Aryan idiom, is now written as literary Welsh.   Lady Guest's rendering, though itself terse and compact, is necessarily somewhat diluted as compared with the original : and we confess that we do not share Mr. Alfred Nutt's apparent hesitation as to whether he might not have made use of M. Loth's translation into French, for that is still more smoothed out and in that way more remote from the spirit of the original.   We are satisfied that, for English readers, Mr. Nutt has done well in adhering to Lady Guest's rendering.   'EIDDIN.'

Revue Celtique.   Paris: Bouillon.   20 *francs* per annum.

In the July number of the *Revue Celtique* the learned editor writes on the interesting subject of Celtic gods in the forms of animals.   Such a god was the famous bull which caused the Tain Bo Chuailgne and other bulls of ancient Gaelic story.   These animals M. d'Arbois de Jubainville shows to have been connected with similar continental gods, and also with personal surnames as, for instance, MacMahon, O'Mahony (and he might have added Matheson) from the bear.   No less than six god animals are instanced.

M. Victor Tourneur continues the Mystery of Ss. Crépin and Crépinien.

The larger part of the number is occupied by Cornish Studies by

Professor Loth, one of the few authorities on that ancient form of Celtic. Reviews of books and magazines form a special feature of the *Revue*.

Leoithne Andeas. By TADHG O'DONNCHADHA.   Dublin: Gill and Son, 1s. 6d. net.

This is a collection of poems by a young Irish poet who also writes under the pseudonym of *Tórna*, and who a year ago had the distinction of composing the Ode for the Oireachtas.   Some of the poems here given are of great merit and read very beautifully.   Perhaps some of the laments are among the best work in the book, but the patriotic poems also show power. Mr. O'Donoghue has tried, very successfully, experiments with some of the old Gaelic metres, and an interesting preface to his book gives some explanation of the metres used and also some notes for the reading of Irish verse.   The reading of verse in any language is an art very insufficiently understood, and comparatively few people realise the full beauty of the sounds used or the labour which a true poet expends in getting harmonious and musical effects. This little book is published under the auspices of the Society for the Preservation of the Irish Language.

An Bhoramha Laighean (The Leinster Tribute).   By T. O. RUSSELL.   Dublin: Gill and Son.   1s. net.

This ancient tract has been put into modern Irish Gaelic by Mr. T. O. Russell in an excellent manner.

Dr. Whitley Stokes has already translated it into English (*Revue Celtique*, 1892).   He calls it a mediæval historical romance, and says that as such it takes high rank.   Describing various incidents, he continues, 'Surely the man who wrote these passages had a poet's eye as well as a poet's power of expression.'   Mr. Russell does not seem to have taken aught from the beauty of the original, and, by putting it into modern Gaelic, he has brought it within the reach of many admirers whose time or talents do not admit of their studying the original.   He has done, in fact, what successive generations of seanchies always did for the folk-tales which were in current recital by the peat-fires, for they modernised them just sufficiently to bring them within the understanding of their hearers without taking away the archaic feeling.   A preface, appendix, and notes supply much interesting information which will help the reader to a better appreciation of the story.

The Colloquy of the Two Sages.   By WHITLEY STOKES, D.C.L.   Paris: Bouillon.   3 *francs*.

Dr. Whitley Stokes has provided for us a translation of this interesting dialogue—with which he also gives the Gaelic text—based on the three oldest copies.   The translator places the date of the composition about the tenth century, but says it can only with certainty be said to have been composed *after* the vikings, 'the men of the black spears,' 'the fair stammerers,' had commenced their raids, and *before* the compilation of the *Senchus Mor*. If we are not mistaken the translation has already appeared in the *Revue Celtique*, but it is well to have it in this more convenient form. The colloquy is in regard to the chief poetship of Ulster and the wearing of the robe and holding of the privileges of the office. These on the death of Adnae in the time of Conchobar Mac Nessa had been bestowed on Ferchertne. This was told by a sea wave to Nede the young son of Adnae, who was studying in Scotland under Eochu Echbél, and he sets out for Emain to claim his father's place. Instigated by Bricriu the ever zealous for evil, he put on the poet's robe and seated himself in the poet's chair in the absence of Ferchertne. On the return of the latter the conversation takes place, and if obscure and difficult to understand in many points is full of interest and of valuable side-lights.

It is difficult to follow the meaning of the sages in many cases, but there are suggestions of hidden depths which might repay investigation. To understand it thoroughly it is necessary to know the social state of the Ireland of the time as well as something of its political conditions. The colloquy ends by Nede acknowledging Ferchertne's greatness as a poet and prophet, and kneeling to him he calls him his father—a thoroughly manly giving up of his own claims to the chief poet's office.

A vocabulary and numerous notes add to the value of this careful rendering by our father of Celtic scholars.

Caledonian Medical Journal. Glasgow: Macdougall, 68 Mitchell Street. 1s.

All Scottish medical men and especially all Highland medical men, resident in Scotland or furth of it, ought to be members of the society which issues this excellent journal. By joining it they will be shoulder to shoulder with their Scottish brethren and will enjoy much good fellowship, but above all they will have the pleasure of helping in the publication of much interesting lore, and perhaps a larger membership would induce the society to prepare and publish some of the Gaelic Medical MSS. in the Advocates' Library and elsewhere, of which Dr. George Mackay gave such an interesting account last year, and one of which was more particularly described some two or three years ago by Dr. Cameron Gillies. This is work essentially for such a society.

The non-member can procure the numbers of this magazine for 1s. a copy, and besides such MS. work as is mentioned above he will find fascinating papers on old Highland cures, second-sight, and other special subjects appearing from time to time. In general, perhaps the layman should not read the purely medical articles—as he may fancy himself possessed of every ailment mentioned!—but every number contains some articles of general interest. A specially interesting one of this kind in the current number is 'Early Scandinavian or Gothic Influences in Caledonia,' by W. Stewart, M.D., the year's president.

An Deo-Ghreine.   Stirling: Mackay.   3*d. monthly.*

This is the magazine of An Comunn Gaidhealach, and is intended to further the objects of the society.   That it is under the editorship of Mr. Malcolm Macfarlane augurs well for its usefulness.   No one with· any knowledge of the working of the Comunn will disagree with us when we say that, during the years of the existence of the society, no member has done so much steady and solid work for it as Mr. Macfarlane.

The present is an introductory number and contains articles in Gaelic and English, several of them of much interest.   We would especially mention that by Mr. Donald Mackechnie.   Future numbers will doubtless deal in a practical manner with the objects which the Comunn has in view, and especially with Gaelic propaganda and how to work it.   The main aim must be to get at the Highland people.   It is earnestly to be hoped that the Comunn Gaidhealach will be supported in this new attempt, and that a fair chance will be given to *An Deo-Ghreine.*   If we took our language seriously there would be no doubt as to the future of this little magazine, but unfortunately many of us are only half-hearted.   The Mòd in Dingwall has stirred the north, however, and perhaps our race will not much longer be describable as ' An Fheinn air a h-uilinn.'   A. MACDONALD.

Guide to Gaelic Conversation and Pronunciation.   By L. MACBEAN.   Stirling:
            Mackay.   1*s.* 6*d. net.*

The fact that this book has gone to a second edition shows that it is proving a help to those for whom it is intended.   It is so comprehensive in its subjects, sentences, and idioms that it cannot but be useful whether the learner regards it merely as a means of getting up sentences, or as a help to a fuller knowledge and a supplement to grammar and dictionary, or to Gaelic acquired by the *viva voce* method.

NOTES

Notes on the Study of Gaelic :—*continued*—First Year's Course

I assume that the aim of a first year's course is to enable the Gaelic-speaking pupil (*a*) to read Gaelic; (*b*) to understand and apply the principles of spelling; (*c*) to know the outlines of Gaelic grammar.

Reading and spelling go closely together.   It will save much trouble if, not only in the first lessons, but throughout the whole course, continuous attention is directed to the value of the vowels and consonants, and their combinations.   This lies at the root of both reading and spelling: once the functions of the letters are understood, there will be comparatively little difficulty.   Further, it will be found that even young children can be interested in the part played by lips, tongue, teeth, and palate in the production of sounds, and if some attention is paid to this from the beginning, it will prove at once an assistance and a practical training in phonetics.

A beginning may be made with blackboard examples, preferably mono-syllables, to illustrate the vowel sounds : e.g. *cas, càs; le, glé, gnè; mir, mìr; tog, òg, bó; cur, cùram.* Diphthongs and triphthongs may be held over, until the representation of the simple vowel sounds becomes familiar. The study of the sounds will, of course, be accompanied by (*a*) pronunciation of further written examples, (*b*) writing of dictated examples. A similar method may be followed with the consonants, mutable and immutable. The 'broad' and the 'slender' (or *palatalised*) values of the mutable con-sonants (*c, d, g, l, n, r, s, t*), will require much illustration : e.g. càch, cioch ; dàn, dé, etc. Specially important is the differentiation of *c, g; t, d; b, p* : e.g. ma*c*, ma*g*; i*t*e, i*d*ir ; lea*p*a, lea*b*aidh. In all these cases the difference is that *c, t, p* are accompanied by a 'puff' or *h*-sound preceding; *g, d, b,* are not. Note also ma*rc*, ma*rg*, ma*rag*. The only *double* consonants in Gaelic are the double liquids *ll, nn, rr,* and these require special attention. Inter-vocalic *ll* is hardly distinguishable from *l*; *cf.* ba*l*ach, a lad, and ba*ll*ach, spotted. Sometimes the only guide is the derivation : e.g. *toll,* a hole ; *Tollaidh,* a hollow place, which, so far as sound goes, might be written To*l*aidh. The others *nn* and *rr* are easier.

After some experience of monosyllables may be introduced the funda-mental rule of Gaelic spelling, *Leathan ri leathan, agus caol ri caol,* 'broad to broad, and narrow to narrow'; or, otherwise, broad consonants must be in direct contact with broad vowels, slender consonants with slender vowels. The famous rule is scientific and intelligible only in the case of the eight *mutable* consonants, with the aspirates *ch, dh, gh.* Here it conveniently marks the distinction of broad and slender consonantal sounds. In the case of the *immutable* consonants (*b, f, m, p*), which admit of no such distinction, the rule is adopted only for the sake of uniformity. Thus *leabaidh* might be spelled *lebidh,* without violence to the pronunciation. It is as well to understand at once that the rule is partly scientific, partly conventional. Its application to words of more than one syllable necessitates some explana-tion of the convoy vowels, clearly set forth by Dr. A. Macbain and Mr. John Whyte in *How to Learn Gaelic,* to which this reference must suffice. Further details of spelling, e.g. the use (not always philologically justifiable) of *th* to separate syllables, may be left to the teacher. It is not necessary or desirable that reading or even composition of simple sentences should be deferred until all these principles are understood : reading, writing, and theory had better go on simultaneously. After some progress has been made, it would be useful to exhibit a chart of the principal sounds, for pur-poses of reference and revision. The pupils might write out examples in illustration.

Gaelic-speaking pupils, or, for that matter, pupils who do not speak Gaelic, can be taught to read Gaelic in a month. There will, however, remain much to be done in respect of (*a*) articulation, (*b*) dialectic varieties, (*c*) expression.

(*a*) Clear and distinct articulation is of the utmost importance. Slurring and indistinctness are the natural enemies of correct spelling; conversely, spelling is immensely helped by proper articulation. This is a principle that holds good for all languages, not least for Gaelic. Some dialects are much more deliberate in enunciation than others : in Kintail, for instance, one can almost time the long vowels by the watch. Perhaps the *Tàileach* over-does it, but the fault is on the right side.

(*b*) It is desirable that in reading—still more in spelling, except for special purposes—dialectic variations should give way to the literary or classical form as represented by the generally accepted spelling. Some such varieties, indeed, are so widespread and so fixed that it is perhaps as well, in reading at least, simply to accept them. It would be hopeless, for instance, to convert the northern Highlander to the orthodox Argyll pro-nunciation of *ao* as in *laogh, taobh*. He will also persist in saying *Tigheirn* for *Tighearna* (the latter to him savours of irreverence), and *feairn* for *fearna*. The widespread diphthongising of *eu* into *ia*, e.g. *feur* into *fiar*, has better claims to recognition in spelling, but even here it is probably better to accept the standard classical form, especially in view of the oblique cases *feòir*, etc. But there can be no manner of doubt as to the incorrectness of -*adh* pronounced as -*ag*; *each* made into *yach*; *duine* into *duinne*; *feusag* into *feòsag*, or the Strathspey *mèur* for *màthair*. All such are intolerable both in reading and spelling. Lists of such as occur in the local dialect should be drawn up and kept for practice.

(*c*) Gaelic reading, like English, is apt to be monotonous. One good corrective is recitation of poetry or prose stories, with proper expression.

Certain common mis-spellings are worth noting at this early stage. The following should have *g* not *d* : *dirigh, deagh, éirigh* (the noun), *sluagh, briagh, laigh*. On the other hand *éiridh* (future tense), and *deidh* require *d*. In point of sound *gh* and *dh* are identical, but the above forms are philo-logically correct. So also are *giuthas, abhainn*.

Exceptions to the rule of 'broad to broad,' etc., are *tigh, so, sud, is* (verb and conjunction).

For grammar, it should suffice for the first year to master the article, noun, and adjective singly and in combination, and *written* composition might well be restricted to this. The power of expression is best developed at this stage by *oral* accounts of what was done or seen on such a day, and such like simple exercises involving observation and description. Idioms and phrases from both languages should be specially attended to.

For beginners in reading no better book can be found than the Gaelic Bible, which might be supplemented by the extracts given in *How to Read Gaelic*. For simple exercises from English into Gaelic Mr. L. Macbean's *Lessons in Gaelic* will be found useful; but in any case the teacher must construct exercises of English into Gaelic from the Gaelic prose pieces read.   W. J. WATSON.

The Distribution of British Ability

Looking through some old numbers of the *Monthly Review* a few weeks ago, my attention was attracted to an article under the above heading. Readers may be interested by a few notes drawn from it, as tending to show how the increased obtrusiveness of the Celtic personality is continuously bringing out fresh evidence from the other side, and how new Anglo-Saxon warriors stand up to battle.

The writer of the article, Mr. Havelock Ellis, is a fair and liberal-minded man enough, but quite satisfied that England's superiority is as great where genius is concerned as it certainly is when it is a question of revenue and resources.

It is often loosely stated that to the Celtic element Great Britain as a whole owes much of her greatness, and I have wondered by what chain of evidence the Celtic enthusiast has arrived at this conclusion. It may not be unprofitable to learn how the other side works out the opposite case.

Mr. Havelock Ellis introduces his subject thus:—'In studying the characteristics of British genius, the first and most elementary question we have to settle is the distribution of British ability in the various parts of the United Kingdom. It is desirable to determine what proportion of British genius is produced respectively by England, Scotland, Ireland, and Wales. In so doing it is obvious that we shall not have classified our British men of genius strictly according to race, we shall not even have determined precisely the contribution of the so-called "Celtic" element to British genius, but we shall have taken an important and interesting first step. This is the question which, in the course of a somewhat elaborate study of the characteristics of British men of genius founded mainly on the *Dictionary of National Biography*, I have made an attempt to answer. I find that among 30,000 individuals included in the *Dictionary* 902 stand out as of pre-eminent ability.'

First let us ask. Is there not an anomaly in talking of the 'contribution' of the so-called '*Celtic*' element to '*British*' genius? Latter-day ethnology rather points to it that the Britains *were* Celts, and that the British survive in the Welsh of to-day. Secondly, why are we to accept Mr. Havelock Ellis's choice of 902 out of 30,000, and the 2 makes us feel there was no particular reason why the enumerator stopped short just then. Why not pause at 900?

There is something very Teutonic in this soul-surrender to a Dictionary—this boiling down of the nation's heritage of genius to 902.

After writing as above our essayist seems to have been struck with the idea that perhaps his selection might not be accepted unknown, and adds in a note, 'It would be tedious to explain here the principal of selection by which these 902 were obtained,' but refers us to a series of articles then appearing in the *Popular Science Journal*. He goes on to show the best way of determining place of origin is not to note place of birth, but by considering the districts to which the subject's *four* grandparents belong. In only a very small proportion of cases has he been able to determine the origins of all four grandparents, and has considered himself fortunate when able to tell where *father and mother came from.* Often, even in his desire to allot his geniuses to different counties, he has had to be content with merely finding out where the father came from. What does this prove as to the Celtic or Saxon origin of British genius? How does the plan of leaving the four grandparents outwork?

Supposing a Scottish servant, bearing the commonest name in Scotland—Smith—accompanied his master's daughter south on her marriage to an English squire, and on being settled in employment in Hampshire he sent for and married his Scottish sweetheart—Margaret Millar—would their son, James Smith, born in the New Forest, be an Englishman because Mr. Ellis failed to find out from their very ordinary names that John and Margaret, his parents, were from Scotland. Supposing James Smith to get a good education, and going into the county town became a clerk, worked his way up married an English girl, Sophia Barker, and fathered a genius of the name of William Smith, would that genius go to the English credit? William Smith, philosopher or scientist, would figure in the Dictionary as the son of James Smith, notary's clerk, of Winchester, and Sophia Barker of Alton, born at Winchester, but father James's sonship to John Smith from Scotland would not appear, and more than likely if we only knew John's father was Alasdair MacGow from beyont the Highland line. But this is a very supposititious case; let us invent another.

Suppose Carroll were the name of some brilliant painter who, rising to fame, would be included in some future National Biography, with or without an R.A. to his name. His birthplace would be given as Cheltenham, his father an Indian officer born in Yorkshire, where his father was a clergyman. The clergyman himself would be found born in London, the son of a famous Dr. Carroll. A good, clear English pedigree, and Mr. Ellis, in all probability, would not feel bound to make further inquiries after the doctor—great-grandfather of the painter. But the painter might hold clear documentary proof that Dr. Carroll was the lineal representative of the Ely O'Carrolls of the King's county, none the less genuine because in his youth Dr. Carroll left Ireland to work under the English husband of his only sister, and through his advice dropped his distinguishing O', because in early nineteenth century days people mistrusted O's and Macs. I have written a pure romance, but will add a third.

The name of Price is above a London shop. Let us imagine a Price in Lancashire whose son became a famous mechanician and inventor—world-wide enough to be included in the fame-branding Dictionary. Price, the inventor, was born at Wigan—like his father before him—but the grandfather's birthplace is unknown to the Dictionary. Local information and the tell-tale P would send a broader minded student over the Welsh border, and, in some obscure mountain village, tradition would tell how young Hugh ap Rice went away in search of work with his Welsh wife and child, and that in Wigan the second son was born and became the father of the famous inventor, but the elder came back and lived and died among old Hugh's people, and so connected the younger with his real place of origin.

I cannot point to any celebrities called Smith, Carroll, and Price. To the average Englishman the possessors of those names would be written down English, but the Celts are not the children of two generations, so they absolutely refuse to be judged by the place of birth of two generations. They go out into far lands and remain Celts. Where would Mr. Ellis place the Glenaladale McDonalds, a hundred years on Prince Edward's Islands?

Let us study Mr. Ellis's exact figures. For some reason he does not analyse the original 902 eminent persons—they have shrunk to 779. 'Speaking generally, it is found that 598 eminent British men and women are English, 117 Scotch, 41 Irish, and 23 Welsh—that is 78·8 per cent. English, 15·3 Scotch, 5·3 Irish, and 2·9 Welsh.' If we are allowed to take up a Pan-Celtic attitude we see 181 Celts as against 598 Anglo-Saxons, not quite a fourth, not so bad a proportion. Viewed as three separate units, the figures afford Mr. Ellis vast satisfaction. 'The preponderance of the English contingent is enormous, but if we take the present population as a basis, it is a reasonably fair distribution, a very slight excess over the first proportion being accountable by the *greater advantages necessarily enjoyed by the English*.' The italics are mine, and every Scotsman will rise up and refute the statement that the English enjoy greater advantages than themselves. Up to thirty years ago the percentage of illiterates was lower in Scotland than in England, her high schools and her universities are second to none. Lowland and Highland have loved learning for its own sake, and before secondary education or continuation classes were thought of, Scottish farm lads attended winter classes round some cottar's fire.

Coming to Wales, Mr. Ellis allows the proportion to be fair, though below what it should be, and for this he accounts according to his own ideas. 'We have to bear in mind the difficulty of a language not recognised as a medium of civilisation. As regards Scotland and Ireland the discrepancy is marked, the contribution of Scotland is much too large, that of Ireland much too small, in relation to the population. We probably have to recognise that intellectual aptitudes are especially marked among the Scotch, and also that the tendency has been fostered by circumstances since, *as is well known*, the lowland Scotch are almost identical in racial composition with the northern English, and there is no *artificial* barriers of language.'

Of what race were the northern English? How sure Mr. Ellis is that it is to English blood and Lowland strength old Scotland owes any little superiority he may allow her. Let him read in the January number of the *Celtic Review* Mr. Ferguson's statement of a clear case against a Teutonic absorption of the Celt in southern Scotland, maintaining there is no record of permanent successful invasion by the Angles of Northumbria, and only a peaceful settlement of Norman barons.

The Celtic Revival has evidently reached Mr. Ellis, but he cannot yet imagine a native language may be an education in itself, that a country may be busy producing native-speaking genius who find no place in his Dictionary or amongst the magic 902.

Listen to his dictum on Ireland:—'The Irish have been seriously hampered by geographical, and to some extent by linguistic, barriers, as well as by unfortunate political circumstances, in contributing their due share to British civilisation.' How do you define British civilisation? I think it is what has made life dull, ugly, commercial, utilitarian; it is what has robbed us of our youth, has clipped the wings of our minds. Perhaps Ireland of the future will be able to teach British civilisation to learn again what it had forgotten—that beauty is the soul of the world.

Wales and the Welsh border are allowed to have produced many soldiers and divines, *to a slight extent*, poets and musicians. The native article is, of course, tabooed. Scotland stands at the head as regards soldiers, a third going to her account, whilst a fourth of the British philosophers, and a fourth of the men of science are credited to her, and nearly all the great travellers, explorers, and adventurers.

Ireland is allowed to have produced more than her share of soldiers, and a very large proportion of British actors and actresses.

Mr. Ellis adds in a kindly spirit:—'The genius of Ireland is a curiously paradoxical subject, and requires a study in itself. Though so many great men have been associated with Ireland, when we analyse them according to race, we find that a remarkably large proportion of them are of English or Scottish descent. Bishop Berkeley, for instance, is often called an Irishman, yet always considered himself an Englishman. The great Irish patriots have *usually* had English blood in their veins, and have sometimes even been proud of the fact. And yet while this is so Ireland has *somehow* had the art of imparting some of her subtlest qualities to those happy Englishmen who have had the good fortune to possess some slight strain of her blood, or be born in her land, or even lived there in youth. The contribution of Ireland to our national genius cannot well be stated in numerical values.'

Here again a native greatness, great for Ireland and in Ireland, does not commend itself to Mr. Ellis. He would not include the O'Clerys, Keating, O'Sullivan Beare, Mangan, or Sir S. Ferguson, but to Ireland they are great. The average Irishman would surrender Bishop Berkeley, in spite of his wise observations in the *Querist*, without a pang, and the great Irish patriots who usually had English blood in their veins more often forgot it than remembered and were proud.

Once more we see the Celt excelling in the lighter, chivalrous side of life—leaders of men, seekers of adventure, imaginative dissemblers on the stage of life. Our article-writer, however, sees but a proof that when conducted on a broad and impartial basis 'a survey of the racial elements of genius effectually puts out of court those who contend that the intellectual

ability of Great Britain belongs exclusively, or even in some disproportion-
ately high degree, to one racial element only.' Certain words of Matthew
Arnold's might be so interpreted, but the Celts themselves do not arrogate
any such position. They only seek to prove by every means in their power
that they are still a living people with a living language, which has a right
to live and shall live, and knowing that if their various peoples gather
together and act in unity, they constitute a formidable and intellectual
nationality from which great things may yet arise.

LOUISA E. FARQUHARSON.

An Undetected Norse Loan-Word

It is the Gaelic *pràmh,* as thus used :—

1. Am bheil ann ach *bruaillean pràmh,*
   A's lionn-dubh mnà, a Dheirdire.

Deirdire, ed. A. Carmichael, 1905, p. 68,

and rendered therein :—

It is but the *disturbance of sleep,*
And woman's melancholy, O Deirdire !

2. 'Nuair labhradh e *pràmhail*
   Bu chràiteach mo chridhe 'm chorp.

Sàr-Obair, ed. J. Mackenzie, p. 382,

where the reference is on the part of a young maid to the depressed
mental state of an old man.

3. Gur e a mheudaich dhomh am *pràmh*
   'S a dh' fhàg mo chadal luaineach.

Oranaiche, ed. Sinclair, p. 7.

4. 'S nuair a ghabh mi'n sin fadachd
   Chaidh mi'n leabaidh *fo pràmh* (*sic*).

Ibid. p. 255.

5. 'Nuair a thug thu do chùl rium
   Shil mo shùilean gu làr,
   Cha'n eil stàth dhomh bhi'g innseadh
   Gu'm bheil m'inntinn *fo phràmh.*

Ibid.

6. Mar shionnach nam fuar-bheann fo phràmh.
   'S mo smuaintean gu truagh dhomh.

Ibid. p. 229.

7. Bu tu mo chiad leannan gun aithne do chàch,
S mi nise fo phràmh ga d'iunndrainn.

Ibid. p. 44.

8. Cha chreideadh tu'n còmhradh nam b'eòl dhuit a mheud
Sa tha do chion-falaich air m'aigne gach là,
S mo spiorad fo phramh 'ga ghiulan.

Ibid. p. 45.

9. priam a chadail.

Dain Iain Ghobha, stanza lxvi., of the poem *An*

Duin' òg 's an seann-duine ;

here *priam* has assonance with *nial.*

10. prèamh at Blair in Athole (Rev. C. M. Robertson).

11. tha a' ghrìan fo phràmh = the sun is eclipsed (phrase).

12. cnàmh-chadail, a slumber, a doze; also craimh-chadail,
cf. pràmh-chadail (Rev. C. M. Robertson, vol. 24, *Trans.
Gael. Soc. Inv.,* p. 356).

But consider here :—cnàmhuin, 'gangrene'; E. Ir. cnám,
'gnawing,' cnamhanach, 'fretting,' or malignant leprosy.
Leviticus, xiii. 51.
cnàmhag theine, 'embers.'

The native Gaelic *cnám,* in sense of 'decay, waste away,' may have led
to some confusion. But the vocalic variants *è, ia, ā,* point to the Norse
kröm, f. gen. *kramar,* a pining, wasting sickness. The verb is *kremja,*
preterite, *kramdi* (M. H. Ger. *krimme*), to squeeze, bruise ; reflex. *to pinch,
to pine,* from a wasting sickness. The primary sense of *pràmh* is that
of *spiritual* or *mental pining, heart-languishing ;* the secondary sense is the
disturbance of sleep which arises therefrom.

The variations in the Gaelic vowels, *priam, prèamh, pràmh,* arise from the
Norse variants, *ö, a, e.* If we start from the Gaelic *fo chnàmh,* it is interesting to recollect the Irish pronunciation of *ch* as *f,* e.g. in the neighbourhood
of Roscommon, as *fuaidh* for *chuaidh,* 'went.' But I do not recollect to
have seen this word in Irish Gaelic. In Scotland *ch* passes readily into
h in such a combination. Recollect also that MacAlpine writes, for Islay,
lŏch-cha, i.e. *leotha,* 'with them.' In the phrase *fo chràmh,* sounded in
quick speech as *fo ʰràmh,* it would, in any case, conduce to ease of pronunciation to introduce the digamma *f,* giving *fo fràmh,* written *phràmh,*
which when 'de-aspirated,' gave *pràmh;* cf. *fosgail,* 'open,' for *osgail;
fradharc,* 'sight,' for *radharc.*

The word is Norse, and still retains its primary sense of 'a pining,
wasting sickness,' especially of heart, mind, and feeling. And in the
light of the introduction of the prosthetic *f,* and of de-aspiration, *pràmh* need
not be classed among the 'few instances of the correspondence of *c* to *p* ';

the original Norse had a *k* sound, and through regular sound changes it has become *pràmh* in Gaelic, with the form *cnàmh*, reminiscent of its original Norse form, and strengthened by the influence of the native *cnàmh*. I agree with Mr. Robertson when he says in his excellent paper on the 'Variations of Gaelic Loan-Words,' that the different forms of this word suggest borrowing. GEORGE HENDERSON.

Fragments relating to the Saxon Invasion from an unknown Canterbury chronicle

A good many years ago I referenced and bound a large number of leaves of MSS. which had been extracted (mostly before 1882) from the covers of Bodleian books. Among them were many Latin chronicle-fragments in similar writing—of the first half of the twelfth century—and of the same dimensions (10×7 in.): moreover, the bindings out of which they had come were all executed (Mr. S. Gibson tells me) in the same Oxford binding about the beginning of the seventeenth century. One of the leaves,[1] commencing a chronicle, is headed, in a twelfth century hand, 'Cronica īperfecta', and I have now no doubt that the entire collection formed part of the volume of 'Cronica inperfecta' which is no. 283 in Prior Eastry's catalogue of the library of Christ Church, Canterbury, recently printed by Dr. M. R. James (p. 49).

In 1899 I saw that these fragments fell into two distinct groups, and I re-referenced them and re-bound them accordingly, after a further and successful hunt for additional related fragments in other Oxford bindings.

The first group now form MS. Lat. misc. d. 30 in the Bodleian. Except the leaf headed 'Cronica īperfecta', which is a chronology of emperors from Augustus to Justinian, they are all part of a chronicle of Old Testament history. *Some* of them, including the *verso* of the leaf in question, have twenty-nine lines to the page. I shall have no need to mention them further.

The second group now form MS. Lat. misc. d. 13. They are part of a general chronicle, cover the period A.D. 70-516, and are all from the pen of one scribe, whose hand is not found in the other group, and who *always* writes twenty-nine lines to the page.

It is with the latter group that this paper is concerned, and I call the chronicle unknown not merely because of my long and unsuccessful attempts to identify it, but because neither the Rev. C. Plummer nor the late Prof. F. York Powell was able to recognise it.

I append notes[2] of passages relating to the Saxon invasion, and of corre-

---

[1] F. 20 in MS. Lat. misc. d. 30 in the Bodleian.
[2] For convenience of printing I have always used dotted *i*. In the fragments there is, of course, no dot, but sometimes a stroke, and sometimes none.

sponding entries in the Anglo-Saxon chronicles. The latter I indicate by the respective letters which Mr. Plummer uses in his *Two Saxon Chronicles*. The dates hardly ever agree.

A.D. 466, the battle near Wippedes fleot. As *fleot* has various meanings, and the water in question is unknown, the words 'prope riuulum qui dicitur Wippedes fleot' are important.

A.D. 484, Ælle's battle 'iuxta torrentem qui dicitur mærcredeſ burna': 'torrentem' is a new particular, important because the stream is still unidentified.

A.D. 487, Beginning of Æsc's reign of 27 years, which Ⱥ B-C call 'xxiiii' winters, E 'xxxiiii.'

A.D. 495, Ælle and Cissa besieged 'ciuitatem andredes'—virtually identical with the Anglo-Saxon version, but 'in ore gladii perimerunt' (i. o. g. is a Biblical phrase) where that has only 'ofslogon'. A Latin entry almost identical is found under 490 in F, and apparently in an earlier form, for it has *perimunt*.

A.D. 497, Invasion of Certic and Kyneric. Similar entry in Ⱥ B-C E, and both in English and Latin in F.

A.D. 501, Invasion of Port, Beada, and Megla. Similarly Ⱥ B-C E (all Bieda and Mægla), also in short English and shorter Latin in F, with Biedda and Mægla (Lat. Mogla).

A.D. 507, Nataleod and 5000 Britons killed. Almost identical Latin entry in F, but its Anglo-Saxon entry, like Ⱥ B-C E, only says that the 5000 were with him: the Latin version is incredible, and obviously arises from an omission of *wera* (or *erant*) in 'wera mid him' (or 'erant cum eo').

The connexion with F (MS. Cott. Domit. A. VIII in the British Museum) cannot be doubted, and that (Plummer, *Two Saxon Chronicles*, II. cxxii) was made in the late eleventh or early twelfth century from an original Saxon chronicle belonging to St. Augustine's, Canterbury, 'for the use of the neighbouring monastery of Christ Church': it is, in fact, no. 318 in Prior Eastry's catalogue of the Christ Church Library printed by Dr. M. R. James (p. 51). Moreover, the details of the *rivulus* and *torrens* point to a special knowledge of the S.E. corner of England, and I have no doubt that the fragments were written at Canterbury.

Entire pages relating to Hengist's invasion closely resemble the *Historia Brittonum*, the Chartres MS. 98, and Nennius, though the narrative, instead of being continuous, is distributed under various years.

The following passages may be contrasted with Mommsen's text of the *Historia Brittonum* and Nennius :—

p. 179, l. 1, 'uocatur lingua regis cantia guoralen id est cantia illius qui uocabatur guoralen.' Here, as in the *Historia* and Nennius, we have a Welsh corruption of Cantwaraland, but the misinterpretation is unique and 'lingua regis' (in the King's English !) is peculiar, the *Historia* and Nennius having 'in lingua eorum.' No such variation could have arisen at the time when the fragments were written (the King's language then being Norman-French), and the phrase suggests a region and period in which part of the population still spoke Keltic.

p. 179, l. 2, 'in nostra autem Chent'—where 'nostra' means British—is omitted, and so is the following passage about the British king Guoyrancgon.

p. 187, ll. 15-16, 'in lingua eorum Episford': 'eorum' is altered to 'nostra'. The following words 'in nostra autem lingua Rithergabail' are omitted.

p. 187, l. 18, 'Categirn'. This name (=*Cat-tegirn*, battle-lord, Welsh *catteyrn* [1]) must have had *tt*. Our fragments habitually use *e* and *g*, but rarely or never *æ*, except in this name, which they write *Catægirn*. This *æ* is almost certainly a misreading of a well-known form of *te*, and indicates an earlier Cattegirn.

The invasion-pages have clearly been edited by an Anglo-Saxon, and in places they are shorter than the *Historia Brittonum*, the Chartres MS. 98, and Nennius, as well as abundant in various readings. The only native author mentioned in the text of the MS., and the *latest* author mentioned, is Bede.

On the mutilated margin of f. 30, against the year 495 (which includes a notice of the capture of Andredes ceastei), is the entry . . . 'oderici'. I conjecture this to mean that the passage referred to is an addition of Theodericus. A Theodoricus or Thodoricius appears as the donor of two books to Christ Church, Canterbury, and Dr. James dates him 'cent. xi, xii': he may have been a monk who brought them with him on his entrance.

I hope some time to ask permission of the librarians of the College libraries in Oxford to examine their Oxford bindings of the early seventeenth century for any other fragments which may still exist of this very curious chronicle. E. W. B. NICHOLSON.

The Scots Magazine, January 1802, contains the following :—

'INVERNESS, *Jan.* 12.—Yesterday Major Macdonald, with the last division of Lord Macdonald's Regiment of the Isles, under the command of Lieut.-Colonel M. Macalister, arrived at Fort George after performing a march of upwards of five hundred miles from Liverpool, during which time the inclemency of the weather was such as would have impeded almost any other corps, except Highlanders. For three successive marches, from Montrose to Aberdeen, they had to cut their way through frost and snow, which they performed with the greatest alacrity, working with their spades and shovels, to the tune of their Gaelic songs, and not a single man of those that marched from Liverpool was left behind. From Aberdeen to Banff the drift and snow was often such as to prevent their seeing one another, and obliged them for security's sake to link each other by the arm from front to rear. Notwithstanding all this, the whole upon their arrival appeared neat and clean, in good health and spirits, and seemingly not in the least fatigued. Although their route from Carlisle was discretionary, yet they still continued their march (the usual halting days excepted) until their arrival at the Fort. It may not perhaps be unworthy of remark that Fort George should now be

---

[1] 'This work' [*i.e.* Nennius] 'introduces Arthur as the Leader of War ("dux belli")' [Mommsen's text is *bellorum*] 'in accordance with the Triads and other ancient Welsh records, in which the federal sovereign is frequently termed—Catteyrn, or War-King,—and his monarchy—Catteyrnedd, or War Sovereignty' (note on page 356 o *Iolo manuscripts*).

garrisoned by the very people to overawe whom it was originally built, a circumstance somewhat curious to think, that in the space of about forty-five years such a change in human affairs should have taken place, an event, however, equally honourable to the government who effected it, and to the Highlanders themselves, for their present loyalty and attachment to the best of Kings.'

A PRAYER TO THE ARCHANGELS

The original of this is contained in a manuscript in the Royal Irish Academy. The Gaelic and translation are given by Mr. T. P. O'Nowlan, M.A., in *Eriu*.

MAY Gabriel be with me on Sundays, and the power of the King of Heaven.
May Gabriel be with me always that evil may not come to me nor injury.

Michael on Monday I speak of, my mind is set on him,
Not with any one do I compare him but with Jesus, the Son of Mary.

If it be Tuesday, Raphael I mention, until the end comes, for my help.
One of the seven whom I beseech, as long as I am on the field of the world.

May Uriel be with me on Wednesdays, the abbot with high nobility,
Against wound and against danger, against the sea of rough wind.

Sariel on Thursday I speak of, against the swift waves of the sea,
Against every evil that comes to a man, against every disease that seizes him.

On the day of the second fast (Friday), Rumiel—a clear blessing—I have loved,
I say only the truth, good the friend I have taken.

May Panchel be with me on Saturdays, as long as I am on the yellow world

.   .   .   .   .

May the Trinity protect me! may the Trinity defend me!
May the Trinity save me from every hurt, from every danger!

AN FHIDEAG AIRGID

Amy Murray

(New York)

THE words of this song were given in the *Celtic Review* for October 1904, and I was so interested by them, that when in the island of Eriskay during last summer I noted down the following beautiful and effective air to which they are sung.

Hi ri liuthil ó, . . Co a sheinneas an fhideag airgid? Hó rŏ hu-ó

hiuthil ó, Mac mo righ-s' air tigh'nn a dh' Alba Hi ri liuthil ó . .

Air luing mhoir thar na fairgeadh, Hó rŏ huó hiuthil ó.

THE GLENMASAN MANUSCRIPT

Professor Mackinnon

GAELIC TEXT

Imtúsa Fergusa do berar ós aird.　As a h-aitle sin do rónsat comarli cred do géndáis.　Agus is i comarli do ronsat glúasacht rompa síar.　Agus rangatar an adaig sin co tech Airne mic Duib Dochlaidh co dúnad Locha nan Airne.　Agus do eirigh Airni mac Duib agus a secht n-derbraithri .i. na h-Airne o'n abar[1] Loch nan Airne, agus do feratar failti fri Fergus co micha*ir* muinntreamail.　Agus do coirged tech an brug*aid* acu.　Agus tugad Fergus is in bruigin ar sin agus Cormac Conloinges agus na maithi ár chena.　Agus ro coirged in tech co sesgar sodhamail, agus do cuired Fergus 'n a shuide.　Agus do suidh Airne mac Duib Dochlaidh ar gualainn Fergusa.　Agus do suid Cormac Conloinges ar a gualainn séin.　Agus do suidetar na secht n-Airne .i. braith*ri* in br*u*gaid ar gualainn Cormaic.　Agus do suidetar na secht laich ba ferrda do'n Dubloinges.　Agus do suid Breac agus Nainnesg dá mac an brugaid is in fhochla fheinned ar an agaid.　Agus do suidh Uaithni Ucht-sholus mac Conaill Cernaig agus Goibninn mac Luirgnigh in a farrad.　Agus do lín*ad* gach ré[2] n-imdaid do maithib Fergusa agus do maithib na n-Airne.　Do freasladh agus do fritheoladh íad do mid agus d' fion agus d' feóil agus do roignib gacha bidh ar chena.　Agus ro dáiled ar na deg laéchaib na deocha sin gur bo subach saithech na sochaide co rabatar ar merugadh meisgi agus mí-c(h)eïlli.

Agus ránic co h-am luide do na laéchaib.　Agus do dergad a imdaid d' Fergus, agus do dergad a n-imdaidi do n(a) h-ard-maithib uile.　Agus do ling gach aon in a imdaid dib ar sin, agus do fagbad Dubthach in a aonar ar in n-urlár.　Agus do fiafraig Dubthach : 'Ca b-fuil mo leab*aidh*-si ? ' ar sé.　'Fiafraig do t' maithib fen,' ar Airne.　Ag a cloistecht sin do Dubthach, do gab a comfua*cadh* imresna *for* Airne.

(Continued from pp. 120, 121.)

ENGLISH TRANSLATION

The proceedings of Fergus are related now. They deliberated as to what they should do, and they resolved to proceed westwards. They arrived that night at the house of Airne son of Dub Docladh, the fort of the Airnes' Loch. And Airne son of Dub (the Black), and his seven brothers, *i.e.* the Airnes after whom the loch is named, rose and gave a warm and courteous welcome to Fergus. And the hospitaller's house was put in order by them. Fergus, Cormac Conloinges, and the other chiefs, were then brought into the hostel. The house was arranged comfortably and luxuriously and Fergus was seated. Airne son of Dub Docladh, sat beside Fergus, and Cormac Conloinges sat beside him. And the seven Airnes, the hospitaller's brothers, sat beside Cormac. The seven noblest of the heroes of the Dubloinges sat (next). And Breac and Nainnesg, the hospitaller's two sons, sat in the champions' seat opposite to them. Uaithne Bright-breast son of Conall Cernach sat down, with Goibnenn son of Luirgnech beside him. And the couches were filled, alternately, by the chiefs of Fergus and of the Airnes. They were ministered to and served with mead and wine and flesh and the choicest of every kind of food. And the stout heroes were plied with liquor until the company were merry and sated, and became excited with drunkenness and unreason.

When bedtime came, his couch was made ready for Fergus, and their couches were made ready for all the high nobles. Each of them thereupon sprang into his bed and Dubthach was left alone upon the floor. Dubthach asked, 'Where is my bed?' said he. 'Inquire of your own friends,' replied Airne. When Dubthach heard this he began

---

[1] *abar*, for the more common *abrar*, v. *supra*, p. 26. Later in the MS. Meave and her army visit this *bruiden*, and the origin of the name *Loch nan Airne* is there explained.

[2] For this idiom, cf. *Sil. Gad*, p. 330, *Rc.* xxiv. 74 : *Sráinis in míolchú for in leoman cach re fecht i tosach*, 'At first the greyhound beat the lion every other time'; and I.G. *gach 're lá*, 'on alternate days' (Din. s.v. *'re*).

Agus do cuala Fergus forniatacht a fregra thug na curaidh,
agus mar do cúala do eirigh tre naire do digail a droch glóir
ar Dubthach. Agus do eirgetar an Dubloinges d' anacal Dubthaich ar Fergus. Agus ro eirgetar bannala agus beg-nertaigh
an baile co buadhnasach. Do cualatar sluagh an dúnaidh
uile an t-uathbas sin, agus do eirgetar an ein (fh)echt
d' innsaige na bruigni .i. muinntir Fergusa agus muinntir
Airne fai sin. Agus do reidiged in righ-bhruigen leó agus do
h-ainced Dubthach. Agus tánic Cormac Conloinges agus
Airne mac Duib Dochlaidh a mach do fechain na slúagh, agus
do b' obair doib an eiterdealugadh re cheile. Agus atorchar
da trichait do muinntir na miled sin iter a muigh agus a
tig(h).[1] Agus do cúaidh cach dib a mesg a muinntiri, agus
do batar co h-anbfosnech ansadail co tanic lá con a lán
shoill(s)i.

Agus ro eirigh Fergus co fír-moch agus ro tinoil a maithe
uile d' a innsaidhi. Agus tanic ar in faichthi agus ro celeabair
do na h-Airnib co h-ainíardha. Agus ro choirigh tosach agus
deredh ar a deg laóchaib. Agus ro fagbadar an tír co tinnes-
nech, agus nír anatar do 'n réim sin agus do 'n ruathar no co
rangatar co dúnad Atha Fen, agus do cuiretar Bricne rompa
gus an m-baili.

Agus rainic sed éin co h-airm a raibhi Oilill Finn agus do
h-aitniged é. Agus do eirgetar cach uile in a agaid, agus do
fersat fír-chain failti fris. Agus do toirbiretar poga imda dó,
agus do fhiafraigetar sgela de. Agus adubairt Oilill : ' Imar-
charidh Bricne dam is in dúnad a nunn.' Do h-imchradh
Bricne is in m-baile iar sin. Do h-esrad agus do h-ur-luachrad
grianana arda uraibne agus tighe lepta logmara doib, agus
adubrad ríu dul d' a tighib lepta d' a frestal agus d 'a fritholam.
' Ní racham ider,' ar Bricne, ' uair ata dail coindme as mó
agus as uaisle aná máid-ne[2] chugaib .i. Fergus mac Roigh

---

[1] *a muigh agus a tigh.* Nowadays we use the article invariably with *tigh,*
tech, but not with *mach* (*mag*), *muigh : a mach 's a steach, a muigh 's a stigh; a*
steach for *i(n) si(n) tech, i(n) si(n) tigh* respectively. We still retain the accusative
forms *a mach, a steach* after verbs of motion, while the dative forms *a muigh, a stigh*
indicate rest : *chaidh e mach,* but *tha e muigh ; thainig e steach,* but *tha e stigh.*

[2] *maid-ne:* the form is not now used independently, being replaced by *sinn, sinne.*
Even in the verb it is being discarded over the greater part of the Highlands of

to fasten a quarrel upon Airne. Fergus heard the violent
language of the champions, and rose from very shame to
punish Dubthach for his ill tongue. And the Dubloinges
rose to shield Dubthach from Fergus. Then the womenfolk
and non-combatants of the stead gathered in a menacing
manner. All the people in the fort now heard the uproar,
and they all, Fergus's folk and those of Airne, came at once to
the castle. And they pacified the folk in the royal hostel and
saved Dubthach from injury. Cormac Conloinges and Airne
son of Dub Docladh went forth to view the crowd, and found
it no easy task to separate the two parties. Threescore of
the people of these warriors fell in the house or outside.
Then each of them joined his own people, and they had an
anxious and disturbed time of it until day with its full light
came.

Fergus rose very early and gathered his chiefs around
him. He came upon the lawn, and bade farewell to the
Airnes in angry mood. He then placed a front and rear
guard upon his goodly champions. They left the country
hurriedly, and did not halt upon that march and on-rush
until they reached the fort of Ath Fen, when they sent Bricne
to the stead to herald them.

Bricne went to the place where Oilill the Fair was, and
he was recognised. All went forth to meet him, and they
gave him a genuine and hearty welcome. They kissed him
many times, and asked tidings from him. And Oilill said,
'Oblige me by carrying Bricne over to the castle.' Bricne
was thereupon brought to the stead. Lofty and very delightful bowers, and richly furnished sleeping apartments, were
prepared and strewn with fresh rushes for Bricne and his
party, and they were told to go to their rooms where they
would be served and attended to. 'We shall on no account
go,' said Bricne, 'for a greater and nobler guest than we
has come, i.e. Fergus son of Roigh, to hold converse and to
make alliance with you; and to seek assistance in weapons

Scotland. For *bhuaileamaid iad*, etc., the common form in the North Highlands is
bhuaileadh sinn iad.

tanic do t' agallaim-si, agus do denam a coraighechta rit, agus
d' iarraidh fóirithnech airm agus eidigh ortsa agus ar an n-
Gamhanraid, uair ni uil an Eirinn uile áo n-egmais Oilella
agus Medba en cara as ferr leis aige ana thusa.' 'Mo chen a
techt agus a thorachtain,' bar Oilill. 'Dogebtar eich agus
eid*idh* agus arm gaisg*id* do 'n turus sin tan*ic*; agus do
geptar coimeirge na Gamanraide ar gach toiscc agus ar gach
turas bas ail leis.' Agus ba failidh iat roim Fergus. 'Ga
fad uaid atá Fergus?' ar Oilill. 'As fagus,' ar Bricne. Do
chuaidh Oilill, agus do reidiged bruiden ríga ro mór aige fa
comair Fergusa mic Roigh.

Agus an uair tairnic an bruiden d' esradh agus d' ullmugadh
adubairt Oilill re Bricne: 'Denam a stech agus denam ar
n-dithad.'[1] Do chuadar and; agus tuccad chuca nua gacha
bídh agus sen gacha saor dighe gur bo subach so-labhartach
saobh-ciallach iad. O do eirigh aigned an ollaman re dim-
saighe na dighe agus re h-udmaille an anrath, agus ro chuir-
estar méd agus meince na sruamand sein meda aigned Bricne
for búaidris. Agus do crom Bricne ar Oilill, agus as ed so
adubairt: 'Maith am, a Oilill, an fedrais an toiscc ima tainicc
Fergus do 'n baile-si?' 'Ni fedar am,' bar Oilill. 'Ar cenn
do mna-sa tán*ic*,' bar Bricne, 'd' a breith leis ar aithed agus
ar elodh.' 'An b-fuil cuid disi fén ann sin, a ollam?' bar
Oilill. 'Ata co deimin,' bar Bricne, 'uair is í do cuir fo
ghesaib é, mana tís*ad* ar a cenn d' a breith leis ar áis no ar
eigin o 'n Gamanraid. Agus do gheall co m-beradh lé an m-boin
mail as dech fuil an Eirinn uile agus a h-airgedha ar chena.
Agus do geall co m-biathf*ad* fir Erenn gacha sechtmad oidchi
ar sluaiged mór Tána bo Cuai(l)gni.' Do b*a* ferr limsa na
b*ad* í sin a toisg,' bar Oilill. Ro leicset secha sin, agus ro
batar ac ól as a h-aitle.

Imtusa Fergusa do berar ós aird. Do cóirigh a muinntir,[2]

---

[1] *dithad*: in S.G. *dìot*, and used in N.H. (North Highlands) for 'meal,' 'dinner.'
Evidently, like English *diet*, a loan from L. *diæta*.

[2] This is the first of several rhetorical passages in this MS., too common in other
Gaelic compositions, old and modern. They are restricted for the most part to
descriptions of armies, fights, horses, chariots, the arming of famous warriors, and
the personal appearance of favourite heroes and heroines. While such passages testify
to the copiousness of the language and to the great command over the Gaelic

and armour from you and from the Gamhanraidh, for, apart
from Oilill and Meave, there is no one in Ireland whose friendship he desires as much as yours.' 'His coming and arrival
are alike pleasing to me,' said Oilill. 'He will receive horses
and armour and warlike weapons as a guerdon of his visit;
and the Gamhanraidh will join him on any quest and expedition he pleases.' And they were blithe to welcome Fergus.
'How far distant is Fergus?' asked Oilill. 'He is quite
nigh,' said Bricne. Oilill thereupon made ready a spacious
royal mansion for Fergus son of Roigh.

Now when the mansion was put in order and made ready
Oilill said to Bricne, 'Let us go inside and have our repast.'
They went; and the freshest of every food and the oldest of
every noble drink were brought to them, and they became
merry and loud-voiced and reckless. The mind of the ollamh
was excited by the strength of the liquor and the fickleness
of ill-luck; and the quantity and frequency of the streams of
old mead (which he quaffed) altogether confused Bricne's
senses. He bent over Oilill and said, 'Good now, Oilill,
do you know the quest on which Fergus has come to this
place?' 'No, I do not,' said Oilill. 'For your wife has he
come,' said Bricne, 'to carry her away in elopement and
secrecy.' 'Is she herself privy to that plot, ollamh?' asked
Oilill. 'She is, assuredly,' said Bricne, 'for it was she who
put him under prohibitions, if he did not come to carry her
away from the Gamhanraidh of her free will or by violence.
And she promised that she would bring with her the hummel
cow, the best in all Ireland, as well as her other herds. And
she undertook to feed the men of Ireland every seventh
night on the great expedition of *Tain bo Cuailgni*.' 'I should
much wish that his quest were different,' said Oilill. The
subject was dropped then, and they continued drinking.

As to Fergus now. He marshalled his people and formed

vocabulary which many native authors undoubtedly possessed, they not infrequently
mar the literary beauty of many of these Sagas and detract from their historical
value. One is not certain that the epithets were in all cases selected for their aptness in accurate description as much as for their merit in securing sonorous and,
above all, alliterative combinations.

agus do rigni tri buidhne aidble osgardha arm-comarthacha,
agus tri coraigthi troma triath-mora toirtemla, agus tri
dirmada data dimóra do-aisneisi do'n Dubloinges. An cet
corugadh do na curadaib .i. fiche cet cath-miled fa Cormac
Conloinges mac Conchobair do roign*ib* na rigdamna a fine
rígda R*ug*raide, co sgiathaib donn-corcra dath-ailli dímóra
dianarda, agus co m-brataib comarthacha comdatha, agus
co n-inaraib *cum*ta crunn-blaithi cimas-milla, agus co
sguirdibh saidbri slim-geala snath-cáola, agus co cloidmib
caol-glasa comarthach(a) cruaidh-géra, agus co slegaib slinn-
gera snas-míne sit(h)-rinnaigthi, agus co luirechaib lerg-dluithi
lán-milla lepar-daingni lasamna, agus co muincedaib maisecha
mong-dualacha maoth-sroill, agus co cennataib socra so-cuma
solus-gemnacha.

A n-urr*adha* agus a n-uaisli agus a n-ard-fla*ith*i a tim-
ceall Fergusa, an aird-righ. Agus is amlaid ro batar co sgiathaib
órdha eng-blaithi uáinega ar clé láim gacha curad, agus co
sleagaib fbada fraoch-búana fuilecha, agus co cloidmib seda
soinemla sith-ridhni ar a sliastaib, agus co m-brataib naine
eochar-blaithi oir-cimsacha umpa, agus co casánaibh grés-
mílla geal-airg*eda* is na brataib ós a m-bruinnib, agus co
minnaib ro cúanna bri*cht*-rinnta rig-maisecha ar foradh gacha
flatha.

A sruithi agus a sinnser agus a so-comarlig, a f*or*bfir agus
a f*or*us-oglá*ich* ar dered na Dubloingsi. A n-amus agus a
n-armainn árrachta agus a n-es-urr*adha*[1] is in m-buidin
n-deigenn*igh* dibh. Daigh is ámlaid ro batar sén co m-brataib
gorma gabaltacha impu, agus co slegaib comfada cinn-géra
colg-rinnaighthi, agus co sg*í*athaib buidi ball-corcra breacht-
naichthi, agus co cloidhmib troma taib-let(h)na toirtemla ar
na trén-feraib, agus co comarthaib imdaib egsamlaib uais*ti*bh.

Rangatar rompo fó 'n innus sin co dúnad Atha Fén. Agus
o t'connairc lucht an baile an slúag sénta solus-mór so-moth*aige*
sin d' a n-innsaige do chuat*ar* ar fuinneógaib agus ar f*oradh*-
múraib an dún*aid* d'á fairgsin agus d'a fechain. Agus ba
c*etfad*ach cach dibh re h-égsamlacht an innill.

---

[1] *es-urradha*, the opposite of *urradha*. The same epithet occurs later.

the Dubloinges in three vast brave weapon-brilliant divisions, and in three imposing princely-great powerful battalions, and in three magnificent huge grand cohorts. The first battalion of the champions consisted of two thousand fighting warriors under the command of Cormac Conloinges son of Conchobar of the *élite* of the crown princes of the royal race of Rugraide, armed with purple-brown beautifully-coloured very large and tall shields, with mantles ornate and of one colour, with well-fitting dun-coloured edge-figured tunics, with scalloped smooth-white finely-woven smocks, and with slender-gray figured sharp swords of steel, and with sharp-bladed smooth-polished long-pointed spears, and with closely-fitted fully-carved long strong and flashing coats of mail, and with handsome hair-plated soft satin collars, and with well-fitting beautifully-shaped gem-flashing headpieces.

Their gentry, their nobles and princes, surrounded Fergus the high king. These carried gold-adorned smooth-gussetted green-coloured shields on the left hand of each hero, and long terror-striking bloody spears, and long finely-tempered sharp-pointed swords on their thighs. They wore green smooth-edged gold-fringed mantles, fastened on their breasts with richly-figured white-silver brooches, while very elegant kingly-beautiful diadems adorned with magic scrolls covered the brow of each noble.

Their seniors and elders, their wise counsellors, their men of trust and knowledge, were in the rear of the Dubloinges. Their mercenaries, their strong officers, and the hired troops, formed the last company. These wore blue peaked mantles, and the powerful men carried long sharp-headed sword-pointed spears, and yellow purple-speckled variegated shields, and heavy broad powerful swords, while many and diverse-coloured banners waved over them.

They marched forward in this order to the castle of Ath Fen. And when the people of the place saw that fairy brilliant well-disposed host approaching they went to the windows and on the ramparts of the castle to behold and view them. And they were all impressed with the spectacular display.

Ranic Fergus ar an faichthi fai sin. Agus o t' conncatar an Gamandrad íat, ro eirgetar a mach a timcell Oilella Finn, agus ro feratar uile fáilti fri Fergus. Agus do cuired a tig leptha íat, úair do bí bruigen mór ar n-á corugadh acu fa comair na Dubloingsi fén. Agus do cuired iatsan innti, agus do togatar a n-airm agus a n-il-faobra ar aidlennaib innti.

Is ann sin tugad maithi na Gamandraidi do cúm Oilella Finn. Agus ro fhiárfaig dibh cá h-ordugadh do bertai ar Fergus, in a tig leptha do bíad no 'n a tig Oilella Finn fén. ' Is córa sin d'íarfaige de fén agus d'a maithibh,' bar íadson, ' ina dínne.' ' Do fiafraiged sin dibh,' (ar Oilill). ' Is i rogha bermaid,' ar síad, ' Fergus agus a maithi do beith a n-aein thig agus [1] Oilill Finn agus maithi na Gamandraidi, innus co m-bía Fergus agus Oilill re coimhéd ar comaind agus ar caratraid.' Ro cuired techta ar a cenn íar sin, agus tugad a sdech íat. Is amlaid so do suidiged iat .i. días do maithib Fergusa im gach n-áin fer do maithib Oilella Finn, agus dias do maithib Oilella Finn im gach n-aoin fer do maithib Fergusa re fritheolam a feirge agus a fúasmada da tegmad coméirghe no esáonta no imresuin etarra, ar bo biáid séin da teallach cruaís agus cothaighthe Leithi Cuinn [2] .i. in Gamannrad Irruis Domnann agus damrad dibeirgi clainni Rugrade.

Do fiarfaig Oilill Finn d' Fergus in d'én táib do beidís, no cach dib a mesg a maithi fen. ' Is ed is ferr do 'n fáilti a tairise,' ar Fergus. Do cuaid Oilill in a imdaid iar sin, agus ro suid a n-inad righ innte, agus do orduigh Fergus in a farrad. Agus ni h-ed sin do clecht Fergus co n-nigi sin, úair ni lamthái rí do radh re nech is in n-oirecht a m-biadh acht a radh fri Fergus. Agus nir lamthai suidi roime a n-inad ríam in ba dual do righ suide nó go tánic go tech Oilella Finn, ri sed éin uaibhrech allata na Gamannraidi. Agus nír miadh

---

[1] In S.G. I would write *an aon tigh ri O.F. agus ri maithibh na G.*, 'in the same house with (and) O. F. and the chiefs of the G.'

[2] The reader will remember that the descriptive name *Leith Cuinn* was unknown until *Conn Cetchathach*, who lived, according to the traditional chronology, in the second century, and *Mogh Nuaghat* divided Ireland between them, the northern part being known as *Leith Cuinn* and the southern as *Leith Mogha*. The boundary was, roughly, from Dublin to Galway Bay.

Fergus then appeared upon the lawn. And when the Gamhanraidh saw them, they all went forth with Oilill the Fair to welcome Fergus. They were put into a sleeping-house, for the Gamhanraidh had prepared a spacious mansion for the reception of the Dubloinges. And these were placed there, and they put their arms and numerous weapons upon the racks.

Then the chiefs of the Gamhanraidh were summoned by Oilill the Fair. He asked them how Fergus should be lodged, whether in the guest house or in Oilill the Fair's own palace. ' That should be asked of himself and of his chiefs rather than of us,' said they. ' But it has been asked of you ' (said Oilill). ' We should prefer,' said they, ' that Fergus and his principal men should be in the same house with Oilill the Fair and the chiefs of the Gamhanraidh, so that Fergus and Oilill can observe the goodwill and friendship of both parties. Messengers were sent for them then, and they were brought to the palace. And thus they were seated : two of Fergus's chiefs on either side of each one of Oilill the Fair's chiefs, and two of Oilill the Fair's chiefs on either side of each one of Fergus's chiefs, to provide against their wrath and fury, in case anger or dispute or quarrel should arise among them, for these were the two (foremost) tribes of the chivalry and bravery of Conn's Half, the Gamhanraidh of Irrus Domnann and the predatory troops of the clan Rugraide.

Oilill the Fair asked Fergus whether they (two) should sit side by side, or each sit among his own chiefs. ' The value of the welcome is its sincerity,' said Fergus. Oilill thereupon went to his couch and sat in his royal seat and ordered Fergus beside him. And until now Fergus was not used to such treatment, for in every assembly in which he was present not (even) a king dared to issue a command to another except through Fergus ; and no one ever dared to sit (even) on a throne before he (Fergus) was seated, until he came to the palace of Oilill the Fair, that haughty and renowned king of the Gamhanraidh. He would yield his own seat to no man. But as for Fergus, he took the seat assigned to him, for he

leis n*ech* eile do cur in a inad.   Fergus, im*orro,* do cuaid is in
n-inadh do h-ordaig*ed* dó, úair nir miadh leis tach*ar* im inadh
fri h-Oilill, or do b*udh* deimin leis a dímíadh do dígail air
fádeoigh.

Acht ata ní chena.   Do gabatar ac ól agus ac aibnes no co
tarrla cáine comraid iter Oilill agus Fergus, gur fiafraigh
Oilill d' Fergus cid ím a tangas a n-Irrus Domnann do 'n
dul-sa.   'Tanac d'iarraidh faigdhe airm agus eididh ortsa
agus ar an n-Gamannraid, agus do denam mo cumainn ribsi
nile.'   'Ni h-í sin toisg do cualamar-ne do bheith agat,' ar
Oilill, 'agus aderait nir ceili-si ar duine ríam ni dá fíarfoch*adh*
dít.'   'Cred da b-fuil agatsa sin ale ?' bar Fergus.   'Is ed do
cualas ám,' ar Oilill, 'gurab ar cenn mo mná-sa tang*ais,* d' a
breith let ar áis nó ar eigin.'   'Ni ceilim-si sin ortsa,' ar Fergus.
'Do b*udh* ferr a cleith itir,' ar Oilill; 'agus ac so, mar do
déna tusa sin, a Fergais,' bar Oilill, 'na cluined nech uaitsi an
comradh sin.   Agus eirich co moch a márach co h-Ath an
Cluithi re Dún an air, agus th' ara carbaid let ann.   Agus
rachat-sa ann agus m' ara carpaid.   Agus gid b'é úaind tí
ass,[1] bid an ben aigi.'   'A dénam amlaid sin,' ar Fergus.   A
n-imthúsa co n-uigi sin.

Imthusa Bricni do berar ós aird.   O'n úair do cuaidh a
ced meisgi de do gab ag fechain an tighi 'n a timchell.   Agus
atconnairc rúamnadh na fergi a n-agaid Oilella agus Fergusa.
Tanic ealla aithrechais dó im a n-derna, agus tanic as a tich
a mach roime.   Agus a(t)conairc an baile ac a linadh a n-oir
agus a n-iar, a n-es agus a thuaith do córaighthib catha agus
do sluaghaib fó'n arm gaisgid.   Agus o t' connairc Bricne sin
tanic a sdech, agus do fiarfaig do Oilill cred na córaighthi
catha agus na socraide sár-móra slúaigecht ran*ic* sa ic linad
an baile.   'Mo muinntir-sa agus mo teglach sin,' ar Oilill
Finn, 'agus do cummoradh áonaig na Samna[2] a marach

---

[1] MS. *as*.

[2] The manner in which the Ultonians used to celebrate the Hallowmas Fair is
described in *Serglige Conculaind* 'The Sickbed of Cuchulainn' (*Ir. T.,* i. 205):—
*Oenach dogníthe la Ultu cecha bliadhna .i. tri lá ría Samfuin ocus tri laa iarma
ocus lathe na Samna feisne.   Iss ed eret no bitis Ulaid in sin im Maig Murthemni oc
ferthain óenaig na samna cecha bliadna, ocus ni rabe is in bith ni dognethe in n-eret*

would not condescend to dispute with Oilill about a matter
of precedence, being certain that eventually he would punish
(that potentate) for this disrespect to him.

But one thing. They drank and made merry, and Oilill
the Fair and Fergus engaged in pleasant talk. Oilill asked
Fergus what brought him to Irrus Domnann on this occasion.
'I have come to ask assistance in weapons and armour from
you and the Gamhanraidh, and to make the acquaintance of
you all.' 'That is not your object as we have heard,' said
Oilill, 'and folks say that you never conceal anything if
questioned about it.' 'What do you mean by that?' said
Fergus. 'What I have heard,' said Oilill, 'is that it is for
my wife you have come, to carry her away willingly or by
force.' 'I do not deny it,' said Fergus. 'It were indeed
better if it could be denied,' said Oilill; 'but look here, if
you mean to act thus, Fergus,' added Oilill, 'repeat this talk
to none. But go early on the morrow to the Ford of the
Game, by the *Dún* of slaughter, taking your charioteer with
you. And I shall go there with my charioteer, and he who
returns of us two shall have the lady. 'Agreed,' said Fergus.
Their affairs thus far.

As to Bricne: When his first stage of drunkenness passed,
he began to look all round the house. And he saw the flush of
anger in the faces of Fergus and Oilill. A fit of repentance
for what he had done seized him, and he went forth from the
house. And he saw the place being filled from east and west,
north and south with battalions in battle array and hosts under
arms. When Bricne saw this he went in and asked Oilill what
these battle cohorts and great armed hosts were that came,
filling all the place. 'My people and my household these,'
replied Oilill the Fair. 'They have come to celebrate the

sin leú acht cluchi ocus céti ocus ánius ocus aibinnius ocus longad ocus tomailt. 'The
Ultonians used to hold a fair every year, viz. three days before Hallowmas and
three days after, as well as on Hallowmas Day. During that time the Ultonians would
be on the Plain of Murthemne holding the Hallowmas Fair each year, and during
that time they did nothing whatever except (engaging in) games and entertainments
and amusements and enjoyment and eating and drinking.' Then follow some of
the ceremonies observed on the occasion.

tegaid.' Agus tánic Bricne a mach a rís agus do condaic buidhen mór a n-des gach n-direch[1] .i. buiden dorcha dimhór dlúth-egairte, agus bruit donna uile impo agus cimsa airgit 'n a n-ur-timcell, agus léinte loar[2] lethna uile impa, agus cloidhme glas-lethna gorma 'n a lamhaib ar luamhain, agus slega midher-gera móra go m-balc[3] lan lamhaib laeich an gac(h) lebar-crannaib dib, agus scéith donna dos-lethna dimóra leu, agus gilla feta foistinech fir-mór a tús na deg buidne sin co forsmacht úadha ortha nile. Do aithin Ailill iad, agus do righnedar an laoidh ann :—

'Fuil buigen sunna do'n dun,
Ni h-úada tí aghaid ar cúl,
Co m-brataib donna datha,
Co sciathaib a comdatha.

'Dáine duba co nert níadh
Co léintib gela ri grían ;
Dáine móra co n-deilb n-duibh,
Do dechadar do'n mor muir.

'Cloidmhe glasa a lámhaib leó,
Trén con bebsadar[4] do'n gleó ;
Slega mergidhe móra,
Fir díregra dimora.'

'Is aithind sunna na slóigh,
Na fir sin co menmain móir ;
Aongas mac Echtaigh a nall
Agus meic oglaeich[5] Arann.

'Ni ríu nach doiligh deabaid ;
Ní h-urusa a n-imdegail ;
Nocha teithid re n-a n-guin,
Co m-(b)a lán an fer d'á fuil.'

Fuil.

Is ann sin tanic Bricne a mach, agus do d'fhech an fhaighti 'n a timcell. Agus adconnairc buidhin móir ar a h-imell

---

[1] An idiom not now used in S.G. Cf. *a thuaith gach n-direch* infra, p. 220.

[2] *loar* ; cf. *leug lothar* (*lomhar*) *nam buadhan*, 'brilliant jewel of virtues' (Ranald Macdonald, p. 287) ; *lothar*, 'wardrobe,' etc. (Dinn.). For *lomar*, from *ló* 'wool,' cf. *casla* .i. *casló*, .i. *olann chas* (O'Cl.).

[3] The sentence is awkward at the best, and possibly corrupt. The MS. reads *ḡmbalcl* (possibly *bald*) *an* etc.

Hallowmas fair on the morrow.' And Bricne went forth
again and saw a great company due south of him, a company,
to wit, dark very large in close array, with brown mantles
fringed with silver round them all, with broad woollen smocks,
and with broad gray-blue swords in their hands flashing, and
great sharp spears with long shafts and thick for a stout
hero's grip, and brown broad-tufted very large shields. A
stately sedate very tall youth marched in front of the noble
company who maintained perfect discipline among them.
Ailill recognised them, and this lay was composed on the
occasion :—

'A squadron is approaching the castle,
  They are not the men to retreat,
  With mantles brown coloured
  And shields of like colour.

'Dark men with hero's strength,
  With smocks shining white in the sun ;
  Tall men of black complexion
  Who have come from the great sea.

'Grey swords in their hands,
  Which strike deadly in conflict.
  Spears pennoned, large,
  Men very tall, not to be gainsaid.'

'I recognise the hosts,
  Those men of high spirit,
  Angus son of Echtach from over (the sea)
  And the youthful warriors of Aran.

'They are men hard to contend with,
  Their protection is hard to obtain,
  These men will not be slain,
  Till the grass is soaked with their blood.
                              (A squadron) is.

Then Bricne went forth, and viewed the lawn all around.
And he saw a large squadron seated upon the edge of the

---

⁴ The unusual form appears to be based on the somewhat uncommon verb *beba,*
bebais, bebsat, 'die,' v. K. M. Contrib., *s.v.*
      ⁵ I take *meic* here as qualifying *oglaeich,* 'young warriors,' not as governing *oglaoch,*
which would mean 'sons of warriors.'

'n a suide, agus samail da chet laoch a línmaire; cet dib co m-brataib corcra[1] cortharacha comdatha, agus cet eile go m-brataib uaine egsamla ill-dathacha impa, agus fer finn-cas foistinech feichemanta, maisech min-corcra maol-tengthach etarra an eiter-medon. Do aithin Oilill iad, agus do rignedar an laid ann :—

'Ata buiden ar an muigh,
  As an foil iad ré a féghain;
  Samail da chet a lín sin,
  Go n-armaib, go n-ilsciathaib.

'Cet dib go m-brataib corcra,
  D' feraib aille admolta;
  Cet dib co m-brataib uaine,
  D' feraip finda fír-uaille.

'Ata ain fer sa buidin
  As aille di feraib fuinidh;[2]
  Laoch mór co finne n-erla[3]
  As co m-binne n-urlabra.'

'Is se sin Muiredhach mor,
  Mac Oilella, lín a t-shloig,
  Nocha teithend se re a lá,
  Dáigh ro fhedar mar ata.'

                    Ata.

A h-aitle na laide sin tainic Bricne a rís ar an faighte agus do dech nime. Agus ba h-ingnad leis an lear[4] slúaig agus na córaighthi catha atconnairc ac techt do'n baile. Agus tanic a sdech, agus atbert fri h-Oilill: 'Ata buiden mór a nois is in slíabh a n-iar, agus samail cethri cet curad a coimlín, agus coiger doinn-fher derrsgaithech deg láoch a tosech an dírma co n-deig cealt taisich im gach triath dibh; fer direch dath-armach donn-ruadh ar deredh na drong-buidhni; agus fer ceinn-lethan cas-mongach ciuin-bríathrach cnes-sholus a(n) etar-medbon na cath-miled ac a cudhnodh.' Do ber misi ait(h)ni ar in m-buidin eile sin,' ar Oilill. Agus is cuma do

---

[1] MS. corcorcra.
[2] Lit., 'the men of the west'; fuin, fuined, fuinim, 'end,' specially applied to 'sunset,' 'close of day,' hence 'west.'

green. They appeared to be two hundred in number; the half of them clothed in purple mantles of one shade and fringed; the other half in green diverse coloured mantles. There sat in the centre of them a man with fair curly hair, sedate, alert, handsome, of ruddy face and lisping tongue. Oilill recognised them, and this lay was made :—

'There is a troop upon the plain,
  Where they can be seen ;
  About two hundred in number,
  With weapons and many shields.

'An hundred in purple mantles,
  Men handsome worthy of high praise ;
  An hundred in green mantles
  Fair and truly gallant men.

'There is one in the band,
  The fairest of the world's men ;
  A tall hero with fair hair,
  And of melodious utterance.'

'That is the great Muiredach,
  Son of Oilill, numerous his host ;
  He will not flee while life lasts,
  Or he becomes a changed man.'

There is.

After that lay Bricne went forth again upon the green, and looked about him. And he was amazed at the multitude of people and the ranked battalions which he saw coming to the place. He returned within and said to Oilill : 'There is a great squadron now on the hill to the west. They look about four hundred warriors in number. Five brown-haired distinguished noble heroes clad in leaders' dress are in the front of the host; a straight light-brown man in bright armour is in the rear of the numerous company ; while a broad-headed, curly-haired, mild-spoken, fair-skinned man is in the midst of the battle warriors, commanding them. 'I recognise

---

[3] Cf. *airla*, 'hair,' (K. M.).   *Urla*, 'lock of hair,' 'beard,' is the current form.
[4] *Vide* vol. i. p. 308, n. 3.

bui ag a rádh, agus atbert Bricne an laid agus ro fregair
Oilill h-é :—:

'Buiden eile sunn sa sliabh,
Ni 'n a n-o(i)r tegaid acht a n-iar,
Na slóig is sotla ar gach seilg,
In a m-broin[1] corcra cro-derg.

'Ataît ar tús na buidhni
Cuiger laoch, lonn a luibhni;
Atá ar deredh treall o'n t-slúagh
Gilli garb direch donn-ruadh.

'Ata ar medhon na miled
Gilla mor seng narsín*edh*,
Duine do réidi*ugh*' gach recht,
Fa'n Eirinn uile an t-oirecht.' ↘

'An Gamannrad sin uile,
Fa Gamain na Sidgaile;
Fer is mó righi 's reabh
Agus is caoime buiden.'

Buiden eile sunn.

Is ann sin tanic Bricne ar in b-faicthi a ris, agus do gabh
ac feithem da gach taeib in a timcell.　Agus atconnairc na
dirmadha data dímóra, agus na toinnti[2] trom-sl*uaig*, agus
na buidni brat-caoma, agus na h-oirechta aidble osgardha.
Agus do gab egla adbal mór é, agus tanic a sdech a ris.
'Sgela let a Bricne?' ar Oilill.　'Ata, imorro,' ar Bricne,
'nair no co n-airmither gainem mara[3] agus duilli feadha agus
drucht for fér agus fér for faichthi, ni h-airemthar sluagh agus
socraide catha, agus cetherna curad agus cath-miled an r*ig*,
agus es-urr*adha* ar faichthi an dunaid-si a trat(h)-sa.'　'Mo
muinntir-sa sin,' ar Oilill Finn, 'ac techt do commoradh an
áonaigh-se a marach.'

---

[1] The word is not uncommon in the sense of 'multitude,' 'crowd.' In the meaning of some article of raiment *broin* is unknown to me.　But cf. S.G. *broineag,*
broineagach, 'rags,' 'tatters.'

[2] *toinnti,* later *toindte,* evidently 'multitudes,' 'ranks.'　In S.G. the verb *toinn*
(N. *toinna,* Eng. *twine*) means 'twist,' 'twine':—

'Freumh ar naduir toinnte dlùth
Mu gach dùil sa' chruinne-ché.'—(*Fear Oiùil,* p. 10).

that other troop,' said Oilill. And as they spoke thus Bricne recited the lay and Oilill responded thereto :—

'Another squadron there on the hill,
They come not from the east but from the west;
Hosts most eager at the hunt,
In their purple blood-red array.

'There are in front of the company
Five heroes, fierce their spears;
There is in the rear, a space apart,
A rough straight light-brown youth.

'In the midst of the soldiers,
A tall, noble . . . youth,
A man fit to decide every case
That may arise in Ireland's courts.'

'Gamhanraidh all of them,
With Gaman of Sidgal;
A man whose sway and good humour is absolute,
And whose troops are the handsomest.'

Another squadron there.

Then Bricne went forth again upon the green, and he kept gazing around him on every side. And he saw the gallant very large crowds, and the serried ranks, and the squadrons in beautiful mantles, and the vast daring multitudes. Great terror took hold of him and he returned within again. Oilill asked, 'Any news, Bricne?' 'I have, indeed,' replied Bricne; 'for until the sand of the sea is counted up, and the leaves of the forest, and dew upon grass, and grass upon green, the hosts and armed troops, the foot champions and battle-soldiers of the king, and the mercenaries upon the green of this castle at the present time cannot be numbered.' 'My people these,' said Oilill the Fair, 'who have come to hold this fair on the morrow.'

[3] The simile is, in whole or in part, not uncommon. Cf. the well-known quat-rains in which Dugald Buchanan endeavours to convey an idea of eternity :—

'Ged dh' àirmhinn uile reulta neimh,
Gach feur is duilleach riamh a dh'fhàs,
Mar ris gach braon ata sa' chuan,
'S gach gaineamh chuartaicheas an tràigh.

''S ged chuirinn mile bliadhna seach
As leth gach aoin diubh sud gu léir,
Cha d' imich seach de'n t-siorr'achd mhòir
Ach mar gu'n tòisicheadh i 'n dé.'

Agus tanic Bricne a rís a mach, agus atconnairc buiden a n-íar-des is in b-faichthi. Agus is í so· a tuarasgbail, am-ail atbert Bricne :—

> 'Atát sunn buiden brogdha,
> D' feraib deg dealba dorrda ;
> Glan a lí [1]
> Cethri cet is trí cethrair.

> 'Sgiath corcra ar clé gach curadh
> Do na triathaib nar tubadh ;
> Atat i minnaib na flatha
> *Bruitne* [2] uaine áon-datha.

> 'Fer dub a tús na fednach,
> Cethri cet triath a teglach,
> Dá dath *for* cuing*id* na cuan,
> Cnes geal, gnuis corcra mar *crúan*.' [3]

> 'Is íad sin clanna Find
> Is mó dho lúaidus linbir [4]
> A coimidecht *Fraoich* na radh [5]
> Eirgid na treoin mar atat.'
>
> *Atat.*

Tanic Bricne ar an b-faichthi, agus do gabustar ag fechain cethr*a* airde an talman in a tímcell. Agus ni fhaca aird dip nach raibi sluagh no socraidi ac techt do'n baile. Agus atchonnairc buiden adbal mór a thúaith gach n-dírech di feraib dorcha dímora, agus br*uitne* [2] endatha nile impe, agus sgeith donna díanarda ar formnaib na fer-óglaoch. Agus nocha tánic amail a samla ar méd na ar miletacht is in faichthi. Agus is cuma do búi ac tabairt a tuarasgbala, agus atbert an laid :—

> 'Is sí so buiden is mó,
> Is fir is ní h-imargó ;
> Nocha tánic sunn co se,
> Buiden amail a lethide.

---

[1] MS. reads *ʃasʃsor*.

[2] Here the word probably means 'spikelets,' a diminutive from *brot*, 'spike,' 'goad.' But immediately below the same form, similarly contracted, must surely mean 'short mantles,' a diminutive from *brot*, *brat*, 'a covering,' 'a mantle.'

[3] Rendered 'red enamel' by W. S. O'Davoren writes : Cruan .i. gne don tsencerdacht (*ut est*), a n-all cruain .i. in derg, ocus creduma .i. in buidhe, maithne

And Bricne went forth again, and he saw a troop on the green in the south-west. And this is their description, as Bricne related it :—

> 'Here is a mighty squadron,
> Of men well-shaped and stern,
> Bright their complexion . . .
> Four hundred and twelve their number.

> 'A purple shield on the left hand of each champion
> Of the chiefs that cannot be challenged;
> In the diadems of the princes,
> Spikelets green of one colour.

> 'A dark man in front of the company,
> His household consists of four hundred lords;
> Two colours distinguish the lord of havens,
> White skin, face purple like *cruan*.'

> 'These are the clans of Find
>
> .   .   .
>
> Accompanying Fraoch of Rea
> The mighty ones will march as you see them.'

There are.

Bricne went (again) upon the green, and kept viewing the four airts of the earth around him. He saw not an airt of them, but with hosts and multitudes coming to the place. And he saw a great vast squadron coming straight from the north of dark very tall men, dressed in short cloaks all of one colour, and with brown very lofty shields on the shoulders of the manly warriors. The equal of these in size or soldierly bearing had not (hitherto) come upon the green. As Bricne was describing them he recited the lay :—

> 'This is the greatest squadron,
> Of a truth no falsehood;
> There has not come up till now
> A troop to match them.

.i. buidhe ocus uaine ocus geal. *Cruan*, *i.e.* a kind of ancient art-work, *ut est*, 'the bridle of enamel,' *i.e.* the red (sort), and *creduma*, *i.e.* the yellow, (and) *maithne*, *i.e.* 'yellow and green and white.' Cf. *Arch. Celt. Lex.*, ii. p. 287.

[4] MS. reads rather *linbar* or *liubar*.

[5] For *Gamhain ruadh na Reeadh* (later *Ree*), *vide* vol. i. p. 296. Here it would be possible, to translate 'F. of the sayings, or maxims.'

' Atat sa droing ar tosaigh,
 Ceithre ced feinnidh fosaidh ;
 Atat sa droing fa dheredh,
 Ceithre ced gan cláon temeal.

' Atát ceithre ced eile
 D' feraib nía móra nime,
 Ar n-eidedh gach fir eolaigh
 Sa m-buidin móir medónaigh.

' Sgiath ar cúl gacha curad
 Do sgiathaib breaca brugach,[1]
 Ata cairthe tróm nach treith
 A n-gústal[2] gacha geil-sgeith.'

' As iat sin na fir a thuaith
 Ó oir-imlib Esa Ruaidh,
 Aedh agus Aongus co m-bloid,
 Da degh mac Cornáin chos duibh.

' Buiden leis a mó a menma
 Tic amail a saine samla ;
 Nocha n-fuil is calma a cli,
 Aderim-si ribhisí.'

                                    As si.

---

[1] MS. reads *bruḡ*. Possibly for *brogach*, 'mighty.'

[2] *custal .i. trusdaladh* (O'Cl.), now *trusaladh* (O'R.), *truisealadh* (H.S.D.),
'tucking up clothes,' 'trussing.'   In the old literature frequently associated with
leinte, 'smocks'; e.g. *leni . . . frí gelchnes i caustul go glunib dó*, 'a smock kilted
up to the knees next his white skin.' Cf. *T.B.C.* s.v. *caustul, custul*. The stones
were evidently strapped to the shields in some way.

'In the company in front
 Are four hundred sedate champions ;
 In the rear company
 Are four hundred equally conspicuous.

'There are other four hundred,
 Tall fierce champions ;
 Each warrior fitly armed
 In the great squadron in the centre.

'A shield on the back of each hero
 Speckled and very large ;
 There is a heavy unwieldy stone,
 Fastened to each white shield.'

'These are the men from the north,
 From the borders of Assaroe,
 Aedh and Angus of equal valour,
 The two noble sons of black-footed Curnan.

'A squadron of highest courage
 That comes in their splendid form ;
 There are not (men) of greater daring or strength,
 I declare unto you.'

                              This is.

                (To be continued.)

MY HIGHLAND BAPTISM

William Jolly

The present Celtic Renascence is but a late, delayed, and natural recognition of a great past Literature, too long despised and neglected by the Sassenach, from various causes—not the least being insensibility to its wonderful charm, reluctance to acknowledge debts to races he despised and drove before him, and, in great part, to the fact that these wonderful literary treasures were hidden, nay buried, in unknown tongues. Now that it is being translated into English, Celtic literature may and will have some chance of influencing British literature in a new and permanent fashion, and of speeding the time pleaded for so eloquently by Matthew Arnold and others in many a glowing paragraph. Now, also, that our universities, notably Glasgow, have wakened out of the sleep of centuries and recognised its importance, Gaelic and Irish and Welsh literature can no longer be ignored.

I came early under the glamour of the Celtic spirit. First, as a lad, when I was electrified by Ossian; though even then, a youthful analysis, comparing his Ode on the Death of Oscar with the Hebrew Threnody on the Death of Saul, proved the coincidence between the two to be so close that it became suspicious, and suggested tampering, by Macpherson, with the Celtic basis. Lowland born, in the old romantic town of the big abbey of Aberbrothock, the 'Fairport' of the Great Wizard, viewing the Highlands through that dim poetic haze, and seeing their hills only from afar off across the broad Strathmore, I was inspired with enthusiasm for the mountains, and fired with ardour to visit the glens and bens. That wish was amply gratified at last, sooner than I could have anticipated, when I was a lad above twenty, more than forty years ago. It was then, on a visit to Loch Rannoch, that I received my Highland Baptism, the virtue of which has ever since permanently influenced life, and will endure to the very end.

In Edinburgh, under the crags of the castle, while still a student in the Normal School there, before University days, which came later, I made the acquaintance of Alister Cameron, from the Highlands of Perthshire. He was son of the old Gaelic teacher and translator, John Cameron, at Innervar, Glen Lyon, where Alister was born. We at once made a covenant of friendship, which has endured undiminished in strength and unbroken by time until this hour. Soon after leaving Edinburgh and Ayrshire, I accepted his warm invitation to spend some time with him in the romantic Rannoch country. The idea was enchanting, and its realisation the fulfilment of a long dream, glorious and unforgotten; and an entry into future labours. Our trysting-place was Kinloch Rannoch, at the eastern end of the lake, where the Tummel leaves it, and where his sister lived. At that time, there was no rail further north than Dunkeld, and thither I sped on my way to what seemed to me the Land of Romance. My recollections of every stage in that long past and picturesque journey are much more vivid than those of yesterday; and have furnished a gallery of imperishable pictures and brilliant associations on the walls of deathless memory. It introduced me to the Highland land, the Highland people, and Highland problems. These became potent factors in my after life, which has, curiously, been spent, in great part, in their investigation; for, in the Highlands, fate determined that I should pass the most important and most laborious days to me, and make my dearest friendships. That early excursion coloured all my subsequent career.

Roaming round Dunkeld in a thrill of delight, I made acquaintance with Birnam Woods, of Shakspearean allusion, the quaint burgh itself, and the interesting cathedral, whose tower still looms large in memory; though I had been accustomed, from boyhood, to the presence of grander ruins in my native town. I had then entered the gateway of the Highlands, and across the porch of my future life work. I still recall with disdain the tricksome mirrors of the summer-house, known as Ossian's Hall, in the grounds of the castle; which found expression to feeling in Wordsworth's indignant remonstrance against these, and its bewildering kaleidoscope of foaming and flashing falls—a travesty of its inherent grandeur, and a violation of their beauty incompatible with their majesty and with true taste. Like Wordsworth,

> ' I mused and, thirsting for redress,
> Recoiled into the wilderness.'

Thence I found my way northwards by open coach, drinking the delights I had looked forward to so ardently that Pitlochry was reached only too soon for full satiation of appetite for the Beautiful. I felt the truth of the Wordsworthian contention, which is the main theme of his 'Prelude,' that these early years of our life have in them a vividness of perception, and a depth and strength of feeling that never do and never can return. They were so intensely real, so powerfully vivid, that they have become imperishable, and cannot even now be expressed in adequate words. Poetry alone seemed the one proper vehicle of utterance; but the irksomeness of poetic diction, even then after considerable practice, seemed to dispel the charm. The reality surpassed all anticipations, however exalted. It was altogether an ecstatic vision, and remains strangely realistic to this hour, as when first seen and felt in all its potency.

I was attracted, first, by the meeting of the great waters opposite Logierait, where the Tay and the Tummel unite; each worthily claiming to be the parent fountain of the mighty river system whose name is dominated by the Tay, THE WATER, as it signifies in old Gaelic, not *Tatha*, smooth, for neither loch nor river merits such a distinction. Geographically considered, however, it is matter of dispute as to which is the parent stream; and I contend that the balance of evidence, in extent, volume and basin, rests with the grander Tummel. But, as the greater Missouri is eclipsed in name by the great but lesser Mississippi, so here the Tay has supplanted its rival.

I visited the Falls of Tummel near Pitlochry, where the stream rolls proudly over the obstructing rocks, with the wondrous cone of Schiehallion, the finest hill in the broad Highlands, set right over its centre, and showing its lovely contour in the glorious lights of a splendid day. Though under twenty feet in height, the Falls combine aspects of form, foam, fierceness and colour, wood, rock and river, which place them above all praise. Even geological Macculloch, in his volumes on the Highlands, written and dedicated to his friend, Sir Walter Scott, is roused to enthusiasm in describing their beauties, scientific soul though he was.

There, also, I made my first acquaintance with *ants' hills*, which, though common in the northern woods, are unknown in Lowland Forfarshire. They often rise several feet in height, formed mostly of the needles of the fir-trees under which they are heaped, and up which the paths of the ever active insects can be traced to their very tops. When left undisturbed, these hillocks look quite lifeless, especially during midday heat; but when stirred with a stick, they at once present a sight of the most marvellous activity, caused by the anxieties of countless thousands of ants to secure their young and repair the damage.

It proves the aptness of the image used by Dugald Buchanan, schoolmaster of Rannoch, and greatest Religious poet of the Highlands, in his remarkable poem on the 'Last Judgment,' when he says that, on that great day, at the sound of the Last Trumpet, the earth will deliver up her dead 'like an ant-hill when stirred!' It is an original and powerful, truly Dantean, comparison; exhibiting also the real source of imagery for all true men and true poets—their own environment, directly observed and artistically utilised. The sight of this curious and striking phenomenon prepared me for being introduced to the works of the Schoolmaster Bard, when I spent these glorious ten days round Rannoch.

I afterwards knew a good parish minister, now gone into the Great Shadow, who was born not far from the Falls. While at school, under a 'boast,' which boys will foolishly make, he said that he would stand in his kilt on the top of an ant-hill for a quarter of an hour. This he accomplished amid the admiring eyes of his comrades and the tears of the girls, but at frightful cost to himself. For the vicious little creatures swarmed up his bare red legs, and underneath his kilt, biting at every step, with the result that he suffered for weeks in bed from blood poisoning—little consoled by his pluck, which was perfect. That pluck never left him in after life; but he chose more appropriate fields for its exhibition, and won, in these, love and enduring fame as a devoted minister and Hebrew scholar.

As a diligent student of English Literature, for Gaelic was then to me a sealed book, though Latin and Greek were not, I felt a peculiar charm in the scenery through which we were driving, in the thought, that the same journey had been made, among others, by Gray and Burns and Wordsworth. Gray's achievement in travel was as remarkable as that of Johnson, for its courage and priority of perception of the picturesque. Yet even he, with his feeling for style and his sympathy for the Celts, was not without the terror which then inspired most Lowlanders. A letter to his Cambridge friend, Wharton, is deliciously feminine in feeling for philological propriety, and, as from an old bachelor, physical formalities. He had just left Glamis Castle, where he had had a good time with that fair poet and lame philosopher, James Beattie. He tells that he saw Schiehallion from the high towers of Glamis, forty-five miles off, which is very accurately stated; and he makes prudishly merry with its extraordinary name, calling the mountain simply ' *That*,' the Latin of scholarly surprise (*ista*). Saying : ' There that *She-Khallian* spires into a cone above the clouds.' Travelling along this same road as myself, he returns to the subject, calling it the Maiden's Pap, and ' that monstrous creation of God ! ' Goodness ! Why shouldn't God make her one of the finest forms in the world, in her way as fine as Cotopaxi or the glorious volcano that dominates Japan !

The junction of Tummel and Tay he rightly deemed ' charming,' assigning the greater size to the Tummel. He thought the road excellent but too dangerous, he confessed ' in all conscience,' though masked indeed by wood that found means to grow where good Gray could not stand. The highway being often without defence, he frankly admitted, dear soul, that he passed it for miles on foot, *partly for fear*, and, no doubt, partly to admire the beauty of the scenery, which the beauty of the weather—it was in June—set off to the greatest advantage. As evening came on, they approached, he continues, the Pass of ' Gillicrankie,' where in the '45 the Hessians, with their prince at their head, stopped short and refused to march a foot farther—falling into Latin like a scholar—' *Vestibulum ante ipsum primisque in faucibus Orci!*' This may be rendered by Scott's *Lady of the Lake*, 'the pass's jaws.' Here they seemed, to the English Lowland poet, the entrance, the vestibule to Hell!

' In short,' Gray concludes, 'since I saw the Alps, I have seen nothing sublime till now.' He asks Wharton naïvely to pray for him; for he also dreaded Edinburgh and the itch, expecting to find very little in any way worth the perils he was to endure. These, it is to be hoped, his virtuous and comfortable couch fully belied!

Schiehallion's name evidently frightened Gray's sensibilities, for, though he gives its probable meaning, he seems to have thought that the first syllable meant Maiden, whereas it is the second that does so; and he prints in capitals, always, the 'SHE'—anticipating Rider Haggard by many years in having feared the ' SHE ' that must be feared, admired and obeyed, here in wild Scotland, as in rude Rhodesia !

Joining the mailcart that runs along the highway above the north bank of the Tummel, I passed the hamlet of Garry, at the entrance of Killiecrankie, with its wealth of wood and its grand gorge. Thence, alone with the young driver, a bright, intelligent and obliging companion, I sped between wooded lanes of birch, redolent with the inspiriting odour from its leaves wet with dew ; combined alder and sienna-coloured Caledonian firs, flecked with sunshine and shade ; and commanding enchanting glimpses of the valley of the Tummel. The glorious peak of the beauteous Maiden's Breast across the vale was ever dominant. Such is the significance of its sweet-sounding name, Schiehallion, from the Gaelic *Sich chailin*) *cailin* being a maiden, and *cailleach* an old woman.

Soon, at an elevated point, the driver kindly stopped, to give his horses needed rest ; but, in reality, to enable me to go through the birch trees to see what is known as 'The Queen's View,' so named since our late Queen visited it. It was an unexpected and magnificent spectacle—to my young eyes *unspeakably* fine. At my feet, though some five miles off, lay Loch Tummel, dented with richly wooded capes and bays, with gentle Schiehallion pictured in its placid mirror ! Beyond, stretched long Loch Rannoch and lone Loch Lydan, or Lydoch, the centres of a wonderful vista ; long-drawn, lovely, and lonely, lighted up by the glowing westering sun ; on to Rannoch's mighty Moor and the Black Forest, with the peaks of grand Glencoe in clear view some fifty miles off!

To my Lowland sight, by the lights of young fancy and unexpected beauty, the scene seemed pure enchantment—the finest I had yet seen on earth. It *is* a sight universally acknowledged as unsurpassed, in its kind, for mingled majesty and beauty, bounteousness, grandeur and wildness.

Then we quickly dropped down on the clachan of Tummel Bridge, where another road crossed ours, amidst mountain masses of boldness and gloom ; all dominated and redeemed by the Maiden's Pap, not less beautiful when revealed on the bosom of wood and wilderness, that partly hid, partly revealed her native comeliness, even at close quarters seen. We then traversed further miles of brighter, better cultivated country as we neared our destination, in a succession of mansions embosomed in foliage, and past Mount Alexander with its old, Scottish, castellated turrets.

At long last, sated but not weary with sight-seeing, sore with the hard journeying, I reached the village of Kinloch Rannoch, across the bridge where the clear Tummel relieves the overburdened lake of its surplus waters. The Loch itself slept in the evening light, huge Ben Alder on its right, twelve miles ahead, where it receives the streams that dash from its rock-bound shoulders.

There I was warmly welcomed by my friend, Cameron, with the heartiest of hand-shakes and the brightest of smiles. He led me to his sister's house, where I spent the happiest of holidays. These were my first taste of Highland hospitality, and digest of great Highland scenery. I was already bitten badly with the sacred thirst of the Celtic fever, the fervour of which still tingles in my blood, dominating life, and, though unknown to me then, anticipating my future fate; but a fate anticipated without sadness or fear, though little increased, in now the long-drawn end, in this world's fortune.

After due and abundant refreshment at my friends' snug house, I had my first sail on a Highland lake, in the glorious glow of an August sunset, with the rising moon to add to its attractions. The impressions I then received are still sweetly beautiful and unforgetable, distinct and clear, and not crowded out by countless boatings since. I felt as if I were, in degree, *King Arthur Redivivus*, gliding along the lonely Mere, as the double oars were dipped in the gleaming waters by my willing companion, while I held the helm, long accustomed to such a task in a seaport town. Happily, no sword descended to terminate the day or our lives. And now, more than forty years since that sweet eventide, we both still wait the final summons to Avilon of the Mighty Mist!

' NOTE.—The Etymology of the name Schiehallion cannot be said to be finally settled. My own opinion inclines strongly towards that given in the text above, which is also the local derivation. This, on account of its own remarkable and singularly striking contour; the fondness of the Celts for this image of a Woman's Breast, as in *Maiden Pap*, in Caithness, on the borders of Sutherland, the *Paps of Jura, Scuir-na-ciche*, or the Scaur of the Pap, at the entrance to Glencoe, *Benachie*, the Ben of the Breast, which adorns the Vale of Alford and Central Aberdeenshire, *Sichnanighean*, in Arran, the Pap of the *Nighean* or Maiden, and many more. Another derivation has been advanced, and is endorsed by the great Gaelic scholar Dr. Macbain, viz. *Sith Chaillin*, the Mountain of the Caledonians or Men of the Woods; like *Dunkeld*, anciently *Duncaillen*, the *Dun* of the Woods, or Men of the Woods.

SOME SUTHERLAND NAMES OF PLACES

W. J. Watson

The county of Sutherland, in its present extent, includes three old divisions—Sutherland proper, the Reay country, and Assynt. Sutherland, *South-land*, was the name applied by the Norsemen to that southern part of their province of Caithness lying between the Ord of Caithness and the river Oykell, with its estuary, the Kyle of Sutherland. 'Mons Mound,' says an old geographer (1165 A.D.), 'dividit Cathanesiam per medium.' Accordingly he writes of this whole north-eastern part of Scotland as 'Cathanesia citra et ultra Montem.' The *Mons* is of course the Ord, and is not to be confused with the modern Mound between Golspie and Rogart, which dates from the early part of the last century. The Reay country in the north from Durness to the Caithness border was, and is, the home of the Mackays ; in Gaelic, *Duthaich Mhic Aoidh*. Assynt is the district on the western seaboard. In 1601, through the influence of the Earl of Sutherland, the south-eastern and northern districts were raised to the dignity of a separate sheriffdom, to which, in 1631, Assynt was added. Previously they formed part of the sheriffdom of Inverness.

Sutherland names fall into three classes—Pictish, Gaelic, and Norse. The two latter are found in varying relative proportions all over the country. The Pictish element is most pronounced in the south-eastern part, though by no means confined to it. This paper attempts to give specimens of the Celtic names, *i.e.* Pictish and Gaelic. The Norse names will be taken separately.

That the Picts, however much they may have been mixed with an older and non-Aryan stock in point of race, spoke a Celtic language of some sort, is generally agreed. It is also the view of most leading authorities that their language had strong Kymric affinities ; that, in other words, it is to-day more nearly represented by Welsh and Cornish than by Scottish or Irish Gaelic. The place-names of Pictland, so far as they have been investigated, bear this out; and Sutherland, though early subjected to strong Norse influence, contributes its own share to the proof. Our earliest authority for this district, Ptolemy of Alexandria, who wrote about 120 A.D., mentions two Sutherland rivers, Nabaros and Ila, one place ὑψηλὴ ὄχθη, High Bank (of a river), and the tribal names Cornavii, Caerēni, Lugi, and Smertae. Nabaros is the modern river Naver, G. *Nabhair* (*bh* = *w*). Its ending -*aros* may be compared with *Tam-aros*, 'the Tamar'; *Sam-ara*, 'the Sambre,' and others. The root *nab- nav-*, appears in several river-names of Celtic origin (cf. Holder, *Alt-Celtischer Sprachschatz*), and is most probably the same as in *nūbes, nebula*, νέφος; Sk. *nabhas*, 'vapour.' For the idea may be compared the Ross-shire river Meig, G. *Mìg*, if that is rightly equated with ὀμίχλη, 'mist,' and its congeners in Greek and Latin. Many of our oldest river-names mean simply water or fluid. As a parallel may be compared the Welsh Nevern. Ila is now in Gaelic *Ilidh* (short initial vowel), the Helmsdale river, connected by Dr. W. Stokes with German *eilen*, older *īlen*, 'hurry.' In point of meaning this is not exactly satisfactory. The river is about 21 miles long, with a fall of 362 feet. The Banffshire Isla falls 1000 feet in 18½ miles; the Perth-shire Isla, G. *Ile* (initial long vowel) falls 3000 feet in 47 miles. The island of Islay is G. *Ile*, with long initial vowel. The latest theory as to the origin of these names, which seem all to hang together, refers them to the root *pi* seen in πίνω, ἔ-πι-ον, *bi-bo*, giving a primitive **pila*, initial *p* being dropped in Celtic. This has the advantage of explaining the island name, as well as *all* the river-names. High Bank, as was pointed out in the first number of the *Celtic Review*, is echoed by Norse *Ekkialsbakki*, 'Oykell Bank,' where Ekkial, G. *Oiceil*, is taken to represent old *uxellos*, 'high,' whence Welsh *uchel*, Gael. *uasal*. The idea is repeated in the name of the township on the bold left bank of the Oykell estuary,—Altas, G. *Alltais*, 'bluff-stead.' Of the tribal names no trace can be found except in the case of the Smertae. These I discovered last summer as commemorated by the Ross-shire hill-name *Càrn Smeirt*, 'the Smertae's Cairn,' in Strathcarron (Kincardine), behind Braelangwell Lodge, and east of *Meall Dheirgidh*, 'lump of redness,' forming part of the ridge between Strathcarron and the Oykell estuary. It does not appear on the O.S. maps. This indicates the location of the Smertae as at least partly in Ross. They probably occupied the valleys of the Carron, Oykell, and Shin. With Smertae is to be compared the Gaulish goddess Ro-smerta, πολύφρων, 'deep-thinking,' from the root *smer*, 'think.' The Smertae were *smart*. This brings us to the end of Ptolemy's names, if we except his names of capes, which, however, seem properly to belong to Caithness rather than to Sutherland. Of the seven Ptolemaic names noted above, it will be seen that four survive to this day, a striking proof of continuity of transmission.

Seven hundred years after Ptolemy's time, the invading Norsemen found in easter Sutherland and Caithness a tribe who called themselves the Cats—*Catti*, 'wildcats'—whence the Picto-Norse hybrid, *Katanes*, 'Cat-promontory,' now Caithness. That these folk were regarded by the Norsemen as Picts is sufficiently proved by the name Pentland Firth applied to the sea that washes their northern coast, which certainly means Pictland Firth. According to mediæval Gaelic legend, Cat was one of the seven sons of Cruithne, *the* Pict, who divided Scotland into seven provinces, of which the most northerly is referred to as *Crich Chat*, 'bounds of the Cats'; *i Cataib*, 'among the Cats' (as Cæsar says *in Sequanis*). This latter expression explains the term *Cataobh* (Cataibh), which is modern Gaelic for Sutherland. With these fierce, wildcat folk may perhaps be compared Herodotus' *Kynetes* or *Kynesii*, 'Hound-folk,' most westerly of European peoples, and next neighbours to the Celts. This old tribal name has impressed itself strongly on the place-names. The southern uplands of Lairg are still in Gaelic *Braigh-Chat*, 'Uplands of the Catti'; northward is *Dithreabh Chat*, 'wilderness of Cats'; the Kyle of Sutherland is *An Caol*

Catach, ' Cat-kyle '; the Earl of Sutherland was *Moirear Chat*, ' Mormaer,' or ' Lord of Cats '; the Duke is *An Diùc Catach*; Sutherland men are *Cataich*.

In Gaelic the primitive Indo-Germanic *qu* sound becomes *c*; in Kymric it becomes *p*; and as primitive *p* is non-existent in Celtic, no place-name involving *p* can be of *Gaelic* origin, unless the *p* has arisen independently, or in borrowed words. If it is Celtic, it must belong to the Kymric branch. Applying the test thus roughly and generally indicated, we find in Sutherland six or seven *pits*; O.G. *pett*, Welsh *peth*, ' a thing,' ' a part.' In Gaelic *pit* is usually translated, generally by *baile*, ' a stead,' which is the meaning of *pett* in the Book of Deer. The Sutherland *pits* are confined to the parishes of Rogart, Lairg, and Dornoch in the south-eastern part of the county. There we have Pitfour (twice), G. *Baile-phùr*; cf. Welsh *pawr*, 'pasturage,' 'grazing.' Pitfour or Balfour is common all over Pictland, and *-fur* appears also in Delfour, Dochfour, Tillifour and Tillifourie, and Trinafour. Once heard in Gaelic, it cannot be confounded with G. *fuar*, ' cold.' The unaspirated form is seen clearly in Porin, G. *Pórainn* (Strathconon), cf. Welsh *poriant*, 'pasture,' and in *Purin*, older *Pourane* (Fife). The aspirated form is as old as the Book of Deer, *nice fùrené*, now Pitfour in Deer. Pitgrudie, `G. *Baile-ghrùididh*, seems to mean ' grit-stead ' or ' rough-stead.' As a river-name Grudie occurs twice in Sutherland and twice in Ross, not elsewhere. Gruids (Lairg) is an English plural of G. *na Grùidean*. Pittentrail, G. *Baile an Tràill*, may mean ' thrall-stead,' in which case it is a post-Norse formation, G. *tràill* being borrowed from Norse *Thræll*. The remaining *pits* appear only on record: Pitmean, Pitarkessie, Pitcarie Petterquhasty. Another *p*-name is Proncy, near Dornoch; Promci 1222; G. *Pronnsaidh*, of which I have no derivation to offer. With it may be compared *a' Phronntanaich*, not far away, which seems to be from the same root with developed *t*, and well-known Gaelic suffixes.

Sutherland shows a fair number of streams with the *-ie* suffix, which is so common in Pictland, while it is scarcely

known in the stream-names of Dalriada, still less in Skye or
Lewis. This suffix probably often represents an old -*ios* or
-*ia*, but there are other possibilities, *e.g.* we have seen that
Ptolemy's Ila is now Ilie. The two Grudies (Durness and
Lairg) have been already noted. In Golspie there are Lundaidh and Màilidh. Lundaidh or Lundie is an extremely
common water-name, and has been referred to a nasalised
form of G. *lod*, 'puddle.' Màilidh is also common : Inver-
maillie and Maillie river in Inverness ; Polmaly in Glen-
urquhart ; Dalmally and Allt-màilidh in Glenorchy, while
Coire Mhàileagan (a double diminutive) occurs twice in Ross.
These may possibly come from the root seen in Latin *madeo*,
madidus, wet ; **mad-l-ios*, cf. Holder's *Mad-onia*. O.G. *màl*,
'noble,' from *maglos*, is also possible. The notion of nobility
appears in Allt Eilgnidh (Brora), from O.G. *elg*, 'noble,'
whence Glen-elg, G. *Gleann-eilg* (where *eilg* is to be regarded
as a stream-name), and Elgin, G. *Eilginn*. In Kildonan there
is Tealnaidh, cf. the Gaulish fountain god Tel-o(n), and (?) the
river Tella (Holder). The Lothbeg river is Labhaidh, which
points to an early **Labios*, *Chatter-y*. The river of Strath
Terry is in G. *Tiridh*. Glengolly, G. *Gleanna-gollaidh*,
implies a river Gollaidh, which it is just possible may be a
dialectic variation of the common *Geollaidh* or *Geallaidh*,
Geldy, etymologised by Dr. A. Macbain from the root *geld*,
'water'; Norse *kelda*, 'a well'; Ger. *quelle*. Sgeimhidh
(Altnaharra) is a rapid stream with a delta, which suggests a
comparison with G. *sgeith*, 'vomit.' On the north-west coast
we have Malldaidh, based on G. *mall*, 'slow.' Further search
would doubtless reveal several more stream-names of this
class. The above will serve as specimens. Besides these
there are two important river-names, Shin and Casley. Shin
is G. *Abhainn Sin* (pronounced exactly like *sin*, 'that').
Ptolemy's name for the Shannon is Senos; in *Trip. Life*
Sinona and Sinna; in Irish *Sinainn*; and Dr. W. Stokes
derives from Sk. *sindhu*, 'a river.' Shin and Shannon are no
doubt ultimately the same; the root, however, seems to be
rather *sĭ, sei*, 'bend,' as seen in σῖμος, 'snubnosed'; *sĭmius, sĭnus*.

This applies physically to both rivers. Casley is in G. *Abhainn Charsla'*; its glen is Gleann Charsla', and its mouth is Inbhir Charsla'; an obscure name; *r* is probably a matter of development in Gaelic. Loch Alsh, G. *Loch Ai(l)s*, in Assynt, is no doubt the same as the Ross-shire Lochalsh, Ptolemy's Volsas; and Loch Awe is a repetition of Loch Awe in Argyll; Adamnan's *Stagnum fluminis Abae*, where Aba simply means 'river,' now the river Awe.

Distinctively Pictish terminations, *i.e.* terminations unknown in Dalriada or in Ireland, are rare in Sutherland. Thoroughly Pictish, however, is the suffix -*ais*, seen in Alltais (Altas) already referred to, and described as to situation. It is also found in Allt Charrais, Rosehall, from root *kars*, 'harsh,' 'rough,' seen in Carron, *Carsona*. This burn flows by the site of an old broch, the stones of which were quarried from its bed. There is another Allt Charrais near Strathpeffer. The ending may be referred ultimately to the root of G. *fois*, 'rest,' ἄστυ, *vostis*, 'a stead.' It is found in such names as Forres, G. *Farais*; Farness, G. *Fearnais*; also in Dallas, Duffus, Geddes, Pityowlish, Durris, Dores, and so on. Another appears in Tressady (Rogart and Lairg), G. *Treasaididh*; cf. Navity, G. *Neamh-aididh* (Cromarty); Musaididh in Stratherrick, from root of G. *mus-ach*, 'nasty'; Welsh *mws*, 'rank.' For the root of Tressady may be compared O. Ir. *tress*, 'battle'; Welsh *treisio*, 'oppress'; *treisiant*, 'oppression.' There is a Tressat in Perthshire. A name which should perhaps have come under stream-names is Banavie, seen in Loch Bhanbhaidh, near Loch Shin. There is Banavie, near Fort-William, several of them indeed; also Glen Banavie in Perthshire, and Benvie in Forfar. All these are to be referred to O.G. and Irish *banb*, *banbh*, 'pig'; Welsh *banw*, 'swine.' *Banba* was an old poetic name for Ireland, and the three pagan queens of Ireland were Eriu, Fodla, and Banba. *Banw* is the name of a Welsh river into which falls *Twrch*, 'hog.' 'Many rivers forming deep channels or holes into which they sink in the earth and are lost for a distance are so called.'[1] Whether

[1] *Archiv für Celt. Lexicographie*, iii. 45.

this applies to any of the Scottish Banavie's I have failed to learn, but the name is more probably a locative form of which our Banff (G. *Bainbh*) and Bamff are the accusatives.   Dola, G. *Dóla*, is near Lairg ; also Loch Dola (O.S.M. *Loch Dùghaill !*), a name puzzling in both root and suffix.   The ending -*la* has been seen in Carsla' (Casley) ; it appears also in Croyla (Badenoch), and in *Sruighla*, the Gaelic for Stirling, and is perhaps a reduced form of -*lach* or -*lann*.

In the south and north parts there are some names not necessarily Pictish, but at any rate of very old Celtic forma-tion.   G. *Magh*, 'a plain,' appears commonly enough as *muigh* (genitive or locative), *e.g.* Drum-muie.   It appears also in Morvich, G. *a'Mhor'oich*, 'sea-plain' ; Ir. *muir-magh*.   Such formations are comparatively modern.   A much older forma-tion, on the model of the Gaulish compounds, is seen *e.g.* in the Irish *Fearnmhagh*, 'alder-plain,' repeated near Inverness in the obsolete Fearnaway, with which cf. Darnaway (? *Durno-magos*).   It is seen also in such names as Multovy (Ross), Muckovie (Inverness), for **Molto-magos*, **Mucco - magos*, 'wedder - plain' and 'swine - plain.'   In Sutherland Rovie (Rogart) stands for **Ro-magos*, 'excellent plain.'   Rinavie (Bettyhill), Gaelic *Roinnimhigh*, stands near a sharp bend of the river Naver, forming a cape, and I take it to be for **Rindo-magos*, 'point-plain.'   Reay is in G. *Meaghrath* ; in the Book of Clanranald Lord Reay is *morbhair meghrath*. The name has been equated with Irish *Moyra*, *Maghrath*, 'plain-fort,' but in view of the Sutherland treatment of *magh* as *muigh*, coupled with the difficulty of the palatalised *m* in *Meaghrath*, the parallel is doubtful.   In Ross we have *Coire nam Meagh* and *Meaghlaich*, both from *meagh*, which is our dialectic form—as it is also in Sutherland—for *mang*, 'a fawn,' and Fawn-fort is an intelligible enough combination. In the Caithness part of Reay there is Downreay, G. *Dù(n)rath*, evidently a Pictish **Dūno-rāton*, 'strong fort.' Reay itself is also heard as simply *Ràth*.

The prefix *far*, which is not necessarily Pictish, though common in Pictland, is seen in Farlary, G. *Farrlaraigh*

(Rogart), 'projecting site' (*làrach*), which exactly suits the place. Elsewhere such places are called *Socach*, 'snout-place.' *Rudha na Farai(r)d*, Englished 'Farout Head,' in Durness, has been wrongly equated with Ptolemy's Virvedrum. It means simply 'projecting cape,' and there is another *Rudha na Farai(r)d* at the entrance to Badcall Bay, much projecting. An old spelling of Farout Head is *Farard* (*Orig. Paroch.* ii. 2. 701). With these may be compared *An Araird*, in Ross, and *Urrard*, in Perthshire, at the junction of Tummel and Garry. The parish name *Farr*, which recurs in Inverness-shire, is also to be compared. Some interesting names in *con-* occur. Ben More (Assynt), or at least its highest peak, is *Conmheall*. This has been rendered as from Norse 'Queen-fell,' but as the name Convall occurs as a hill-name elsewhere where there is no possibility of a Norse origin, the true meaning seems to be rather *con-mheall*, 'combination of lumps'—which describes Ben More well, as it has four peaks. *Kuno-mellos*, 'high lump,' is also possible. Between Altas and Lairg, a bold and striking rock of oblong form rises out of the moor, with distinct traces of an old hill-fort. This is *Conchreag*, probably meaning 'high rock'; cf. the hill Conachar, near Lubcroy (Ross), which may be *Kuno-carson*, 'high rock.' The other Sutherland *Conchreag* I have not seen. There is also *Coneas* on the Glengolly river, 'combined fall'? In all these cases *con*, 'dog,' is possible, but there are so many of them all over Pictland which are physically either 'combinations' or high places, that one doubts the applicability, especially as *cù* is quite rare in other combinations. All these names may be regarded as on the debatable ground between Pictish and Gaelic. It may be noted here that *Clais nan Cruithneach*, 'the Picts' hollow,' is near Stoer in Assynt.

There are some interesting purely Gaelic names. *Longphort*, 'encampment,' 'shieling,' which becomes elsewhere Luncart, Lungard, Luncarty, Luichart, is in Sutherland *laghart*. *Seann laghard an t-sluaigh*, 'the old shieling of the folk,' occurs in a poem contributed by Rev. A. Gunn to the Gaelic Society of

Inverness (*Trans.* xxiv. 8). Rob Donn has *Allt an Fhaslaghairt*, 'burn of the stead-shieling.' Evelix (Dornoch), Aveleche 1222, is an English plural form of G. *Eibhleag*, 'a live coal,' and applies primarily to the sparkling Evelix Burn. Dornoch represents an old *Durnācon*, 'place of hand-stones, or rounded pebbles,' an accusative form, of which the locative appears in the common name Dornie, wrongly ascribed to G. *dòirlinn*, 'an isthmus.' Bonar, 1275 le Bunnach, is in Gaelic *am Bannath*. The site of the present Bonar was known up to the building of Telford's Bridge in 1812 as *Baile na Croit*, 'hump-stead. The real *Bunnach* (doubtless a misreading for *Bunnath*) was half a mile lower down, where a long ford, which can still be pointed out, ran from near the beginning of the present wood on the Sutherland side to a spot near Kincardine Church on the Ross-shire side. Bonar must mean *Bonn-àth*, 'bottom ford,' the lowest ford on the Kyle. Bona, at the north end of Loch Ness, is *am bàn àth*, 'white ford,' from its white pebbles. There has been no ford there since the deepening of the outlet for the canal. A quaintly Anglicised form is seen in Patter-gonie (Oykell), a corruption of G. *Bad a' dhonnaidh*, 'clump of the mischance.' Shinness on Loch Shin is commonly supposed to mean *Shin-ness*, 'Shin-point,' a hybrid which may indeed be paralleled by Katanes, Caithness. The modern Gaelic, however, is (*Aird na*) *Sinneis*, and the oldest spellings are *Schenanes* 1548, *Schennynes* 1563, pointing unmistakably to *seann innis*, 'old haugh.' There is another Shinness in Strath Dionard, Durness. Dail Teamhair in Glencasley has been noted already (*Celtic Review*, i. p. 286). No satisfactory derivation has been offered of the parish name Criech, 1223 Crech, G. *Craoich*. But for the old spelling, it might be explained as *Crao(bh)aich*, 'place of trees,' but this can hardly hold. Of the common explanation *crìch*, 'boundary,' is out of the question. Of the other Gaelic parish names Lairg, 1230 Larg, is from *leary*, 'a sloping hillside; Clyne, 1230 Clun, G. *Clìn* is the locative (dialectic), of G. *claon*, 'a slope.' It has been wrongly ascribed to *cluain*, 'a meadow.' Farr, Dornoch, and Reay have been mentioned.

Eddrachilles, G. *Eadra-chaolais* for *Eadar-dha-chaolais*, 'between two kyles.' Loth is O.G. *loth*, 'mud.' Kildonan appears to mean St. Donan's Church, but 1223 Kelduninach points to *Cill-Domhnaich*, Lord's Kirk. There is no space to deal with the church-names, but it may be noted that there are seven *Cill's* in Strath Brora: *Cill-Brathair*, 'the Brother's Kirk'; *Cill-Pheadair Mhór* and *Cill-Pheadair Bheag*, 'little and big Kilpeter'; *Cill Caluim Cille*, 'St. Columba's Kirk'; *Cill Eadhain*, 'St. John's Kirk'; *Cill Mearain*, 'St. Mirren's Kirk'; and *Cill Ach-Breanaidh*. *Circ*, borrowed from Norse *kirkja*, occurs once or twice, *e.g. Innis na Circe*, Kirk Haugh in Glencasley, not far from *Badintagart*, 'priest's clump.' The island on the north coast which appears on O.S. maps as *Eilean nan Naomh* is given in G. as *Eilean na Neimhe*. It has an old dedication to St. Columba, and I suspect that it is really from O.G. *neimhidh*, Gaul. *nemeton*, 'a sacred place.' Another name which may be referred to this is Navidale, 1563 Nevindell, G. *Nea'adail*. There was a sanctuary here in olden times (Sir R. Gordon, *Earldom of Sutherland*), and though the formation is Norse, it is none the less possible that the Norsemen named the dale after the 'Nevie' which they found there. In addition to the Nevies noted in *Place Names of Ross and Cromarty*, there is yet another at the head of Glenlivet. All these were doubtless pagan shrines of the Picts, later taken over by the Celtic Church.

In conclusion, some rare or obsolete Gaelic words may be noted as occurring. *Eirbhe* or *airbhe*, 'a wall of stone or turf,' is found repeatedly, as it also is in Ross, *e.g. Eilean nan airbhe*, 'isle of walls'; *Allt na h-Airbhe*, 'burn of the wall' (at least thrice), Englished Altnaharra. Some of these walls are said to extend for many miles, disappearing in soft ground to reappear further on. *Uar* is the regular Sutherland word for a scree, a landslip, also, a water-spout, and is extremely frequent in the names, *e.g. Coire Uairidh*, 'scree corry'; *Beinn Uairidh*, 'scree hill'; *Allt Uairidh*, applied to burns whose banks slide, leaving scaurs. It occurs only once in Ross: *Srath-uairidh*, in

English Strath-rory, and the only other instance outside Sutherland known to me is *Allt Uairidh*, behind Abriachan, Inverness. It is probably a Pictish survival. Another term extremely common is *rabhann*, pronounced in some parts *rafan*, a species of grass growing in lochs of which sheep and cattle are fond. From it we have *Bada-rabhainn*, 'clump of ravan,' and such. It is probably to be connected with Welsh *rafu*, 'to spread'; *rafon*, 'berries growing in clusters.' *Lòn* in Sutherland means 'a slow burn,' as in Skye. *Saidh*, 'bitch,' occurs several times, as in *Coire na Saidhe Duibhe*, 'corry of the black bitch.' *Preas* regularly means 'copse,' not 'bush.' Diminutives in *-ie* are very common, *e.g. alltaidh*, 'a burnlet'; also *dailidh*, 'a little dale.'

ST. SECHNALL'S HYMN TO ST. PATRICK

Circ. A.D. 452; Translated from the original Celtic Latin by

Fr. ATKINSON, S.J., Wimbledon College

With Introductory Note by Fr. POWER, S.J., Edinburgh

[Among Celtic scholars there is as much unanimity as to the very early date of the Hymn of St. Sechnall, as there is about the genuineness of the two documents written by the hand of St. Patrick—the *Confession* and the *Epistle to Coroticus*.

St. Sechnall's Hymn in honour of 'The Master of the Scots' cannot be dated later than A.D. 452, that is, about twenty years after the arrival of St. Patrick in Ireland. It is thus by far the earliest document, metrical or otherwise, written in Celtic Latin. Tradition ascribes it to Sechnall (Secundinus), the contemporary and kinsman of the Apostle of the Scoti.

The internal evidence (see especially Stanza I.) points unmistakably to the fact that when the poem was written St. Patrick was still alive and in the zenith of his fame.

Haddan and Stubbs, Bishop Dowden, and many others have remarked on the absence of any reference in the panegyric to the miracles of the man celebrated in Irish legends as the greatest Thaumaturgus since the days of the Twelve Apostles. The traditional explanation of the Irish legend is, that Patrick not only fell foul of his panegyrist, but ruthlessly revised many passages which he considered too complimentary to the 'rusticissimus peccator.' However that may be, the whole composition tends to show that all Scotia (Ireland) became Christian in an incredibly short time.

The evolution of the Continental Latin, first introduced with its script into Scotia by St. Patrick, is another interesting fact attested by the pseudo-classical alphabetic poem of St. Sechnall. No one, as far as I know, has yet noticed the extraordinary resemblance of St. Patrick's Latinity to that of St. Gregory of Tours. The latter wrote in what is now admitted to have been the vulgar tongue of Christian Europe in the fifth century. St. Sechnall, who must have been taught by some Italian of the Celestino-Palladio-Patrician mission, shows a marked advance on the portentous syntax of the uncouth Gaulish Latin of St. Patrick. The improvement was steadily maintained till it reached a very fair degree of perfection in the Latin works of St. Columbanus of Bangor, Iona, Luxeuil, and Bobbio.

The accompanying hymn was printed for the first time by Muratori. Its popularity in modern days has been quite eclipsed by the Eucharistic Hymn of St. Sechnall, found in the Antiphonary of Bangor, and beginning—

Sancti venite,
Christi Corpus sumite.

A good translation of the latter from the pen of Dr. Neale may be read in *Hymns Ancient and Modern*.

The best MS. of the 'Praise of St. Patrick' is to be found in the *Book of Armagh*. There is another venerable copy with a few variants, formerly preserved at St. Isidore's, Rome, but now transferred to the Franciscan monastery, Merchant's Quay, Dublin. This MS. in Stanza III. gives the reading *Petrus*, instead of *Petrum*, and is followed— I do not know why—by Haddan and Stubbs, and Cardinal Moran.

A rhymed translation of the following poem has been printed by Miss Cusack on pp. 597 *sqq.* of her immense volume, *Trias Thaumaturga*. Father Atkinson's version will, I think, be preferred. The worst that I can say of it is that, as a piece of poetry, it is superior to the original. The task of the translator was a difficult one. St. Sechnall's composition, however historically interesting, is little better than prose cut into lengths. Father Atkinson's duty was to eschew ornament, like his original, and yet to write poetry. His fidelity to St. Sechnall and his self-restraint in the use of poetic diction can only be appreciated by those who will compare his rendering with the Latin Hymn as given in Canon Warren's noble edition of the *Antiphonarium Benchorense*.

Readers acquainted with the muscular conciseness and elliptical Latin of St. Sechnall's Hymn to St. Patrick, beginning—

Audite omnes amantes,

may at first blush be surprised that the new translator, who is not new to poetry, should have chosen the far-extended line of the hexameter. Like other translators, he is under the law of faithfulness to the meaning of the first Irish poet, but no one would require of him to render a congested verse of somewhat 'barbarous' Celtic Latin by an equally short verse of English that would puzzle the modern reader and jar on the musical ear.]

LISTEN ye lovers of God as I tell you of Patrick the Bishop,
  Man whom the Master hath blest, hero of saintly deserts ;
How for the good that he does upon earth, he is likened to angels,
  How for his life without flaw, peer of Apostles he stands.

Every tittle he guards of the mandates of Christ the All-Blesséd ;
  Bright in the sight of the world glitters the light of his works ;
Wondrous and holy indeed the example he sets and men follow,
  Praising the Lord for it all, praising the Father above.

Steadfast is he in the fear of his Maker ; his faith is unshaken ;
  Firm as on Peter the Church rises up-builded on him ;
God hath allotted to him the place of Apostle within it,
  'Gainst it the portals of hell never are strong to prevail.

Him hath the Master elected a teacher of barbarous races,
  Cunning with seine of the truth, fishing for men with his net,
So that from waves of the world he may win unto grace the believing,
  Making them follow their Lord up to His throne in the skies.

Christ's are the talents he sells, the excellent coin of good tidings,
  Claiming them back from our clans, fruitful with usury's gain ;
Certain for meed of his toil, for price of his prodigal labour,
  Some day with Christ to possess joy in His heavenly realm.

Faithful in service to God is he—God's most glorious envoy,
  Model and type to the good what an Apostle should be,
Preacher with word and with action to such as God calls for His people,
  So that if word be too weak, action may urge them to good.

Christ hath his glory in keeping, yet here upon earth is he honoured,
  Worshipped by all who behold, e'en as an angel of God ;
Yea, for as Paul to the Gentiles, so God hath sent him His Apostle,
  Guiding the steps of men home, unto the Kingdom of God.

Humble in spirit and body, the fear of his Maker hath filled him,
  Though for his goodness the Lord loveth to rest on his soul ;
Deep in his flesh that is sinless he carries the mark of the Master,
  Patiently bearing nor e'er glorying save in the Cross.

Dauntless and restless he feeds the believing with heavenly banquets,
  Lest they that journey with Christ, faint as they walk on the road,
Furnishing forth unto all for their bread the words of the Gospel—
  Lo ! as the manna of old—multiplied still in his hands.

Chaste for the love of his Lord, he warily keepeth his body
  Wrought and adorned as a shrine, meet for the Spirit of God :
Yea, and the Spirit for ever abides amid works that are cleanly,
  Yea, 'tis a victim he gives living and pleasing to God.

Light of the world is he, kindled ablaze, as was told in the Gospel,
  Lighted and set on the stand, shining far out to mankind :
Stronghold is he of the King, a city placed high on the hill-top—
  Plentiful riches are there, stored for the Master of all.

Surely shall Patrick be called in the heavenly kingdom the greatest,
  Who what his holy words teach, bodies in goodness of deed ;
Pattern and model of all, he guides the van of the faithful,
  Keeping in pureness of heart trust ever clinging to God.

Boldly he blazons the name of the Lord to the infidel races,
  Giving them grace without end, out of the laver of life.
Day after day for their sins unto God he makes his petition,
  Slaying for health of their souls victims worthy of God.

Worldly acclaim doth he flout, that God's law may yet be established,
  While at God's Table he stands, all is as dross in his eyes ;
Thunder of this world may crash ; undaunted he faces its crashing,
  Glad in the tempest of wrong, since that he suffers for Christ.

Shepherd so faithful and true of the flock that the Gospel has won him,
  Chosen by God's own self ward of the people of God,
Chosen to pasture His people with teaching appointed from heaven,
  Risking his life for the flock, after the pattern of Christ.

Him hath the Saviour raised to be Bishop because of his merits,
  Counsellor unto the priests fighting the battle of God,
Giving them raiment to wear and food from a heavenly storehouse,
  Holy celestial words, quitting his task to the full.

Lo! to the faithful he bears the call of the King to His nuptials,
  Wearing the nuptial robe, clad with the garment of grace.
Heavenly wine doth he draw without stint in celestial vessels,
  Bidding God's people approach unto the heavenly cup.

Hid in the sacred Books, a sacred treasure he found him,
  Seeing the Godhead clear under the Saviour's Flesh,
Holy and all complete are his merits that purchase the treasure.
  'Warrior of God,' is he called, looking on God with his soul.

Faithful witness is he of the Lord in Catholic precepts,
  Precepts carefully stored, salt with the message divine;
So that man's flesh may never corrupt into food for the earth-worms,
  Kept by the heavenly juice fresh to be offered to God.

Labourer noble and loyal is he in the field of the Gospel,
  Sowing in sight of the world seeds of good tidings of Christ;
Sowing with lips that God guards seed in the ears of the wary,
  Making their hearts and their minds tilth of the Spirit of God.

Christ for Himself hath made choice; His deputy here hath He placed him,
  Out of two tyrants' holds setting their prisoners free—
Ransoming slaves from the chains of men who held them in bondage,
  Freeing from Satan's rule numberless souls that were his.

Hymns and psalms doth he sing to the Lord with St. John's Revelations;
  Chanting to hasten his work, building the people of God.
Into their keeping he gives the law in the Name of the Triune,
  Teaching the Persons are Three, simple the Substance of God.

Girt with the girdle of God, by day and by night never ceasing
  Unto his Lord and his God, riseth his prayer without rest;
Mighty the toil is, and sure the guerdon that waits for his labour—
  Lordship along with the Twelve over the people of God.

Listen ye lovers of God as I tell you of Patrick the Bishop,
  Man whom the Master hath blest, hero of saintly deserts;
How for the good that he does upon earth, he is likened to angels
  How for his life without flaw, peer of Apostles he stands.

FEARCHUR LEIGHICH

CAPTAIN WM. MORRISON, ARMY MEDICAL STAFF (RETIRED)

TRADITION is an unreliable basis on which to dogmatise. It has therefore to be taken with the proverbial grain of salt, except so far as circumstantial environments confirm the tradition. Among the many traditions current in Highland *ceilidh* around the fireside, in my early days, few were given such credence as the story of Fearchur Leighich, physician to the Mackays of Farr.

One of the earliest recollections of my life was the recital of how he came into possession of all the islands and sea-girt rocks between Rudha Storr in Assynt, and Rudha Armidale in Farr. My family was closely related by marriage to a man who claimed to be in the direct male line from this noted physician. He delighted to relate to willing listeners the success of his progenitor in the healing faculty, and the influence he exercised over King Robert the Second in consequence. He was called, it is said, to treat the king after the court physicians had failed to diagnose the ailment from which the king suffered. According to the tradition, the treatment was the acme of simplicity. It was said to be a decoction of boiled milk with wilks and seaweed, a treatment which has to some extent been resuscitated, if we are to believe the advertisements regarding the efficacy of the various patent medicines now extracted from seaweed.

The first charter to confer royal favour on the Leighich was granted by Lord Alexander Stuart—better known in history as the Wolf of Badenoch, fourth son of Robert the Second, and at that period governor of the regions to the north of the Grampians. It conferred on the recipient certain lands in Melness and Hope, and was dated 4th September 1379. This mark of royal favour was confirmed in a second charter, dated 31st December 1386, by King Robert, to which were added all the islands above referred to. The fact that the 'Wolf' made the first grant would presume that it was

he, and not the king, who came under the physician's treatment, but believers in the tradition in my native parish
would probably not accept my theory, the belief being that
it was King Robert who was really the patient.

The Durness tradition concerning Fearchur is that he was
one of nature's physicians, born in Glengolly, in the Reay
Forest, a few miles to the west of Loch Hope, of which Rob
Donn says :—

'Ged a gheibhinn gu m'ailghios,
Ceann 't-Sàile Mhic Aoidh,
'S mòr a b' annsa leam fanadh,
An Gleanna Gallaidh nan craoibh.'

Here he had ample opportunities of acquiring an intimate
knowledge of the medicinal properties of the numerous plants
and herbs that adorned that lovely glen, finding in nature a
cure for all the varied ills of life.

A writer in Scottish *Notes and Queries*, vol. iv., 2nd
series, page 163, gives the following information regarding
the subject of our sketch—'Bethune, Farquhar, Wizard
Doctor. The most famous wizard doctor of the Highlands,
and the first of a family long famous as doctors there. He
was called "Ferchard Leche," and was the leech who, for
services to a royal patient, obtained a grant of land from
Robert ii. in Sutherlandshire in 1386. Strange legends have
crystallised round this wizard, who was a native of Islay.
He is said to have become omniscient through taking
serpents' broth.'

That the Leighich was a medical migrant from Islay of
the name of Beaton was never accepted in the traditions
concerning him in Sutherlandshire, and it would be interesting to know where the writer in *Notes and Queries* found the
information on which he based his note.

The first to give the Leighich the name of Beaton was the
parish minister of Eddrachillis, the Rev. Alexander Falconer,
in his Report of the district in the *Old Statistical Account of
Scotland*, vol. vi., 1793, in which he refers to the grant of the
islands as made to 'Ferchard Beaton, a native of Islay.' No

such tradition as to the Islay origin of the Leighich was ever current in Durness. There were Beatons in Sutherlandshire about the fifteenth century, but they were connected with the Dornoch Cathedral.

I have examined the charters in the Register House, Edinburgh, but the name of Beaton is in neither of them.[1]

The parish minister of Eddrachillis above referred to, in continuation of his remarks, adds the following information regarding the Leighich.—' This Ferchard was physician to the Mackays of Farr, and received from them in exchange for his right to these islands (named in the grant of 1386) a piece of ground near Tongue called Melness, where he lived himself, and some of his offspring after him; but the Mackays found means to recover possession of Melness long since, and yet it is said Ferchard's posterity remain still in the country under the name of Mackay.'

It is difficult to reconcile the different versions of the possession of lands in Melness and the Davoch of Hope. One is the statement in the charter found in the Dunrobin Charter Chest by the Commissioner of the Sutherland Estate—James Loch. This charter runs :—'This is Donald Our M'Corrachy's letter of procuratory as descendit frae Farquhar Leiche to resign all the lands of Strathnaver within written in our Souerane Lordis handis.' On this deed James Loch has written, ' This deed is endorsed in a handwriting of 1660.' The other is the transfer of the same lands from Sir Hugh Mackay of Farr to Donald MacCorrachy under the following circumstances. This Donald was a grandson of Iain Mor, Chief of the MacLeods of Assynt, and at the instigation of the Morrisons of Ashir and the Mackays of Durness he murdered his cousin, James MacLeod—a claimant for the lands of Eddrachillis—in order to put Donald Mackay, a natural son of Sir Hugh Mackay, in possession of the western portion of that district. This Donald Mackay was,

[1] It would interest only a few to insert the charters in this sketch, but if any of the readers of the *Celtic Review* would care to wade through the legal Latin of the period, I shall supply a copy of both charters.

according to the Rev. Alexander Falconer, the founder of the Scourie branch of the Mackays, but Sir Robert Gordon, makes the founder of that house to have been a son of Iye Mackay by his wife, a daughter of Hugh Macleod of Assynt. Here again we encounter the traditional discrepancies. Donald MacCorrachy could not have renounced in 1511 what he did not possess until about the year 1580. If it was he who renounced the Melness and West Moin in 1511 he must have been a veritable patriarch at his death in 1619, one hundred and eight years after he had renounced the Melness lands. After obtaining the West Moin estate, Donald MacMhorchadh Mhic Iain Mhor lived in Fresgill, and was regarded as a scourge to the district. His son William is buried in the old churchyard on the west side of Loch Hope. His grave is marked with a stone bearing a death's head, cross bones, and other symbols of our mortality. If William's father is the Donald MacCorrachy of the 1511 charter, 'descendant frae Farquhar Leiche,' he must have been in the male line, which would have made the Leighich a Macleod instead of a Beaton, and this cannot be disposed of by the crude opinion that the Mackays not only took the lands of their neighbours but obliterated the family names of those whom they despoiled.

The Beatons of Islay did not come into prominence until the year 1511, when one of the name is enrolled for the first time in the records of the Glasgow University. There is an Islay tradition that an Englishman named Cockspur was murdered in Islay in 1370, and that his servant, Duncan Beaton, was rescued by a girl named Grant, whom he afterwards married, and by whom he had two sons, one of whom became a bishop, the other a noted physician. If this tradition has a shred of truth, the dates of the charters above referred to dispose of the legendary connection between Fearchur Leighich and the prominent physicians who came into royal favour during the first quarter of the seventeenth century.

On page 77, *Caledonian Medical Journal*, 1902, Dr. H. Cameron Gillies enrols Fearchur Leighich among the Mac-

Beaths of Islay with as much authority as the Rev. Mr. Falconer had in making him a Beaton.

My object in writing this paper, however, is not so much to prove whether Fearchur was a Beaton, a MacBeath, or a Mackay, as to print the song of the islands which, I believe, has not before appeared in print. I have not heard it recited since I was ten years of age, when its singularity, if not its rhythm, fixed it in my memory. I have failed to trace the author, who, I imagine, must have been a sailor who traded between Lochinver and the Caithness ports. The *Old Statistical Account* gives the islands as from Rudha Storr to Stroma, from which it may be inferred that the song was current in those days, as the charter goes no further than from Rudha Storr to Rudha Armidal in the parish of Farr.

ORAN NAN EILEAN

1. Chi mi Suana mhór 's an tide,
   Beagan an taobh shios do Arcudh,
   Chi mi Dungasbaidh is Stròma,
   Far an tric na sheòl mi seachad.

2. Chi mi Ceanna Dhunnat gu mór ann,
   Ceanna Thoi'thidh 's an Ceanna beag ann,
   Mach bho na sean chi mi Sannsaid
   'S fad a thall bhuam chi mi Arcudh.

3. Chi mi Rudha Shrathaidh gu h-iosal,
   Far an tric 'n a lion mi mo sheòl air,
   Eilean nan Naoimh bhithinn taghal,
   'S mi fradhraic Eilean nan Ròn ann.

4. Chi mi eileanan an t-Seana Ghoill,
   Ma thimchioll gu tric 'n a stad mi,
   Eilean a' Chaoil 's e glé bhòidheach,
   Sgeir an Òir 's an t-Eilean Cragach.

5. Chi mi sean an Ceanna geal ann,
   'S na tha do dh' eileanan fo air,
   Eilean Hothan 's an Dubhsgeir,
   'S ann an Ruspuinn gheibhinn còmhnuidh.

6. Chi mi Goillisgeir is Clobhraig,
   'S n' thaobh thall tha sgeir a' Bhuic ann,
   Eilean a' Chòbhairidh shuas ann,
   Far an tric an robh sguaib agus guit ann.

7. Chi mi 'n Fharaid ghorm mur b' àbhaist,
   Is na pàirceachan aig mo Lord ann,
   Chi mi 'n Gairbh Eilean mór air a tharsuinnt,
   'S chi mi Glaisleacan nan eòin ann.

8. Chi mi 'n Clò 's Creag na Seobhaig,
   'S bu tearc a bha 'n leithid 's an Roinn-Eòrpa,
   'S ainmig chaidh mi riamh seachad
   Nach do shràc mi mo sheòl oirr.

9. 'Sealltuinn suas air a gualainn,
   Chi mi 'n Dùnan làn do chòsaibh,
   'S mach bho 'n sin chi mi 'n Duisleac,
   Sùla-sgeiridh agus Ròna.

10. Chi mi 'm Balg 's Rudh' a' Bhuachail,
    'S mi 'g amhairc suas air m' aghart,
    Chi mi 'n Dubhsgeir 's na Clobhsaich,
    'S bith na Clobhsaichean na m' fradharc.

11. Chi mi Eilean a' Chonnaidh,
    Suas bho na sean chi mi Aisir,
    A' Ghlaisleac an taobh thall do 'n chaolais,
    'S i sìnt ri Lochan Ceann Sàilidh.

12. Eilean nan Ròn 's e glé ainmeil,
    Is na tha thimchioll air do sgeirean,
    Chi mi sean Eilean a' Chruadal,
    Suas gu Eilean na Saille.

13. Chi mi eileanan Loch Lusard,
    Far an tric an robh mi le bàta,
    'S lionmhor acarsaid gun iomradh,
    Tha eadar 'n Inbhir 's an Spàrdan.

14. Mach bho na sean Rudha 'n Tiompain,
    'S Eilean Shannda air a tharsuinnt,
    Eilean a' Bhuic is an Cruachan,
    'S ged fada bhuam, chi mi Ghlaisleac.

15. Chi mi eileanan Bhad-choill ann,
    Ma Eilean a' Chùirn gun do stad mi ;
    Tha Eilean a' Bhreithimh gun dórainn,
    Calbha Mhór 's Calbha Bheag ann.

16. Eilean Alldanaidh glé bhòidheach,
    Rudha Stòrr an ceann na h-uidh,
    Buinidh gach aon dhiubh do mo Lord-sa,
    Ach 's ann a bha chòir bho Fearchur Leighich.

17. 'S iomadh oidhche fliuch is fuar,
    Ri tonnaibh cuain is muir tarsaint,
    'S cha do reub mi de cuid seòlaibh
    Feadh an oirlich do thombaca.

18. Ged tha mis an diugh gun bhàta,
    Dearbh cha b' abhaist domh bhi do h-eas[bh]uidh,
    Ach Mhic-Aoidh mu rinn thu m' fhàgail,
    Gu m' fad 's an àit thu cumail ceartais.

TRANSLATION

1. I see Suana in the tide,[1]
   Somewhat below Orkney,
   I see Duncansby and Stroma,
   Often have I sailed past them.

2. Dunnet Head is looming largely,
   Hoy and Holborn in the distance,
   Sandside I see out from them,
   And far over from me I see the Orkneys.

3. Lying low I see the point of Strathy,
   Where oft the breeze has filled my sails,
   I would sight the Isle of Saints,[2]
   While viewing the Isle of Seals.

4. Near me are the Isles of Strangers [3]
   Where in safety oft I've anchored,
   Isle of the Strait in rich adornment
   Near Gold Skerry and Rocky Island.

---

[1] There is no apparent reason why the author of the song should have begun at Suana, unless to emphasise the difficulty of navigating the Pentland Firth. The islands of Suana and Stroma formed part of the Orcadian parish of Wall and Flotta. The velocity of the tide at Hoy Head in spring tides is seven miles an hour, and three in neap tides. This was sufficient reason for any careful mariner to keep at some distance from either shore.

[2] The first of Fearchur's possessions are at the mouth of the Kyle of Tongue. Eilean nan Ròn is of considerable size and supports twelve families in comparative comfort. The soil is fertile, the whole island being under cultivation. Passing under the island is an arch one hundred and fifty feet span and seventy feet broad. The rocks are conglomerate, resting on red sandstone, more prominent in the north end of the island, and stratified in the direction of W.S.W. at an angle of 10°.

Eilean nan Naoimh bears trace of a sacred edifice having been there at some remote period. It was probably used as a burial ground when wolves prowled the Sutherlandshire forests. It has several caverns through which the sea in rough weather spouts to a height of more than thirty feet.

[3] Eilean nan Gall, originally Islands of Strangers, better known now as the Rabbit Islands, are three in number. The soil, being sandy, provides excellent cover for the rabbits.

5. Viewing now the Whiten Head
   With the isles that lie beyond it,
   Isle of Hoan and the Black Skerry,[1]
   But in Rispond I could tarry.

6. I see Goileskeir and Clourig,[2]
   And on the far side I see the Buck-rock,
   Island Choarie lying westward,
   Here sheaf and fan denoted plenty.

7. Farout Head, green as was its wont,[3]
   Is apportioned to my Lord,
   Great Garveilan I see lying across,
   And I see Glaisleac, haunt of birds.

8. The Nail-stack and the Hawk-rock[4]
   Scarce their like is found in Europe,
   Seldom I passed beyond them
   But my canvas was torn.

9. Looking o'er the Black-flag shoulder
   I see the Dunan with caves in plenty,
   Out beyond I see the Duisleac,
   Sulaskerry and Rona.

10. I see the Blister and Shepherd's Headland,
    And, glancing westward before me,
    I see the Black Skerry and the Cleft Isle,
    With the Cleft Rocks full in view.

11. I see the Isle of Brushwood,
    And up from that I see Ashir,
    Grey-flag on the far side of the strait,
    Stretched beside Loch Kensaly.

---

[1] Eilean Hoan, a mile in length and half a mile in breadth, once supported five crofters (enjoying a portion of the mainland hill pasture), until expatriated in 1838 by the tacksman of Rispond. Of these, two families emigrated to America, the others were compulsorily settled on the congested and arid crofts of Lerin and Smoo.

[2] Eilean Chlobhraig, near the inner end of Loch Eriboll, once supported three crofting families, but is now attached to the Eriboll farm. It has a valuable limestone quarry which, owing to cost of transport, has for some time been abandoned.

[3] Farout Head is a formation of grey slate, while the region lying between the Kyle of Durness and Loch Eriboll is an immense bed of limestone of unknown depth.

[4] The Hawk-rock is the extreme point of the Farout Head, and like Stack Clo (on the opposite side of the Bay of Balnakeil), is about six hundred feet high, and is the summer residence of thousands of the puffin tribe who hatch their young here. These feathered sojourners have immunity from raiders since the passing of the 'Wild Birds' Protection Act,' and are now as great a pest in those waters as the steam trawlers, but, unlike the latter, they are outside the jurisdiction of the Sheriff Court.

12. The renowned Isle of Seals,
    And all the reefs there are about it,
    Eilean Chruadal I see there,
    And up to the Isle of Fatness.

13. I see the islands of Loch Laxford,
    Where oft I have taken a boat,
    Anchorages lie in numbers,
    Between the Inver and the Roost.

14. Outside of these stands the Knoll Point,
    With Handa standing there obliquely,[1]
    Buck Isle and the Cruachan,
    And though far away I see the Grey-flag.

15. I see the islands of Badcall,
    And I have tarried at the Isle of the Cairn,
    The Judge's Isle is now less baneful,[2]
    Great Calva and Little Calva are there.

16. Isle of Oldaney most beautiful,[3]
    Near Point of Storr, where ends my journey;
    All those islands own his Lordship,
    But their right came from Fearchur Leighich.

17. Many a cold wet night I voyaged
    Ocean waves and cross seas,
    Nor e'er destroyed of her cordage,
    The length of an inch of tobacco.

---

[1] A cluster of islands, about twenty in number, lie between Shegra and Assynt. The most notable of these is Handa, rising perpendicular to a height of six hundred feet, and in its crevices myriads of sea-fowl sojourn for the season.

The geological formation of this island is most interesting, lying horizontally as if superimposed by the ingenuity of man. Handa once was tenanted by twelve families, but was added to the factor's farm when the eviction fever spread over Sutherlandshire. It was once the residence of Iain MacDhoil mhic Huistean of the Assynt MacLeods, a branch of Siol Torquil of Lewis. This warrior was the murderer of John Morison, the Lewis Breitheamh, in revenge for the murder of Torquil Dubh.

[2] After the murder of John Morison by MacLeod of Handa, a party of Lewis men took the judge's body from Inverkirkag for burial in Stornoway. They were driven by storm on to one of the islands in the Bay of Badcall since called Eilean a' Bhreitheimh. Here they disembowelled the body, and proceeded on their journey when the storm abated. This incident took place in the year 1601. The murderer went over to Lewis and married his victim's widow, from which the inference is that the possession of Bathsheba was the real cause of the murder rather than the avenging of Torquil Dubh's death.

[3] Of the islands in the Bay of Badcall none appear to be of much value except Eilean Auldney, which now forms part of the pasturage of the sheep farm of Ardvaar.

18. Though I'm now without a boat,
    Sure 'twas not my wont to be without one,
    But Mackay, though thou hast forsaken me,
    Long may'st thou remain to give us justice.

THE FIONN SAGA

(Continued from p. 153.)

GEORGE HENDERSON, M.A., B.Litt., PH.D.

THE CAMPBELL OF ISLAY RECENSION—*(continued)*

Fionn's Return

AT that time (as Mac Cisaig said in Uist) people were few in Alba. There were great empty glens with a man in them here and there, not as it is to-day when men abound in Scotland. There were many deer in these days, and men hunted them.

Fionn knew by his knowledge that his father's men were there and in great straits. So he set off to seek them. They were on the land of the king of Lochlann, as it appears; and the king would not keep them in meat. They had oaken skewers in their bellies to keep them out from their backs, they were so gaunt, and thin, and starved. They had to hunt for the king, but he did not give them enough to eat. They lived in a cave, or, according to others, in a sheiling (*bothan-àiridh*).

Fionn, with his sword under his arm and Bran at his heels, walked to the dwelling and looked in.[1]

'I will go in and stay,' said he, 'unless I am turned out.'

There was no living thing there but the fire. Swords were there leaning against the wall, rusty old swords and spears, and there were beds and benches.

As no one was there to hinder him, Fionn leaned his sword, *Mac-A-Luinn*, against the wall, and stretched himself

---

[1] According to others Ireland was the place; or Lochlann, to which the lad walked after he had walked all over Ireland.

on the floor beside the fire, and Bran lay down beside him and went to sleep.[1]

They had not been long thus when Fionn heard a murmur (*torraman*) of voices, and trampling and rattling of feet and arms coming towards the dwelling, but he lay long still and feigned sleep. He looked secretly and saw great, wild, tall, stalwart, terrible strong men coming, unlike the others in the land of giants, who were under enchantments (*sgleð*) and glamour, and who were phantoms.[2] Seven of them came home, and they had *sailearach fhèidh*, a hind with them, which they killed. They flayed the hind and tossed it into the great kettle that was on the fire, and when it was cooked it gave them but *biteag*, a morsel apiece.

When they had the kettle ready for the fire they noticed the lad and the hound and the sword, and they began to talk.

'Is not that hound the likest to Bran that ever was in the world?' said one.

'Did ever man see a sword that is liker to *Mac-A-Luinn*?' said another.

'But look at this lad,' said a third, 'who is sleeping there, are not these the two eyes and the cheeks and the very face of Cumal?'

Then they awoke him and asked him to share what they had, though it was but a morsel for each.

'It is little enough for yourselves,' said Fionn.

'My lad,' said one, 'eat your share, we are ever thus since the black black day.'

'But who are you?' said Fionn. 'I never saw men like you for stature and for grand terrible looks.'

One of them sighed, and then another; and then one said :—

'We have seen the day when we were not ashamed to tell who we are, but you are a stranger, I trow.'

'Yes,' said Fionn, 'I never trod on this ground before'; and that was true.

---

[1] Or—he slept at a roadside inn and put his sword into a press in which he found a lot of rusty old swords. So curiously do these old stories change without their losing their identity.　　　　　　　　　　　　[2] Unreal shams.—J. F. C.

'Did you ever hear of *An Fhinn*, "The Feen" (Fayne)?'
said one.

'Yes,' said Fionn, 'I have heard about the Feen from my
nurse, that they were the grandest men that ever were seen
in the world.'

'So we were on a day,' said the warrior; 'but that day is
gone.'

And then he told how the kings of Lochlann and Eirinn
had slain Cumal by treachery, how they had shared Alba
between them and turned the Feen into slaves and . . . for
them, all as it has been told already at the beginning.

'But will the Feen ever be better off than you are now?'
said the lad.

'*Aileaganan*, "little darling,"' said the warrior, 'twelve
times better than we were ever; under Fionn mac Cumhail,
for it was so in the prophecies that he was to come and
recover the land.'

'We shall never see him,' said one.

'Ai! Ai!' said another, and so they sighed and lamented.
They did not know who he was, but he knew them.

And so they talked all night of the ancient glories of the
Feen and their sorrows and hardships and their woes, and
then they fell asleep about the fire, the old warriors of Cumal
and Fionn mac Cumhail, whom they did not know. In the
morning they had nothing but a gulp of venison broth (*bolgum
de shùth na sailearaich*); they had no right meal, nothing.[1]

He had a venomed claw (*spuir nimh*) which had a sheath
upon it. That he lost in the realm of the giants in fighting
the monster, as I have told you already, and there, as they
could not make another like the one he had lost, they made a
golden sheath for it. (*Bha cuarain òir air an spor nimh.*)
There was a golden buskin upon the venomed spur of Bran.[2]

---

[1] According to another version they took the king's fat beeves from his cattle-fold.
He opened the gate and took out the stots by the nose, one for two, or one for three,
or one for each, and then they feasted till the skewers burst in their bellies. This
scarcity of food is characteristic of the class who remember these stories.

[2] To me this seems to indicate some recollection of hunting leopards in the
Aryan land.

Bran always killed more than Fionn. If Fionn killed 600 of men or of beasts, Bran killed 700, always a hundred more than his master.

When Bran came from the dwelling, Fionn loosed the golden sheath from his foot, and he set him at the herd of heavy stags. When he had gone Fionn followed, and before they stopped he and the great hound had killed nine nines.

Then the old soldiers fell a-talking. One said: 'Is not that like Bran?'

'This one is as good as Bran any day,' said another.

'That is not Bran's colour,' said a third.

'They had the same mother,' said Fionn.

'But take up the deer and let us go home. If men come to blame you I will take the blame.'

They took nine great stags, and they feasted so that one of the oaken skewers broke in the belly of each of the old warriors that night. Next day they took nine more home, and so day by day, and nine by nine they brought home the nine nines, and feasted so well that all the oaken skewers broke in their bellies.

As each one ate his meal the splintering was heard of the oaken skewers that they had in their bellies to keep them from their backs.

Fionn's First Battle[1]

On one of these days Fionn was tired and lay long asleep. While he slept two young lads sprang in.

'What is your news, lads?' said one of the Fayne.

'Not much,' said one, 'but the king of Lochlann has set a battle with the king of Eirinn (or the king of the East—*aird an ear*), and we have come to fetch you.'

Now one of these lads was in the king's service, and his name was Ubhal Lamh Fhad (? Ule Long-hand). He was

[1] There is great variety in this next bit, but all versions agree as to the main incidents. The arms are taken, Fionn recovers his mystic sword, and with it beats the foe. The arms are taken out of a press in an inn, or out of the bothy, or out of the cave, while Fionn is sleeping. The battle is with the king of the East or the Easterlings in one case, but the name of the man who takes the arms always is the same, and he appears again later on in the story.

so called because his finger touched the ground when he stood upright.

'We will never fight on that side,' said the Fayne.

'Then I will take these swords and old arms,' said the lad.

Fionn's mother's brother was king in Lochlann at that time, and his man Long-hand gathered up all the arms and took Mac-A-Luinn with the rest while Fionn slept, and because he had that sword Bran got up and followed him.

When Fionn awoke the arms were gone and Bran and the men; and there was no one within but a little lad.

'Where are the arms?' said Fionn.

'They are taken away,' said the other, 'by Long-hand, the king's man, for there is to be a great battle with the Easterlings, and the Fians are to fight.'

'Why did you not awake me?' said Fionn.

He feared that he would lose his sword for ever, so he got up and went out after the Lochlanner, Ubhal Lamh Fhad.

He went fast and round about by a hidden path and met Long-hand with the load on his back.

'What is the news?' said he.

'Not much,' said the other, 'but that there is to be a fight with the king of the Easterlings and the king of Lochlann. There are some people called Fians, and these are the weapons with which they are to fight.'

Fionn followed, thinking how he was to get his sword again, and he said :—

'Hi! ha! hu!	'Hi! ha! hoo!
Fuil air fear,	Blood on man,
Gaoth air sluagh,	Wind o'er hosts,
Cath ga chuir,	Battle a setting,
'S truagh gun Mac-A-Luinn.'	Wae without the Son of Lunn.'

'What's the matter?' said Long-hand.

'Only a little bit of a sword of mine that is lost,' said Fionn.

'What would you do with it if you had it?' said the Lochlanner.

'I would keep off a third of the battle,' said he.

The Norseman cast down the sheaf of arms and gave him one of the swords. Fionn took it and shook it and brandished it and it broke. Then he said :—

> [' 'Tis one of the black-edged glaives
> Not Mac-A-Luinn my blade;
> 'Twere no danger if drawn from sheath,
> A lamb it would not behead.'[1]]

and then he said as before—

Hee! ha! hoo! blood on men, wind o'er hosts, battle on-setting, wae without the Son of Lunn!

'What would you do with it if you had it?' said the Lochlanner.

'I would keep off two-thirds of the battle,' said Fionn.

'There, take it,' said Long-hand, and gave him another sword.

But that was no better than the first, so Fionn repeated his two rhymes, and if he repeated more they have never been said to me by any reciter, though many have said these rhymes.

'What would you do with the sword if you had it?' said the Long-handed Lochlanner for the third time.

'I would stake all I saw,' said Fionn, 'and fight the battle alone.'

'Here is a gate,' said Long-hand, 'and if you can get your sword while I open and shut it take it.'

He cast down the sheaf of swords, and Fionn sprang upon it and sheathed his sword.

'I have you,' shouted he, 'and I will never let you out of my grasp again.'

'Let us see if you will be as able as you say when the fight comes,' said Long-hand.

Then Fionn sat and fell a-thinking, as he always did according to the stories and ballads which describe him.

'I have come,' said Fionn; 'I would not like to fight against my mother's brother, but I should like to show him

---

[1] [Cf. *West Highland Tales*, iii. 337, where there is a better version, the Gaelic of which I have preferred to the one followed by Campbell in this recension.]

what I am. This day I will help him against the Eastern men.'

So he went to the king and said: 'May I go to the battle?'

'What would you in the battle?' said the king of Lochlann, 'and what will you have?'

'The battlefield will be mine at all events,' said Fionn.

Then the Easterlings came, and Fionn loosed Bran his hound, and took the golden sheath off his venomed claw, and grasped Mac-A-Luinn his father's sword.[1]

Fionn's First Fight

Then the fight began and the Easterlings fled with Bran after them. Not a Lochlanner stirred; they sat on a hill and looked on.

When the battle was done there was no word of the lad who had fought so well.

The Fayne went to Tulach Oireal, where they used to stay, and they talked together.

'Who was that lad who was better in the fight than we?' said one.

'It was said that Fionn mac Cumhail was to come,' said another.

'If it be he, and if he be alive, he will not wait to take the long clean road, but he will come by the foul short way here, if it be the man whom we suppose,' said a third.[2]

Fionn went to the king after the battle, and the king knew who he was.

'I had that sword,' said Long-hand; 'it was in a bundle of old arms, and I wish that he never had got it from me. I took it from him and he got it back, and now I am going to ask a favour of him and that is my life. If he grants me life I will do all he asks.'

---

[1] [The description of the fight is not elaborated here; it formed a 'run' such as occurs in other Gaelic romances. Campbell took down Gaelic notes which need not be here elaborated; they have nothing peculiar.]

[2] Alludes to the tale called The Three Counsels.

The king had his hat off to meet him and his hands spread, and the rest of them were on their knees in ditches begging for mercy from Fionn mac Cumhail. Fionn knew the king though he had never seen him, and he said—

'I am going away, but it may be that I shall see you and the king of Eirinn, your friend, in spite of you both. Begone or your head will be off, sweep your men to Lochlann and let the Irish go to Ireland, or if not I will come to Lochlann and ruin the realm.'

And when Fionn had said this he went away.

Then Fionn sat and thought how he was to get to his own people again. He put his finger under his wisdom-tooth and found that he must seek them at Bogach O Criaragan in Eirinn.

He did not know where that was, but he went all alone with his sword and Bran, and where he did not know the way his finger told him where to go.

The Feinn were watching at Tulach Oireal where they used to be, and when they saw him coming they raised a great shout. 'It is he! with the dog of our beloved (*cu m' fheudail fhēin*) and his mighty sword. It is Fionn, the son of Cumal. He is come at last.'

Then he was made Righ na Féinne, king of the Fayne, and the Fayne (Féinne) gathered about him from all the places where they had fled when Cumal was slain. And many a cheery happy day they had with that man, Fionn mac Cumhail, over here in Alba.

CAMPBELL'S RECENSION ENDS

CHAPTER II

IV: ALASDAIR RUADH MAC IAIN'S ACCOUNT

[This reciter lived in the isle of Eriskay. His name was Englished as Johnson, but he himself knew no English. He was about eighty-five years old when I met him in 1892. His progenitors came to Eriskay from Trotternish in the isle of Skye, where an ancestor had taken refuge after the Massacre of Glencoe. He was descended of

the Maciains of Glencoe. Circumstances were not favourable for my
writing out his version in full, but this was done by Father Allan at
his leisure, and the result placed at my disposal. The narrator's
dialectal peculiarities are noticed in footnotes; the folklorist can
rely upon the whole as faithful to oral tradition. Certain touches
of a ruder age are left unobliterated, but will be sufficiently indicated when I translate. When Father Allan died last September
there passed away from the Highlands one who was possessed
in a double measure of the spirit of his race, from the world one of
its nobles. His many-sided virtue it would be impossible to praise
too highly, or the aptness of his mind for story, and fun, and wit.
His treasures of delightful anecdotes have died with him, but his
collections of folk traditions have happily been secured. As long as
any knowledge of the literature and old folk life of the Highlands
exists, the sweet unspotted memory of the Rev. Allan Macdonald of
Eriskay will endure. I could write much of him. I have associations
of him discoursing of Spain, where, at Valladolid, he was educated;
of his work at composing Gaelic hymns, which appeared in his
Laoidhean Spioradail; of his teaching music to the young so far as
to render some pieces in Latin, in Gaelic, and in English; of the
many hours spent in jotting down many unrecorded words and
phrases my pencil notes bear witness. One of the small books I
cherish is a copy of MacEachainn's Gaelic rendering of the *Imitatio
Christi* which he gave me. In May 1905 he wrote me: 'I am in
better health than I was when you were here last, and as happy as a
king. The Bishop offered me the charge of Fort William, for which
I thanked him. I told him I had much sooner stay where I was,
and I was left in peace.' He was ardent in his own faith and equally
sincere in charity. He had no liking for Greek, which must have
been the fault of his instruction, nor for philosophy, which may have
been in part his loss, if not his wisdom. I shall not soon, if ever, see
his equal, as fellow-countryman, as friend, as conversationalist, as
exemplar of love and goodness and courtesy; had he lived in a former
age his name would have come down as *Naomh*, Sanctus, Holy.
There was in him a sincere wholeness of heart and mind, which
remains to me and to all his friends a legacy which, to our lasting
grief, his death has so recently left us. He loved Eriskay.—G. H.]

An Fhéinn

Aig sìn-sinnseanair Rìgh Eirinn o 'n chòigeamh glùn 's ann
a lionsgar na Fiantaichean. 'Se dithis agus triùir a bha iad

a faighinn a h-nile bliadhna de dhaoine mora agus boirionnaich
as an robh sia troidhean.　Bha'd 'gam pòsadh sin ri chéile
agus an sliochd a bha tighinn bhuapa bha mìodachd mhór
mhór unnta gus na rinn iad reisemaid mhór dha na
Fiantaichean.

'Nuair a fhuair iad a nise na fiantaichean cruinn 's ann
airson a bhith 'nan saighdearan agus 'nan luchd-dìon air a
rioghachd air[1] na Lochlannaich.　'S ann airson 'cur as do na
Lochlannaich chaidh 'n togail 'n toiseach.

Nuair a fhuair iadsan iad fhéin cho làidir chuir iad litir
gu Righ Eirinn nach ruigeadh e leas dùil a bhi aige ri 'n
cuideachadh-sa ri' bheò no ri 'bhàs.　Rinn iad righ dhaibh-
pfhéin an sin air[2] Cumhal.　Bha naoi naonan ann dhiubh an
toiseach ga b'r'i' am barrachd a bh' ann 'nuair a rinneadh righ
a Chumhal.

Cha chuala mi riamh co bhuaithe thainig Cumhal ach bha
Diarmad, Goll is Oscar 'nan clann peathar do dh' Fhionn.
'Nuair a thainig 'n triùir-sa bho righ Eirinn gu ruig an
t-Eilean Sgitheanach chumail nam fiadh bho na Fiantaichean,
ach an aona fhear bu dona air a ghreigh, 'se sin an aon fhear
bh'air a chur a mach dhaibh gus a mharbhadh dhaibh féin.
Cha robh'd ach leigeadh greim dha fheoil agus balgam dhe
shùth dha 'n h-uile fear do na Fiantaichean.　B'fheudar dhaibh
a bhi cur deilgnean daraich 'n am broinn 'ga cumail a stigh.
Bha iad mar sin riamh gos an d' thainig Fionn orra.

A chlann a thainig bho nighean Chumhail, piuthar Fhinn,
b'.iad sin Diarmad is Goll is Oscar.　Bha iad càirdeach do
Fhionn ged nach robh iad càirdeach do na Fiantaichean.　B'e
Fionn brathair am màthar.

BÀS CHUMHAIL

'Nuair a bha Cumhal 'na righ orra cha robh 'chridh' aig
duin' an tilleadh ged a bha gu leoir air fheadh an t-saoghail
na bu treasa na 'ad.

---

[1] Idiomatic use of *air* in sense of 'against.'

[2] Idiomatic use of *air*, meaning 'of,' but best rendered by a direct objective, *e.g.*
they elected C. king.

Chuir an righ Cumhal a mach lagh nach robh duine dhianadh cron nach sgaradh 'ad 'bheatha. Bha aon fhear a sin ciod e rinn e ach laighe le mart. Rug 'ad air a bhoin agus mharbh 'ad i agus chuir iad cuid na bà (seach,[1] arca na bà) mu amhaich, agus dh' fhuaith iad e air chor 's nach tugadh duine 's am bith as e. Chuir iad air falbh bhuath buileach e agus cha chanadh iad facal ris ach Arca Dubh.

Chaidh e gu pàilis Righ Eirinn e fhéin 's a bhean. Chuir e brath a stigh thun an righ gu robh gnothuch beag aige ris. Thainig a righ a mach agus mhuthaich e dha agus dh' fhoighneac e dheth gu de 'n duine bh' ann. Thuirt Arca an sin gu 'm b' esan fear dha na Fiantaichean.

'Nach tu a chaill do nàire nuair a thainig thu 'n am aodunn, an déis dha m' shìn-shinnseanair ur cur cruinn agus sibh a dhealachadh bhuam a rithisd, is nach *ligidh*[2] sinn leas dùil a bhith againn cuideachadh fhaighinn bhuaibh?'

''N tà,' os Arca, 'a chionn gur a mise bha 'g iarraidh orra thus a leantail chuir iad so mu m'amhaich mar thàmailt 's chuir iad bhuath mi. Thainig mi far robh sibh-pfhein gos sibh a thoirt dhomh cuideachadh.'

'Cha 'n urrainn domhsa cuideachadh a thoirt dhut a leithid de dhuine mór.'

'Cha 'n iarr mi ach iasgach na h-aibhne agus cumaidh mi iasg ribh-pfhein air[3] ur braiciost.'

'Gheibh thu sin agus innis dhomh ciamar a chuirear Cumhal gu bàs?'

'Cha do thog Cumhal,' os Arca, 'sùil ri gin riamh ach boirionnach ro bhriagh.'

''N ta,' os a Righ, ''s ann agamsa tha an aon bhoinne-fala as àille tha fo'n ghréin. 'S còir dhuinn litir chur ga ionnsuidh.'

Sgriobh Righ Eirinn litir a sin gu Cumhal e thighinn far an robh e gu faigheadh e maithte na rinn e 'na aghaidh. Dh' fhalbh Cumhal an sin agus chaidh dha 'n phailis aig Righ Eirinn. 'S 'nuair a rainig e chuireadh dinneir gu feum dhaibh. Shuidh 'ad aig bord 's cha robh Cumhal a' leigeil a shul bhàrr nighean Righ Eirinn.

---

[1] Otherwise.   [2] =ruigeadh; *l* for *r*.   [3] In sense of 'for.'

'Cha chreid mi nach eil thu air gaol a ghabhail air a nighinn.'

'An tà,' osa Cumhal, ''si 'n aon bhoinne-fala as docha leam a chunna mi riamh.'

'Mas i, pòs thu fhéin 's i fhéin mata.'

Phòs 'ad a sin agus oidhche na bainnseadh[1] aca chuireadh Arca Dubh 'n aon seomar riutha a' falach. 'Nuair a chunnaic Arca sin an t-àm (gun robh a thrì meanmachd fir ga chall air muin na mnatha) thug e 'n ceann bhàrr Chumhail le chlaidheamh fhéin 'Mac-a-Luin.' Bhuail a bhean a basan. Nuair a chunnaic Bran Mac-A-Luin aig Arca lean e Mac-A-Luin agus Arca.

BREITH FHINN

Dh' fhàs a bhean trom 's chuir a righ a mach achd nam b' e nighean a bhiodh ann gum biodh iad coma mu déidhinn, nach togadh i tòrachd a h-athar; ach nam b' e gille bhiodh ann gun rachadh a mharbhadh cho luath 'sa thigeadh e dh' ionnsuidh an t-saoghail.

Ann an ceann nan trì ràithean thuisleadh ise air leanabh nighinn agus le toileachadh 's le toilinntinn a rinn an righ cha robh duine bha mu 'n champa nach robh marbh leis an daoraich.

A bhean-ghlùin bu ghiorra dhith thuirt i rithe :—

'Seall gu dè th' agam an dràsd?'

'Tha agad an dràsd,' os ise, 'pàisde-gille.'

'Eirich thus',' os i-fhéin, 'agus falbh leis agus tog e.'

''N ann,' os ise, ''s mi air mo mhionnachadh nam b' e gille bhiodh ann gun reachainn a thoirt suas dha 'n righ gur e gille bhiodh ann?'

'Falbh thus' agus tog e is cho fada 's is bonnach dhomhs' e 's bonnach dhuits' e na nì eile a bhios agam 's leatsa do chuid dheth ach tog an gille.' Dh' fhalbh a bhanaltrum, a bhean-ghlùin, 's thog i leithe 'm pàisde 's mach a ghabh i.

[1] In Eriskay dialect I heard many old genitives still in use among the old men, and by analogy such genitives were extended.

Mar a dh'eirich do bhrathair na te a theich le Fionn

Bha 'brathaïr roimpe 'san rathad 's e 'na shaor. 'Eirich, eirich,' os ise, 'cho luath 'sa rugadh tu thoir a choill ort is dian bothag dhomhs' s mi air cron a dhianamh air nighean a' righ.'

Dh' éirich esa agus mach a thug e; thug e choill air 's rinn e bothag dha phiuthair. 'Nar a rainig ise bhothag bha i ullamh aig a brathair roimpe.

Dh' fhoighneac e dhith : 'gu dè th' agad an sin ?'

'Cha 'n eil ach ni a thug mi bho nighean an ruigh.'[1]

'O cha 'n e idir. 'S ann a th' ann Mac Chumhail. Thoir dhomh-s' e 's gun cuir mi 'n ceann dheth leis an tuaigh.'

'Falbh a stigh is gearr,' os ise, 'a sprod ud tha san fhardoruis mu 'm bi mo cheann-sa bualadh ann a tighinn a mach na dol a stigh.'

Chaidh e stigh agus dhìrich ise dha 'n tobhtaidh ('s ann a muigh a bha iad air a chnoc) 's an tuagh aice. Air tighinn a mach 'a brathair air an dorus bhuail i faobhar na tuaighe air ann am mullach a chinn 's chuir leth air gach gualain dhe ceann a brathair. Chuir i sin a mach air a loch e (an saor) 's chaidh i fhéin a stigh 's bha i' cumail a ghille air aghart cho math 'sa b' urra dhith.

Mar a thogadh 'na leanabh e Is mar a mharbh e 'n dubh mhiol-chu

'Nar a thainig an gille sin gu coiseachd theirig am biadh an sin dith thug i leithe o thigh an righ 's chaidh i chon a bhaile far an robh nighean a' righ. Fhuair i uiread 'sa b' urra dhith thoirt leithe 'bhiadh, agus nuair a bha i 'falbh de rinn miol-chu a bha 'n tigh a' righ ach a leantail air fàileadh na feola. Chaidh i dhachaidh.

Bhiodh an gill' aice air fheadh an taighe 's bha sguab dhreathann aice 'g éirigh air mu na casan 'ga ionnsachadh ri cruadal.

---

[1] Dialectal for *righ*.

Theirig am biadh a rithist di. Bha i dol a dh-ionnsaidh a bhaile a dh' iarraidh tuillidh 's 'nar a nochd i ris an aitreabh far robh nighean a righ smaointich i gun do dh' fhàg i a' mhìol-chu a stigh 's gun robh 'n gille air ich aice. Thill i cho luath 'sa b' urra dhi dhachaidh dha 'n bhothaig. Bha 'n gille agus ceann a mhìol-choin aige 's an darna laimh agus an druim as a laimh eile an deaghaidh a' cur a cnaimh na h-amhuich. 'Nar a chunnaic i 'n t-euchd a rinn e ghrad thill i thun a bhaile is dh' inns' i 'nighean a righ gun do chuir an gille an dubh-mhìol-chu a cnaimh na h-amhuich.

'Tog thus e,' os i fhéin, 'is fhad 's a bhios mise beo cha chaill thus' air.'

Thill i dhachaidh dha 'n bhothaig.

MAR A DH'IONNSUICH E CRUADAL 'S MAR A BHAISTEADH E

'Nar a fhuair es' e fhéin cho làidir dh' éireadh e air a chaillich leis a sguabaidh chor 's nach d' fhàgadh leoba*dh* feola na fala*dh* air a casan.[1] Rachadh i sin a mach air a loch leis gus an ruigeadh an t-uisge na cìochan aice 's greim aic' air chùl cinn air 's air smigid 'g ionnsachadh snàmh dha. Bheireadh i air chul cinn air agus chuireadh i fo 'n uisg' e 's dh' éireadh e ann am miadhon a locha thall.

Chaidh i dha 'n bhaile dh' iarraidh tuilleadh bidhe. Bha i 'ga thilleadh ach cha ghabhadh e tilleadh bhuaip. 'Nar a nochd i sin ri colaisde bh' aig Easbuig ag ionnsachadh sgoilearan bha uair a chluichd aca 's bha 'ad ri snàmh a muigh air a loch. Mach esan le chuid aodaich 'nam measg. Bheireadh e air chùl cinn air feadhainn diu 's chuireadh e fo 'n uisg 'ad 's bha e 'gam bàthadh mar sin. Co bha' ga choimhead a muigh 'romh 'n uinneig ach an t-Easbuig agus dh' eubh e sin: Có leis an gille Fionn bàn a tha bàthadh mo chuid sgoilearan ?

'Taing do Dhia,' os a chailleach, 'fhuair mi baisteadh dha 'm mbac. Tha dhiol uisge timchioll air.'

[1] Datives and genitives as in Eriskay.

· 'O fhuair,' os an t-Easbuig 'Fionn mac Cumhail.' Cha robh ach chuireadh reiseamaid timchioll a locha bonn ri bonn gus a mharbhadh.

MAR A FHUAIR FIONN TEICHEADH LEIS A CHAILLICH 'S MAR A THUGADH AN T-AINM AIR LOCH LURGAINN

Bhuail a chailleach a dà bhois ri chéile is lig i lasag as. Nar a chual esa ràn a mhuime thug e aghaidh air tìr 's cha robh duine bha roimhe nach do mharbh e gus na ràinig e 'chailleach. Rug e air dhà lurgain oirre (orra)[1] is thilg e air fras-mhullaich a ghual*adh*[2] i. Thug e aghaidh air a bhothaig 's 'nar a rainig e sin a bhothag leig e as a chailleach 's cha robh aige dhith ach an dà lurgainn. Thilg e 'n dà Lurgainn sin a mach air a loch ann an Eirinn. Tha Locha Lurgainn sin an Eirinn fhathast tha iad ag ràdh.

MAR A CHOINNICH E IASGAIR MÓR NA H-AIBHNE 'S MAR A DH'IARR E BIADH AIR

Cha robh fios aig air an t-saoghal de dhianadh e ach 'se *sgeuma* rinn e, lean e 'n abhuinn a thachair ris is chunnaic e duine mór mór ag iasgach air an abhuinn agus chaidh e far a robh e.

'Gu de do naigheachd 'ille bhig,' os an duine mòr a bha sin.

'An tà cha 'n eil agam-sa guth,' os an gille, 'ach b' fhearr leam nan dugadh tu dhomh breac dhe 'n iasg a th' agad 's mi gu bhi marbh leis an acras.'

'N tà,' os esa, 'ma tha shealbh ort fhéin 's gu 'm marbh mi breac an dràsda gheibh thu e.'

Mharbh e sin breac 's cha do mharbh e leithid riamh cho mór ris.

Os an duine : cha 'n fhaigh thu 'fear-s idir. Cha do mharbh

---

[1] *orra* was pronunciation of reciter for 3rd pers. sing. fem.
[2] Eriskay dialect.

mi leithid riamh o thainig mi agus bithidh e ro-mhór ann an suilean a Righ leithid so dh' iasg thoirt h-uige. Ach gheibh thu 'n ath fhear mharbhas mi,' os e fhéin.

Mharbh e sin fear 's bha e na bu mhua na chiad fhear a mharbh e. 'Cha 'n fhaigh thu fear-s idir,' os e fhéin.

'Od,' os an gille, 'cumaidh tu mise gu bràch gun bhreac thoirt domb, 'gealltuinn a h-nile fear a thoirt dhomh 's gun thu ga thoirt dhomh.'

'An tà 'ille mionnaichidh mi air bàrr na slaite ged 'iodh e urrad ris na dhà gum faigh thu fear-sa.'

Mharbh e sin breac, 's bha e na bu mhua na gin a mharbh e.

'N tà, 'ille mhath,' os e fhéin, 'so dhut a nist e. Cuiridh tu 'n teine air an taobh ud dha 'n allt agus cuiridh tu 'm breac air an taobh-sa dheth. Ma leigeas tu ball dubh na losgadh air cha 'n fhaigh thu sgath dheth.'

MAR A BHRUICH E 'M BREAC 'S MAR A FHUAIR E FIOSACHD

Chuir an gille 'n teine air an taobh thall dha 'n allt agus am breac air an taobh-sa. Mar a bha 'm fiodh cho leumach de bha ach splang a dh' fhalbh as an teine agus bhuail e air taobh a bhric. Leum an gille null air an allt 's chuir e mhiar air a phoc a dh' éirich air a bhreac agus dh' fhàisg e stigh am poc ris an iasg agus loisg e 'mhiar 's chuir e 'mhiar 'na bhial is fhuair e fiosachd gur a sud am fear a mharbh 'athair Cumhal 's gur e 'n cu bh' aig 'athair an cù bha comhla ris aig an abhuinn 's gun robh 'n claidheamh bh' aig 'athair, Mac-a-Luin fo leabaidh aige.

'Nuair a bhruich esan an sin am breac thug e taing do dh' Arca Dubh a chionn a thoirt dha.

MAR A FHUAIR FIONN MAC A LUIN

Dh' fhalbh e sin 's chaidh e gu ruig tigh Arcaidh 's thuirt e ri bean Arcaidh gun a chuir Arca e dh' iarraidh a chlaidh-

eimh. Thuirt ise sin ris :—' Cha 'n eil dùil leam gu bheil
claidheamh aige ach an claidheamh a th' air a thaobh.' Thuirt
esan an sin rithe-se gu robh e fo leabaidh. Dh' fhiachadh fo
leabaidh 's cha d' fhuaradh e. Chaidh e sin a mach 's bha e
'nòdachadh [1] gur e rud air choireiginn a chaidh 'na cheann
fhéin nar a smaointich e air a leithid. Chuir e 'mhiar a
rithist 'na bhial agus fhuair e mach gur ann *bho* [2] phosta na
leapa bha e air a thiodhlacadh. Thill e stigh 'n sin 's thuirt e
rithe gu 'n robh e 'g ràdh gur ann fo phosta na leapadh [3] a bha
e air a thiodhlacadh. Thog 'ad an leaba, fhuair 'ad Mac a
Luin. Rug e air Mac a Luin agus dh' fhalbh e sìos far a robh
Arca Dubh.

MAR A THOG E TORACHD ATHAR 'S MAR A FHUAIR E BRAN

' Tha thu air tilleadh a rithisd 'ille,' os Arcabh.[4]

' Tha,' os an gille.

' De tha thu 'g iarraidh nis-de ? '

' Cha 'n eil ach gu bheil 'ad ag ràdh gur thu fhéin a
mharbh Cumhal.'

' An tà 's mi,' os esan. ' An ann dol a thogail a thòrachd
tha thusa.'

' Cha 'n ann ach tha mi cinnteach gur ann agad a bha
spòrs air.'

' *Leabhar* is ann,' os e fhéin,

> ' Bhèiceadh e mar mhuic
> Bhramadh e mar ghearan
> Is ceann mo shleagh 'na thiomban.'

' N tà,' os esa, ' mhic na galadh, s e 'toirt tarruinn air Mac
A Luin, ma bha sin agad-s air m' athair, bithidh e agam-s
ort-sa', 's e leigeil ceann Arca leis an abhuinn.

'Nar a chunnaic Bran an sin Mac a Luin ghrad dh' éirich e
agus lean e Fionn. Bha so Fionn a' smaointeachadh co dhiubh
a reachadh e gu baile na dh' fhanadh e as. Ach chaidh e

---

[1] Surmising.   [2] Dialectic for *fo*.
[3] Eriskay genitive ending in this word.   [4] *Sic* reciter here.

dha 'n choillidh[1] dh' fhiachainn gu de stuth bha 'Mac-a-Luin. Thòisich e air na craobhan 's bha e 'leagail nan craobhan mar gum biodh an t-arhbar fo fhaobhar na spealadh.

(*To be continued.*)

L'ANKOU

Frances M. Gostling

(Song of the Ankou)

'In the green lane as thou camest homeward, little daughter,
As thou camest between the banks where trees meet overhead,
Hast thou seen aught to fright thee that thou tremblest,
That thy knees shake, and thy lips are pale as the hawthorne?'

'As I came down the lane, mother, the sad grey dusk was falling,
The dusk was falling from the trees above my head,
And the bird that had been singing ceased his sweet song at my passing,
His song that till then had filled my heart with music.

'"Little bird, little bird, wherefore art thou silent?
Why art thou silent when all things are so still?
Now in the evening, at the fall of silver evening,
Thou shouldst be singing loud and clear, little bird."

'But softly whispered the bird, "Hush, dost thou not hear it?
A sound before which every song is still,
A sound of sorrow and of mourning, coming from the road that is before thee,
The shadowy road that thou must travel before thou reachest thy home."

'"I hear no sound except the dewdrops falling,
Heavy crystal tears from the green roof overhead;
Tell me, oh little bird, thou that sittest on high upon the tree top,
Thou that sittest on high upon the tree top, what dost thou see?"

'"I see a man leading his horses toward thee,
Leading two horses harnessed to a heavy cart."
"It is my father, foolish little bird, leading our horses homeward,
Oh, say it is my father, leading our horses that plough the furrows."

---

[1] Dative case distinctly in use in this and many other words. While in the nominative case *coille* has l *mouille*, in this dative form the pronunciation changes to aspirated l.

' "Nay, they are never thine; though one be fat and well-looking
His fellow is lean as Death, his bones press sharp against the skin,
They limp and are aweary with the sorrow of their burden,
Their burden that is the sorrowful burden of all mankind."

' "Tell me, oh bird, what is this burden they are drawing,
This burden by reason of which they limp and are aweary ?"
"Nay, thou shalt see it thyself, is it not even here beside thee ?
'Neath the Calvary at the turning to the churchyard shalt thou see it."

' Then through the dusk and gloaming I saw it coming toward me,
The horses straining and stumbling with the weight they drew,
The whip fell, the whip of the man who led them,
Drawing the cart swaying and rocking behind them, yet never a sound, a
    sound.

' I saw the cart as it rocked, and I saw who sat within it,
A sudden moonbeam broke through the dusk as he passed,
And I saw, ah, hold me, mother, dear little mother, his face turned full upon
    me,
It was l'Ankou who sat there, l'Ankou the terrible Reaper, even now he is
    coming to reap.'

The moon was shining bright when the death cart came to the door,
A sound of wailing and bitter crying was in the air—
Of bitter crying and sorrow, a sound that l'Ankou loves,
Smiling he entered in, smiling he bore her out in her white, white gown,
    her white face turned to the moonlight.

In the old Breton churches of the past were many wonderful things, the like of which we shall never see again.
Strange minglings were there of the old faith and the new;
curious survivals of paganism that have at last all but disappeared before the ever increasing light of Christianity. In
the chapels that were raised upon the old worshipping places
of Druid and pre-Druid times, many objects found place that
must have reminded worshippers of the past. The crocodiles'
heads that held in their mouths the ends of the tie-beams,
the grotesque figures carved on the wall-plates, the altars to
' Our Lady of the Lights,' reminding one irresistibly of Isis,
our lady of Flames, the Saint Venus worshipped at Langon
for so many years transformed at last into St. Agatha; St.
Michael and his golden balance, the dragons and their slayers;

the sacred wells and the saints of the fountains replacing the Korrigan and the Duz, all the strange paraphernalia connected with the lighting of the sacred fires—the dragon, the torch, the disks, remnants of ancient sun-worship, how wonderful they were! But amongst them all none was more interesting than a certain figure once commonly found all over Brittany, now rarely to be met with, though still remembered and held in reverence in some remote districts.

Sometimes this figure took the form of a tall thin man with long white hair and face shadowed by the broad felt hat of the country, sometimes of a skeleton, draped or undraped, whose skull turned on a pivot as though to signify that in a single glance it beheld the whole district over which it ruled. But whether man or skeleton, it always held in its hand a scythe, the blade of which was turned forward, and it signified l'Ankou or Death. Many are the beliefs and superstitions connected with l'Ankou, and though the representations of him have, as I have said, all but disappeared from the land, the people in many parts believe in and fear him as their ancestors did in the past. They believe, for instance, that the last man who dies in the village during the year becomes l'Ankou for the year ensuing. That he has his chariot or cart in which he makes his royal progress, spreading terror and desolation wherever he goes. That he is usually drawn by two horses, one fat and well-to-do, the other lean as Death himself. They say that he uses a human bone to sharpen his scythe, and goes about quite silently—he, his horses, and his cart. His great friends and helpers are supposed to be Plague and Dysentery, the former of whom being lame cannot move over flowing water by herself, but has to be carried by some one. The story is still told of her that when the plague was ravaging Europe in the sixteenth century she was brought to the town of Elliant by a young miller. He found her sitting in a white dress on the edge of the stream bewailing herself that she could not reach the town in time for the Pardon. Very beautiful she looked to the young man, and when he discovered her trouble he was only too willing to lift her on to his horse and carry her over the river. 'Young man,' said she when once she found herself on the other side, 'you do not know what you have just carried across. I am the Plague; I am making the tour of Brittany, and am now going to church where mass is being celebrated; all whom I strike with my cane will die suddenly,' and she spoke truly, for we are told that the entire village was depopulated with the exception of the miller and his mother.

The tax on salt was also once a great ally of l'Ankou, but it is said that the Duchess Anne extinguished it. The story of her doing so is curious and perhaps worth repeating. It has been related by M. Anatole le Braz in his *Legende de la Mort.*

When the Duchess Anne was living at the Castle of Korrec in Kerfot her husband said to her one day—'The meeting of the states is about to be held; I must go to it.'

'Well, be careful what you are about then. Above all put no new taxes upon my Brittany.'

'No, certainly not.'

So he started, attended the congress, and returned to his castle.

'Well?' inquired the Duchess.

'Heu!' he answered, 'I was obliged to consent to the imposition of the salt tax.'

'Ah!'

Then without another word the Duchess rose and went out to the kitchen, where she whispered a few words in the ear of the servant who was stirring the soup for her master's supper.

A few minutes afterwards the servant brought the soup in all boiling hot, and the Duchess's husband put his spoon into it.

'Pouah!' cried he at once, 'they have forgotten to put in the salt.'

'Hé,' answered the Duchess in a jeering tone, 'what does that matter?'

'This soup is simply abominable, I tell you.'

'You will have to eat it as it is nevertheless. You must do it as an example to the peasants. You have deprived them of their salt. . Deprive yourself of it in like manner.'

'I tell you that I insist on having my food properly flavoured.'

'Then abolish the salt tax.'

'I cannot ; I have sworn to help to maintain it as long as I live.'

'As long as you live ?'

'Certainly.'

'Oh, very well, that shall not be for very long,' said the Duchess Anne, and taking from the table a thin-bladed knife, she plunged it into the heart of her husband. Then she ordered one of her servants to go and announce that the salt tax was dead.

But the nobles protested.

'Your husband,' said they, 'swore to maintain the tax as long as he lived.'

'Just so,' answered the Duchess Anne, 'but he is dead, and with him we are going to bury the salt tax.'

And since that time no one has heard any mention made of this scourge of humanity.

So l'Ankou now has only his two assistants.

As to the duties of l'Ankou they are very arduous. Not only has he to strike down the living and to collect the dying, but he has to rule the dead. 'He is the Mayor of the Dead,' filling in fact somewhat the same position in Celtic mythology that Osiris did in the Egyptian. There is an old Mystery Play in which his creation is described.

'I am about to create Death,' says God the Father, 'who shall be royally merciless. Oh cruel Death, I order thee from this hour to go marching through the world, and to kill all without pity.'

One of the things that must strike every traveller in Brittany is the respect that is paid to the dead. It is indeed a cult, the cult of Death, the most ancient, deep-seated, and ineradicable cult of these Armorican Celts. They seem to have a positive love for all that pertains to Death, and it is only necessary to see the size of a Breton funeral to realise how attractive this l'Ankou is to all but the stricken one. His storehouse, the cemetery, always lies in the very heart of the village, and if some cottages can be built whose back windows look out over the crowded enclosure, so much the better. It is the playground of the children, the meeting-place of lovers, the favourite spot where old women knit and gossip, and their menfolk smoke the evening pipe. Yet they fear l'Ankou, as who does not? Only they love to have their dead in their midst, and resent any attempt towards a more sanitary arrangement. When cholera was last busy among them more than one attempt was made by the authorities to establish cemeteries outside the villages, but this movement always provoked the greatest opposition.

'The bones of our fathers lie here in our midst,' the people would say, 'then why do you wish to separate them from those who have just died? If you bury them away out there, they will hear neither the singing nor the services. Here is their proper place where we can watch their graves from our windows. The dead cannot kill us, Death only comes by the will of God,' and so they continue to bury their dead in their midst, to dig them up at the end of a few years to make room for others, to store their bones in charnel houses, and to draw water from the fountain that as often as not comes flowing out of the churchyard.wall.

But it is a different matter to meet l'Ankou going his rounds in the dusk of evening. Even the bravest will blench and shudder at that. He travels usually by the little old lanes does l'Ankou, lanes where the high banks rise on either hand, and trees meet overhead. In these green tunnels he is often to be met of an evening, and woe to those who meet him, for they fall into a fever when l'Ankou has breathed upon them and it is not long before he calls at their house and carries them away in his cart.

Formerly in the old church of Ploumilliau there stood one of the skeleton figures of l'Ankou. It was held in great reverence by the people of the neighbourhood who came from far and near to its shrine. Did any wish for the death of an enemy? there was l'Ankou ready to be interviewed. Was a husband, a son in danger? l'Ankou must be propitiated by prayers and offerings. How long he had stood there no one could tell. Carved in oak and painted, he might have been any age, and as it is well known that primitive peoples pay more reverence to ancient statues than to new, it is probable that the Ankou of Ploumilliau was extremely old. Was, I say, for he has disappeared from the church where he reigned so long. The story of his removal is interesting as showing how firmly rooted are the ancient beliefs of these Armorican Bretons. At the time when l'Ankou used still to hold audiences in Ploumilliau church, there was in the neighbourhood a certain person who made himself notorious by his contempt for the ancient superstitions regarding the Death cult. It brought him into conflict with many of the peasants, and especially with a certain old woman who took his conduct so much to heart that she resolved to rouse the Ankou to avenge himself. Kneeling before the skeleton she explained the matter at length, dwelling on the blasphemous conduct of the accused and finally calling down destruction upon him in the proper, authorised manner. Then she went home and awaited events. But to her surprise nothing happened. The weeks, the months passed, and the sinner continued to flourish as a green bay tree. What was the reason? The Ankou must have heard her, she had even shaken him by the arm, as was usual in extreme cases, crying aloud, 'Let him wither away on his feet even as a plant injured in its root, let him die before the time appointed, and may there be none to help!' In her perplexity she went again to the church and gazed long at the little god. Certainly he was very old. Quite gray with age, his paint all lost under thick layers of dust. No doubt that was the cause of his silence. If he could be rejuvenated he would surely feel more able to act in the matter. No sooner said than done. A pot of red paint was procured, and one afternoon when the church was empty Ankou was transformed, turned into a new red Ankou, and his worshipper left him sure this time of his ability to help the good cause. But Sunday came, High Mass was in progress, M. the rector mounted the pulpit and was beginning his sermon, when he noticed a great turning of heads in the direction where stood old Death. He looked himself and could scarce believe his eyes. There, red and staring, stood the little figure, and no doubt equally red and staring, stood the good priest looking at it, very angry that any one had dared to take such a liberty in his church. And because of this, and no doubt because also he knew of the practices that were in vogue with regard to this same figure, he banished it to the chamber over the porch, and allowed no one to visit it henceforth, till gradually the remembrance of it has all but died away. But the people still believe that the Ankou walks among them with his scythe. They often meet him in the narrow lanes at night, driving his cart towards a cottage where some one is lying ill.

It was after a long, long search and many vain inquiries that we found the ancient Death last year. We found him standing in a dark old chamber over the south porch of the church, hidden away, forgotten, the very key that locked him from former worshippers itself kept under lock and key in the vestry. After the breezy tramp through gorse and golden genista, the church seemed doubly dim and mysterious, and it was with something of a feeling of dread that we climbed the ancient spiral staircase whose granite steps had been hollowed by generations of forgotten feet and found ourselves before a heavy oak door that groaned dismally as it turned on its disused hinges. Across a floor, velvety with dust, into the light of a tiny loophole, and we stand in the presence of the Ankou, the great, the terrible Ankou, and find the sightless orbits gazing up at us in mute appeal. It was a strange sensation to find oneself lifting the little figure out of its dark corner and placing it in the light that streamed in through the unglazed window. It seemed to look out over the churchyard that had for so many hundred years been its undisputed realm, with such a wistful gaze, it was so long since it had looked at its own, so long since it had been shut up there in the dark.

The sacristan's wife was watching us in scared silence—'It is strange to be photographing the Ankou, is it not?' I said as cheerfully as I could.

'Mon Dieu, oui,' she muttered, crossing herself; and turning her back on the unholy work, she moved to the far corner of the room.

Presently, however, seeing that nothing untoward happened, she thawed a little, and told us how in her mother's time the Ankou stood in the church, and that no one thought of visiting Ploumilliau without paying his devotions to the mysterious Ervoanik Plouillo as it was called.

'Madame knows that it is Death?' she concludes, crossing herself; and I remember how in old time the ancestors of these same Bretons, the early shadowy Celts of whom Cæsar has left a record, boasted of their descent from a great god of death, 'Thus,' or, as the Romans called him, 'Dis-pater,' and in the strange little figure before me I seem to recognise one of those primitive religious survivals to which I have already referred.

To the imaginative mind of the Celt, as to that of the ancient Egyptian, death early became personified, and was worshipped as one of the greatest powers of the universe, a power at all costs to be propitiated.

Druidism, with its more enlightened teaching, limited the powers of the earlier elemental gods and by telling of one supreme Spirit, degraded these powers of nature into attributes of the great 'one God.' And later, Christianity, brought over from Insular Britain at the time of the Celtic immigration as Druidism had been a thousand years before, strove to replace the worship of death by the worship of life.

But still, through every change, through every age, the Death cult lingers; and it is the religion of Death that one finds in Brittany to-day, though the Ankou has been hidden almost out of existence.

It is a strange worship, this worship of Death, and the strangest thing about it, is that the people themselves would deny and resent that it exists at all. A Breton priest to whom we spoke of the cult of the Ankou, indignantly replied that the people were all good Catholics, though somewhat superstitious in certain districts. And so no doubt they are, for as one of their own writers has well expressed it, 'Christianity has merely blessed those things it was powerless to destroy,' and thus it was that l'Ankou formerly found a throne on the altar of the dead in Plou-milliau church. He held high state at the festival of Toussaints, when every house provided supper for its dead, leaving the front door open for the Anaon or souls of the dead to enter, to eat and to warm themselves. He had his warnings that he sent before to announce him, *Traou spont*, as they are called in some parts, and he had his great song, the ballad of the Ankou, of which I may here give a few lines :—

'Old and young, take my advice. It is my wish to put you on your guard—For death comes nearer every day—As for one, so for all.

'"Who art thou?" cried Adam. "I am terrified at the sight of thee. How thin thou art, and how frail—Thou hast not an ounce of flesh upon thy bones."

'"It is I, the Ankou, friend ; it is I. I plant my lance in thy heart—I turn thy blood all cold. I am thy nearest companion—I am at thy side night and day—only waiting the bidding of God—only waiting the bidding of God. Poor sinner, I come to call thee—It is I, the Ankou, who walks unseen across the world. From the height of the Ménez, with a glance, I kill five thousand at a blow."'

As I focussed the terrible little figure before whose coarsely carved feet so many generations had knelt and trembled, before whose glance, whether by witchcraft or more direct means, men had quailed and withered away, I seem to feel his gaze upon me, and the photograph once taken, I hurriedly closed the camera and left him alone once more in his solitude. There he stands, and will stand for many and many a day ; and though the priest may lock and double lock the door, l'Ankou will find his way out of the dismal chamber, and reap and reap again the harvest that is his due.

A GAELIC CLASS IN NEW ZEALAND

Rev. D. S. Maclennan (Waipu, New Zealand)

Gaelic in the colonies is not a quantity to be reckoned upon in the future of that language. The revival of patriotism in the Old Country may do something even yet, along with the spread of a more generous scholarship, to keep alive the ancient tongue ; but in the colonies these two factors must be very largely discounted, and Gaelic is rapidly falling before the march of the utilitarian movement. There are doubtless exceptions, but my experience is that the typical Colonial is a Vandal of the Vandals. To him nothing is sacred. He has had no past and he cares not for the future ; he lives for the present and is essentially selfish and self-centred. Culture for its own sake he does not understand nor desire. Money and pleasure engross his interests. He is really influenced more by America than by the Old Country, which he looks upon as somewhat antiquated, choosing to think that it remains where his father, a poor crofter or ploughman, left it, fifty or eighty years ago. It is clear that in such environment Gaelic has no chance. The only hope for Colonial Gaelic is in Eastern Canada, particularly the provinces of Nova Scotia and Cape Breton which were so largely settled, about one hundred years ago, by whole communities from the Western Highlands, who carried with them their language and no other, and necessarily taught it to their children ; but the third and fourth generations are now springing up and the promise is not likely to extend much further. A Gaelic news-paper, *Mac Talla*, published in Cape Breton, and kept up with some spirit for a long time, has eventually died through lack of readers. In fact, Canada is three thousand miles too far away from the Hebrides, and a dividing ocean not merely of waters but of interests and conditions of life rolls between the old country and the new ; so that there is little likelihood that Gaelic will flourish long in Canada. All honour to those who have done their best to prolong its life in that country. Their energies should be devoted more to the preservation of anything precious that has come down from the past, that their old people carried with them from the old land, whether in the way of tale or song or well-turned phrase. From the point of view of the modern Celtic Renascence it is a thousand pities the Gaels ever left their native country to mingle with colonial populations as they exist at present. It is bad for them sentimentally and bad for them religiously, and it ultimately means their complete absorption in the new population with the loss of their language and their characteristics. No doubt the gain to the new population will be considerable. But the abiding together of the Gael at that transition period at which the great emigrations took place would have greatly enriched the Scotland and Ireland of to-day with a patriotic, religious, and morally clean country population, and would have provided for a larger and more powerful Celtic influence being brought to bear upon the English language and English genius. It might not be too much to say that we should have one or more English poets to-day, one or two English statesmen, more than one man of science, and probably a few great preachers. Certain it is that Gaelic would have increased its chances of life at least ten-fold. For the emigrants of one hundred years ago were really the cream of our West Highland population.

From the current of emigration that flowed at that time towards the North American shores there was, fifty years later, a deflection, and in this deflection and the fate of the Gaelic which it carried in its course towards a still newer and much more remote country I wish to try to interest the readers of the *Celtic Review*. Amongst the emigrants to Nova Scotia one hundred years ago or more there were families from Gairloch, Lochcarron, and Lochalsh, chiefly Mackenzies and Mackays, who settled at St. Anne's, and had as their minister a man bearing the distinguished name of Norman Macleod, a native of Assynt in Sutherland. A son of his became a wanderer and found his way to Australia in the late forties. In the course of time he sent news to his father (who had given him up for lost) of the pleasant winterless land that lay under the Southern Cross ready to receive a population. . Tired of contending with the Canadian winters, many of the Highland settlers listened with eager interest to the wonderful news, and in the course of a year or two five shiploads of people started from Nova Scotia to seek a country in the southern seas. They carried their minister, as Israel of old did the Ark of the Covenant, in their midst and braved the dangers of two oceans in vessels built and manned by themselves until at last they reached Australian shores. But they soon found that Australia was not to their mind. Virgin bushland with Highland hills in the background awaited their arrival in New Zealand, and so this most remote of all lands received its contribution of settlers from the wandering Gael. Were the circumstances better known I have no doubt this migration would rank as one of the most remarkable in history. It was carried out without disaster and indeed without serious misadventure by the people themselves. There was no one to promote, none to lead the expedition; they had little knowledge of navigation, and no experience at all of the seas they were to traverse. It was the largest body of immigrants which New Zealand received at one time, and the descendants of these Highlanders have now occupied a con-, siderable portion of the northern peninsula of the colony. It seems to be the peculiar destiny of the Gael that he should be found in largest numbers in the most remote and inaccessible parts of a country, and the rule holds good in regard to our New Zealand friends. At the time of their arrival the whole colony was before them and they could have chosen the best land in it. But having made their choice, such as it was, they doggedly stuck to their farms and to one another.

A question in which I was greatly interested when I came among the Highlanders here was: How would the Gaelic language, already transplanted from Scotland to Canada, bear this second transplanting? At first it seemed to stand it well. The first generation born in this colony grew up bi-lingual, Gaelic being for the most part the mother-tongue, but the younger generation, and indeed nearly all under thirty, were strangers to the Gaelic, and, I regret to say, some of them affected to treat it with contempt. On asking a young lady, whose parents spoke Gaelic chiefly, whether she would join my Gaelic class she answered that she did not wish to learn Gaelic as it would 'spoil her English.' She spoke with that beautiful soft accent which is only found in Gaelic-speaking communities, and was quite unconscious of the fact that she owed the sweetness and purity of her English to her parents' Gaelic. The young people formed the notion that Gaelic has been a hindrance to their fathers, and that the sooner they get rid of it the better it will be for their future advancement. Such notions were not uncommon in Scotland a generation ago, but happily they are extinct now, and the Scotch Highlander is rightly proud of his Gaelic. He has come to see that the power to use two languages implies a certain mental culture which is a valuable asset to him in the battle of life. With Gaelic as the mother-tongue English comes inevitably nowadays. But with English as the mother-tongue Gaelic is rarely well acquired. It is clear that, with such false notions prevailing, Gaelic has no future in this large Highland settlement, and therefore none in Australasia, for this is the only district in the Southern Hemisphere in which the language is spoken and preached habitually.

When I spoke of forming a class for instruction in Gaelic the matter was pooh-poohed by the older people who told me that I should not have a dozen pupils. My object was to create an interest in the parent language among the people generally; to show them that their language deserved better treatment than it had received amongst the descendants of the pioneer settlers; to show them in short that if they would be in the fashion they should learn Gaelic; and above all to improve the attendance at the Gaelic service on Sundays. What was my surprise to find a class of over fifty on the opening night, and this attendance kept up with a tendency to increase rather than diminish every week throughout the winter months. The majority of the class were young men and women, and, as most of them knew very little Gaelic, I had to adopt a popular and easy method of instruction. Much use was made of the black-board, and easy sentences, such as the familiar *ciamar tha thu*, were written down and rigorously pronounced. By and by we came to the *pons asinorum* of Gaelic pronunciation, *Dh'ith laogh òg ubh amh*, and the blunders made by the various aspirants after an orthodox enunciation of the gutturals were hugely enjoyed by the audience. We used no text-book at first as we had to wait for three months to get some from Scotland. But we got through the phrases in common use, the numerals, the days of the week, and the months of the year (so far as names can be found for them in Gaelic). We also took up some Gaelic proverbs, in which a few of the old men gave useful assistance ; and we even attempted Gaelic poetical renderings of such English classics as 'Mary had a little lamb.' After three months of this work I thought it time to make a start with Gaelic grammar, and here my first difficulty arose. Our Gaelic grammars, even the most elementary I have yet seen, are founded upon Latin, and none of my class, although most of them had the ordinary colonial education, knew any Latin. Even the provincial teachers in this colony have no knowledge of any language but their own. Consequently it may be said they have little real knowledge of grammar. *Case*, in Gaelic, with its Latin terminology, *Nominative*, *Genitive*, *Dative*, etc., was utterly strange and puzzling to them. The older people used *case* all their lives, as Monsieur Jourdain used prose, without being aware of it. *Gender* also was a little puzzling but afforded some amusement. I explained to them that the gender of a noun in Gaelic had nothing to do with sex (as in English) ; that both *boirionnach* and *firionnach* were masculine ; that *uan* was masculine, even when described as *uan beag boirionn* (a little ewe lamb) ; and that *gabhar fhirionn* (a he-goat) was feminine. I fancy this was considered a joke. Of course I explained to them that some nouns were followed by an adjective in its plain form, and these were classed as *masculine* by grammarians, others taking an adjective in its aspirated form were described as *feminine* ; that *clach* was feminine because it might be described as *clach mhòr* or *clach bheag*, and that *tigh* was masculine because it could be spoken of as *tigh mòr* or *tigh beag*. But I found that I should have to abandon declensions or else lose my pupils. The text-books I sent for were, *How to Learn Gaelic*, by Whyte and MacBain. The lessons and extracts were devoured with avidity. I found the tale *Murachag is Mineachag* most useful as an exercise in pronunciation, and also as affording practical illustrations of the use of *case*, and many of my pupils easily learned to repeat it in Gaelic from beginning to end. The grammatical part of this useful little book is, however, not so simple as it might be made for beginners.

By and by a senior Gaelic class, consisting of a dozen of the best readers, was formed, and we got through some of Dugald Buchanan's and Duncan Bàn Macintyre's poems, during which some of the pupils made remarkable progress. One young lady can now read almost anything in modern Gaelic, and can write the language very creditably. It may be interesting for readers of the *Celtic Review* to know that an English translation of Dugald Buchanan was made by Donald Macleod, son of the worthy old minister of this settlement, who himself was known for a rhymster in his youthful days. It was published in Auckland in 1856, and seems to be, on the whole, a highly creditable performance. The translator has been most successful with *The Skull*, but here he has used too much liberty with the original, both in words and metre, and we have a poem after the manner of Pope's *Iliad*. I shall close with an extract :—

> 'Wast thou a maiden, comely, graceful, fair,
> With brilliant eye and fascinating air,
> Who in the world performed the loveliest part,
> Whose soft attractions snared the youthful heart ?
> Now every grace that caused the generous fire
> In each fond suppliant, conquered by desire,
> Is turned to loathsomeness and foul disgust,
> To every eye a mass of vilest dust.
> Cursed be the grave that ruthlessly defaced
> Thy perfect form by art and nature graced.'

BOOK REVIEWS

Old-Irish Paradigms. By JOHN STRACHAN. Dublin: School of Irish Learning; and Hodges, Figgis and Co., Ltd. London: D. Nutt. 1905. 2s. 6d. *net.*

Multum in parvo fitly characterises this little volume of 83 pages. Designed to serve as a skeleton for a course of lectures on Old-Irish Accidence, and to be used along with Professor Strachan's *Selections from the Old-Irish Glosses* it well serves its purpose ; it embodies, so far as is necessary in reading Strachan's *Selections*, the results of the more recent investigations in the study of Old-Irish grammar. Let us hope that the welcome accorded it may incite Dr. Strachan to write a comprehensive grammar in this difficult but important field. No section is given to the infixed pronoun,—what is requisite for the *Selections* being embraced in the vocabulary. There are also no paragraphs on adverbs, nor on prepositions, nor on the comparative ; nor is what was given in the *Selections* on the copula and substantive verb repeated. The Old-Irish verb Dr. Strachan has studied very thoroughly ; he well knows in what respects Windisch's *Irish Grammar*, which has served its own day well, needs revision. Zimmer has long since, to give but an instance, discussed the so-called *t*-future, *b*-preterite, and *u*-imperfect which Windisch gives as verbal forms, and all things of this sort are of course absent from Strachan's *Paradigms*. Absolute, conjunct, and relative forms of the verb are clearly distinguished. The types of the present active here given are :—I. A. (1) *berim*, I carry ; (2) *benaim*, I strike ; (3) *-gninim*, I know ; *ara-chrinim*, I perish. I. B. *gaibim*, I take ; II. *marbaim*, I kill ; III. *léicim*, I leave. There are full paradigms of the *-s-* subjunctive and of the *-s-* future, the verb illustrated being *guidid*, prays. Deuterotonic and prototonic forms are carefully distinguished as in *asbiur*, I say : *-epur* ; *dobiur*, I give : *-tabur*. Of the deponent unfortunately no complete paradigm can be constructed. A careful comparison with forms given by Windisch will often reveal differences, *e.g.* the dative fem. of *tri*, 'three,' is given as *trib*; the form is *teoraib* in the glosses on the St. Gall Priscian, as in Stokes' and Strachan's *Thesaurus* (vol. ii. p. 178): *donaib teoraib personaib uathataib=* 'in the three persons singular.' Praise must be given to the full classification of the declension of nouns. It is thus:—A. Vocalic stems—1. stems in -*o*-, the examples given being masc. or neuter; 2. stems in -*ā*- which are fem. of course (and this it were as well to have stated); 3. stems in -*io*-, the examples being masc. and neuter; 4. stems in -*iā*-; 5. stems in -*i*- (examples being from all three genders); 6. stems in -*ī*-; 7. stems in -*u*-; 8. stems in -*ū*-; 9. stems in a diphthong, e.g. *bó*, 'cow'; gen. *bou*, *bó*. B. Consonantal stems: 10. stems in a guttural, of which four types are given (a) *cathir*, 'city'; (b) *malae*, 'eyebrow,' n. pl. *malaig*, in some modern dialects distinctly preserved as *malaigh*, or *mailghea* from the old acc. pl. (?), and without any weak -*n* ending; (c) *rí*, 'king'; (d) *lie*, 'stone'; 11. stems in a dental: (a) *cin*, 'fault'; (b) *tene*, 'fire'; (c) *fili*, 'poet'; (d) *bethu*, 'life'; (e) *carae*, 'friend,' and other words, some of which have *a* or *u* in the nom. The neuter *dét*, 'tooth,' belongs here; 12. stems in a nasal, masc., fem., and neut. examples being given; 13. stems in -*r*-, as *athir*, 'father'; 14. stems in -*s*-, which are neut., e.g. *tech*, 'house'; but *mí*, 'month,' is cited as a masc. stem in -*s*-. This classification is more accurate than that in Windisch who did not distinguish -*o*- stems, as Stokes did in his *Celtic Declension*, published in 1886. The examples given under Adjectival Declension are rather scanty. Confessedly a 'skeleton,' the living voice is needed to supplement the written statement, as otherwise the beginner in the School of Irish Learning will be at a loss to understand the scheme of classification, or to comprehend why *teg*, 'a house,' is an -*s*- stem; *muir*, 'sea,' a stem in -*i*-; *ech*, 'horse,' a stem in -*o*-. That an exhaustive grammar of Old-Irish, giving all historical and proto-Celtic forms is what we are justified in looking for from Dr. Strachan the present work clearly reveals. The sooner the better.

GEORGE HENDERSON.

Deirdire, and the Lay of the Children of Uisne. Orally collected in the Island of Barra, and literally translated by ALEXANDER CARMICHAEL. Edinburgh: N. Macleod, 1905. *3s. 6d. net.*

Of the many treasures from the storehouse of Gaelic legendary lore, which lovers of that lore owe to the editor of the *Transactions of the Gaelic Society of Inverness*, few are more prized than the exquisite oral version of the Deirdire romance collected by Mr. Carmichael, and translated with his wonted intimate and delicate grasp alike of the original to be rendered and the medium through which it was rendered. Mr. Carmichael has laid all students of Gaelic literature under a fresh obligation by reprinting text and version, and by adding a lay, likewise collected and translated by him, which gives an entirely independent version of the legend and presents many points of the greatest interest.

The Deirdire story stands out pre-eminent among the too scanty remains of early Irish literature. Full of interest to the antiquarian, full of charm to the artist as is much of that literature, it must be admitted that, as a whole, it is deficient in architectonic faculty, and in that mingling of realistic presentiment and imaginative inspiration which, in varying degrees, constitutes the excellence alike of Greek and Scandinavian heroic and mythic legend. Its beauties are too often those of detail rather than of structure, specimens of a conventionalised (true an exquisitely conventionalised) rather than of a direct and vigorously observant art. The Deirdire story in its oldest form escapes this criticism. It has an austere compactness of structure together with details of the most touching pathos, which, even in the imperfect form under which it has been transmitted to us, give it a high place among the masterpieces of tragic story-telling. Such is the essential force of the elements of which it is composed that, had it fallen into the hands of a first-rate literary artist, it would certainly have ranked among the half-a-dozen greatest stories of all literature.

It is fascinating to follow the fortunes of such a theme as displayed upon the self-centred and limited stage of Gaelic story-telling. Upon the whole it must be said evolution has not been progress. Great as is the charm of the twelfth century version contained in the Glenmasan MS., due, it cannot be doubted, to an Argyleshire story-teller who had the same passionate love of his native hills and moors, lochs and streams, as the centuries later Duncan Ban, still the effect is weaker, the note is that of romance rather than of realistic tragedy or ballad. The tendency is further accentuated in the version published by Dr. Douglas Hyde in vol. i. of the *Zeitschrift für Celt. Philologie*, which may well be the production of an Irish artist of the seventeenth or even the eighteenth century. It is equally apparent in the version under review, but this is characterised by such charm of detail, by such direct and limpid beauty of presentment as almost compensate for the loss of the old stern tragic note. Nor must we forget (as, alas, we have so often to recall in the case of oral literature!) that the version is not the best that Mr. Carmichael might have procured could he have foreseen the future, not the version of Alexander but of John 'who never could take a tale in and never could give a tale out,' a decidedly unjust piece of fraternal criticism if we may judge by this example of John Macneill's skill. Doubtless though, Alexander's version would have been more rounded and, here and there, more coherent.

The folk-lore questions raised by both tale and lay are many, and I must reserve discussion of them for another place. I must, however, record my conviction that the tenacity of the Loch Etive localisation is due to the fact that the author of the Glenmasan version was an Argyleshire man, and that his version won a well-deserved local popularity. The Inverness localisation to which Mr. Carmichael alludes (pp. 135-136) may testify to a lost Inverness version.

It is work of supererogation to praise the merit of Mr. Carmichael's

BOOK REVIEWS

rendering. Yet the sun has spots. I would at least submit the following cases to Mr. Carmichael's considered judgment. I do not like *Scandinavia* for *Lochlann.* The ideas the English reader associates with the one word are all too different from those which the Gaelic narrator calls up by the other. Scandinavia is *not,* as Lochlann is, a mysterious realm inhabited by formidable and uncanny wizard warriors. I do not like (p. 39) a '*confidential* love,' and a '*conversational* mate.' I cannot believe the Gaelic has the same effect as the English. P. 67, lines 6 and 7, the English word 'harmless' is ambiguous. The preceding dialogue, if Mr. Carmichael renders faithfully, must be corrupt in the Gaelic. In the mediæval texts the position is clear: Fergus urges the claim of native land in preference to the alien country, however great be the advantages of living in the latter. I do not like 'mercenaries' for 'amhusg' though I can suggest no better rendering.

Optimist and believer in progress though one may be, one cannot but be filled with sadness at the thought that such an exquisite and genuinely popular art as is here revealed is fast fading away. The greater our gratitude to those whose loving and zealous skill preserves the last fragments of a wonder-world of beauty which all too soon will have vanished for ever from the popular ken. ALFRED NUTT.

The Place-Names of Elginshire. By D. MATHESON, F.E.I.S. Stirling: Eneas Mackay. London: David Nutt. 6s. *net.*

Mr. Matheson's work is a handsome volume of over two hundred pages, and in printing, paper, and binding does credit to all concerned in its production. Illustrations of burgh seals and coats-of-arms, and an index to the twelve hundred names discussed add to its interest and usefulness. A few slips, as Balluack for Barluack, and Brunthill for Bruntland, and omissions, as Coltfield, p. 38, Delnahatnich, p. 110, Knockando, p. 157, etc., require attention. The names of each parish are grouped together and the parishes taken in alphabetical order. Not a few names occur several times, and in some cases the same derivation is repeated, and in others, without apparent reason, a different one is given. Cognates of the explanatory terms are usually given and also repeated. The forms that ' white,' for example, takes in Dutch and other languages are given under Whitehouse (p. 139), under Whitewreath (p. 141) and under Whiteriggs. Where the authorities are followed all this, whether necessary or not, is correct enough.

In the case of Gaelic words Mr. Matheson does not follow authority, but attempts to supply the cognates on his own account. His independence is scarcely justified by the results. The applications even of Grimm's Law to Celtic are not observed. *Baile* is said to be allied to Greek *polis,* *aill* (rock) to English *hill,* and *beinn* to Welsh *pen.* *Aber,* it is said, ' is derived from *ath,* a ford, and *bior,* water, and is generally supposed to belong to the Welsh rather than to Gaelic.' *Aber* is a Pictish word cognate with Welsh *aber,* and comes from the root seen in Gaelic *beir,* English *bear,* Latin *fero,* with a prefix *ad*, *to*, or *od*, *out*. *Pit*, stated in different places to be from Gaelic, from Pictish, and from Welsh or Brythonic and allied to Latin *puteus*, is a Pictish cognate of Welsh *peth*, Gaelic *cuid*.

The nearest Norse place-name is beyond Beauly, yet Norse derivations are numerous. Braes and Kirkton are examples. Clones is held to indicate the presence of the Norsemen, and yet derived from Danish. Latin, French, German, Dutch and Welsh are drawn upon without sufficient consideration. Crosshill is referred direct to Latin *crux*, and Cockmoor is taken from English *cock*, and Dutch *moer*, but Cockmuir from Danish *kok*, a heap, and Norse *mor*, *moer*. Hybrid derivations, as here, are freely advanced.

Haste and lack of revision are evident even in the composition. One article has been allowed to stand thus :—'*Ladycroft.*—This is an old word.' "Our Lady" of the Catholic ritual signifies the Virgin Mary, and was so called because this piece of land originally belonged to the Church of St. Fillan.' The dedication to Dr. Andrew Carnegie has two slips in its one sentence, and the statement (p. 186) that *mo*, my, and *do*, thy, prefixed to names of saints of old 'are now substituted by the term *Rev.*,' is attributed, if the sentence be strictly construed, to the Irish histories. An extensive acquaintance with the vocabularies of the various languages mentioned is evident, and much ingenuity is shown in the solution of many difficult names. The lists of names and the old spellings are important aids to the study of place-names, and not a little may be learned from the volume as to the forms taken by Celtic names in the local 'doric,' and the past physical, social, and ecclesiastical condition of the county.   C. M. R.

NOTES

Notes on the Study of Gaelic :—*continued*—Second Year's Course

A year's training may reasonably be expected to result in good facility in reading, a general acquaintance with the methods of spelling, and some familiarity with the combinations of article, noun, and adjective. A second year's course will include a more detailed acquaintance with special points in spelling, a general knowledge of the grammar and syntax, easy composition and idioms, all this with reference to the reading.

For reading purposes may be recommended without reserve *Uirsgeulan Gaidhealach* (E. Mackay, Stirling : 6d.) which is cheap, varied, and well and accurately printed; but as it does not contain enough matter for a year's reading it requires to be supplemented. For this purpose nothing could be more suitable than the good old text-book, *Leabhar nan Cnoc* (Northern Chronicle Office, Inverness: 2s. 6d.). Apart from semi-religious matter, this contains enough secular reading of a high order to last, together with the other, for more than a year.

A word of warning with regard to spelling is possibly necessary, as its importance may be apt to be underrated. Accurate spelling is as essential in Gaelic as it is in English, and though in the initial stage of an experiment, such as the Leaving Certificate in Gaelic, a certain amount of laxity may be overlooked, it is to be expected that the standard will materially harden in this respect. In any case good spelling is sure of its reward; inaccurate spelling cannot be other than prejudicial to the candidates. Fierce controversies have raged about Gaelic spelling. Much ink has been spilt, and friendships have been severed over the presence or absence of the letter *h*—which after all is stated on good authority to be no Gaelic letter—and over the claims and position of apostrophe and hyphen. This was in the pre-scientific days, when the study of the old forms of the language in the light of comparative philology was only just beginning or had barely begun.

Now, thanks to the work of specialists, we are in a position of greater certainty, and it would add much to the teacher's own interest if he made himself acquainted, as far as possible, not only with the right way, but also with the reason for its being right.

The use of *h* to indicate aspiration is sufficiently set forth in the grammars. Whether the aspirated consonant occurs at the beginning or in the body of a word, the theory of aspiration is the same: it takes place when the consonant originally stood between two vowels. The influence of analogy, however, causes the modern language, especially in speech, to extend the practice; *e.g.* we seldom hear *féin*, self, but rather *fhéin*. So with genitives of feminine proper nouns, with regard to which there is some variety in usage. They are generally unaspirated: *banais Màiri*, Mary's wedding; but they are also heard aspirated, especially, I think, after liquids: *Tobar* Mboire, Tobermory; cf. *loth na h-asail fhiadhaich*, the wild ass's colt; *cliù na h-ainnir chaoimh*, the gentle lady's renown. A word may be said on the difficult subject of *h-* prefixed to a word beginning with a vowel.

This is not to be explained by the easy and time-honoured *euphoniæ causa*. Apart from instances in which it may be due to analogy, *h* here represents the terminal consonant of the preceding word in the old language. The commonest case is where it stands for the final *s* of the old article: this explains its universal use after *na* of the article: *bruach na h-aibhne*, the river's bank; *na h-iomairean*, the ridges. In other cases it stands for the final *th* of a verb: *gu ma h-olc*, may it be evil; *gu ma h-anmoch*, may it be late. The old Irish form is *co m-bath olc*. Further examples are *a h-aon*, one (alone); *a h-athair*, her father; *a h-uile fear*, every man; *na h-abair*, say not; *gu h-àrd*, on high; *ge h-àrd*, though high; *tha e 'g a h-òl*, he is drinking it.

Here we meet one great use of the hyphen, viz. to connect prosthetic consonants that originally belonged to the preceding word. This use is further exemplified in prosthetic *t* and *n*. In such combinations as *an t-each*, the horse; *an t-slat* (nom. fem.), the rod; *an t-saoir* (gen. mas.), the carpenter's, *t-* is really part of the old article. So with *ar n-athair*, our father; *bhur n-athair*, your father: *n* properly belongs to *ar* and *bhur*, the primitive forms of which ended in *n.*[1]

The other main use of the hyphen is to separate the two parts of a compound word when the stress accent is on the second part of the compound, e.g. *fir-ruith*, runners; *mac-talla*, echo—a sensible and useful convention, which should be strictly adhered to. A third and subordinate use is to mark off the emphatic particles *-sa*, *-san*, affixed to nouns and adjectives, e.g. *mo chù-sa*, my dog; *do chù dubh-sa*, your black dog.

The apostrophe is properly used to indicate the suppression of a letter, and is often necessary *e.g.* with certain forms of the article. But it is well for the sake of simplicity—not to mention appearance—to refrain from its use except when it is necessary. It is often used in writing when it would be better to give the word in full: we *say, am bail' ùr* the new town, but it is surely better to write, *am baile ùr*. It should not be used, says Professor Mackinnon, to stand for suppressed words, 'such as *a* the possessive pronoun, *a* the so-called relative, *ag* of the present participle, and *do* of the infinitive. In such cases the practice ought to be in Gaelic as in other languages, to use the apostrophe only when ambiguity may arise.'[2] Thus it is correct to write *tha mi dol*, I am going; *chunnaic mi athair-san*, I saw his father; *am fear chluinneas*, whoso hears; *am fear thuit*, the man who fell, (in the two last the verbs are already relative in fòrm, the construction being in 'parataxis'); *tha mi bualadh*, I am striking. Professor Mackinnon would, however, write *cha'n*, not *chan*; *gu'n*, not *gun*.

In grammar the pronouns should receive special attention on account of the difficulty in spelling these small particles. A list of the uses of the relative should be made. (Note that the oblique cases of the relative *an*, *am*, are really the *article* singular.) In the verb two things may be noted as deserving special study, (*a*) the idioms of the verb *to be*, such as, *is mòr leam*, I value; *ge b'oil leat*, in spite of you; (*b*) the idioms of the passive voice, which consists almost wholly of periphrastic forms, e.g. *théid mo bhualadh*, my striking will proceed, I shall be struck; *chaidh a mharbhadh*, his killing went, he was killed. The irregular verbs must of course be got up.

Gaelic syntax presents many points which are better omitted at this stage, where the aim is to keep to the great main roads and to avoid by-paths and exceptions. The pupil must know, for instance, that the so-called infinitive is a verbal noun, and therefore requires the genitive after it. It may be questioned whether it is necessary at this stage to trouble him with the construction of the noun in apposition, and of such phrases as *tigh bean a' chlobair*, the shepherd's wife's house. What to omit and what to include is a matter for the discretion of the teacher. He will find Dr. H. C. Gillies's *Gaelic Grammar* useful here. It is a pity that its price puts it beyond reach of the ordinary pupil.

---

[1] On these points Dr. A. Macbain's *Etymological Gaelic Dictionary* may be consulted.   [2] *Celtic Review*, ii. 86.

In the early stages of composition it is much the better plan to prevent mistakes being made from the beginning, than painfully to eradicate them when they are made. It is important also that the learner's mind should not be confused by having to face too many *new* difficulties at once. The vocabulary and syntactical points involved should be thoroughly known before putting pen to paper. Further, it is a good plan to go over the exercise on the day before it is written, giving translation and explanations freely, but allowing no notes to be taken. The result will be a much nearer approach to accuracy, and the correct rendering will stick to the memory as a model for future occasions. Again, when the translation from Gaelic into English has been gone over, the pupils should write part of it in idiomatic English. This is a first-rate exercise in English composition, and brings out idiomatic differences better than anything else; Highland English, even of non-Gaelic speakers, is saturated with Gaelic idiom. When this has been looked over, the English should be turned back again into Gaelic, and compared with the original. This will be found to be a powerful method. In connection with composition, Gaelic idioms are of the utmost importance. Dr. H. C. Gillies gives a fairly good list, but it needs supplementing. Idiom is of the essence of a language, and Gaelic is intensely idiomatic.   W. J. WATSON.

The Ruin of Britannia

Mr. Wade-Evans's interesting article on 'The Ruin of Britannia' will appeal to a wide circle of readers, dealing as it does with a period of the common history of northern and southern Britain of which so little is as yet accurately known. His researches, following up those of Daniel H. Haigh (1861) and Dr. W. F. Skene (1865), by maintaining a series of dates for important events of the fifth century, much earlier than those still generally relied upon, open up many new and inviting lines of inquiry. To these, very probably, qualified students are already addressing themselves ; but perhaps some brief amateur comments and queries may not be deemed an encroachment on your valuable space.

If 502 be the true date of Maelgwn's death (as both Mr. Haigh and Mr. Wade-Evans have it), and 462 of Dewi's birth, then from both data Cunedda's birth may reasonably be placed about (or before) 340, which allows but 30 years for each descent ; for Maelgwn could scarcely be less than 42 when he died ; and Cunedda may have been 60 or more when Einion (his tenth son according to Humfrey Lloyd) was born. Thus three generations from Cunedda to Maelgwn may agree with four from Cunedda to Dewi. But Cunedda's birth might be placed much earlier even, looking to the fact that about 400 he had nine, eleven, or twelve sons, all warriors (we are not told how many daughters), and one grandson grown up. If 80 in A.D. 400, his birth would be A.D. 320, and his mother, Gwawl, daughter of Coel Godebog by Stradwen, might be born about 295, when Coel was about 65 years old. This would admit of Coel's having had Helen Lluedawg by a wife of his youth in 246, and of her giving birth to Constantine (as wife of Constantius Chlorus) in 274, and dying in 327, when over 80, after visiting the Holy Places in Jerusalem. (See an able paper on Helen's British origin in *Archæologia Cambrensis*, 1847, by John Jones, Llanllyfni.) May not Cunedda's migration from Manau have been earlier than 400,— say about 384, when the departure of Maximus for Gaul and Italy left Britain denuded of troops and open to the raids of Picts and Scots, who had had time to recover from their defeats by Theodosius in 368? As to Cunedda's age at the Migration, 80 seems quite a moderate estimate. In later Welsh history (*tem.* William Rufus) we read of Iestyn, succeeding his father Gwrgan (who died aet. 126), as Prince of Glamorgan, when 106 years of age, and after making war against Rhys ap Tewdwr, King of Deheubarth, dying aet. 111, *leaving 440 descendants!*

But there are other difficulties connected with this early date for Maelgwn's death; as, for instance, his interview with Kentigern (Cyndeyrn) during the latter's retreat from Strathclyde to North Wales, in which period Dewi of Menevia died [*Life of Kentigern*]. Kentigern's mother was daughter of Loth (Llawdin Lluedawg) whom Arthur made King of Lothian after the defeat of the Picts at Mynydd Agned (Edinburgh), the date of which battle Mr. Wade-Evans fixes as October 470. The death of Loth, and birth of Kentigern, coincided within a day, and Haigh says that Loth died in 492, Arthur in 493. But in that case Kentigern would be only 10 years old at Maelgwn's death. Again, Maelgwn was present at the battle of Ardderyd, which the *Annales* place in 573, a date which Skene accepts. How, then, could he die 71 years before? Were there two Maelgwns? The death of Dewi (St. David) during Kentigern's location at Llanelwy makes it clearly impossible that the former could have survived till 601 as in the *Annales*.

It is thought that Columba's kingly convert, Brude mac Mailcon, may have been a son of Maelgwn Gwynedd by a Pictish princess. If so, since Brude began to reign A.D. 555, he must then have been 53 years old at least (for Maelgwn died in 502). Why, then, did he not come to the throne at an earlier age? It is noticeable that the two preceding Pictish kings reigned (alone) but one year each, and that they were preceded by five reigns amounting in all to 29 years, at the beginning of which period Brude's age must have been at least 22. At that time two Drests reigned together, both probably grandsons, by different parents, of Drust son of Erp (? Erc),—since among the Pictish kings ancestral names seem to have descended in the same family through long periods. These reigned 5 years, after which one of them reigned alone 5 years more. He was followed by his two brothers, who reigned in succession 7 and 1 or by another list 6 and 6 years. These short reigns look as if they were for fixed periods by arrangement. The next reign is of 11 years and is followed by another Drest, perhaps sister's son to one of the former Drests; he reigns 1 year, and is followed by Galam cennaleph for 1 year, with whom Brude mac Mailcon reigns jointly for 1 year more, before his sole reign of 30 years begins. Galam was perhaps grandson of a king of the same name who reigned 512-524, preceding the two Drests (*Da* Drest, whom Innes lists as another king!) From their reign to that of Galam cennaleph (which Innes reads Galam *cum* Aleth) the law of succession may have required that two, or three, collateral lines should reign successively, or jointly, till they were exhausted, before Brude, a younger generation by a sister, should come to the throne. Bede's 'ninth' year of Brude may date from his joint reign with Galam, coinciding with the 'eighth' (*octavo*) of the old Chronica on which Innes chiefly relies. As Columba's arrival from Ireland seems fixed to Pentecost 563, the reigns from Drust son of Erp, when readjusted, show that the latter king began to reign A.D. 409 (giving Nectan morbet, Drust's younger brother, 24 years as in the Chronica, and not 25 with Innes.) The correspondence of this well-attested era with that of the departure of the Romans from Britain should not be overlooked. The Chronica also tells us that in Drust's reign, '*ix. decimo anno "regi" ejus Patricius episcopus sanctus ad Hiberniam pervenit insulam.*' Also that under Nectan morbet, '*tertio ·anno regni ejus Darlugdach abbatissa Cilledara de Hibernia exulat pro Christo ad Britanniam*'; and that '*secundo anno adventus sui immolavit Nectonius Aburnethige Deo et Sancte Brigide, presente Dairlugdach que cantavit alleluia super istam hostiam.*'

'*Optulit igitur*' (it proceeds) '*Nectonius magnus filius Wirp, rex omnium provinciarum Pictorum, Apurnethige Sancte Brigide, usque ad diem judicii, cum suis finibus, que posite sunt a lapide in Apurfeirt usque ad lapidem juxta Ceirfuill, id est, Lethfoss, et inde in altum usque ad Athan. Causa autem oblationis hec est. Nectonius in vita julie* [? hodie] *manens fratre suo Drusto expulsante se usque ad Hiberniam Brigidam sanctam petivit ut postulasset Deum pro se. Orans autem pro illo, dixit : "Si pervenies ad patriam tuam Dominus miserebitur tui : regnum Pictorum in pace possidebis."*' As Dr. Skene, in *Chronicles of the Picts and Scots* says, 'the phrase "in vita *julie* manens" is nonsense,' and I would suggest '*hodie*' as above, but do not pretend to say whether that would imply that the record *is a contemporary one.*

This episode, connecting at so early a date as A.D. 450 (the third year of Nectan) the foundation of Abernethy with Patrick's famous convert, Brigid, the daughter of Dubhthach maccu Lugair, chief bard to King Laeghaire, is extremely interesting, as showing the intimate relations of Erin with Alban in those early days, and the spread of Christian teaching among the Picts independently of the labours of Ninian. The note regarding Patrick, as having gone to teach the Irish in the 19th year of Drust, *i.e.* in A.D. 427, is probably affected with the same error as the popular date 432; for there can be no doubt that Patrick was labouring in Ireland long before either date. If 461 be the true date of his death, and he spent 60 years preaching in Ireland, he must have arrived there in 401.

The Pictish reigns before Drust, as far up as that of Gartnaith loc, are worth considering. The years ascribed to each are generally moderate and probable. Two seeming exceptions are: Talarg achivir, 75 years; and Gartnaich diuberr, 60 years—Drust's immediate predecessors. But as Drust himself *lived* 100 years and reigned 45, and as many sovereigns have reigned over 60, and some over 70 years (as Louis XIV. of France, 72 years), the exceptional character of these two may be held to be in their favour. If accepted, the date of accession of Gartnaith loc is 222. The MSS. disagree *in toto* as to the reigns before this epoch, and need not be pursued further.

This Gartnaith, we are told, was the progenitor of four Gartnarts who reigned subsequently. As *five*, or by combining two lists, *six* kings of the name appear to have followed, does this imply that the note in question was made between the dates of the fourth and fifth of these, *i.e.* by Innes's Chronology, between 640 and 661? Innes inserts after Gartnaith loc, a King 'Vere,' to whom he gives 9 years. The '9 years' are those of Gartnaith himself, and 'Vere' is simply the end of the word *regnavere* in the entry opposite his name, which is as follows:—

'Gartnaith loc, a quo Garnart iiij. regna*vere, ix. annis regnavit.*'

The otherwise most careful essayist gives the 'iiij' as *years* to Gartnaith, and out of the remainder of the sentence (here underlined) he makes a new King 'Vere' with a reign of 9 years! This and the fictitious 'Dadrest' already alluded to throw out Innes's reckoning of the '70 kings' of the Picts from Cathluan to Constantine, which would require readjustment. After Gartnaith, Breth son of Buthut reigns 7 years; Vipoig namet, 30; Canatulachama, 4; Wradech vechla, 2; Gartnaich diuberr, 60; and Talore son of Achivir, 75 years, ending A.D. 409. According to these numbers Vipoig reigned from 237 to 267; but Fordun's Chronicle inserts after him a King 'Blarehassareth' with 17 years. This entry cannot be got rid of so easily as the two which follow it: 'Frachna[1] albus, 30' (a repetition in Gaelic form of Vipoig); and 'Thalarger Amfrud, 16' (a strange transposition of 'Talargan filius Amfrud,' *i.e.*, Eanfrid of Northumbria, who reigned about 400 years later!): if accepted as genuine (for otherwise where did he get the name?), it places Vipoig's reign from 220 to 250, entirely coinciding with the testimony of the votive tablet of Lossio Veda, nepos Vepogeni, found at Colchester in 1891, and inscribed to the Emperor Alexander Severus, who reigned from 222 to 235.

Many other considerations besides the foregoing may arise out of Mr. Wade-Evans's ingenious efforts to re-construct the chronology of these early periods of British history, and it is to be hoped that the subject may be taken up responsively by some of your able Scottish contributors.

JAMES SIMPSON.

---

[1] *Fiachua* in the List in Appendix V. of Innes.

THE CELTIC REVIEW

APRIL 16, 1906

A WELSH BALLAD

J. Glyn Davies (Welsh Library, Aberystwyth)

I took down the following ballad and its tune from the singing of my mother, Mrs. John Davies of Liverpool, who had heard it sung at Talysarn, Carnarvonshire, nearly half a century ago, by her eldest sister. I do not know of any other instance of its existence in Wales, nor indeed of any other ballad of a similar type.

It is obviously fragmentary, and must have been so when my mother heard it, for the last verse was regarded as an anticlimax *pour rire*.

From the fairly regular distribution of stressed and unstressed syllables, I would assign the utmost age-limit of the present form of the ballad to the mid-sixteenth century.[1] The phrase 'claf iawn yw f'*enaid*' [very sick is my soul] I should not expect to find in Welsh popular poetry much after the close of the sixteenth century. Between metric and diction, I feel tempted to put the ballad down to the first half of the seventeenth century.

In the following arrangement of words and tune, each of the first two lines is repeated :—

---

[1] I hope to publish shortly an account of metrical changes in the sixteenth century, where the data for this statement will be given.

1. { O fy mab anwyl ble buost ti ddoe: { yn hela sgwarnogod: mam
   { O fy mab anwyl ble buost ti ddoe: { yn hela sgwarnogod: mam

{ cweiriwch fy ngwely ;
{ cweiriwch fy ngwely ;   Claf iawn yw f'enaid yn ymyl ter - fynu.

2. O fy mab anwyl be gefist ti'n fwyd :
   Neidar lle slywan :[1] mam cweiriwch fy ngwely ;
   Claf iawn yw f'enaid yn ymyl terfynu.

3. O fy mab anwyl be roddi di'th blant :
   Bendith Duw nefoedd : mam cweiriwch fy ngwely ;
   Claf iawn yw f'enaid yn ymyl terfynu.

4. O fy mab anwyl be roddi di'th wraig :
   Cortyn i'w chrogi : mam cweiriwch fy ngwely ;
   Claf iawn yw f'enaid yn ymyl terfynu.[2]

When I took down the words, some five years ago, I had
hela pysgodyn [hunting a fish] instead of *hela sgwarnogod*[3]
[hunting hares]. *Neidar lle slywan* in the second verse points
to a North Walian origin : to pack *llysowen* into two syllables
would be difficult, without mutilating it beyond recognition.

    I am indebted to Owen Rhoscomyl for the identification
of the Welsh ballad. It is 'Lord Randal,' and the nearest
approach I can find is Version B, Child's *Ballads*, 1905.

1. 'O whare hae ye been a' day, Lord Donald, my son ?
   O whare hae ye been a' day, my jollie young man ?'
   'I 've been awa courtin : mither, mak my bed sune,
   For I 'm sick at the heart, and I fain wad lie doun.'

---

[1] *slywan*, N. Wales metathesis of *llysowen*.

[2] 1. O my dear son, where hast thou been yesterday : hunting hares ; mother
make my bed, very sick is my soul, near its end. 2. O my dear son, what hadst
thou for food : a snake instead of an eel ; mother, etc. 3. O my dear son, what wilt
thou give to thy children : the blessing of God of Heaven ; mother, etc. 4. O my
dear son, what wilt thou give to thy wife : a rope to hang her ; mother, etc.

[3] Spoken W. for *ysgyfarnogod*.

2. 'What wad ye hae for your supper?' etc.
   'I've gotten my supper:' etc.

3. 'What did you get to your supper?' etc.
   'A dish of sma' fishes:' etc.

4. 'Whare gat ye the fishes?' etc.
   'In my father's black ditches:' etc.

5. 'What like were your fishes?' etc.
   'Black backs and speckl'd bellies:' etc.

6. 'O I fear ye are poison'd?' etc.
   'Oh yes! I am poison'd:' etc.

7. 'What will ye leave to your father?' etc.
   'Baith my houses and land:' etc.

8. 'What will ye leave to your brither?' etc.
   'My horse and the saddle:' etc.

9. 'What will ye leave to your sister?' etc.
   'Baith my gold box and rings:' etc.

10. 'What will ye leave to your true-love?' etc.
   'The tow and the halter, for to hang on yon tree,
   And lat her hang there, for the poysoning of me.'

There are many versions of 'Lord Randal,' and I have only access to three. Possessors of Child's large edition may be able to find closer parallels, but at any rate, there can be no doubt as to the identity of the Welsh ballad. It will be observed that the metric is practically identical with Version B, the only difference being the repetition of the second line, which I look upon as an excrescence. Verses of five lines are rare in Welsh, and of a different type from this, whereas the same *Langzeile* occurs in rhyming couplets, and is common in quatrain form.

I am indebted to my colleague, Mr. David Jenkins, Mus. Bac., for revising my score of the curious and hitherto unpublished tune, and to my brother, Mr. G. M. Ll. Davies, for sending me a fresh and attested copy of tune and words.

THE GLENMASAN MANUSCRIPT

Professor Mackinnon

GAELIC TEXT

Et tánic Bricne a mach a rís, agus do búi ac fechain na faichthi 'n a timcell. Agus atconnairc buiden an-aithnidh ingantach ac ti*chtain*[1] a thuaith ar lorg na cet buidhne, agus samail da chet laoch a línmare. Agus ni raibi laoch gan laig*in* dibh, na cath-milid gan cloich commoir a cobr*aid* a sgeith, agus ain fher ard-mór osgardha amulcach a n-eidermedón na n-ánr*ad* agus folt cas clechtach croch-buide fair. Tánic Bricne a sdech, agus do innis do Oilill na sgela sin agus adubratar an laid etarra ann :—

' A fhir d' féchus na buidni,
Seall orra ar ái do ruibhni,[2]
Ma ro-d-aithni innis dam,
Cia an buiden mor-sa sa magh.[3]

' Ab*ar* rím, a Bhricni bhúain,
Err*adh* sunnradach an t-sluaig,
Co n-inniser duit ule
Tuarasgbail gach en duine.'

' Baramail da chet láoch lonn,
Mo do dáinibh na gach drong ;
Derg a sgeith is buidi a fuilt,
Agus is a thuaith tegait.

' Go n-a dá chet laighni lethna
Mar tisdáis an dail debtha,
Co n-da chet líag-nertaib nia
A n-gust*a*laib a crom-sgíath.

' Ogláoch amulcach menn mór,
In fer sin fá suidh an slóg
Geb*aid* tairis ós tel*aig*
Folt cas cruthach caoim slem*ain*.

---

[1] MS. *tī*, which perhaps is an anticipation of the verbal noun in the modern language *ti*[*ghin*]*n*.

[2] Verses attributed to Ossian and found in LL. fol. 161b, and the Advocates' Library MS. xxxviii. p. 154, give *ruibne* and *luibne*, both glossed. LL. glosses

(*Continued from pp.* 222, 223.)

ENGLISH TRANSLATION

Bricne went forth once again, and viewed the green all round.   And he saw an unknown strange troop coming from the north in the track of the first squadron, about two hundred in number.   Each hero had a spear, and each battle-soldier a very large stone in the hollow of his shield. In the centre of the warriors marched a very tall brave beardless man with plaited curls of saffron-yellow hair. Bricne went within and told these tidings to Oilill, and this lay was recited by the two of them :—

'You who look on the hosts,
   View them in the line of your spear ;
   If you recognise them, tell me
   What this great company on the field is.

'Describe to me, persistent Bricne,
   The distinctive garb of the warriors,
   That I may give to you
   An account of each individual.'

'I judge them to be two hundred fierce warriors,
   Taller than the men of other troops,
   Red their shields, yellow their hair,
   From the north they have come.

'With two hundred broad spears,
   As they come into the thick of conflict ;
   With two hundred heavy champion stones
   Fastened to their curved shields.

'A tall beardless stammering warrior,
   Is he around whom the hosts sit,
   Over his crown there flows
   Hair curly beautiful soft smooth.

---

ruibne by *sgiath*, 'shield,' and *luibne* by *sleg*, 'spear.' The Edinburgh MS. reverses matters, glossing *ruibne* by *sleagh* and *luibne* by *sgiath*. O'R. has *ruibhne* (1) 'a lance,' (2) 'a numerous host.' From *ae*, 'cause, knowledge, science,' developed the phrase *arai*, used in various shades of meaning : 'on account of,' 'in spite of,' 'nevertheless.' The exact force of the phrase here is to me uncertain.

[3] MS. $\frac{d}{m}$.

'Is síat na fir sin, aderi,
An macrad o Muigh Eme ;
In fer mór, miad gan ceilg,
Fermenn mac Dara dreach Deirg.

'Is mairg re curid a n-gleó,
Gibé h-uair gabait angó,[1]
Is mogénar fer am n-dib
Les an gabait airm, a fhir.'

A *fhir.*

Imthusa Ailella Finn imorro. Do gab ag suarcus ar Fergus, agus as ed adbert ris : 'Cid ima tangais do'n tir-si a Fhergais?' ar Ailill. 'Do cúalais cena,' bar Fergus. 'Ma sed ni tibra-sa mo t-sheoid ar mh' aimles,' ar Oilill. 'Ni caithim fein do biad-sa no do deoch,' ar Fergus, 'oir ni ghonaim-si (duine)[2] sa biad chaithim do gres.' Agus do eirig Fergus a mach. Agus adubairt Ailill do guth beg re Fergus : 'Na cluined an Gamanrad sin. Agus tarra moch-trath ar Ath an Cluiche, agus na cluined duine sin acht ara do carbaid. Agus ní cluinfe duine uaimse h-e acht ara mo carbaid. Agus denam comracc, agus gipe uain tí ass, bíd an ben aige.' Ránic Fergus a mach agus lenais Dubthach agus Aongus h-e re cách. Agus do fhiafraighedar fa lana feirge de, agus ni b' áil leisen a indisin doib. Agus do gab tenn forra gan a indisin do neoch eile. Agus do indis doib as a h-aitle. Agus

---

[1] *angó,* an uncommon word, 'alas!' (K. M.). The meaning here is evidently 'wrath,' 'anger' (*an,* intensive, + *gó* 'deceit'?).

[2] MS. reads *do* followed by what looks like *gonatt duine* scraped out. The repetition of the incident is interesting (cf. *supra,* p. 212), for the version now given is in some respects like those of LL. LU. and Egerton (Brit. Mus.), printed by Prof. Windisch in *Ir. T.,* ii. p. 208 *et seq.* Here follows the corresponding passage from LL. Fergus and his party arrive at the palace of Ailill the Fair :—*Ferthair failte friu.* '*Cid fris-tudchábair?*' ol *Ailill Find.* '*Co ro anam celide lat-su,*' ol *Fergus,* '*dáig ata debaid dunn ri Ai(lill) mac Matach*' (*Magach*). '*Ni anfa-su lim-sa ém,*' ol *Ailill Find.* '*Mad nech immorro dot muntir, no (ni) ainfed. Dáig adfiastar dam-sa not chara mo ben.*' '*Etar ascaid di chethra din dúnn. Atá eicen mór forn.*' '*Ni béra-su ascaid uaim-se,*' ol *Ailill,* '*dia n-ana chelide lemm.*' *Doberar dam co tinniu dóib cona dú di chormaim dia feiss.* '*Ni chathiub-sa do biad-su ám,*' ol *Fergus,* '*uaire na biur th'ascaid.*' '*Assind liuss duit dín,*' ol *Ailill.* '*Rot bia són,*' ol *Fergus,* '*ni gebthar forbasi fort.*' *Dos-cumlat ass iarum.* '*Tairceth fer i n-áth,*' ol *Fergus,* '*fochetóir i n-dorus ind liss.*' '*Ni éraibther ocus ni erbbaibther dom inchaib-se ém,*' ol *Ailill.* '*Ragat-sa féin,*' ol *se.* '*Cia úann ragas ar a chind ind fhir, a Dubthaig?*' ol *Fergus.* '*Ragat-sa ar a chind cid me,*' ol

'These men, I tell you,
Are the chivalry of Muigh Eme ;
The tall man, pride without deceit,
Is Fermenn son of the handsome Dara the Red.

'Woe to those against whom they fight,
Whenever their ire arises ;
Happy indeed the chief
With whom they take up arms, O man.'

                                                   Thou.

Now as to Oilill the Fair. He made himself pleasant to
Fergus, and this is what he said to him : 'What has brought
you to this country, Fergus ?' asked Ailill. 'You have heard
already,' replied Fergus. 'In that case, I shall not give of my
wealth to my hurt,' said Oilill. 'I, for one, shall not taste your
food or your drink,' rejoined Fergus, 'for I have never slain
(a man) after partaking of his food.' And Fergus went out.
Ailill whispered to Fergus : 'Let not the Gamhanraidh hear
this. But betake thee early to the Ford of the Game, and
let no one hear of it but your charioteer. And no one shall
hear of it from me but my charioteer. Let us fight, and
whichever of us survives shall have the lady.' Fergus went
out and Dubthach and Angus followed at his heel. They
asked what the cause of his wrath was, but he did not like to
tell them. And he charged them to tell no one else. He then

*Dubthach.   Dothét Dubthach iarum issin n-áth ar a chind.   Benaid Dubthach sleig
tríit co n-dechaid tria di shliasait.   Dolleci-seom dana gai do Dubthach co m-bert
crand tríit.*   They were welcomed. 'What has brought you thither ?' asked Ailill the
Fair. 'To stay with you,' replied Fergus, 'for we are at feud with Ailill son of
Magach.' 'Neither you nor any of your people shall stay with me,' said Ailill, 'for I
have been told that you are in love with my wife.' 'Give us some of your cattle then,
for we are in great straits.' 'You shall have no gift from me, nor shall you stay here,'
said Ailill. An ox and bacon with a due supply of ale were given them for food.
'I shall not eat your food,' said Fergus, 'not having received your gift.' 'Out of the
castle you go,' said Ailill. 'That will be to your advantage,' said Fergus, 'for you
will be safe from attack.' They went forth thereafter. At the gate of the castle
Fergus added, 'Let a champion appear at the ford forthwith.' 'You will not be
baulked, nor shall my honour be entrusted to another,' said Ailill, 'I shall be there
myself.' 'Who from our party will meet the man, Dubthach ?' asked Fergus. 'I
shall go myself,' said Dubthach. Dubthach thereafter went to meet him at the ford.
Dubthach struck him (Ailill) with a spear which went through his two thighs. Ailill
hurled a lance at Dubthach which went through his body, shaft and all.

do iarr Dubthach a legen fein do chum an comraic sin re h-Oilill. Adubairt Fergus nar fer dingmala dó itir eisium agus gur leic tairis comrac etorra do dhenam an an comroinn sin ; agus adubradar an laid ann as a h-aitle :—

'A Fhergais a n-anfa-sa
Re gach n-decair n-dein n-doghraing ?
Ca fáth im a rachá-sa
Romamsa do chum an comlainn ?

'Ní thicc dibh a(f)rithaileam,
Nocha n-uil an bhar línuib,
Tuccaid oraib a íniccin,
Ní thánic dib a dhíguil.

'Ailill Finn an flath ruire,
Flath Irruis íarthair Banba,
Nocha comlann comadhais
A cenn rig Ulad amra.

'Teilgfed-sa an sleg slinnger-si,
Co h-Oilill Átha Fernais,
Nocha n-uil laoch ri m' lamha
Madh dá n-an-sa a Fhergais.'

A *Fhergais.*

Acus ránic Fergus d' a tigh-lepta iar sin, agus rucadar as an adhaig sin. Agus do eirigh Fergus co moch ar na márach, agus do dhúisigh a ghilla. Agus do gab sein a eich agus do innill an carpad. Agus ger moc(h) ranic, fuair Oilill ar an Ath. Agus tugatar achmusán agarb ainíarmartach d' a n-armaib tren-gera treathan-luatha teilcti an agaid a cheile. Agus do fritheoiletar na h-ogláich co h-aithnidh na h-arma, co nach raibe fargamh no fuilechadh ar na flaithibh, agus do t-shoillsich an lá ar na laechibh.

Agus do mhothaich Dubthach agus Aonghus Fergus d 'imtecht uatha agus do ghabhadar an arma, agus tangadar do chum an Átha. Agus fúaradar na curaidh a comlann ar an Áth, agus tucadar fargam gach áin fir[1] ar Oilill, agus tucastar Oilill fargamh ar gach áin fer dib sen. Et do mhothaigh Cormac Conloinges mac Concubair agus Uáitne Ucht-sholus mac Conuill Cernaig Fergus d' imtecht a mach. Agus tánic

---

[1] The MS reads *fer*, but the correct form *fir* is written in full in corresponding passages later.

told them. Dubthach requested (Fergus) to allow himself
to fight Oilill. Fergus said that he had given up the idea
of fighting (Oilill) on that issue, for he was by no means a
worthy opponent of his; and thereupon this lay was repeated
by them :—

'Fergus, will you abide
Every fierce angry quarrel?
Why should you undertake
This conflict in preference to me?

'It does not become you to meet him,
The man is not of your rank;
To succour him might be suitable work for you,
Not to avenge (his insolence).

'Ailill the Fair, the lordly prince,
Prince of Erris in the west of Ireland,
Is not a fitting opponent
To the famous King of Ulster.

'I shall hurl this sharp-pointed spear
Against Oilill of the Ford of Fernas;
There is not my equal in the fight,
Saving you only, Fergus.'

Fergus.

Fergus thereupon went to his sleeping apartment, and
the night passed. He arose early on the morrow, and
wakened his attendant, who caught the horses and yoked
the chariot. Early though they arrived they found Oilill
at the Ford. And the two brandished their very sharp,
mighty-swift, easily-hurled weapons against each other, and
made a fierce but undecisive attack. The warriors handled
the weapons dexterously, so that there was no mark nor
blood on the princes until the day dawned on the heroes.

Dubthach and Angus observed that Fergus had gone
forth, and they seized their weapons and made for the Ford.
They found the champions fighting at the Ford, and each of
them made a thrust at Oilill, and Oilill made a thrust at
each of them. Cormac Conloinges son of Conchobar and
Uaithne Bright-breast son of Conall Cernach observed that

Cormac (agus Uaithne) a mach rompa. Agus do connaic na curaidh a comlann, agus o d' connaic, ro indsaigh íad. Agus tucc (Cormac) forgam ar Oilill, agus tuc Uáithne forgamh eile fair ; agus do ghon Oilill gach ain fer acasan. Is and sin tanic Birrderg mac Ruaidh agus Edar mac Eogáith agus Fiacha mac Fireaba a mach, agus tucadar forgamh gach áin fir ar Oilill, agus tug Oilill trom-ghuin ar gach trein-fer dib sin. Is ann sin tanic Gobhnend mac Luirgnigh agus Suanach mac Salgabann, comhalta Cormaic, agus Lugaid Laimdercc mac D. . . agus Sith. . . mac Edghait co h-inath na h-imresna, agus tugadar forgam gach ain fir ar Oilill, agus do ghon Oilill gach ain fer acasan. 'Cid duitsi, a gilla Oilella,' ar gilla Fergusa, 'gan a indisin do t' mat(h)aib [1] trena san eicin adbal a fuil ? ' 'Is briathar damsa am,' ar an gilla, 'an cein bus cudroma a comrac nach indeósa sgela o cach dib.'

Cid tra acht o dered oidc(he) co h-ard trath-nona do bi doib ar in luinni sin, co clos fó'n longport ledgaire na cloideam 'gá comtócbail agus tinnt . . . na colg ris na cathbarraib, agus sithe na sleg ris na sian-gaothaib. Agus adclos a pupall clainni Fidhaigh na fuasnada sin. Atrachtadar sein co dígáir dasachtach agus co fraochda forníata agus co menmnach mi-cheillidh, co clos a fuaim agus a fothrom a nellaib nimhe agus co cuasaib crand agus carrac garba greagan gailbech gúasacht-ach gresedacht buan greghan na Gamandraidi ac éirge, agus olbacht [2] na n-ánradh ac a n-eidedh agus meall-gal na macradh ac a moch-dusgadh, muisec na min-daeine ac mall-asgnám, cresnugthi agus comairleda na fer-cuinged agus na forusogláoch ac tennad na trén-fer agus ac greasacht na gillannrad agus ac laind na luath-chos do tarrachtain an mer-tresa agus do digail a n-ancraidi ar an Dubloinges. Agus tangatar rompa co ro dían in a n-doiredib dlut(h) crann-gera díanarda duaibsecha, agus in a m-buidnib roda rían-garba recht-búana, agus in a

---

[1] In the dialogue of the two attendants several words are indistinct in the MS. and the reading offered is to some extent conjectural.

[2] MS. olbs or albs. Possibly for ollbach (allbach) 'wild shout.' Cf. bach .i. greis no dasacht (O'Dav.), and oll, 'great,' 'vast.' The reading is clear, but the word is obscure to me.

Fergus had gone out. And Cormac (and Uaithne) went forth. They saw the heroes fighting, and when they did they approached them. And (Cormac) made a thrust at Oilill. Uaithne made another thrust at him, and Oilill wounded both of them. Birrderg son of Ruad and Edar son of Eogaoth, and Fiacha son of Fireba thereafter went forth, and each of them attacked Oilill, and Oilill inflicted deep wounds on each mighty man of them. Then Goibnenn son of Luirgnech and Suanach son of Salgaba, foster-brother of Cormac, and Lugaid Lamderc (Redhand) son of D . . . and Sith . . . son of Edgat went to the scene of the conflict, and each of them struck at Oilill, and Oilill wounded each man of them. 'How is it, servant of Oilill,' said Fergus's servant, 'that you did not tell your mighty chiefs the dire extremity in which (Oilill) is?' 'It is a vow of mine,' replied the lad, 'as long as the combat is equal to say nothing about it.'

And so it was that from the end of the night until full afternoon they fought in this furious fashion. There were heard throughout the camp the clash of swords raised on high, the clang of blades against helmets, and the whistle of spears mid the tempestuous winds. The din was heard in the tent of the clan Fidach. These rose up furiously madly angrily valiantly courageously recklessly so that their rush and tramp were heard in the clouds of heaven and in the hollows of trees and rough rocks; the wild dangerous urgently-persistent uproar of the Gamhanraidh as they rose up; the . . . of the warriors as they donned their armour; the shout of the youth at their sudden awakening; the frown of the young folks as they rose reluctantly; the inciting and counselling of the champions and warriors as they pressed the mighty, and urged the attendants, and hurried the swift-footed to exert their battle-frenzy and avenge their enmity on the Dubloinges. They marched forth very swiftly in close columns sharply pointed very lofty terrible, and in roughly marshalled doggedly furious battalions and in agile troops with banners displayed on red standards,

ceithernaib clisdi crann-ruadha comartac(h)a co rangatar co
h-inadh na h-imresna agus co lathar an laoch-bhúailti.

Is ann sin do eirgetar an Dubloinges co díghair, agus
co badba baoth égciall*ach*, agus co fraocha foistinech, co
n-dernatar mainner aghm*ar*[1] aithesach fhaobar-cruaidh ogal-
borb ainntreannda, agus leibenn lethan-cruaidh laóch-niata
lorg-remar l*aoch*-lonnach, agus buaile bir*ech* barr-derg brath-
aigméil breac-dhathach bán-corcra. Tangatar rompa fo'n
réim sin in a cipi dluith-mer do-rí*artha* doiger-mor do-
oconeta,[2] agus in a toindte togdha toirtemla tuait(h)-echtach
tholg-ainntreannda, gur gabatar lathair fhairsing imbúáilti ar
uilinn oirrt(h)eraigh an Atha, gur gáirset agus an Gamandrad
co cómnart agus co curata d' a cheile, co clos co nellaib a
n-ilach, co n-ar bó leir soillse os na slogaib an comairet ro
batar na frasa fír-móra fog*a* ac f*erthain*, agus na bera barr-
géra brath-neimnecha bodha ar luamain os na láochaib.

Agus do crom*ad* na cliatha crann-remra catha ac na
curadhaib, gur lub*ad* agus gur loinn-brised na crainn ris na
cath-sgiathaib, agus gur beicet*ar* na fraighi ris na fuasnadaib,
agus gur gairid*ed* na luir*igh* ag á luath-gerrad*h*, agus gur
loinntesgadh na laic(h) tres na laoc(h)-bruinnibh, agus gur led-
r*adh* na cinn tres na clogataib, agus gur aimréidighit fuilt do
na fíar-lannaib, agus gur dalladh suile do na sruithlinntib fola
fichidi forruaide ac tuitim co for-lethan ar na fairgsinaib. Agus
do chuaid in cath in a comlannaib agus in a cendairc fo chetóir,
co clos co fada o na fednachaib sin cathus na cath-miled,[3] agus
fedmenna na feinned, agus ruathar na righ-damn*a*, agus
torann na triath, agus brosgar na m-buiden ag a m-báolugadh,
agus claidr*eam* na ceithernac(h)a clódh a cernaib an catha ;
meall-ghal agus menmnannrad na macr*ad* agus na maoth-
oglaoch ; atm*ar*echt na tren-fer ac a tesg*adh* ; imarc*aid* na
n-úasal ar na h-ur-íslib ; ard-ghotha na n-uasal-rígh agus na
n-oire*cht* agus na n-armann ac tennad in tresa agus ac greasacht
na gliadh agus ac laind na laoch.

Cid tra acht o rangatar a fedhmanna catha ar cach ro

[1] MS. *admar*.
[2] The reading is clear, the word is unknown to me.

and arrived at the place of conflict and the scene of hard blows.

Then the Dubloinges gathered fiercely terribly restlessly recklessly wrathfully firmly, and formed themselves into a phalanx warlike victorious steel-edged awe-inspiring rough, and into a bulwark broad and stern hero-valiant thick-shafted hero-furious, and into a palisade pointed red-tipped fateful dangerous speckled pale purpled. They marched forward in that order in dense masses insatiable large-speared, . . ., and in select powerful featful rock-firm columns, and selected a spacious trampled field at the eastern angle of the Ford. They and the Gamhanraidh shouted vigorously and exultantly on seeing each other, so that their pæan reached the clouds. And over the heads of the hosts the great heavy showers of brandished spears and flashing sharp-pointed deadly venomous javelins shut out the light.

And the thick-shafted battle spears of the champions were twisted, and the shafts were bent and broken in splinters against the battle shields; and walls echoed the din; and coats of mail were shortened by the frequent hacking of them; and heroes were slashed through their valorous chests; and heads were cloven through helmets; and hair was twisted by curved blades, and eyes were blinded by the fierce red streams of blood that fell thickly upon the ground. The battle became at once a series of duels and strife, so that far away from the actors could be heard the onset of valiant soldiers, the mighty efforts of the champions, the onrush of the crown princes, the thunder of the lords, the clamour of the troops warding off danger, the sword play of the brave foot-soldiers in all parts of the field; the spirit and eagerness of the young and tender warriors; the ire of the stalwart men as they were being hacked; the arrogance of the gentry towards the plebeians; the loud voices of the nobles and officers and warriors in pressing the fight, inciting the charge, and urging the heroes.

Now when their battle supports reached the others Fergus

[3] The phrase, word for word, is used by the Four Masters (F.M.) 1504. Cf. K. M. Contrib. *s.v.* cathas.

gabh Fergus agus Aóngus agus Dubthach ac túargain a sgeith
ar Oilill a áonar, agus do gab Oilill ac tuargain a tri sgíath
orrason.   Sgibis Fergus ar cúlaib, agus crothais an cráoisech
catha, agus gonais Oilill fochetóir fó cumus.   Crait(h)is Oilill
an manáois móir-lethan o h-innsma go h-urloinn gur gonastar
Fergus co fortamail.   Agus gonais Dubthach agus Aongus
Oilill, agus gonuis Oilill iadsum co h-amnas[1] gur bo cósair cró
na curaidh ó na craoisechaib.

Agus o do cualatar an Gamannrad na tri béimenda bodbha
sin ar aon sgéith Oilella Finn co foillsechdha, do freagratar
grinne fraochdha forníata do Gamannraid Irrnis íad .i. Ghamain
seng na Sidgaile con a dá Gamain mar aon ris.   Agus tuairged
a triar brathar do tri béimennaib brath-aidble a sgiath co
h-ainíarmartach ar Fergus.   Fregrais Fergus co fraechda
fedmannta sin.   Tangatar triar tren-fer toirtem*la* do'n Gamannraid cetna *cu cath*, agus tucatar tri beimenna aidble osgarda
do'n aird-rig co cúalatar na maithi nile íat.

Cid tra acht ro b' adhbar uathbais agus uiregla[2] do lucht
an catha sin eístecht re buaidersaidh na m-badb agus na
m-brais n-én na h-ealt*an*[3] agus na h-énlaithi, agus re nuall-
guba na con agus na cuanart ac urnuidhi áir agus abaige, re
selgairecht na sideng, agus re h-eitea*laigh* na h-énlaithi
aérda ac toirnem ar na trochbuidhnibh.   Bá h-imda ám ré
h-ed na n-athgairit ann sin feinnidh frasgonta, agus curaidh
crechtnaigthe, agus laochrad laim-gerrtha, agus triath ar
tuisl*e*daigh, agus taisech tróm-gonta, agus mail ar mertnige,
agus brug*aid* broinn-tesgda, agus forb-fir fiar-gerrtha, agus
buidhne brat-corcra, agus cinn co comarth*ach*, agus suile saob-
dalla, agus beoil ar m-bán-glas*adh*, agus suile saob, agus bruinne
ag bolg*f*annaig, agus cosa ar cam-lúainn, agus troigthi truaill-
gerrtha, gur bo torann toghdha tuaithbil tubaistech triath-
gonta troch-digbál*ach*, agur gur bá cath-buaile coimnert cleth-

---

[1] In the modern language *ealt, ealta*, is of the *n*-declension.   Cf. D. B. M'Intyre :

'Bha eoin an t-sléibhe 'n an ealtainn glé ghloin.'

[2] *uirghioll* in I.G. and S.G. is 'speech,' 'talk,' 'eloquence.'   Alliteration probably decided the use of the word here.   To the survivors, no doubt, the scene would
be the subject of talk and comment.

and Angus and Dubthach charged with their shields Oilill alone, and he with his three shields charged them. Fergus leapt back, brandished his battle spear, and wounded Oilill below the belt. Oilill brandished his great broad spear from shaft to point and wounded Fergus right valiantly. Dubthach and Angus wounded Oilill, and he in turn fiercely wounded them to such purpose that the heroes were a mass of gore from the spear-thrusts.

When the Gamhanraidh heard clearly these three terrible blows upon the single shield of Oilill the Fair, the flower of the fiery chivalry of the Gamhanraidh of Erris responded, viz. the slim Gaman of Sidgal and his two (brother) Gamans along with him. The three brothers delivered three tremendous fateful but indecisive blows of their shields upon Fergus, which the latter met with fury and effect. (Other) three mighty valiant men of the same Gamhanraidh joined the fight, and gave three furious compelling blows to the high king which were heard by all the chiefs.

Howbeit it was a source of terror and dread to those engaged in that fight to listen to the screaming of carrion crows and birds of prey of bird-flocks and bird-tribe, the bowling of dogs and dog-packs hungering for carnage and entrails, the watching of wild birds, and fluttering of the birds of the air as they swooped down on wounded men. For there indeed within a short space could be seen many a warrior sorely wounded, many a champion mangled, heroes with their hands hacked, lords fallen, chiefs mortally wounded, princes outdone, yeomen with bosoms ripped, stout men hacked, troops with bloody mantles, heads cut, eyes half-blinded, lips locked and pale, eyes turned, breasts panting, knees cross-swaying, and feet chopped. So that after the fierce encounters the field was one continuous ominous confused tumult of wounded lords and churls, and one stout strong firm-armed phalanx of broken shafts whittled swords and cloven helmets, and one purple path of broken swords

---

[3] Cf. vol. i. p. 107, where *sieng*, S.G. *sithionn*, means, as now, 'venison.' *Sideng* here is evidently the same word, but the meaning must be 'birds of prey.'

armach crann-brisde colg-shnithe clogat-gerrtha, agus gur ba
céide corcra colg-brisde corp-línmar cnes-oslaïcte cubar-bolgach
cru-línmar na faighte da n-éis ó n-imláidib, gur imdaigedar
na h-echta, agus gur aimréidhigedar an fhaigthe re h-imad na
cráeisech agus na cloideam agus na cath-sciath agus na coland
cros-gerrtha comarth*ach* agus na sláod-óclaoch sínte sec-marb
agus na miled mormenmnach mudhaigte agus na n-gilla
n-éidechi n-atbregda; gur cuired ár na Gamhanraide san
gleo sin, agus co n-dorcradur dronga di-áirmhide do'n Dubloinges .i. deich cet ar n-a comairemh.

Cidh tra acht o d' connairc Fergus a muinntir 'g a
marbadh agus 'g a mughugadh agus an Gamhanrad ac
tocht tairsib, do gabustar ac tócbail a menman rig-mileta os
aird .i. ac telgadh na trom-cloideam, agus ac trascradh na
trein-fer, agus ac fabhairt na foga,[1] agus ac corcr*adh* na crann,
agus ac tregdadh na triath, agus a comroinn na corp, agus ac
meirrdíth na m-buidhen, agus ac scoltadh na sciath, agus ac
broghadh na m-beimenn, agus ac urtógbail a ferge; oir mas
fhir do na sgelaigib ni eirged fercc Fergusa no co roichedh a
fhadhbrann d'a fhuil. Sínis laim d' a cloideam .i. do'n Calad-
colg, agus ní fhuair 'n a truaill ider h-e. Is amlaid ámh tarla
sin .i. aon do lo ro búi a coimriachtain re Meidbh ré taib
craibe cuill a Cruachain, agus fuair Ailill íad amlaid sin.
Agus do ben an Calad-colg as a thruaill, agus do cuir cloideam
crainn co n-imcoimed 'n a inad.[2] Agus ó d' connairc Fergus
an ní sin bá dóich leiss gur mheabhal do ronsat Connachtaich
air. Agus do fhócair do Bricni imthecht, agus a rádha re
Cormac Connloinges an cath d' facbail, agus a fédfa d'a
muinntir do breith leis. 'Agus ni ber-sa troigh tech*id* re
m' re no re m' reimes.' Rainicc Bricne d' indsaige Ulad agus
ro ráidh a theachtairecht riu. Rainicc Cormac as an cath o
d' connairc nert na Gamanraide ag tocht tairsib, agus tuc
sgiath tar lorg[3] d' á muinntir.

[1] The plural is frequently *fogada*.
[2] Cf. vol. i. p. 228, where the incident is related in detail.
[3] Lit., 'shield over track,' the common phrase for 'covering a retreat.'

and carcases wound-gaping foam-bubbling all-bloody. The slaughters were multiplied and the field made impassable by the number of spears and swords and battle-shields, the hacked and mangled carcases, the unwieldy warriors stark dead, the high-spirited soldiers destroyed, and the attendants as they lay hideous and swollen (?). Such was the slaughter by the Gamhanraidh in that fight, in which fell a countless host of the Dubloinges,—(not less than) a thousand in number.

Now when Fergus saw his people being slain and destroyed, and the Gamhanraidh gaining upon them, he began (afresh) to show his royal military spirit,—wielding the heavy swords, laying mighty men low, plying the gapped spears, hurling the shafts, piercing princes, cutting bodies in two, annihilating troops, cleaving shields, driving home his blows, and rousing his wrath; for according to the historians Fergus's wrath did not attain to its full fury until he waded ankle deep in blood. He stretched forth his hand for his sword—the Hard-blade—and found it not in its scabbard. And this is how it was: one day as he was in dalliance with Meave by a hazel-tree in Cruachan Ailill caught them in the act. And he removed the Hard-blade from its sheath and put a wooden blade in its stead. When Fergus observed this, he thought the Connaught men had done it to insult him. So he ordered Bricne to go and tell Cormac Conloinges to leave the fight with as many of his people as he could bring with him. 'But as for myself I shall not retreat one foot during my career or my course.' Bricne went to the Ultonians and told his message to them. Cormac then withdrew from the battle when he saw that the forces of the Gamhanraidh were so much superior, and covered the retreat of his men.

(*To be continued.*)

CHILD-SONGS IN THE ISLAND OF YOUTH

Amy Murray (New York)

'In the Island of Youth, between Neil and Allan, on the true edge of the Great World,' say. the songs they sing and the *sgeulachdan* they tell at *céilidh* round the fire on the floor. On the map it is Eriskay ('Eric's Ey'—that shows the Lochlanners were there), and you will look south of Uist and north of Barra for it among the Outer Isles.

A half-eyed man could see how its neighbours got their naming ; from whom but those who lorded them before the sheep crowded out the men—Mac Niall and Ailein Clan-Raonuill?—what better namesakes than their old-time chieftains ? But no one knows why Eriskay is 'Eilean na h-Oige'; the very name of the namer is forgot.

Was he not *taibhsear*, I am thinking ? for thus he might have had the sight of a day when *An Domhan Mór* should be so graceless in her old age that she would house no more the blessed things of youth—faith, confidence, and joy ; when they should shelter in waste places—cold mountains, lonely glens, bare islands,

'Where few are the sowings of seed,
Where many the sowings of storms.'

Far ahead is the seeing of the Gael ; it might even have been that the nameless one who named the island had the forward vision of a pilgrim who should come from *An Domhan Mór* to the edge of the world before the passing of Father Allan, to find things dead to her for many a day were warm and living in the Island of Youth.

If one should be told there is neither a tree nor a bush on Eriskay ; if one knew how the wind can card the thin pasture and the tattered barley, and pelt the thatches with flying sand and spin-drift ; if one were to think upon the sort of living to be got from rock and bog and sea, one would not look there for the 'forgotten art of gayety.' But there, and in the one heart and mind with the deep seriousness of a God-fearing folk living close to the workings of the elements, it may be found. 'God gives us this because we have so little,' said an Eriskay woman once to me.

There is no myth for which Father Allan had not some measure of tolerance, but for that of 'Celtic gloom!' That is a fiction of the tourist and the alien—I may myself have helped it on a bit on this side the water—for it is the weird, the sad, the unusual that first attracts the collector of tunes ; and so is he likely to bring away with him a showing for one side only of the Gael. But Father Allan taught me that for fishing in such waters as lie round Eriskay the line alone is not enough—better to take the net —better yet to go a-trawling.

Real sorrows are plenty in the Outer Isles, and they have their poignant utterance ; there is a quality of sadness, more-over, in many lovely Gaelic airs which is more elemental than human. We read our own vain longings and world-weariness and regrets into them, even as into the voices of the wind and the wave ; then we say the folk-song of the Gael is altogether sad.

But in truth it does not hold itself too high for any mood of his, and he has a social soul and a cheery. Besides the love-songs and laments that are his symbol to the *Sasunnach* across the Minch and the *Sasunnach* across the Atlantic, he has songs to work to, and songs to dance to, and songs to raise a laugh, and the children have their own songs too.

'A songless web is unlucky.' There are fine slashing rhythms in *Orain Luathaidh,* the waulking-songs ; fifty coup-lets to a song, and the pitch raised twice while the cloth is shrinking and the women swinging and pounding. 'I *do* wonder how they can be making up so many choruses!' a girl once said to me. There is indeed endless ingenuity in the stringing of syllables meaning nothing in particular that answer to the couplets, and give the solo-singer breath-ing time.

For other songs you go to *céilidh*, and over the peats—
the fire on the floor that burns the whole year round—you
will get them till morning. You may happen upon the first
hearing of an *Oran na Feannaig* that a man made himself
in his boat last night; a song of an eight-line stanza and a
little line croaked out at the end to give the assonance-
rime (you seldom get finals rimed in the English fashion)
for the next verse. They are always comic, the crow-songs,
and the men are always making them.   There was a man from
Uist ploughing over on the mainland who made one on his
own splay feet ; he was looking down on them as he trod the
Lowland furrows, and thinking they were 'wanting back' to
Uist, and their homing fancy was the burden of his song.
Another man got the notion of a song while he was gathering
tangles, and slipping in the wet and cold on the rocks and
the sandbanks. Another man yet was ill and had to lie abed ;
the hens were harrowing his nerves by going in and out
among the dishes on the dresser, and he made an *Oran na
Feannaig* to console himself.   There would not seem to have
been much 'Celtic gloom' in any of those men.

Sometimes at *céilidh* the stools will all go back against the
wall, and the couples stand up for a reel. Then you will
hear a lively *Port-a-Bial* ; one of the company will take the
tune, and the rest will all lift on it.

They are not easy noting, the *Puirt-a-Bial*, and not alone
by reason of the pace and the volleying of the words. But
they do not quite 'follow the stick.'   To be sure, the singer's
boot comes down steadily enough on the clay floor, and the
tune goes along at the same gait apparently. But the two
do not always quite keep step, and it is a puzzle sometimes
to know where to put in your bars. Perhaps it would be
well for folk-song writing to go back to the old ways of the
Elizabethans, as Herbert Hughes is doing in *Doire nan
Eala*—the long phrase with the bar at the end gives so much
better scope to the natural inflections of the voice.   It is
the words that have first place in Gaelic song throughout,
and the time and tune must follow them. Moreover, it

would sometimes appear that the singing of them is rather 'a way of doing it' than consciously a way apart from speech. That was Father Allan's idea, and together we came upon it and upon the child-songs in the Island of Youth.

I was walking one day with a grey-eyed girl towards *Coilleag a' Phrionnsa*, where Prince Charlie first set foot ashore for the '45—white sand underfoot, grey rocks on the one hand, blue water on the other.

Before we reached the bay there were rocks to be got over. The tide had left them wet and ruddy and garlanded in strange ways with dripping sea-grass, the 'long-haired one,' with tawny-edged 'ruffles' and bronze blob-wrack, with the dark-coloured *duileasg* they boil in the black houses, and with what not else that grows or harbours in such places. Here and there lay the great tangles, long as coach-whips, that they burn on Uist for the kelp-making. They say they are like waving palms on the floor of the sea, but out of water they always put me in mind of the-one-we-won't-mention. And let me say to any one who wonders, that the tangle is blackish, and you can bend it this way and that; it is thick as your wrist at one end, and there is a tassel of limp leathery leaves at the other.

The girl stooped and lifted one. 'Look you,' she said, 'when we were children my mother would get these in the springtime and roast them, and we would bite a piece out *here* and throw it in the fire. Then we would rub them in our two hands and say some rimes,' and she fell to rubbing the leaf between her palms (*deiseil*, I suppose) and to chanting thus :—

LIATHAG—'TANGLE RIME'

In talking time, and in a droning voice.

Li - a - thag bheag mhìn, Thug an t-ìm a Eir - inn,

Li - a - thag bheag bhàn, Thug an càis a Al - ba,

Blas a' ghuail air cuid a' ghobh - a,

Blas na meal - a air mo chuid fhéin.

Little smooth tangle,
Took the butter from Erin ;
Little white tangle,
Took the cheese from Alba.
Taste of coal on share of smith,
Taste of honey on my own share.

'Then we would get them to eat. But we must always say the rimes first,' she added.

When such a thing as this comes to one who has the Gael's blood in her, to one who aye feels black houses homely because her forebears came from them, it is as though she climbed the thatch of such a house, and looked down through the smoke-hole upon the bairn-time of her own great-great-great-great-grandmother!

'You must let me have that!' I said.

'I will,' said the girl. 'You'll get it when Father Allan comes back.'

Some days later we sat all three in the little room the girl kept clean and cheery for Father Allan. Many a song she gave me in there, so that at last she wondered herself. 'I didn't think I had so many!' she said. Against the wall stood a small harmonium, of a most grudging temper. Many a tune I fingered on it, nevertheless, that never had fingering before, to the girl's delight. 'Isn't it *nice*! I didn't think it *was* so nice!' she would say.

Two windows looked over the smoking thatches down in the Baile, and across the loveliest blues and greens and heather-colours in the whole world, to the hills of Barra, always sending us showers and mist.[1] Father Allan sat by the quiet

[1] 'When Neil puts on his cap and Allan his bonnet, we will get rain,' they say in Eriskay.

kindly fire of peats, and the girl, her hands always at the knitting, was singing strange airs that never took the turn you looked for. I was putting them on paper, and Father Allan was watching lest some wee note should slip away.

The Tangle-Rime came into my mind; I asked for it, and got it just as at *Coilleag a' Phrionnsa.* Father Allan wrote the words in his little book. 'Now I will take down the tune,' said I.

'But there isn't a tune in it at all,' said the girl.

'Surely there is!' said I (and I do not know which of the two of us was the more surprised).

'Indeed, there isn't any,' she said earnestly. 'It's just nothing at all but rimes.'

'Will I play it for you?' I asked (for the shall and will of the Highlander, when he takes to the English, are those of the Lowlands).

The turn she gave to her head said 'yes' to my question, and 'no' to my thought. I began at the pedals, and with their usual ill grace the keys yielded up

Eriskay girls have their own wild laugh. 'Ha-*hà*! I-*bhò*!'—and if I never heard it before, I heard it then.

'Do you *know*,' the girl said, wiping her eyes, 'I never knew I was singin' it!'

'It's only a way of doing it[1] to them,' said Father Allan, when she had gone out to look after her bannocks, 'but they always do it the same way.'

The instinct that leads them would seem to be a strangely blind one, or it might be more just to say that they seem strangely blind to it. For example, the way they sing 'Màiri Bhuidhe,' a waulking-song with a triple chorus.

---

[1] 'Is there a tune in it?' he asked a woman who said she had the 'Song of the Smithy.'

'There's a sort of edge (*caoin*) to it,' she answered.

There are fine Ossianic lays, chanted in the bardic way, to be had in the Outer Isles for the asking.

The ways of the notes in the first and third are not the same, but the two women who were teaching me the song could see no difference between

and—

'Aren't they just the same *words*?' they asked. But they regularly brought in first one and then the other.

'*Aithne bliadhna aig fear na h-aon oidhche,*'[1] they say in Eriskay, and I am not in the pulpit. But I would counsel any one coming after me to think a little upon the old modes of the plain-song (taken as they were from the use of the people into the service of the church), and upon the old scale with the flat leading-note as you get it on the chanter, before he puts the Gaelic tunes to paper. Many a tune will lose its edge if it is thrust into a modern scabbard.

Here are two bits of Hebridean plain-song. I got the tune of 'Luchag is Cat' in Eriskay, and the words (which seem a sufficient variant upon those of Campbell of Islay to be worth setting down) from Donald M'Donald, piper, at Dalibrog in Uist.

LUCHAG IS CAT—'MOUSE AND CAT'

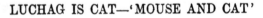

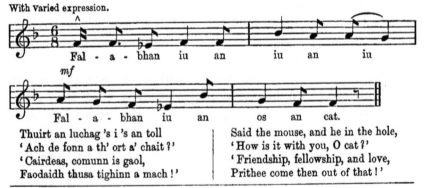

Thuirt an luchag 's i 's an toll	Said the mouse, and he in the hole,
'Ach de fonn a th' ort a' chait?'	'How is it with you, O cat?'
'Cairdeas, comunn is gaol,	'Friendship, fellowship, and love,
Faodaidh thusa tighinn a mach!'	Prithee come then out of that!'

---

[1] 'A year's knowledge with the man of the one night,' meaning that a stranger often claims more knowledge than those who have been in a place for a long time.

'Mhairbh thu mo phiuthar an dé,
Fhuair mi féin air eiginn as ;
'S eòlach mi air an dubhan chrom
A fàs am bonn do chas, a chait !'

'You killed my sister yesterday,
Scarce myself got out of that ;
Knowledge have I of the crooked hook
Growing on the sole of your foot, O cat !'

AN CÙ BÀN—'THE WHITE DOG'

In a swinging measure, and not too fast.

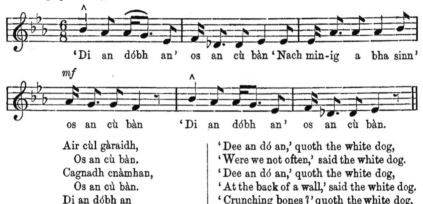

'Di an dóbh an' os an cù bàn 'Nach min-ig a bha sinn' os an cù bàn 'Di an dóbh an' os an cù bàn.

Air cùl gàraidh,
  Os an cù bàn.
Cagnadh cnàmhan,
  Os an cù bàn.
Di an dóbh an
  Os an cù bàn.

'Dee an dó an,' quoth the white dog,
'Were we not often,' said the white dog.
'Dee an dó an,' quoth the white dog,
'At the back of a wall,' said the white dog.
'Crunching bones ?' quoth the white dog,
'Dee an dó an,' said the white dog.

The white dog must growl now and then—'*Dirrrra dóbhan, os an cù bàn.*' 'Where does this come in?' I asked. 'Och, just anywhere you like,' said the girl.

I fancy that a sort of insight into the beginnings of plain-song might now and then be got through the singing at St. Michael's. It is done by a bunch of girls in the loft, and has a really touching sound of youth and reverence; the music, however, for my first Sunday in Eriskay had been chosen by a *Sasunnach*. There was not much of it, and even had the tunes been better, that would have been just as well, for there was no one there (nor anywhere, I believe) who could sing the Gaelic and the Latin as Father Allan could speak them. When he would lift his voice in the prayer before the Mass,

'*O Thighearn Ios, a Mhic an Dé bheò,*'

it was as the talking of the elements, and my only wish was to hear on and on, and to have no break.

But one morning, after the women came back from the

fish-curing in the Shetlands, the voices struck with deeper volume into a fine archaic measure that made me prick an ear. 'What was it?' I asked over the porridge afterwards. Father Allan's face fell a bit. 'It is an old "Cradle-song of the Blessed Virgin,"' he answered, 'but they have spoiled it. Do you hear how *plain* it is?—but what can I do about it? —each one of them had her own way of the tune, and no two of them the same, and how would it do for each one to be putting in her own twists and turns? So they have had to leave them *all* out, and now there is not a woman on the Island can sing it in the old way, so far as I know.'

I suggested that the plain-song doubtless had gone through such a stage, and that after a season of bare boughs the tune might—'Sprout out again!' he exclaimed, his face brightening.

Unless one sees the shape of a tune the first time through, one may have trouble with it. The second thoughts of a man who is giving one a tune are not his best; he is sure to leave out something, or to take another turn, and not to know it. And it is of no manner of use to tell him of it, or to ask a question.

> ' Instinct right, reflection wrong,
>   When you get a man to sing a song!'

—said Father Allan with a laugh one day. I was always listening when the grey-eyed girl was singing over her work, and getting another and another wee note to enrich the melodies I had already on the paper.

Again, the very good-will of the singer may cheat you. 'Is it *so*?' you ask, doing your best with a slippery phrase. 'Och, yes,' he will say gently, thinking to himself the while that your way may not be just his own way, but no doubt it will be just as good, whatever. You love him for this, the sign in him of that old culture which every one of his race inherits and hands down. But you may lose the edge of your tune by it.

'It makes me happy to give you this,' said a *cailleach* of

nigh to fourscore years and ten, knitting all day long in the place-that-is-most-honourable beyond the fire. She had not a word of English, and I with my little of the Gaelic was trying to get words and tune together of an *Oran Luathaidh* she had (and that is the only way to do). She fairly shouted them at me to help my wits, standing up to it at last; she clapped me on the knee when I got them; we rocked together in gales of laughter over my mistakes. Sometimes, while I was puzzling over a phrase with my eyes in my book, the room would fill up without a sound. I would look up to see a ring of neighbours round, men, women, and children; all speechless, and every one with his eye on me. After we had grown merry together, they would all lift on the tune, or join in the laugh they dearly love—but I must always be the first at that.

Three more child-songs the grey-eyed girl gave me, and there must be many more. There is none without its '*blas na meala*,' the heritage of him who is born to the speaking of a bardic tongue, and there is a good feeling for bird-notes in them.

ORAN NA SMEÒRAICH—'THE MAVIS' SONG'

In a calling tone.

'Son of the servant of Mary,
Son of the servant of Mary,
Come home, come home!
To dinner, to dinner!'
'What dinner? What dinner?'
'Hard reed-bread, oat-bread;
Be quick! be quick! be quick!'

ORAN NA H-UISEIG—'THE LARK'S SONG'

In a scolding tone.

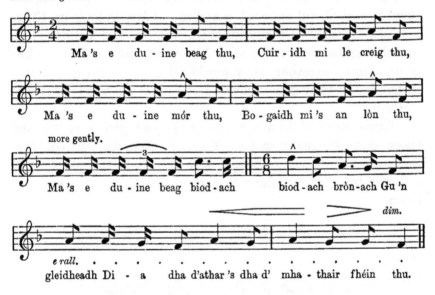

The lark is seeing boys coming to harry the nest—she sings :—

If you be a little man,
I'll put you over the rock;
If you be a big man,
I'll dip you in the dub;
If you be a poor little, wee, wee fellow,
May God keep you for your own father and mother!

PORT NA FEANNAIG—'THE CROW'S TUNE'

Quick and lively.

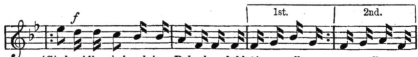

'Sùgh cridhe sùgh coluinn, Robachan dubh!' os an fheannag, os an fheannag.

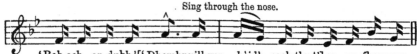

'Rob-ach an dubh'['Dhomhnuill gur bòidh-each thu!']os an fheannag.

'Little rough black one, essence of my heart and body!' said the hoodie-crow,
'Little rough black one!' ['Donald, how fair art thou!'] said the hoodie-crow.

The crow is always ' Domhnuill,' and the reason is not far
to seek (say it aloud, Gael-fashion). An Eriskay mother trots
the two-year-old, in his little *leine-Chriosda*,[1] to this tune, and
he keeps his laugh for ' *Domhnuill gur boidheach thu*,' which
she always sings through her nose.

My best tunes came from youngish singers, strong *gillean*
and young women who had in mind their mothers' ways, while
she still had heart for the high notes. When her strength
fails a little, she ' makes it easy for herself,' and the daughter
keeps the better tradition. I have never heard much sound
of passion in an Island treble, but rather the clear plaintive-
ness, the almost sexless quality, of a young lad's voice. It
fits the music strangely well.

'She has *her own* voice,' said a girl once when we were
coming away together from a woman who had been singing
wonderful lullabies, while she rocked her twelfth *leanabh* in
her arms. The girl came from *Bun-a-Mhuilinn*, where they
sing high and shrilly, and the woman's voice was like a
wonderful deep reed, that ran easily an octave below my own
low pitch. It fascinated me; so did the mellow deep-sea bass
in which a sailor sang for me one night, in the grey-eyed girl's
kitchen, the strangest tune I ever heard.

'It's a great deal of trouble I am making you,' I said one
day to the mother of twelve (and she was a youngish woman),
and she answered with a most beautiful grave kindliness, 'I'm

---

[1] Perhaps *leine-chneas*, skin-shirt. This was also the term applied to the retainers
who went with a bride to her new home and settled there.

sure if we have anything, we 're glad to give it to you.' They
are willing enough, the dear people. But give them a little
time to 'mind' their songs, so they may know what they
know. 'If you would just come down some time when I will
be mending my nets!' said a young fisherman who had given
me one fine sailor-song, then found himself aground.

Some girls came in one day (this was on another island
near-by, and I was just coming away) to see the *clàrsach*. I
played and sang a while, then the good woman who was
housing me said to them, 'Now you must give Miss Murray an
Oran Luathaidh.' But nothing came from them but giggling,
with uneasy looks from one to another, until I said, 'Och, I
know how it will be with myself. I can never think on a
song when I want it.' 'Yes, indeed!' said the oldest girl
gratefully, 'it will be just that. We have plenty, and we
will not be home before we will be thinking on them. But
we can't mind them now.'

'I am sure,' I said, 'if you had just the time, you would
give me plenty *Orain Luathaidh*.'

'We will that!' said she. 'If you would come again, we
would be all ready for you; if you would let us know, so we
could be thinking them over.'

There are plenty songs in the Outer Isles, plenty of the
best of good people to sing them. I love them for the sake of
my own blood, and I saw them for a space through Father
Allan's eyes—he never saw Eriskay looking grey but once, he
told me. Grey and lonely it will be now without him.

There is a way of saying among Highlanders concerning
the things they know past forgetting; it is that they 'have'
them. So may we say, we who had the joy of knowing Father
Allan, that though he may have gone away, we have him still;
he will stand to us for all time as the symbol of what a friend
and a man and a servant of the Lord should be, and of what
a chieftain might have been.

There was neither any fiery cross nor any changing of old
ways in his wise thoughts for the bettering of his people's fortunes, nor would he see them take the world beneath their heads.

`More pasture for the cow, more milk for the children, more bannocks for everybody he would have indeed.   But he knew a man could live a life complete on the edge of the great world as well as in the heart of it; he knew *An Domhan Mór*, and what a man would stand to lose therein—ways of un-worry and of brotherly love, tradition of bardic speech, trick of happiness. He would rather see him take his chance with the sea and the sand, and his children herding barefoot, than that they should crowd a back land in a city slum—it were better that the grey-eyed girls should be carding and spinning at home, living their mothers' lives in the black houses and thinking the old deep thoughts of their mothers' mothers, than to be gossiping in the servants' hall somewhere on *Mórthir*.   And while they waited for the coming to their misty shores of better times, he would have them sing and be merry; the faith for which he stood had no quarrel with the piper nor the *seanachaidh*; the first reel at the weddings was always in his own house.   'We know,' he said, 'how necessary it is for our poor people to be happy;' and again, 'you cannot get nearer Heaven than here.'

Even as he said this, his destiny was cast, and he was at the yonder end of time.   Only a fortnight more, and his people put him in his grave down by the *Baile*.   They paid such tribute to him as they could—they took the clods up with their hands, and with their hands heaped them above him.   So now will we who are in *An Domhan Mór* be bringing what we may to lay upon the grave of Maighstir Ailein. It would be none the less to him, this poor offering, for all that it came from underfoot, in his own Island of Youth.

BARDACHD IRTEACH

[THE poems and fragments here printed are a collection of native verse made by the Reverend Neil Mackenzie in St. Kilda.   Mr. Mackenzie was born in Sannox, Arran, in 1796, and died in Glasgow in 1879.   He went to St. Kilda as missionary in 1830, and remained there until 1843. Thereafter he was successively minister of Duror, Kilbrandon and Kilchattan, and Kilchrenan and Dalavich. During his stay in the island Mr. Mackenzie taught the people to read and write, and the last three extracts here printed are in the handwriting of one of his pupils. These are printed *literatim*—as the forms show a few peculiarities of local pronunciation. Mr. Mackenzie himself wrote in the literary orthography, but probably the influence of the island dialect accounts for the frequent suppression of *n* before *c, g, t*, and a few uncommon combinations. In a separate note on the St. Kilda dialect, Mr. Mackenzie makes no mention of these, but states that the language of the islanders is like that of Harris 'with very little difference. This difference consists in the idea which they attach to a few words, and the way in which they pronounce words in which *r* rough, and *d* or *g* in some combinations are sounded. The *r* they uniformly pronounce like *l*, as in the word *ruith*, "run," which they pronounce *luith*.' The notes attached to the various pieces are also by Mr. Mackenzie. Quite apart from any literary merit which they may possess, these pieces are not devoid of interest. With the exception of the Christmas *Nuallan* and a religious poem, they are all of one type, elegies for friends and relatives who had, nearly all of them, perished by falling over the rocks. It is to be hoped that this sad wail expresses only a phase of the life passed in the lonely island. The young will, no doubt, have their songs, and one would be glad to get samples of them. The thanks of the editor are due to the Reverend J. B. Mackenzie, Kenmore, for kindly sending his father's collection to the *Celtic Review*.]

1

NUALLAN NA CALLUINN

Which was used in St. Kilda till 1830. It was customary for the one half of the houses to prepare for the *Calluinn*, year about in rotation, and the other half to go with this *Nuallan* from house to house of those whose turn it was to make ready. After collecting the bread, the cakes were compared one with another. The biggest (*bannock*) was deemed to be the best, as it indicated the greatest skill in baking, and also the liberality of the good wife of the house. Some of these *bannocks* or barley cakes were as broad as the stone of the quern, or about the size of a shield, and frequently contained above seven pounds of meal. The cheese and bread were then equally divided among all the men, and carried home to be used :—

'Thainig mise 'n so d' ur n-ionnsaidh,
A dh' urachadh dhuibh na Calluinn;
Cha ruiginn leas sud innseadh,
Bha i ann o linn mo sheanar.
Theid mi deiseal air an fhardaich,
Is tearnaidh mi aig an dorus;
Gabhaidh mi null mar is coir dhomh,
Culaibh comhla fhir an tighe.
Craicionn Calluinn 'na mo bhaca,
Is maith an ceol thig o'n fhear ud;
Cha 'n 'eil neach gheibh (fh)àileadh
Nach bi gu bràth dheth fallan.
Gheibh fear a(n) tighe 'n a laimh e,
Is sparraidh e cheann anns an teallach;
Theid e deiseal air na paisdean,
Ach gu h-àraidh gheibh a bhean e.
Gheibh a bhean, is i as fhiach e,
Lamh riarachaidh na Calluinn.
Leis an tart tha air an dùthaich,
Cha 'n 'eil dùil againn ri drama;
Rud beag de thoradh an t-samhraidh,
Tha mi 'n geall air leis an aran.
Is ma (tha) sud againn ri fhaotainn
Ma (dh') fhaodas sibb, na cumaibh maille air.'

2

By a woman to her husband, who lost his life by falling over the rocks when in search of birds :—

'Ach (a) Righ, 's goirt mo thuireadh,
Ged 's goirt, 's eigin domh fhulang,
Ged dh' fhalbh mo chraobh mhullaich féin.

'Thug sud leagail air m' inntinn,
'S chaidh mo bheadradh a dhìth orm,
'S truime m' inntinn na pìob chaidh gun ghleus.

'Is nach mi bh' air do chùlaibh,
An uair dh' fhàilig do dhùirn thu,
Agus acfhuinn lan lùis bhi 'n ad dhéidh.

''S mi chuireadh ri t' fhasdadh,
No dhiobradh mo phearsa,
Is cha bhitheadh deò neirt agam féin.

'Na h-earb [1] a gaol an fhir-phòsda ;
Ach dealachadh cho òg,
Rinn mo chridhe leonadh gu m' eug.

'Ge nach b' ard thu o'n talamh,
Bu docha leam na fear-baile thu,
Ged bhitheadh tu falamh o spréidh.

'Ge nach b' chraobh a bha àrd thu,
Bu chraobh mhaith a chum stà thu,
Dh' aithnichinn thu a(n) gàradh leat fein.

'Gur fliuch cluasag mo leapa,
An déidh mo chur 's mi tigh'n dachaidh,
'S iomadh té bha 'n a dalta dhomh féin.'

3

The following elegy was made by a woman here to her
husband and brother who were lost together in the rocks.
Her name is 'Marad Ni'n Ruairi Mhoir' :—

'Bheir mi toiseach mo thuiridh
Dha mo chuileana gaolach ;
An dithis bha tapaidh,
'S a bha air leacaig 'n an sineadh.
Cha 'n e clann rinn mi fhagail,
Ach fir dhaicheil dheas dhireach ;
Gu ma geal a gheibh 'n anam
Ann gleannan na saorsa.
Ehir nach (dh') bhagair mo bhualadh,
'S nach chuir gruaimean air m' inntinn,
Dh' aithnichinn t' iomram air bata
Tigh 'n far thonnan a chaolais.
'G a iomradh 's 'ga eigheach,
'S tu bu bhinn leam bhi 'g eisdeachd ; [2]
'S mor bha theist aig an tuath ort,
'S bu tu ruagair' nan caorach.
Dh' aithnichinn bris-cheum do choise,
'S bu leat an toiseach a dheanamh ;
Gun luadh air m' oganach tapaidh
B' e fath nan creach thu bhi dhith.
Chaill do mhathair a fradharc,
'S chaidh a roghainn a dhith orra ;
Chuir thu moille air a h-astar
'S cha dirich cas-bheinn an fhraoich i.'

---

[1] or creid.   [2] or cluinntinn.

4

The following poem was made by the widow of a man called Somerled (*Somhairle*) after his death, which took place one evening as he and his daughter intended to watch the *Làmhaidh*. As they passed a ledge, a wave swept them both into the deep :—

(A FRAGMENT)

'S goirt a dh' fhairich mi bhliadhna,
'S cha b' e biadh a bha 'n aire orm ;
Cha b' e crodh air na blàraibh,
Ged a dhràbhadh iad seachad.
Ach mi bhi 'g amharc, 's gur cruaidh,
Far na sguabadh a mach sibh ;
Ach gur muladach tha mi
Ann am àros, 's tha sac orm.
'S gu bheil mise fo mhì-gbean,
'S mi dìreadh na cas-bheinn.'

5

The following elegy was made by the same woman on the death of her second husband, who was drowned in the loch when attempting to land with a swell on the shore :—

' 'S tric mi 'g amharc gach là,
A ruin, an roilig do bhàis
'S ann a muigh air an tràigh chaidh cunnart oirbh.

' Thu bhi muigh gu fliuch fuar
Ann an iomall a' chuain
'S gu 'n ann a t' fhardaich, a luaidh, an fuireachd ort.

' Do chlann bheag air mo sgàth,
'S nach urr' iad do stà,
Bhi 'g an iomain gu càch, gur duilich leam.

' Co sheall anns a' ghréin,
No cheangail oirre bréid,
Nach bitheadh mo sgeula duilich leatha ?

' Bhi faicinn an t-sliochd,
Rinn i arach fo crios,
Aig té eile gun mhios, gur duilich leatha. '

'Lamb deanaimh an stà,
Thoirt an fhraoich chum an làir,
Cha bhiodh tu a d' thàmh, 's cha b' fhurasd' leat.

'Lamh deanaimh nan cruach,
'S a cheangal nan sguab,
'S tu nach leigeadh orm cruas, 's bu duilich leat.

'Ormsa thainig a' chlaoidh,
S cha b' e roinn chur a m' mhaoin,
So tha mise 'g a caoidh, gu muladach.'

6

This was composed by . . . on the death of her daughter :—

'Cha 'n e uisge nan gleannta
Dh' fhag mo cheann-sa cho tinn;
Ach na thriall uam dhachaidh
Air an astar nach till.

'Cha 'n ann chionn mi 'g a ràdh,
Tha meur an t-snath orm a dhìth;
Cha deach cist' ort no anart,
Ach filleadh tana gun dìon.

'Ged bhiodh fuachd ann is frasan,
Cha ruig thu fasgadh mo thaoibh;
Seachd beannach(d) do mhàthar
'G ad chumail sàmbach, a laoigh.

'Ach a Thì na leig uait mi
Ged sguabadh tu mi.'

.   .   .   .

7

The ensuing elegy was composed by Mairi Ni'n Shom-hairle to a man who went out to waylay the *Làmhaidh*, and was precipitated into the sea and drowned :—

''S tric mi 'g amharc, 's gur cruaidh leam,
Far na sguabadh a mach thu;
Far na choinnich an t-aog thu,
'S nach do fhaod thu tigh 'n dhachaidh.

'Chaidh mi 'n iomall nan càirdean,
'S tha mis' an dràst gun chul-taice;
'S gur mairg ni bun as an t-saoghal,
Ged chinneadh caoirich is mairt leis.

'B' fhearr bhi tric air na gluinibh
Gul an urnuigh bheir ceart leis,
Na bhi le[1] moit no le[1] ardan,
Chuir Dia mu lar e 's bu cheart sin.

'Fhuair mi roimhe('n)tùs m' òig' e
'M fleasgach . . . a bha tapaidh;
Is o nach b' airidh mi fein air,
Thug Mac Dhe uam e dachaidh.'

8

The following verses were made by a man here to his
wife who lost her life in Congar. Her husband, having laid
snares for *fulmar*, went away with the boat to Boreray. On
their return they saw an object on the sea, below where he
laid the snares, which they took to be a drowned sheep, and
which they passed as the swell would not permit them easily
to go where it was. When they were approaching the shore
he was singing a song which he composed on the death of a
son who lost his life by falling off a horse which was frightened
by foolish boys. The name he gave to the verses he called
'Iorram na Truaighe.' His brother, observing that his wife
was not down with the other wives as she was wont to be,
said to him, 'I am afraid that you never had reason to sing
Iorram na Truaighe till now.' The suspicion was too true.
The object they took to be a sheep was his own wife:—

'N uair dh' fhalbh uait an todha,
'S nach robh mo lo(mha)in ri feum dhuit,
Chaill mi iuchair mo dhoruis,
Is pairt dh' onoir mo cheud ghraidh;
Chaill mi 'n stiuir bha air m' fhar(d)aich,
Is cuid am bàta an aite eigheach;
Chaill mi cearcall-èarraich mo thighe,
Is m' aighear gu leir leat.

_____

[1] ri (?).

'N uair thilleas mi dachaidh
O thional eunlaith is uibhean ;
Gun tein' gun lòn air mo chionn,
'N uair thig mi á eilean ;
Cha choinnich (thu) air traigh mi,
Is bidh mo chridhe bristeadh
A' faicinn mo phàisdean.'

9

These verses were composed on the following occasion. A man and his son went to the *Dùn* in spring to waylay the *Làmhaidh*. The son was below in the rock and the father on the end of the rope above. Being encumbered by the rope he put it off. These birds come in a body. In his eagerness to catch one going away he overbalanced himself and fell into the sea. His poor father saw him struggling with the billows till his strength failed, when he sank to rise no more. His mother made the poem :—

'S mi gun suigeart 's mi gun sòlas,
'S mo leanabh uam feadh na fòlaibh ;[1]
Ach tha mo dhuil a(n) Righ an domhain,
Gun ghlac do Mhaighstir còir ort,
Mur do phill do pheacadh mòr thu.
Mo cheist ! a ghruaidh a bha boidheach
Gus na rinn an t-aog do leonadh.
Dh' fhag thu t' athair dubhach bronach,
Cha dirich cas-bheinn an fheoir e ;
Ach ged 's mise dh' araich og thu,
Si tha truagh dheth do bhean phosda.
Dh' aithnichinn t' fheannag,[2] 's cha bhiodh sgòd oirr'.'

10

The following lines were composed by Anna nighean Fhionnlaidh mhic Dhomhnaill, to the memory of her brother and sister who died within a short time of one another :—

'S gur mise tha gu dubhach
O shiubhail an t-aon la ;
O chaill mi mo phiuthar
A bha gu subhach 's gu faoilidh ;

---

[1] tonnan.   [2] A 'lazy-bed' of potatoes.

Bha gu maiseach ciatach,
Bha gu fialaidh ro' dhaoine.
Cha leig mis' thu air di-chuimhn'
Ged liathainn san t-saoghal.
O dh' fhalbh a d' mhnaoi oig thu,
'S e mo bhron-sa mar thachair,
'S cha'n 'eil deò ann am sheorsa (?)
Mar tha smuaintean a' bhàis,
H-uile là tigh'n a steach orm.
Chaidh mi 'n iomall nan càirdean,
O là chàradh an leac ort.
Chi thu, 'Righ, mar tha mise,
'S mi 'g am chlisgeadh 's 'g am chiùradh ;
Mar tha mi 'g ionndrainn na gibht ud
Tha fo'n lic air a dunadh.
Chaidh mi 'n iomall nan càirdean,
Mar tha 'm bàs air mo spùilleadh ;
'S tric 'n am chridhe-sa sàthadh,
'S e mo bhrathair-sa b' fhiù sud.
Bu tu sguid-fhear na guaille,
An am gluasad a' bhàta,
Le ar ruigheachd a' chruaidheachd,
Bhiodh tu shuas air ramh-bràghad ;
'S gu'm (bu) bhinn thu gu éigheach,
An àm éirigh na bàirlinn.
Bha thu foinnidh, deas, treubhach,
Gur mairg céil' rinn thu fhagail.
Gnuis an àigh, cha bu bheag orm
Thu thigh'n thugam air chéilidh ;
Mar bu mhiannach leam tachairt,
Thu thigh'n dachaidh là féille.
Bu tu an solu(s) ro' d' chairdean,
'S mor a' bhearn thu 'g an treigsinn,
Och is Och ! mar a tha mi
'S mi 'g 'ur n-àireamh le chéile.'

11

RINNEADH AM MARBH-RANN SO LEANAS LE BEAN ÀRAIDH AIR BÀS A FIR

' Gur mis' tha fo ghruaim ;
'S tric snidh' air mo ghruaidh ;
Cha chaidil mi uair gun dùsgadh.

'Lamh a dheanadh an stà,
Bu mhaith t' fheum anns gach àit,
Cha bu lapach an dàil na tùirn thu.

' Mi ri amharc leam'fhéin,
Do chuid uidheam ri stéil,
Lamh deanaimh an fheum gun dùil ris.

' 'S an tulach ud shuas,
Chuir mi m' aighear 's mo luaidh,
Fo lic dhainginn nach gluais 's nach tionndaidh.

' Ciste chaol an da thaoibh,
Chuir mi lasaich ¹ chuim,
Nach fidir thu caoidh no ionndrainn.

' Mo thruaighe mi féin !
Gun fhear-tighe 'n ad dhéidh,
Gur dubhach tha céis do ghiùlain.

' Gu'n dhubh sud mo ghruaidh,
'S cha till thu a d' shnuadh,
Chaoimh-fhir a bha suairc a d' ghiùlan.

' Ach a Thi as mor gloir,
Neartaich fein a shliochd òg,
Tha gun taice gun sgòrradh cùil.

' 'S tric mi smuaineach leam fhéin
Air grad theachd mhic Dhé,
'S a ghiorrad gus ('n) éigin cunntas.'

12

' Bha sgeula air fhoillseachadh
Air machaire nan coilltichibh ;
Is buachaillean na h-oidhche,
Ghabh oillt is crith.

' Na gabhaibh sgàth deth,
'S e thubhairt na h-aingle,
Tha slaint' air foillseachadh
Bha seinn a gloir ann.

' Is rugadh an trath-sa dhuibh,
Ann am baile Dhaibhidh,
An Slanuighear grasmhor,
'S an stabull neo-dhòigh(eil).

---

¹ lasgaidh.

' Gu ceartas a dhioladh,
'S gu saoradh o phiantaibh,
'S an lagh a choimhlionadh,
A bha dian air an tòir.

' Bha thrusgan cho suarach,
'S e paisgte ma chuairt da,
'S cha sheomar duin' uasail
A fhuair e gu còmhnuidh.

' Bha reul na h-oidhche
Mar chomharra cinnteach,
'S i falbh air *loine*,
Roimh Dhruidhean an dòchais.

' Cha luaithe chaidh innseadh
'Luchd-àitich na tìre,
Bha('n) cridhe fo mhì-ghleus,
'S a(n) Righ gun bhi Dòigheil.

' Thainig guth anns an oidhche
Gu Ioseph " Gabh greim air,
Is falbh leis an naoidhean,
Is naimhdeas cho mor da."

' Bha sgeul ud cho prìseil,
Cha d' fhan e san tìr-sa ;
Tha e 'g imeachd 's na Innsibh,
'S h-uile mìr do'n Roinn-Eòrpa.

' Is thainig i ('n) tùbh-sa,
Cha d' fhagadh air chùl e ;
Tha slainte ri fhaotainn
Do aois is do dh' òige.

' Tha ('n) sgeul ud air innseadh
An Sgrìobtur na firinn,
Ma bheirear a rìs sinn
Gur e Criosd t' fhear-pòsda.

' Cha dean beatha no bàs,
No nithe tha làthair,
Air sgaradh gu bràth
O Ard-righ na glòire.

' Cha'n fhaca 's cha chuala,
Cha'n urrainn neach luadh air,
Sonas tha shuas ann,
Do'n t-sluagh a gheibh còir air.

'Cha chuala mi riamh e,
 Aithris air trian deth;
 Tha sonas neo-chriochnaicht' ann
 Gu sior(ruidh) cha traogh air.'

The above was composed by Finlay Macqueen, younger,
in 1842.

13

The following verses were composed by Neil Ferguson,
1841 :—

AIR FONN

'Ochoin a Thi nach foir thu mi
 O 'm smuaintean gu faireachadh,
 Mu('n) tig a(n) t-am a theid mi dhìth
 'S nach bi ann tìm gu aithreachas.'

14

An elegy on the death of Neil Macdonald, who lost his
life by falling over a rock when killing the *fulmar*, by a
female relation of his own.

''S ann Di-h-aoine roimh 'n Domhnach,
 Fhuair sinn sgeula gun sòlas
 Bhi caoidh a fhir orduidh (?),
 Thug deoir air mo ghruaidh.

''S truagh nach mi bh' air ceann t' acair
 'N uair chaidh thu as t' fhacail (fhaicill ?) ;
 Dheanainn dichioll (air) t' fhasdadh,
 Gu do sheachnadh o'n uair.

'Tha do phaisdean gun taice,
 A chuid tha làidir is lag dhuibh,
 Ma chas deanamh an tapaidh,
 'S nach bu lapach sa' ruagadh.

'Tha do bhean air a ciùrradh,
 O beulaobh 's o culaobh,
 'S i bhi caoidh a fir ducaich (?),
 Dh' fhalbh a cuid as gach uair.

'Mo cheist, colann na ceille,
 'S e do bheul nach robh breugach,
 O1 's tu nach labhradh na breugan,
 'S tu nach labhradh a' cheilg.

'(Ach go ro-bheusach suairce)
Brathair mo mhàthar,
A ghortaich 's a chràidh mi,
Bidh a m' fhaire gu bràth thu,
Gus a(n) càirear mi 's uaigh.'

15

[These verses, with one or two more quatrains, are printed in
Gael, v. p. 54.]

'Bliadhn' an t-samhraidh-sa 'n uiridh,
Rinn na h-uibhean mo léireadh ;
Gur ann thall ann an Soädh, dh' fhag
Mi 'n t-òg nach robh leumach.

'Is tu nach falbhadh le m' fhacal,
Is tu nach innseadh na breugan ;
Gur diombach do'n eug (mi)
Cha'n fhear gaoil domh fein e.

' 'N uair thug e uam Iombar,
Fath mo mhisnich gu léir e ;
Bidh mo chuid de na h-uibhean
Aig a' mhuinntir as tréine.

'Bidh mo chuid de na h-ianaibh,
Anns na nialaibh ag eigheach ;
Thu bhi muigh sa' gheodh' chuinge,
'S gur cianail dubhach ad dhéidh mi.

'Bha do bhuill' air a chloich ud,
'S bha do lot an deigh leum air ;
Thu bhi muigh air na stuadhan,
'S muir 'g ad fhuasgladh o chéile.

' 'N uair thainig do phiuthar
Cha robh sin subhach le céile ;
Cha tig thu gu d' mhathair
Gus càradh do léine.

' Ach seach(d) beannachd do mhathar
'G ad chumail samhach ri cheile.'

THE SAME

' 'S gur ann san t-samhradh a shiubhail
Rinn na h-uibhean mo léir-chreach,
'N uair a thugadh uam Iomhar,
Fath mo mhisnich gu léir e.

'S gur ann thall ann an Soädh
Dh' fhag mi('n)t-òg nach robh leumach ;
Is tu nach falbhadh le m' fhacal
'S nach innseadh na breugan.

'Thu bhi muigh sa' gheodh chumhainn,
Gur cianail dubhach ad dhéidh mi ;
'S thu bhi muigh feadh nan stuadhan,
'S am muir 'g ad fhuasgladh o chéile.

'Ach seach(d) beannachd do mhathar,
'G ad chumail sambach ri chéile ;
Gu robh fhuil air a chloich ud,
'S lotan an déidh leum air.

''S gur diombach de 'n eug mi ;
Cha chaomhail leam fein e ;
Nach leig thu gu d' mhathair,
Gu i chàradh do léine.

'Bidh mo chuid de na h-eunaibh
Anns na neulaibh ag eigheach ;
Is mo chuid de na h-uibhean
Aig a' bhuidhinn as tréine.'

16

Composed by Christian Gillies on the death of Mr.
M'Leod, missionary, St. Kilda, the grandfather of the present
proprietor :—

''S mor a(m) briseadh a dh' eirich,
Dh' fhairich sinne gu leir e,
Ceann ar Creidimh air eugadh,
  'S nach 'eil slàn e.

''N àm bhi dunadh do chiste,
'S a bhi togail do lice,
Bha na fir air droch mhisnich,
  Bhi 'g ad fhàgail.

'Is ann bhiodh thu s(a') chlosaid,
A' leughadh 'n ad aonar ;
Thug thu t' uidh [1] d' Tì mhor ud,
  B' e ro fhearr leat.

''N uair thigeamaid dhachaidh,
'M beul na h-oidhche 's sinn acrach,
Bheireadh tu nasgaidh
  An gràine dhuinn.

---

[1] for *aigne*.

' B' e sud ceann a(n) fheumaich,
'S nan diolacha déirce ;
'S tric fhreasdail thu fein e,
    'S gun e t' àiridh.

'Sud m' athchuing' air Criosd
Do chlann dhol air éiridh (?),
'S gu'n dean iad toilinntinn
    Do do ghràdhaig.'

17

The following fragment was composed by a female called
Cathrin Og (elsewhere said to be the woman who composed
the verses on Mr. M'Leod), about sixty years ago :—

    ' Is olc leam mar thachair,
    Ceile mo leapa
    Air a ghlasadh gun airidh (?).

    ' Their gach te rium ni mo ruigheachd
    Gur ro-righinn leam fein t' eirigh ;
    Cha dh' fheithe fbada is tha mi,
    Am luidhe a taobh a tighe gun eirigh.

    ' Cha dean leighean slàn mi,
    Ged do bhiodh làmh rium na ceudan :
    'S ann tha mo dhuil a dhol dachaidh,
    Gu meach'nais a(n) Dé mhoir.

    ' 'S gur truagh nach taitneadh mo bheus riut,
    Cha dh' theid a fhalach an cùil mi,
    Is mo dhroch chuis dhomh 'g a stéidheadh.'

[The following fragments are in plain handwriting (not Mr.
Mackenzie's) and are given *literatim.*]

18

Rinneadh a Marbh-ran so le boireanach araidh a bha san
aịt, da m-ainm Anna Nighinn Mhoil Domhnaich da brathar
is da dithis mhac :—

1. ' Bithidh mo bhrathar aịr thus
    Gu bu chomain sud dhuin
    Gu bu shilteachd do shuil mam chradh.

2. ' D' e cha deach mi steachd
    Sann a ghaoil na do theach
    O la thugadh tu mach as marbh.

3. 'Mi mam Dhomhul ur og
   Bheathaich mi thu gle og
   Gur e Ruaire thug bron seach cach.'

19

5. 'Gur a mise tha air mo chlisgeadh
   Smi ri leughadh do litreach
   Gad a ghleidh mi mo ghibhtean
   Fhuair mi fios air a bhron.

6. 'Tha mo cheist an tog speiseil
   Cha do rinn thu riamh eucoir
   Bu tu beannachd na feumach
   A reir sna bha d' bhoca.

7. 'Tha mo cheist an tog fearlail
   Stric a fhuair mi cheanal
   Agus seudan gun da cheanach
   On fhear tha Shiol Leoid.

8. 'Co bhean no co mhathair
   Rinn gillean riamh arach
   Nach creid mar a tha mi
   Smi air fagail mo dheo.'

20

Rinneadh a marbh-rann so leis a bhoireanach cheudna dan aon fhear :—

1. 'Tha mo cheist a Leodach
   Ga math gha tig a cota
   Na fhuair mi gha do sholos
   Na aobhar broin domh tras.

2. 'Lamh gheal bu mhaith gu sgriobha
   Gu m-aluin as a rile thu
   Nam tarruing dhuit na file
   Co t-aon neach bheireadh barr ort.

3. 'Gur mise mhathair mhuladach
   Comhnuidh ris an turaman
   Smuaineachadh air m uireasaibh
   Thuit buileach orm a garadh.

4. 'Cha gharadh a rinn clachairean
   Dh' aireamh mi san fhacal ud
   Ach aileachd na fear mhaiseach
   Chuir mi tasgaidh uam a caradh.'

THE RUSKINS

ALEXANDER CARMICHAEL

THE land of Lorne is one of the most diversified districts in Scotland, and one of the most picturesque and interesting. It is striking and panoramic, full of hills and dales, lakes and rivers, plains and mountains, long attenuated peninsulas and long convolving arms of the sea, winding from ten to forty miles among the straths and mountains, while the old keeps and castles, the old churches and temples, and the old sculptured stones and crosses are of surpassing interest.

But it is with a small section of the land of Lorne that I have to do here, with the part called Muckairn. Muckairn lies along the shore of Loch Etive, and is a long, wide district rich in agricultural and pastoral land. It is rich also in story and tradition. Place-names in Muckairn and the adjoining parishes commemorate Deirdire and the Sons of Uisne, who found rest in their flight by the beautiful shores of Loch Etive. The extensive and varied district of Muckairn was thickly peopled, from the River Awe at the base of Cruachan to the River Lusragan beyond the foot of Di-choimhead, and from the edge of Loch Etive to the mountain-chain several miles inland. And probably a more robust race of powerful men and handsome women than these people of Muckairn could not be found within the British Isles. They were chiefly Macdougalls, MacCallums, and MacCalmans, the latter predominating.

Glenlonain, 'the glen of the marshy river,' is a few miles inland, and runs nearly parallel with Loch Etive for several miles of its length. It is a beautiful glen, with a long range of high hills on the landward side and a long ridge of high land on the seaward side. A striking, grand, and picturesque view is obtainable from this high ridge between Glenlonain and Loch Etive. On the east shoulder of this ridge is a cluster of ruined dwellings. The place is called Barraglas, 'grey-green ridge,' Barraglas nan Calman, 'grey-green ridge of the Calmans,' Barraglas Chlann Chalman, 'grey-green ridge of Clan Calman,' and Barraglas nan Rusgan, 'grey-green ridge of the Ruskins,' Barraglas Chlann Rusgain, 'grey-green ridge of Clan Ruskin.' There are no Calmans, no MacCalmans, no Ruskins, no MacRuskins there now, all having been ruthlessly swept away in the raging clearances. An itinerant teacher revisiting his native Barraglas said :—

> 'Tha tri fichead 's a tri bho 'n a b' aithne dhomh 'n gleann,
> Tri fichead 's a tri dhe m' chairdean a bh' ann,
> 'S e bas agus bairlinn chuir mo chairdean dh' am dhi,
> An ait an tri fichead gun ann ach an tri.'

> 'Threescore and three since I first knew the glen,
> Threescore and three of my kindred therein,
> It was death and eviction that reft me of these,
> In place of threescore and three now only the three.'

Another native poet said :—

> 'These are the homes
> Where my fathers dwelt—
> There are no houses now.
> These are the floors
> Where my fathers knelt—
> And now the rushes grow.'

There are just three families of big farmers now where there had been previously threescore and three families of comfortable crofters and small farmers.

A family of the MacCalmans of Barraglas had a tanning-house down on the bank of the Neannt River, immediately below the present railway station of Tigh-an-uillt. The situation was well and wisely chosen, near the sea and on the bank of a large clear mountain stream, intersecting a large and rich grazing and agricultural district full of people and cattle and sheep. The sites of the tanning-house and of the tanning-pit were pointed out and traced to me by a native of the spot, together with the sites of the houses of the workmen of the tannery. From these sites one would infer that the tannery must have been of considerable extent, employing many men.

From his occupation a man who removes the bark from a tree is called *rusgan* in the south and *rusgair* in the north Highlands—'a peeler, a bark stripper,' from *rusg*, 'rind, peel, bark.' The term is also applied more remotely to a man who dresses stone, wood, or iron.

From their occupation the family of MacCalmans who had the tannery had to bark trees for tanning purposes. Hence they were known throughout the district as na Rusgain, na Rusgairean, 'the peelers,' 'the bark peelers,' and Clann Rusgain, 'the bark peeling family,' losing their clan name in their occupation name, like many other men and families throughout the Highlands.

This native industry was killed out about the middle of the eighteenth century by an English company who established an iron-smelting foundry at Bunawe. This company bought up all the wood of the district for many miles around, using the branches and the more worthless woods for smelting purposes and for converting the ore which they brought from England into iron. They also imported coal, flour, stoneware, and tanned leather, and shipped from Bunawe to England the valuable wood, kelp, hides, and tanning bark. The quality of the Bunawe smelted iron was of the best, fetching the highest price in the market and enriching the English company.

When 'Iain Ruadh nan Cath,' Red John of the Battles, Earl of Argyll, went to meet the Earl of Mar in 1715 he took with him all the available men of the country. Probably several of the Muckairn Ruskins went, but at least one Ruskin went with the earl.[1] He was severely wounded at the battle of Sheriffmuir. His comrades carried him from the field to a farmhouse. Ruskin was a young man of good presence, good ability, and good manners, and the family of the farmer were good and kind to him :—' Agus ma bha gach neach gu math

[1] I asked both the late and the present Duke of Argyll if any record of those who went from the county on that occasion was available, but neither knew of any such. Possibly there may be some buried in the crypts of the War Office.

dha bha nighean an taighe gu sonraichte. Bha i ga chaithris
a latha agus a dh' oidhche gu 'n an tug i dhachaidh bho 'n
bhas e. An sin phos Mac Rusgain bho Mhucarna agus nighean
an tuathanaich ann an siorrachd Pheairt. Bha seann daoin'
a seanchas gu 'n tug Mac Rusgain thun na h-obair abhaistiche
air an robh e eolach, ann am baile Pheairt.'—'And if every
person was good to him, the daughter of the house was
specially so. She was watching him by day and night till
she brought him home from death. Then Mac Ruskin from
Muckairn and the daughter of the farmer in the sheriffdom
of Perth married. Old people were saying that this son of
Ruskin betook him to the accustomed work with which he
was acquainted, in the town of Perth.' Ruskin never came
back again to Muckairn, except to see his people.

From this Ruskin of Muckairn and his wife John Ruskin
was descended. Of this descent the late Clerks of Duntannachan, Glenlonain, a scholarly intelligent family of whom
the Rev. Archibald Clerk, LL.D., Kilmallie, was one, had no
doubt whatever, and they knew the whole history of the
Ruskin family. John Ruskin himself has told us that his
grandfather came from Perth, but he could not go back
beyond his grandfather. When the writer informed him of
the further tradition regarding his family and descent Mr.
Ruskin was keenly interested.

The last of the Ruskins of Muckairn was a certain woman
known as 'Ciorsdan Dhughaill Fhigheadair,' Christina,
daughter of Dugald the weaver. Her father was a Mac-
Calman and her mother was a Nic Rusgain, Ruskin. Christina
MacCalman was a woman of remarkable character, and of
special interest. In youth she was tall, slender, and handsome, but in age she stooped considerably. Men and women
who had known her well described her minutely, mentally
and physically, and these descriptions strikingly resembled the
characteristics of her distant kinsman, John Ruskin. Donald
Sinclair, crofter, aged 88, said :—'The wisdom of the Ruskins
was in Christina, the daughter of Dugald the weaver. It was
with the Ruskin sept, the people of her mother, that she went

—people sensible, capable, eloquent, beautiful in person, in language, and in work. They were full of natural ability and of knowledge of life, and they were dignified and handsome along with that. Christina could be described in one word— thorough. The most trivial action of life was to her a matter of supreme importance, and she performed it as if the visible God were standing before her.'

Angus Macniven, tailor, aged eighty-five, said : ' Ciorsdan Dhughaill Fhigheadair had the most beautiful eyes I have ever seen in the head of a woman. They were dark-blue, large, expressive, and deeply set. Her eyebrows were large, and full and bushy for a woman. Her hair was nut-brown, abundant, and somewhat wavy. Her cheeks were ruddy-brown, round and prominent, her mouth full and expressive, and her chin strong and ample, while her nose was strong and straight with open nostrils. You would hardly call her features fine, but they were full of the beauty of character, of love, and of goodness. In person, character, and surroundings she was pure as the snow of Cruachan. She had a perfect passion for colours and could discriminate and differentiate between and discourse upon shades where ordinary persons could see no difference. If ever woman lived in the eye of her Master Ciorsdan Dhughaill Fhigheadair did. She knew her Gaelic Bible from beginning to end as probably no minister in the country knew it. She was a beautiful speaker, a born orator, and were you to hear her you could not but listen, and it was not of trifles that she would converse. When she died people came from far and near; rich and poor, gentle and simple coming long distances to pay their tribute of love and admiration for this poor cottar woman of Glenlonain.'

Three highly intelligent men accompanied me one day to the scenes of the Ruskin homes in Muckairn. We went into a ' tobhta,' roofless ruin, and I showed them a likeness of John Ruskin, covering the name and beard. I asked the men who that was and they called out simultaneously, ' Ciorsdan Dhughaill Fhigheadair,' and the three praised the likeness, for the three had known the woman well and spoke of her admiringly. After the three men had gone over each feature of the face and head I drew the paper from the beard. Then they said at once, 'Donnachadh Dhomhuill! nach e tha coltach ris!' 'Donald's Duncan! isn't it like him!' I asked who was 'Donnachadh Dhomhuill' and they said that he was a Duncan MacCalman, from Muckairn, living in Glasgow, and one of the Ruskin MacCalmans.

Still concealing the identity of John Ruskin I showed a likeness of him when young. Two of the men said together, 'Oh, your brother John, Malcolm, is it not like him! the nose, the eyes, the brows, the cheeks, the mouth, the chin, the head, the hair, they are just his.' The two men praised and praised the likeness, and appealed to Malcolm to confirm them. But Malcolm did not speak. I looked up over my shoulder to see why he was silent, and I saw a stream of tears down his cheeks. When speech came back to Malcolm he asked me where I had got the striking portrait of his brother who had died years before, a young man of great ability and promise, and who was most dear to him. Malcolm Campbell Macphail is a man of remarkable capabilities and, for his opportunities and education, a man of great mental endowment. He is a poet, too, of no inconsiderable merit. His mother, Mary Campbell, acquired English, and during the Crimean War she translated as she read the news of the day to the neighbours who crowded her house at night. Her brother, Donald Campbell, was known as 'the learned blacksmith.' After testing him, Mr. Donald MacCaig, minister of Muckairn, said that Donald Campbell knew the Gaelic, Greek, Latin and Hebrew Bible probably better than any minister in the Presbytery of Lorne. The mother of this brother and sister was a certain Moriad Rusgain, Moriad Ruskin, of Muckairn. She was a highly endowed woman. She knew her Gaelic Bible from beginning to end and was never tired expounding its doctrines, eloquently and effectively, to her less endowed neighbours. All these members of the Clan Rusgain were self-educated, and they are forcible examples of the general truth of the Gaelic sayings, 'Bu dual da sin'—'That was hereditary to him, and, ' Theid an dualchas air aghaidh ge b' ann an aghaidh nan creag'—' Heredity will go forward though it should be against the rock.'

Near Barraglas, the ancient home of the Ruskins, is a low mammilated hill called Mam nan Rusgan, the hill of the Ruskins, and a rock called Creag Rusgain, the rock of the Ruskins, while not far away is a place called Creag Mac Righ, the rock of the son of the king. Several pieces of ancient sculpture were scattered about the valleys and among the neighbouring heights. One of these was a slab on which runes or oghams were inscribed. My intelligent informant, Mr. Allan Macdougall, of the Duntannachan family, searched with me for this slab, but unsuccessfully. We afterwards learnt that the local roadman had built the inscribed stone into the bank of the road at Cladh nam Macraidh, the burial-place of the young men. Mr. Allan Macdougall also told me of three human heads sculptured in stone in the neighbour-hood. They lay at a distance in another direction, however, and I had to leave. Before I came back again to the place my informant was dead, and my memory failed to follow his minute directions among so many hillocks and hollows over-grown with rushes, ferns, and brushwood.

Within a few hundred yards of where this inscribed slab is buried stands a pillared stone with a Roman cross deeply incised on back and front. Immediately below the cross on front is sculptured in high relief a figure resembling a New Zealand war club. From an incised ring near the centre of the boss nine incised lines radiate at nearly equal distances. What the club-like figure with its round boss of nine rays may mean it is not easy to say. Possibly the nine lines may represent the nine rays of the sun so often mentioned in Gaelic oral literature. But whatever this figure on the hard granite pillar may mean it is very ancient, probably more ancient by far than Christianity in Scotland, and older by centuries than the crosses on either side. This pillared block with its incised crosses, raised ' club' and sunk rays lay under the feet of beasts in the ancient burial-place, now the farmyard, of

Cladh nam Macraidh. Macphaidean, a strong young man, a
farm servant in the place, scrubbed and cleaned the block in
the adjoining River Lonan, and then carried it on his back
to the top of the knoll above the road, where it now stands.
Macphaidean went to America, was wounded in battle, and
died in hospital. It gives me pleasure to record the name
of this intelligent young man.

Some miles from the home of the Ruskin MacCalmans
is an island of Lochawe called Innis Draoinich, isle of the
sculpture, and Innis nan Draoineach, isle of the sculptors.
This was one of several schools of sculpture scattered through
the Highlands, where the much admired Celtic crosses and
tombstones were carved. Near Innis Draoinich is Innis Aill,
Innis Aille, and sometimes Innis Aillidh, beautiful isle. There
had been a house of Cistercian sisters here, with a church
and a place of burial. Some families still bury in this green
beautiful isle of the nuns. There are ancient sculptured stones
here, probably unsurpassed for beauty of design and execution
in the British Isles. Ornaments in gold and silver have
been made from these designs, and worn by Royalty. It
was the tradition of old people in Muckairn that the Ruskin
MacCalmans had somewhat to do with these sculptures of
Innis Aill and with the school of sculpture of Innis Draoinich
and with the sculptured fragments found scattered over the
district. The Ruskin MacCalmans were also famous for
making dyes and tartans. An old saying is :—

> ' Gartan Chlàidich agus tartan Mhucarna,
> Lann Lios-móire agus daga Dhuine.'

> ' The garter of Claidich and the tartan of Muckairn,
> The sword of Lismore and the pistol of Doune.'

These were the best and always got the prize at the
famous Feill Chonnain, St. Connan's Fair, and at the no less
famous Feill Roid, Rood Fair, of Glenorchy, and their excellence
passed into a proverb. Dealers with strings of pack horses
came to these Fairs from the towns of the south to buy these
garters, tartans, swords, pistols, linens, woollen cloth, and

other native productions. Quantities of home-made tartan were sent from the Highlands to England. The proscription of the tartan and of arms killed out these and other manufactures of the Highland people.

THE FIONN SAGA

(Continued from p. 272.)

George Henderson, M.A., B.Litt., Ph.D.

Mar a fhuair Fionn Eòlas air na Fir Mhóra

Air greis dha 'bhith ris a sin chunnaic e soitheach (saghach) 'dianamh dìreach air an a robh e agus ag acrachadh agus dithis dhaoine móra tighinn aisde air grunnachadh, 's ghrad chuir e 'mhiar 'na bhial fiach am faigheadh e mach gu de'n fheadhainn a bh'ann. Fhuair e sin a mach gur a feadhainn a thàinig a rioghachd na' Fear Móra 's iad a' tighinn a dh'iarraidh Fhinn 'ic Cumhail 's gu robh blast aca ann a rioghachd na' Fear Móra 'tighinn air tìr a h-uile là agus a' faighinn duine ri ich[1]; gu robh mac a righ gu bhi aic' air deireadh na seachduinn 's gu robh e 'san dailgneachd gur e Fionn mac Cumhail a mharbhadh i agus gur e draodhachd a bh'orra fhéin bha 'gam fàgail cho mór' sid 's nan tugadh e liad sìa sgillinnean a dh' fheoil 's a chraicionn bho mhullach an cinn nach biodh iad ach mar dhaoin' eile.

Thainig iad far a robh e. 'Gu dé do naigheachd 'ille bhig?' os àsan.[2]

'Cha'n eil guth, a dhaoine móra,' os e fhéin, ''s b'e sin sibhse na daoine móra nach fhaca mise riamh 'ur leithidean.'

'Ach,' os àsan, 'an aithne dhut cà bheil Fionn Mac Cumhail a' fantail?'

'N tà,' os esan, 'chunnaic mi a cheart duine sin ach cha'n eil ann am Fionn ach duin' òg. Cha'n eil an duine sin ach seachd bliadhna dh'aois. Gu de'n gnothuch a th'agaibh-sa ri Fionn?'

'N tà,' os 'ad fhéin, ''s ann a rioghachd na' Fear Móra

---

[1] = ith.   [2] = iad-san.

thàinig sinne agus 's ann a dh'iarraidh Fhinn 'ic Cumhail a
thàinig sinn agus biast againn ann an Rioghachd na' Fear
Móra 'tighinn gu tìr a h-uile là 's tha i 'faighinn duine h-uile
là tha i 'tighinn gu tìr ri ithe (iche) agus tha i gos a bhi aig
mac a righ air deireadh na seachduin' 's bha e 'san dailgneachd
gur e F. M. C. bha gos a marbhadh.' ' 'N tà,' os esa,
' innsidh mise duibh a cheart duine th'ann a sin ma leigeas
sibh dhomh buille bheag dhe'n chlaidheamh so thoirt dhuibh.'

'Gu dé nì do chlaidheamh don' ðirnne?'

Dh'fhalbh e agus thug e siab do'n chlaidheamh 's thug e'n
dà cheann diubh.

Mar a chaidh Fionn do rioghachd nam Fear Móra

Cha d'rinn e sion ach an ceann thoirt dhiubh 'nar a thainig
soitheach (saghach) eile. Dh'acraich e 's thàinig iad air tìr
mar a rinn càch is ghabh esan sios m'an coinneamh is
dh'fhaighneachd iad dha[1] : 'Gu de do naigheachd 'ille bhig?'
os àsan. 'Cha'n eil guth, a dhaoine móra, etc. etc.' 'Ach
am faca tu'n fheadhainn a bha 'sa bhàt ud?' 'Chunnaic 's
tha iad shìos ann a sud, an ceann an taca riu, 's s'ad sìor
ghaireachdich aig Fionn Mac Cumhail an deaghaidh an dà
cheann thoirt diubh.

' 'N tà, 'se Dia nan gràs thug dhut innseadh dhuinn, gad
a rachadh a righ fhéin uice cuide ri'mhac cha teid sinne
seach so m'an doirear na cinn dhinn mar a rinneadh air
càch.'

' 'N tà b'fhearr leam nan dugadh sibh mi fhéin libh air-
son innseadh dhuibh gun dug e na cinn bharr na feadhnach
eile.'

Thug iad leo 'nan achlais a mach e thun an t-saghaich is
sheol 'ad gu rioghachd na' Fear Móra. 'Nar a ràinig dh'acraich
'ad 'san acarsaid agus leum esa a mach air a mhuir agus
shnàmh e gu tìr.

Co bha 'san tràigh ach buachaille bh'aig Righ na' Fear
Móra agus thachair Fionn ris.

' 'N tà,' os e-fhéin, ' 'se Dia chuir orm thu 's mi gheibh an

---

[1] = dheth 'of him.

duais o nighean an Righ air-son do thoirt ga h-ionnsuidh air-son thu 'bhith nad' dheudaig aic' air a bhòrd.'

MAR A DH'ÉIRICH DO DH'FHIONN ANN AN RIOGHACHD NA FEAR MÓRA AGUS MAR A MHARBH E BHIAST

Dh'éirich 'sin am buachaille agus rainig e pàilios righ na' Fear Móra is thachair nighean a righ ris.

''S mi bheir dhuibh an deideig snasail,' os esa.

' Gu de sin ? ' os ise.

Thug e Fionn agus Bran as a phòca. Thug e 'nighean a righ 'ad agus a h-nile uair bhiodh is' aig biadh bhiodh esan air a bhòrd aice, e-fhéin is Bran. Bhiodh e h-nile oidhche comhla rithe 'san leabaidh agus mar bha na ciochan aice-sa cho mór bhiodh 'ad ga mhurt-san. Bha e so oidhche dhe na h-oidhcheannan comhla ri ann sa leabaidh agus thòisich is' air caoineadh.

''Ne mise bhi comhla ruit tha toirt ort bhi 'caoineadh mar so ? ' osa Fionn.

' O cha'n e. Tha mo bhrathair gos a bhith aig a bhéisd an earar agus 'se sin tha 'toirt orm a bhi 'caoineadh. Bha e 'san dailgneachd gur e Fionn mac Cumhail bha ris a bhiast a mharbhadh. Chuir m'athair air falbh dà shoitheach[1] dh'fhiach a faigheadh 'ad e. A chiad shoitheach[1] chuir e air falbh thachair e riutha agus mharbh e'n dìs dhaoine chuir e 'ga iarraidh. 'Nar a chuala sgioba 'n t-soithich eile gun a mharbh e 'ad thill 'ad dhachaidh. Cha'n fhac iad alt deth.'

' Gu dé bheireadh sibh do dhuine a reachadh thun na béisteadh airson 'ur brathair ? ' osa Fionn.

''N tà gad a reachadh na tha 'rioghachd na' Fear Móra a dhaoine thun na béiste cha teid thus' h-uice.'

''N tà,' os esa, ' sud an rud a ni d'athair-se. Dianadh e gàradh chlachan anns am bi sia traidhean, faigheadh e sia sailbhean daraich agus trì slabhruidhnean iaruinn chumas mo chù-sa.'

' Ud,' as[2] Fear a bha timchioll, ' cumaidh aon duine againn an cù.'

---

[1] Shaghach—Eriskay pronunciation.   [2] = os, ars'.

'Beiribh air na thoilleas timchioll air is fiach an cum sibh e.'

Dh'fhalbh an sin na thoilleadh timchioll air a chù is rug 'ad air agus ghearr Fionn fead ris a chù agus an duine nach do chuir e bharr cnàmh na h-amhaich chuir e bharr na guail*eadh* e. Bhrist e cas fir agus mharbh e feadhainn eile dhiubh.

Chuireadh brath air clachairean an sin agus rinneadh an gàradh ann san robh sia traidhean. Chuireadh trì slabhruidhnean iaruinn air Bran agus trì sailbhean daraich air ceann a h-uile slabhruidh.

Thug esa an sin Mac-A-Luin as a thruaill agus dh'fhalbh e. Thainig a bhiast air tìr an sin agus a chiad tarruinn a rinn i air a h-anail thug i traidh air aghart esan ga h-ionnsuidh agus ghearr esa an sin fead bharr a ghuail*eadh* agus bhrist Bran té dhe na slabhruidhnean. Tharruinn i rithisd a h-anail agus tharruinn i Fionn traidh eile air aghart. Ghearr esa fead eile bharr a ghuaileadh agus bhrist Bran an darna te dhe na slabhruidhnean. Smaointich Fionn an so nan leigeadh e Bran a stigh am broinn na beist*eadh* air thoiseach air fhéin, gu robh cho dòcha Fionn fhéin a thòiseachadh air Bran is toiseachadh air a bhéisd agus chuir e sin a mhiar fo dheud fios a dh'fhiach *cud* a gheibheadh e.

' Theirig thusa stigh air thoiseach am broinn na béisd*eadh*,' os an fhiosachd, is gheobh Bran *arr* [1] fhàileadh thu.

Tharruinn ise so gaoth ga h-ionnsuidh agus ghearr Fionn fead bharr a ghuaileadh agus stigh am broinn na béisd*eadh* a bha e agus stigh Bran as a dheaghaidh. Thug ise so a h-aghaidh air a locha,—seadh, a bhiast. Thòisich Fionn air an dala taobh dhi agus Bran air an taobh eile. Thàinig 'ad a mach an sin air gach taobh dhi. Cha robh gas gaois*neadh* air Bran 's cha mhua bha gas gruai*geadh* air Fionn.

Mar a fhuair Bran a spor neimh 's mar a fhuair e 'dhath

'S ann an uair-sa fhuair Bran an spor neimh a broinn na beisd*eadh*.

---

[1] =air do (Eriskay).

Dh'fhalbh Fionn an so is thug e'n loch air 'ga nigh fhéin agus a nigh' a choin. 'Nar a nigh e e fhéin thug e sùil bhuaithe 's co chunnaic e nuas g'a ionnsuidh ach mac righ nam Fear Móra agus claidheamh rùisgte aige g'a ionnsáidh. Chuir e'n so 'mhiar fo dheud fios fiach cā 'n robh 'gill 'dol. Fhuair e mach gur ann gos an ceann a chur bharr Fhinn a thainig e 's gos e fhéin a chur 'san ainm gur h-e fhéin a mharbh a bhiast.

'Cā bheil thu dol?' osa Fionn.

'Thàinig mise,' os e fhéin, g'ad ionnsuidh gus an ceann a thoirt dhiot.'

''Ne sin mo thaing-se,' os Fionn, 'airson tighinn a dh'ionnsuidh na beisde*adh* orra[1] shon-sa? Ach ma thogas tu mo nàdur nas mua na tha i cha 'n eil fear agaibh ann an rioghachd nam Fear Móra nach ruith mi fhéin 's mo chù throimhe ann an aon uair an uaireadair.'

Thàinig an so an righ fhéin a nuas agus thuirt Fionn ris, gum b'olc an taing a thug a mhac-sa dhà air-son a dhol air a shon-san dh'ionnsuidh na béis*teadh* 's tighinn g'a ionnsuidh air-son a cheann a thoirt deth 's gum biodh e fhéin fo ainm gur e mharbh a bhiast.

Dh'fhalbh athair a ghille, an righ, an so agus rug e air *tàs* a bh 'aige agus cnap luaidhe air ceann a h-uile meanglan di, agus dh'éirich e air a ghille 's nach d' rinn e sìon air ach gun a dh'fhàg e beò e.

'Cuiribh a nis,' osa Fionn, 'gaoisid air mo chù.' Rinneadh sin agus dh'fhàgadh donn air fad e.

'O,' osa Fionn, 'cha 'n e sud dath bu mhath liom-sa chur air mo chù idir.'

'Ciod eile,' os an righ, 'an dath as math leat a chur air?'

'Dà thaobh dhonna agus tàrr glas
Agus dà chluais chorracha chrò-dhearg
Air dhath na seilge.'

Bha sin air Bran an an tiotadh aca.
Chuireadh falt bàn air Fionn fhéin.

[1] =air do.

MAR A FHUAIR FIONN RIOGHACHD NAM FEAR MÓRA FHÀGAIL 'S A THÀINIG E GU SLÉIBHTE

Os a rìgh : 'Cha 'n -eil agams' ach an aon nighean. Gheobh thu ri pòsadh i.'

''N tà,' osa Fionn, 'cha ghabh mise i sin bhuat. Ach,' os esan, 'rud a dh' iarras mi oirbh mo chur do'n Eilean Sgiathanach.'

Chuireadh a mach an sin a bhìrlinn agus dh' fhalbhadh leis agus dh' fhàgadh ann an Sléibh*teadh* e.

'Nar a chaidh air tir ghabh e suas air feadh Shléibhte agus chunnaic e na bothagan a bh' ann an sin agus chaidh e gu ruige té dhiubh. Cha robh creutair an sin ach teine beag agus shuidh e air pluic na rudeigin agus cha b' fhada bha e ann an sin 'nuair a thàinig làn na bothaig' dhachaidh dhe na Fiantaichean, aon fhiadh beag bìdeach aca eatorra.

MAR A CHAIDH FIONN ANN AN SEANCHAS RIS NA FIAN-TAICHEAN'S MAR A DH'INNIS IAD DHA MAR A MHARBHADH 'ATHAIR, CUMHAL

Rug iad air an fhiadh is bhruich 'ad e agus 'nar a bha e bruich 'se aona ghreim dhe shithionn ràinig air na bha 'stigh agus aona bhalgum dhe shùgh.

'Seall orm,' osa Fionn, 'an e sud an seol bidhe a th' agaibh daonnan ?'

''N tà, se,' os àsan, 'os cionn ghr*eiseadh*.'

'Gu de a chuir cho beag 'sin sibh ?'

'N tà bhuail 'ad air caoineadh feadhain diubh.

''N tà,' os àsan, ''nar a bha sinne cruinn ann a so bha aon duin' againn 'na rìgh agus bha Eirinn fo 'smachd uile. Cha ghabhamaid bacail o dhuine 'sam bith. Rinn sinn an sin lagh, duine 'sam bith dhianadh cron dhe na bh' againn, gun cuireamaid air falbh bhuainn e. Fhuair sinn a sin fear dhiubh laighe le mart agus chuir sinn bhuainn am fear sin agus àrca na bà mu 'amhaich. Dh' fhalbh e bhuainn agus ràinig e rìgh Eirinn agus fhuair e bho rìgh Eirinn abhuinn cheud air-son iasgaich agus air-son iasg ùr a chumail ris an righ. Mu'n d' fhuair e sin bho 'n righ cha 'n fhaigheadh e sion gos an innseadh e ciamar a gheibheadh 'ad Cumhal a chur gu bàs.'

'An tà,' os Arca, 'cha do ghabh Cumhal gaol air gin riamh bho nach robh boirionnach ro bhriagh ann.'

''N tà,' os an Righ, ''s ann agam-sa tha 'm boirionnach as briagha tha ri fhaighinn agus 's ann as fhearr dhuinne litir a chur ga 'ionnsuidh.'

Sgriobh rìgh Eirinn litir e thighin ga 'ionnsuidh 's gun robh e maithte aige gach sion a rinn e riamh air. Fhuair Cumhal an litir agus leugh e i. Dh' fhalbh e ga Pailios Rìgh Eirinn agus 'nar a ràinig e'm pailios bha lamhan sgaoilte romh Chumhal, leithid a dhuine ruighinn.

Chuireadh dinneir mhór gu feum dhaibh agus shuidh 'ad mu 'n bhòrd agus bha nighean a Righ mu choinneamh Chumhail's cha robh Cumhal a' leigeil na sùl di.

'Cha chreid mi fhein,' os an Righ, 'a Chumhail, nach eil thu air gaol a ghabhail air mo nighinn.'

''N tà, thà,' osa Cumhal, 'is i an aon té a b'fhearr leam agam dhe na chunnaic mi riamh.'

Bha nighean i-fhein deònach air-son Chumhail a phòsadh is chuireadh fios air pears' eaglais ('se sagairt a bha'nn 'nuair sin tha mi cinnteach). Phòs 'ad agus oidhche na bainnse chuireadh Arca am falach 'san t-seomar as an robh āsan dol a chadal. 'Nar a chunnaic Arcaidh 'n so an t-am aige e-fhéin éirigh rug e air Mac-A-Luin a bh' aig Cumhal is thug e 'n ceann bharr Chumhail. Ghrad bhuail ise na basan, nighean an Righ. 'Stigh ghabh 'ad dha'n t-seòmar is bha Cumhal an deigh an ceann a thoirt deth agus thog' blith air ad a mach e.

Thuirt an Righ an so ann an ceann nan trì ràithean nam b' e gille bhiodh aig bean Chumhail gu marbhte e, agus nam b' e nighean a bhiodh ann gum biodh 'ad coma air a son,—nach togadh a nighean tòrachd a h-athar gu bràch. Dh' asaideadh an sin i, os na Fiantaichean, air pàisde nighinn agus dh' innis 'ad so a h-uile car mar a thachair 's mar a rugadh Fionn, mar a tha air a chur sìos agaibh ann an toiseach na sgeulachd a cheana. Rinn an gille so, os āsan, móran marbhaidh ann an ceann a sheachd bliadhna agus thog ar cridhean[1] 'nar a chuala sinn a leithid a bhith ann. Agus, os āsan, 's ann air sgoilearan bh' aig Easbuig gan ionnsachadh rinn e sgaid a bha 'n sin. Thuirt an t-Easbuig a sin, 's e 'coimhead a mach air uinneig: 'Co leis tha 'n gille Fionn tha 'bàthadh mo chuid sgoilearan?' Thuirt a mhuime 'n uair sin 's i air a chùl: 'Tha 'dhiol uisge timchioll is tha mo mhac-sa air a bhaisteadh.' 'Thà,' os an t-Easbuig, 'Fionn mac Cumhail.'

Cha 'n eil ach bha e còmbla riutha an oidhche sin anns a bhothaig gus an tàinig[2] an latha là-na-mhàireach.

AN T-SEALG A RINN BRAN

'Nar a thàinig an latha dh' fhalbh iad dha 'n bheinn-sheilg agus dh' fhalbh Fionn comhla riutha ann. Rainig iad innis nam Fiadh. Chunnaic.iad dream dhe na feidh a' dol seachad orra.

'Nach tilg sibh,' osa Fionn, 'orra sud?'

'O cha tilg,' os āsan, 'cha 'n 'eil a chridhe air ar cluais tilgeil orra, ach 's suarach an dream ud seach an dream a tha 'tighinn as ar deaghaidh.'

Thàinig sin an làn-dhamh, an fheadhainn mhóra.

'Nach tilg sibh orra sud?' osa Fionn. 'Cha tilg,' os āsan. 'Cha 'n eil a chridhe againn, ach an aon fhear as dona th' air deireadh a speil 'n an deidhidh so.'

'Nach fhaigh mi cead,' os Fionn, 'mo chù leigeadh unnta so—na daimh mhóra bhrèagha tha 'dol seachad.'

'Gu de,' as āsan, 'ni do chù dona orra? Nach lig thu ā?'

Leig Fionn Bran gu siubhal is chanadh an dala fear ris an fhear eile: 'O nach collach[3] a dh' fhalbhas e ri Bran.'

'Mar e Bran 'se bhràthair e,' os fear eile dhiubh. Air a chiad dhol m' an cuairt a rinn Bran orra leag e naoi làn daimh le bun iorbaill agus air an ath dhol m' an cuairt leag e naoi eile agus bhuail Bran air an leagadh gus na dh' iarradh air Fionn an cù a chasg. Chaidh iad so far robh na feidh is

---

[1] Plural of *cridhe*, used by reciter.   [2] Pronounced *dàinig*.   [3] =Coltach.

dh' fhoighneac Fionn diubh : ' Gu de nisd,' os e fhéin, ' an t-eallach bu mhua bheireadh cù leis ? '

' Bheireadh,' os na Fiantaich, ' naoi làn daimh dhiubh sin. Bheireadh e leis sin air a mhuin. Bheireadh Bran leis naoi eile a làn daimh air bun iorbuill. Gad 'imide (bhitheamaide) làn bidhe is dibheadh bha ar dìol againn a dhà 's a thrì thoirt leinn diubh.'

Cheangail Fionn naoi làn daimh do Bhran agus cheangail e naoi làn daimh eile dha fhéin agus thug cach leo aon fhear agus an còrr cha b' urra dhaibh thoirt leo leis cho lag 's a bha 'ad.

MAR A DH' INNIS FIONN DO NA FIANTAICHEAN GU 'M B' ESAN FIONN MAC CHUMHAIL

Chaidh 'ad dhachaidh agus thug ad làmh air a choire mhóir, am fear nach tugadh làmh air bho mharbhadh Cumhal. Lionadh le feidh e agus bhruich 'ad na bh' ann an sin. Thòisich iad air iche 's a h-uile fear mar 'iodh e làn bheireadh e dealg daraich as a bhroinn. Thilgeadh 'ad a dh' iochdar na bothaig i.

' 'N taing do 'n t-Sealbh cha robh sinne cho làn bho mharbhadh Cumhal 's a tha sinn a nochd. Mar a tig fodha so fhathasd ! '

' Ciod a rud a thig fodha ? ' osa Fionn. ' An tà,' os àsan, ' clann peathar Fhinn. Chuireadh,' os iad fhéin, ' os ar cionn an so 'ad gus na féidh 'chumail bhuainn ach am fear bu dona air a ghreigh.'

' Siuthadadh sibhse agus ithibh 'ur dìol is cha 'n eil ann an Eirinn na bheil a chridhe facal a ghradh ribh. 'S mise Fionn mac Cumhail.'

(*To be continued.*)

SOME SUTHERLAND NAMES OF PLACES

W. J. WATSON

THE Norse occupation of Sutherland and Caithness lasted from about 880 to 1200 A.D., when William the Lyon finally established the authority of the Scottish crown in these northern parts. The names from this source, therefore, may be over 1000 years, and cannot be less than 700 years old. While it is true that Norse names may be found almost any-where in Sutherland, even in its very centre, there are several indications that the occupation was not nearly so complete as it was, *e.g.*, in Lewis. There the old Celtic names have suffered a clean sweep; almost all the Gaelic names are 'phrase-names' of the type of *Allt na Muilne*. In Suther-land, on the other hand, there survives quite an appreciable number of Pictish names, dating long before the advent of the Norsemen. We also find a free use of suffixes in forming Gaelic names—such as -*ach* with its old locative -*aigh; -lach*, -*an + ach*, and other combinations of an antique cast, which could hardly have been formed after 1200, and probably date much earlier. The Norse element is very strong on the north coast, much weaker in the interior and in Sutherland proper. It is noteworthy, however, that many of the principal hills and dales are Norse. Fresh-water lochs are mostly all Celtic, as also rivers. Village names are divided, with a preponder-ance in favour of Norse which does credit to their choice of site. The evidence of the place-names, then, goes to show that the Norsemen held the whole of Sutherland as its over-lords, but did not occupy it to the extent of displacing the native population or their language. At the same time, it is highly probable that there was a good deal of bi-lingualism during this long period of 300 years; this also is, to some extent, reflected in the names.

We shall take first the principal terms found in combination :—

á, river, genitive *ár*, appears terminally in Brora, G. Brùra, N. Brúar-á, Bridge-water, a name found in Iceland; also in Borgie, Fort-water. The genitive case is seen in Arscaig, ár-skiki, 'river's strip,' with which we may compare Ascaig, 'river-strip.' Amat (Oykell and Brora), G. àmaid, is á-mót, 'river-meet,' 'confluence,' found also in Ross. Calda Beag and Calda Mór are two parallel streams that flow into Loch Assynt: kald-á, Coldstream. The district between them is Edrachalda for Eadar-dha-Chalda, 'between two Coldstreams.' Abigil, G. àbigil, may be á-bæ-gil, 'river-stead-gully.' Aberscross is in G. àbarscaig and àbairsgin; in 1512 Abbirskor, 1525 Estir and Westir Abbirschoir ; 1563 Westir Abberscors, showing the modern English form to be a plural. The G. àbarscaig would represent á-búr-skiki, 'river-bower-strip'; in Iceland there is Búrá, 'bower-stream'; but in view of the variant forms the last syllable must be held uncertain. In any case the initial long vowel shows that we are not dealing with a Pictish *aber*, as has been commonly supposed.

Bakki, a bank, is seen in Ekkiallsbakki, Oykell-bank. Hysbackie is hús-bakki, 'house-bank,' and Coulbackie, G. Callbacaidh, is kald-bakki, 'cold-bank.' The first part of Crasbackie is not clear. Backies, near Golspie, is an English plural, Banks.

Bólstaðr, *ból*, a homestead, is not uncommon. Arnabol is either 'Arni's stead,' or, less probably, 'eagle or erne stead.' Gylable is gilj-á-ból, 'gully-river-stead.' Erribol, G. éiribol, is eyrr-ból, 'gravel-beach-stead.' The Gaelic of Embo is also éiribol, but it appears as Ethenboll, circ. 1230 ; Eyndboll 1610 ; and may mean 'Eyvind's stead.'

Unapool in Assynt is Una's or Uni's stead. Kirkibol and Crosspool, Churchstead or Kirkton, and Roodstead, are two of the few Norse church-names in Sutherland. Leirable, 1563 Lyriboll, occurs in Kildonan, apparently mud-stead, N. leir, whence in Lewis Lurebost. With it may be compared Duible, 1527 Doypull, perhaps from dý, 'a bog,' 'bog-town.' Colaboll is either 'Kol's stead,' or 'charcoal stead.' Scrabster appears in the *Orkneyinga Saga* as Skára-bólstaðr, 'seamew-stead.' Torboll in Dornoch and Torrobol in Lairg both represent Thori's stead. Eldrable, G. Eildirebol, 1563 Altreboll, 1610 Eltribol, has been explained as Altar-stead, but more probably contains a proper name such as Elldjárn. The N. altari, 'altar,' is late and Christian. Skelbo means 'shell-stead,' the Gaelic Sligo and Sligachan. Skibo, G. Sgiobul, appears about 1230 as Scitheboll, which may be either 'Skithi's stead,' or, from skíd, 'firewood-stead.' The local authorities take it from G. sgiobal, 'a barn,' but the ancient spelling has to be taken into account. Ribigil is in 1530 and 1610 Regeboill, which might be reyka-ból, 'reek-stead,' but though reykr, 'reek,' is common in Icelandic names it seems always to be applied to places near hot springs. A suggested derivation is rygjar-ból, 'housewife's stead'; the difficulty here is that Norse *g* between vowels would certainly have been aspirated. Ulbster in Kildonan is probably Ulfr's stead, but may be Ulli's stead, Ulli being a pet form of Erlend.

Borg, a fort, appears in Borve Castle, Farr, G. Borgh; here G. *gh* must have been sounded *v*, a pronunciation which we know from other instances to have been formerly common, and which is still heard. Near it is Borrogeo, borgar-gjá, 'fort creek.' Borrobol is 'fort-stead'; there is a broch within about a mile of it. Burragaig Bay in Durness appears to be borg-vík, 'fort-bay.' There is also Loch Borralaidh, from borg-hlid, 'fort-slope.' In Assynt in Loch Borrolan, at Altnacealgach, borgar-land, 'fort-land.' The river Borgie is 'fort-river.'

Dalr, dale, is found terminally in many names. Armadale in Farr, is 'Arm dale' or 'Bay dale.' Mudale, G. Muthadail, 1570 Mowdaill; 1601 Mowadale, is possibly módadalr, 'muddy-river dale.' Strathalladale, a hybrid, is helga-dalr, 'holy dale'; the personal name Helgi is also possible. Trantlemore and Trantlebeg, 1527 Trountal, contain the name Thrond, the full genitive of which appears in Trotternish, Skye, G. Trondairnis, Throndar-nes. Langdale is simply Longdale. Rimsdale, 1630 Rimbisdale, and Achrimsdale are from rymr, roaring, 'roaring dale.'

Scalmasdale in Kildonan is hard to dissociate from Skálmar-dalr, 'sword-dale'; 'cloven dale,' in Iceland. Skelabosdale is skela-bólstadr-dalr, 'shell-stead dale.' Strathskinsdale is from skinn, skin, cf. Skinnet in Caithness. Oulmsdale is the present equivalent of Ullipsdale, 'Ulfr's dale.' Keoldale, G. Cealdail, 1559 Kauldale is possibly Kaldi-dalr, 'Cold-dale.' Torrisdale is 'Thorir's dale.' Astle or Asdail in Dornoch is in 1222 Askesdale, 1275 Haskesdale, meaning 'Ashdale.' Swordale, G. Suardail, 1275 Swerdel, is 'sward-dale.' Ospisdale is probably for Ospak's dale; Spinningdale, G. Spainigdail (long *n*), 1464 Spanigidill, 1467 Spainzidell, 1546 Spangzedaill. It has been referred to spöng, gen. spangar, 'a spangle,' which would, however, result in Spangadail. The second syllable *ig* is doubtless vík, 'a bay'; the first may be spann, 'a pail' or 'measure,' possibly with reference to the shape of the small bay on which Spinningdale stands. Migdale, G. Migean, 1275 Miggeweth, 1561 Mygdaill, an obscure name. Helmsdale is known from the Sagas to be Hjalmund's dale.

Ey, an island: Boursa is búrs-ey, 'bower-isle.' Soyea, sauda-ey, 'sheep-isle.' Handa, sand-ey, 'sand-isle,' with *s* aspirated. Calbha Bheag and Calbha Mhór, 'calf-isle,' a name commonly applied to small islands standing off the shore. Howga of 1570 is in 1601 Haga, now Hoan. Oldaney, G. Alltanaidh, though applied to the island is really a mainland name, and probably Gaelic; the island is Eilean Alltanaidh, the Isle of Oldaney. It is supposed to represent Jura of Ferchar Leighich's charter of 1386; dýr-ey; 'deer isle.'

Erg, shieling; borrowed from O.G. áirge; now àirigh. The classical instance is *Asgrim's ergin* (*Orkneyinga Saga*), which is now Askary, in Caithness. In Sutherland it is rather common terminally as *-ary*. Fiscary, in Tongue, is 'fish-shieling,' and about a mile from it is *Ach-an-iasgaich*, 'fishing-field.' Toscary, from tosk, a tooth, tusk, means 'tooth-shieling.' Scottarie comes from skot, a shot; 'shot-shieling,' cf. skot-bakki, shot-bank, *i.e.* butt. Modsary probably contains a contracted form of a personal name, *e.g.* Mötull, and so with Kedsary, which may be Ketill's shieling. Halmadary, famed for the legend of *Tuiteam Halmadairigh*,[1] is most likely 'Hjalmund's shieling.'

Sleasdary, in Creich, is doubtful. Creag Thorairigh is 'the rock of Thori's shieling.' Scourie, G. Sgobhairigh, is probably from skógr, a shaw, wood; 'shaw-shieling.'

Fjall, a hill, fell, has in several cases been replaced terminally by G. *beinn*, as has happened elsewhere, *e.g.* Goatfell is in G. Gaodabheinn; so Blaven, 'blue-fell,' and others. In Sutherland Sulven, G. Sulabheinn, is for Sula-fjall, 'pillar-hill.' Fashven, G. Faisbheinn, with its tapering peak, is hvass-fjall, 'pointed fell.' Sgribhisbheinn is not clear as to its first part; perhaps it contains *sgriða*, a landslip, scree. Foinaven, G. Foinnebheinn, may be pure Gaelic, meaning 'wart-hill,' from its peaks. On the other hand it may represent vind-fjall, 'windy-fell,' just as *vindauga*, 'wind-eye,' becomes *fuinneog*,

---

[1] *Inverness Gael. Soc. Trans.*, xx. 99.

uinneag, window. It has been thought that *fjall* has also been replaced by G. *meall*, lump, in Farrmheall, as for Fær-fjall, 'sheep-fell'; but the name is more probably pure Gaelic meaning 'projecting lump'; cf. Farrlary. At least four hills in Sutherland are called Maovally, G. Maobhalaidh with old people; now becoming Mao'alaidh; 1564 Movell. All these present the same rounded, semi-elliptical appearance, and I take them to be from maga-fjall, 'maw-fell' or 'paunch-fell'; the aspirated *g* would be sounded *v* as in Borve above. Another name which recurs three or four times is Saval, G. Sàbhail. There is a Saval near Lairg, and in Assynt are Saval Beag and Saval Mor, with a gap between called *Bealach eadar dha Shàbhail*. Eastward is *Lurg an t-Sàbhail*. Sàbhail seems to be a Gaelic form of há-fjall, 'high-fell.' Norse initial *h* before a vowel is usually treated in Gaelic as if it were an aspirated *t*; thus há-bakki, 'high-bank,' becomes in Lewis Tàbac. But this *h* might equally well be taken to stand for aspirated *s*, and of this we have one certain instance in Hjaltland, Shetland, which becomes in Gaelic Sealtainn. It may be noted that Sutherland names happen to present no clear instance of Norse initial *h* becoming *t* in Gaelic. Ben Loyal, west of Loch Loyal, near the Kyle of Tongue, is in G. Beinn Laghal; 1601 Lettirlyoll. As far as phonetics go this may represent laga-fjall, 'law-fell,' or laga-völlr, 'law-field.' Another suggestion is leið-fjall or leið-völlr, 'leet-fell' or 'leet-field,' *i.e.* places where certain public meetings were held; but, though this makes good sense, it would become Laoghal, rather than Laghal in modern Gaelic. Ben Arkle, where the deer in Sir Robert Gordon's time had forked tails, is G. Airceil, and is thought to mean 'ark-fell,' 'chest-fell,' from its shape. It may equally well be Gaelic *airceal*, a hiding-place, a name which occurs in Lochbroom. In any case it can hardly be erg-fjall, 'shieling-fell,' as has been sometimes suggested. Beinn Smeòrail is 'butter-fell,' or 'butter-field,' (völlr).

Fjörðr, a firth, appears in Loch Inchard, G. Loch Uinnseard, probably engis-fjörðr, 'meadow-firth,' and in Loch Laxford, G. Lusard, 'salmon-firth.' Strath Dionard probably contains the Norse name for the Kyle of Durness, into which it opens, and may be dýn-fjörðr, 'noisy-firth.'

Garðr, a garth, yard, court, occurs as *-gary*, *-chary* : Odhrsgaraidh is 'Ögr's garth.' Ach-cheargary is from kjarr, copse; 'field of the garth by the copse.' Griamachary, at the foot of Ben Griam, is

'Grim's garth.'   Halligary may be either 'sloping garth' or 'Hallr's garth.'

Gil, a ravine, gully, is so common that only examples can be given. Fresgil, in Durness, may be from fress, tomcat; fraes, noise, 'noisy gully,' has also been suggested.   Eirigil, from eyrr, means 'gravel-beach gully.'   Báligil, bálagil, is 'bale or flame gully.' Abigil (à) seems to be á-bæ-gil, 'river-stead gully.'   Allt Thàisgil is from háls-gil, 'hause (throat) gully'; cf. Gob Thàis in Lewis, and Thàisgil in Gairloch.   Achrìdigil, field of Rìdigil, probably rjóta-gil, 'rowting or roaring gully.'   Achŭrigil, Rosehall, is not to be compared with Loch Urigil, in Assynt, which has the initial vowel long, and may be from úrr, wild ox. The Rosehall Urigil is rather from urð, 'a heap of stones.' Achriesgil is from hrís, copse; 'field of the copse gully.' Connagil is from kona, woman, Sc. quean; cf. Cuniside, G. Caonasaid, qvenna-setr, showing the genitive plural.   Bréisgil may be explained as breið-áss-gil, 'gully by the broad rocky ridge.'   Allt Thòirisgil means 'burn of Thorir's ravine.'   Sgrigil is 'scree or landslip gully'; Tràligil, 'thrall's gully.'   Réigil, 1601 Raygill is given as Gaelic of Rhifail, and has been given me also as Rifagil.   The double form may be explained as rifgil or régil, 'big gully.'   Suisgil in Kildonan, G. Sìsgil, 1527 Seyisgil, 1545 Suisgill, has been referred to seyðisgil, 'seethe-gil.'   With it may be compared Gìsgil, 'gushing gil,' from geysa, gush, whence geysir, gusher.   Lastly may be taken Dun Dornadilla in Strathmore, in Gaelic Dùn Dornagil, which may well be Thorna-gil, 'thorn-gully.'

Gjá, a creek, has been taken over into Gaelic as *geodha*, and appears terminally as -*go* or -*geo* in Port Vasgo for hvass-gjá, 'tapering creek'; Lamigo, 'lambs' creek'; Borrogeo, 'fort creek'; Sango, 'sandy creek'; Glaisgeo, (?) 'glass creek,' but it may be G. 'green creek.'

Hlíð, a slope, genitive hlíðar, occurs in Swordly, 'sward-slope.' Leathad Darnlaidh is probably 'hillside of the thorny slope.' Tuirsligh is for Thursa-hlíð, 'giant's slope'; cf. *na Tursaichean* in Lewis, applied to the standing stones.   Rudha Armli is 'Cape of the bay slope,' cf. Armadale, and Borralaidh is 'fort-slope.' Fastly is probably hvass-hlíð, 'pointed slope,' cf. Faishven. Flìrum, a rocky islet off Durness, is probably hlíðar-holm, 'sloping isle'; Rob Donn has *leac Fhlìrum*.

Nes, a headland, cape, occurs only thrice: Melness, 'bent-grass cape'; Unes, 1275 Owenes; 1566 Unis; G. Jùneas; often mentioned in connection with the 'ferry of Unes,' now the Little Ferry, *am Port Beag*, at mouth of Loch Fleet. Durness, G. Diùranais, 'deer-cape'; cf. Diurinish, Skye, and elsewhere.

Setr, a stead, shieling, appears in Sutherland terminally as -*said*, which becomes in English -*side*. Caonasaid has been noted above; 1601 Kennyside. Linside, G. Lionasaid, is for lín-setr, 'flax-stead.' Loch Staonsaid is from stein-setr, 'stony shieling'; Loch Coulside, G. Cùlasaid, is kúlu-setr, 'knob-stead,' from kúlu, a rounded hill; cf. Culbo, in the Black Isle. Hòrasaid is 'Thori's stead or shieling.' Dionsait may be 'noisy stead,' from dynr din. Fealasaid is fjall-setr, 'hill-stead,' in English Fallside. Bowside, búsetr, 'dwelling-shieling.' Bracsaid is brekka-setr, 'slope-seat.' Sandset, now Sandside, is 'Sandseat.' Clanside, G. Claonasaid, and Clayside are doubtful.

Skiki, a strip: Arscaig and Ascaig have been mentioned. Overscaig is ofarr-skiki, 'over or upper strip.' Poulouriscaig, G. Poll-aorisgaig and Poll-éirisgeig, is from eyrr, meaning 'pool or hollow place of the gravel-beach-strip.' Boarscaig is búdar-skiki, 'bothy strip.' Malmsgaig, from málmr, sand, with secondary meaning of metal; 'sand-strip, or ore-strip'; cf. Malmö in Sweden, and Málmey, Iceland. Calascaig is 'Kali's strip'; cf. Calascaig in Lochbroom. Ramascaig is from hrafn or hramn, a raven: 'ravens' strip,' while Ròmascaig is rauma-skiki, 'giant's or clown's strip.' Truderscaig cannot come from trúdr, a juggler, for d would drop. It is probably Throndar-skiki, 'boar-strip' or 'Thrond's strip'; cf. Trantle, above. Skibbercross, G. Slobars-gaig; 1360 Sibyrs(k)oc; 1562 Syborskeg, Schiberskek; a difficult name; possibly siðu-búr-skiki, 'side-bower strip'; siða, 'a side,' is common in Norse names. Gordonbush has been given me in Gaelic as Gar-éisgeig, where *gar* is Gaelic meaning 'copse'; éisgeig may be eyði-skiki, 'waste-strip.'

Völlr, a field, gives Carrol, kjarr-völlr, 'copse-field.' Rossal is hross-völlr, 'horse-field'; its grass is injurious to cows, though harmless to horses. Langwell is lang-völlr, 'long-field,' and Sletell, 'even-field,' from sléttr. Musal, 1560 Moswell, is 'mossy-field'; Marrel, mar-völlr, 'seafield.' Brawl, G. Breithal, is breið-völlr, 'broadfield.'

Some names may be added which do not come under these headings. In addition to the personal names already noted, we have Craig Shomhairle and Airigh Shomhairle, 'Somerled's rock and shieling.' Poll Amhlaibh is 'Olaf's or

Anlaf's pool,' Druim Manuis, 'Magnus' ridge'; Eilean Eglei is 'Egill's ey or isle.' Dalharrald in Farr contains the common Harold, possibly in this case Earl Harold, who was defeated by King William in 1196. Cyderhall is an interesting name. In 1230 it appears as Sywardhoth; 1275, Sytheraw; and Siddera on Blæu's map; clearly 'Sigurd's how' (*haugr*), the burial-place of Earl Sigurd, who died from the effects of a scratch from the buck-tooth of Mælbrigit, Mormær of Moray, whose head he carried at his saddlebow. Sigurd, says the Saga, was 'laid in how' at Ekkiallsbakki. The Gaelic is *Siara*, which may represent Sýr, a pet form of Sigurðr: the full form would be expected to yield *Siarda* in Gaelic. Asher or Oldshore, G. Aisir (à) was in 1551 Aslar, 1559 Astlair, and has been regarded as a contraction from Asleifarvík, Asleif's bay, where King Hacon touched in 1263. Leac Bhiurn in Strathnaver is 'Björn's flagstone.'

Golspie is in 1330 Goldespy, G. Goi(ll)sbidh; the latter part is bær, býr, a stead, village; the first part has been referred to *gil*, a ravine, which is impossible; also to *gull*, (older *goll*), gold, which, in default of a personal name, is the most probable explanation. Strathfleet, G. Srath-fleðid, comes from fljót, flood, a common stream-name. Eilean Klourig (Clobhraig) on the north coast, is klofar-vík, cleft-bay; the island is cleft right through by a narrow channel. Sandwood in Durness stands for sand-vatn, sand-water, the only instance known to me of *vatn* in Sutherland and the mainland of Ross, whereas it is so common in the Western Isles. Two parishes bear Norse names, Tongue, from *tunga*, a tongue; and Assynt, ascribed to áss-endi, rock-end. The difficulty with the latter is that the initial vowel of Assynt is short in Gaelic. The suffixed article is seen in Merkin, the march (mörk), Akran, the acre, Pólin, the ból or stead. Syre, G. Saghair, is rather uncertain. If we accept initial *s* of Gaelic as arising from Norse *h*, as was suggested in the case of Saval above, it would represent *hagar*, pasture-lands; on the other hand there is a Saghair in Ireland. Storr in Assynt, G. Stòr, is usually supposed to be from *stór*, big, the latter part of the name having dropped. But the name occurs in the *Orkneyinga Saga* as Staur, and there is another point of the same name in the *Heimskringla*, with suffixed article, Staurinn, both apparently from *staurr*, a stake, point. Ben Hope is from *hóp*, a bay, whence Gaelic *òb*; as Ben Horn is from *horn*, a horn. Ben Clibreck is in G. Clìbric, and may be klif-brekka, 'cliff-slope' but Gaelic *ì* makes this doubtful; in any case the latter part is *brēkka*, a slope. Grumbeg and Grummore are interesting. In 1570 they appear as Grubeg and Grubmore, and farther back in 1551 Gnowb Litil and Mekle, from gnúpr, a peak, common in land-names. Loch Merkland is mörk-land, 'march-land'; it is on the watershed. Strath-vagastie appears to be from vaka-staðr, 'watching-stead.' Heilem, which appears in Rob Donn as Hilleam and Huilleum, is in 1530 Wnlem, 1542 Unlem; 1551 Handlemet; 1601 Hunleam and Houndland, and may be hund-holm, 'hound isle'; it is a mushroom-shaped peninsula. Fors, a waterfall, gives Forsinard and Forsinain, upper and lower waterfall respectively. Cape Wrath, G. am Parbh, is from *hvarf*, turning-point, cf. hvarfs-gnípa, Cape Farewell, in Greenland. Solmar, in Durness, is sól-heimar, 'bright-ham,' Brighton, a name found in Iceland. Ben Armin is from ármaðr, gen. ármanns, a steward, controller, whence G. ármunn, a hero. The Italian looking Ben Stomino, east of Loch Loyal, is said on good authority to be a mere map-name. It appears on a map of Sutherland dated 1823, and has kept its place since. The Gaelic form is Beinn Staim and Loch Staim lies north of it, apparently from the by-name Stami. Druim-basbaidh in Farr probably contains a shortened form of a personal name with the -*by* suffix, seen in Golspie; bads-bær, 'bath-stead' is possible. Drumholli-stan, east of Strath-halladale, is 'the ridge of the holy stone.'

In dealing with the Norse element I have had the advantage of consulting a paper contributed some years ago by Dr. A. Macbain to the *Highland News*, of which he kindly permitted me to make use.

THE RUIN OF HISTORY

(A reply to 'The Ruin of Britannia')

IN *The Celtic Review* for July and October 1905 Mr. A. W. Wade-Evans aims at showing that the *De excidio et conquestu Britanniae* which bears the name of Gildas 'was composed about 700,' and that the invective by which it is followed is alone the composition of Gildas, and was written by him 'before 502.' And as part of his argument he seeks to prove that Vortigern invited the Saxons in 428. I shall here show that the 428 date hopelessly breaks down, and that each of Mr. Wade-Evans's preliminary contentions also collapses.

He begins with the *Annales Cambriæ*, 'and the important event from which the *Annales Cambriæ* compute appears to be St. Germanus's 2nd Advent to Britannia, which it fixes in the year which would be in our reckoning A.D. 445 . . . Annus I is 445 . . . Annus CCCLXIII is 807, and so on.'

Now (1) the *Annales* do not give the number 445 at all, while both Mommsen and Mr. Phillimore, their latest editor, reckon their Annus I. as 444; and (2) *they do not mention Germanus at all.* It is merely Mr. Wade-Evans's assumption that they date from the 2nd Advent of Germanus, and, to those who abide by Bede's dating, it is manifest that they begin with the supposed year either of Vortigern's accession or of the Saxon landing. Finally, the *Dictionary of Christian Antiquities* and the *Dictionary of National Biography* both place Germanus's 2nd Advent in 447.

He proceeds to say that the compiler of the *Annales* had before him several chronicles computing from different eras, and jumbled up their entries without reducing their dates to a common era. He gives 'three examples out of the many' —

(1) 'It is universally admitted that St. Patrick died in 461. . . . Now the *Annales Cambriæ* place it'—his death—'opposite Annus XIII., which in the era of 445 gives a wrong date, viz., 445 + 12 = 457; but which in the era of 449 gives the right date, viz., 449 + 12 = 461. Therefore this event was extracted from a chronicle which computed from 449.'[1]

Patrick's death was an *Irish* event, and is dated 488 by the *Annals of Innisfallen*, 489 by the *Chronicon Scotorum*, 492 by the *Annals of Ulster*, and 493 by the *Four Masters*. Here are four divergent dates within a period of

---

[1] It was doubtless stated by tradition or in some early chronicle that Patrick died 58 years after coming to Ireland, and this was misinterpreted as referring to his mission to Ireland (about 432), instead of his captivity (about 403). I find that Prof. Bury has the same explanation. 457 was given for the death of Sen Patraic (Bury, p. 284), and was the year of Patrick's *retirement* (*ib.*, p. 206).

six years; does Mr. Wade-Evans really suppose this arises from four different eras having been adopted within that period ?

A glance over Dr. Whitley Stokes's edition of Tigernach in the *Revue Celtique* would have shown him that similar divergences among the Irish chronicles are incessant. To account for these it is not necessary to postulate the concurrent use of a number of eras, varying only a year or two from each other, *and none of them known ever to have been used at all*. It is enough to seek their origin in well-known causes. One of these may have been the different dates at which the Roman consular and the Christian ecclesiastical year began. Another very common one was the omission or miscopying of numerals. In a number such as CCCLXXVIII., for instance, it was quite easy to drop or repeat a [, an X, or an I. Where ink was faint or corroded, or vellum dirty, it was easy to read C as L, X as V, L as I, U as II.

If Mr. Wade-Evans will look at p. 145 of Mommsen's edition of the *Historia Brittonum*, he will find in the various readings of the MSS. a *series* of such mistakes, where there *can* be no allegation of the use of different eras. The number of years between Adam and the Babylonian transmigration according to Jerome's translation of Eusebius's Chronicle—which can hardly fail to have been the ultimate basis of computation—should be IIIIDCLXX, yet every MS. on this page gives IIIIDCCCLXXVIIII, or adds another X. Some scribe had let his eye slip to adjacent numbers, from which he had inserted additional figures; thus the superfluous VIIII is the end of the number before that which he was copying.

(2) The *Annales* place the death of Cadwaladr opposite Annus CCXXXVIII, *i.e.* according to Mr. Wade-Evans, 238+444=682; according to Mr. Phillimore, 238+443=681. Mr. Wade-Evans quotes the authors of *The Welsh People* (p. 127) as saying, 'If, from the few data we have to rely on, the matter is traced out, there can be no doubt that the year 681 is too late, and that in all probability it was in or very near to 664 Cadwaladr died.' 'We know from Nennius,'[1] says Mr. Wade-Evans, 'that he died in a pestilence . . . between 642 and 670, and also that a great pestilence commenced in 664 . . . Now Annus CCXXXVIII in the true era of the Invitation is 428+237=A.D. 665.'

Now the entry of the *plague* is in all three of the MSS. included in the Rolls edition of the *Annales*, but the *death of Cadwaladr* is only in A, the other two (B and C) having instead varying forms of a statement that he fled to Brittany—a statement taken from Geoffrey of Monmouth. And, although these other two MSS. are of the late thirteenth century, and are only partially transcripts of the *Annales*, 'they are both largely based . . . on a MS. (or MSS.) of those *Annales* that is now lost, and was in places a

---

[1] He should have said 'the *Historia Brittonum*,' which is earlier; Nennius omits all this matter. I have in *Keltic Researches* similarly confused the Nennian redaction with the earlier form, and abase myself accordingly but nothing has turned on the point.

more correct transcript than the now unique existing one' (Mr. Phillimore in *Y Cymmrodor*, xi. p. 139). I suggest that the original text of the *Annales* had only the entry of the plague, and that a later scribe, saying to himself, 'This must have been the plague in which Cadwaladr died,' added the statement of his death.

, (3) 'Opposite Annus CLXXXVI the *Annales* place this dark entry—'Guidgar comes and returns not,' which Annus makes 445 + 185 = 630. It obviously refers to some early well-known settlement whose best remembered leader was 'Guidgar.' The only known settlement of the kind of which we are reminded is that of Wihtgar and Stuf in the Isle of Wight in 514.' And he proceeds to explain by what combination of errors an event which took place in 514 was ascribed to 630.

It is really enough to point out that the *Annales* have not mentioned any other Anglo-Saxon settlement, that the elements of the name Guidgar (*i.e.* wood-lover) appear in Welsh pedigrees in Guid-cun, Guid-gen, Cyn-gar, and that 'comes and does not return' is far more likely to refer to a Cumbrian or Breton paying a visit to Wales and stopping there than to a Jute invading the Isle of Wight. On these considerations alone Mr. Wade-Evans's case ought to be ruled out of court.

But his explanation of how the dislocation of 116 years was brought about is far too instructive to be missed :—

'Two mistakes were made. A scribe had before him the date 'A.D. DCXIV,' *i.e.* 514. The first mistake was to read DC as 600 instead of 500 (that being once a common way of writing 500). Having thus obtained the number 614, he proceeded to compute in the era of St. Germanus's 1st Advent, viz. 429. In other words, if 429 is made the Annus I, then 614 will be 614 – 428, which is Annus CLXXXVI *as above*. Afterwards a second scribe, neglecting the era, inserted it without change in his own era of 445, so that the event was thrown 116 years out of its true date !'

Whether any one ever dated anything 'in the era of St. Germanus's 1st Advent' we need not stop to inquire. It is enough that no one who knew the Latin numeral system could possibly write DC for 500, or interpret it as anything but 600. D stands to C in exactly the same relation as L to X and V to I, and Mr. Wade-Evans might just as well have told us that LX was 'once a common way of writing' 50, and VI 'once a common way of writing' 5. Here he has been misled by two earlier writers.

He next shifts King Maelgwn's death from 547 to 502, on the hypothesis that it was computed 'in the era of Stilicho.' The sole ground for disturbing the date is that St. David was born in year 14 of the era of the *Annales* (= 456), that according to 'genuine pedigrees' he was fifth in descent from Cunedda, whereas Maelgwn was fourth—and that consequently 547 is too late for the death of the latter.

First note that *in the oldest MS. of the* Annales *David's birth is not mentioned.* He only appears in one of about 1286, so that in their most ancient text there is no discrepancy between the dates assigned to him and to Maelgwn.

The next thing which strikes one about these 'genuine pedigrees' is that in that of David 'Cedig' and 'Sant' are not real persons at all. The first seems merely a faulty repetition of the preceding name (Cedig *i.e.*) Ceredig, and the second simply the epithet *sant*, 'saint.'

And, if this be so, then David, instead of being a generation younger than Maelgwn, was a generation older, and the accepted date of Maelgwn's death receives the strongest confirmation.

On referring to the genealogies in the Harleian MS. 3859 of the *Annales*, the index to the Book of Llan Dâv, and the index to the Red Book of Hergest, one finds no Welsh name Cedig, and no Welsh name Sant.

The article on St. David in the *Dict. of National Biography* ingeniously observes that David's father Sant was 'apparently evolved from the title *mabsant* (patron saint), which admits of being mistranslated "the son of Sant".'

As regards Cedig, the *Dict. of Christian Biography*, the *Dict. of National Biography*, and Rees's *Cambro British Saints* all ignore him, and (though there are late Welsh pedigrees which give him), if Mr. Wade-Evans will refer to the very useful index to Old-Welsh genealogies published by Mr. Anscombe in the *Archiv für celtische Lexicographie*, he will find that in the thirteenth century Cotton MS. Vesp. A. xiv David's alleged father Sant is twice given as the son, not grandson, of Keredic, even though in one place the MS. allows this Keredic a son named Kedic or Kedich.

In short, so far as the evidence before us goes, there is not the least reason why David should not have been Maelgwn's senior, and why he should not have been buried (as Geoffrey of Monmouth states) by Maelgwn's orders at Menevia.

But something still remains to be said about the *Annales* and David. The oldest MS. has against the year 157 this entry :—'Sinoduſ urbiſ legion. Gre-goriuſ obiit in *christ*o. Dauid epis*copuſ* moni iu-deor*um*.' It is commonly said that this is a statement that St. David died in Menevia in 601, and, if so, it would of course cut the ground from under Mr. Wade-Evans's feet. He simply ignores it; but I shall shortly show elsewhere that the final place-name should be *moniu aerô*, and indicates an earlier seat of David's bishopric at Moniu near the Aeron, now Hen Fenyw, 'Old Menyw.'

He next sets to work to determine to what era the date of Maelgwn's death should be ascribed. It is 'not difficult to discover'—nothing would be when 'discovery' is conducted on his methods. And this is how he does it.

The oldest MS. of the *Annales* is interpolated in the text of a copy of Nennius's redaction of the *Historia Brittonum*, where it is preceded by a string of badly blundered chronological notes. This is a translation[1] of these notes from A.D. 29 onwards :—

'Also from the two Gemini, Rufus and Rubelius, until Stillitio consul are 373 years.' (*They are only* 371 ; the Gemini were consuls in 29, Stilicho in 400.)[1]

---

[1] The Latin is on p. 209 of Mommsen's edition of the *Historia*.

'Also from Stillitio until Valentinianus son of Placida and the reign of Guor-thigirnus 28 years.' (*But V. became Caesar in 424 and Augustus in 425.*)

'And from the reign of Guorthigirnus until the discord of Guitolinus and Ambrosius are 12 years, which is Guoloppum, *i.e.* Catguoloph.' (*The only Guitolin we know was Vortigern's grandfather,*[1] *and Catguoloph means 'free from battles,'*[2] *which was surely not true of any 12 years of Vortigern's reign.*)

'Guorthigirnus moreover held *imperium* in Britain when Valentinianus and Theodosius were consuls' (i.e. 425, *which contradicts the '28 years' already given*).

'And in the 4th year of his reign the Saxons came to Britain, Felix and Taurus being consuls, in the 400th year from the incarnation of our Lord Jesus Christ.' (!!!)

'From the year in which the Saxons came into Britain and were received by Guorthigirnus until Decius and Valerianus are 69 years.' (*The consulship of Decius and Longinus in 486, only 58 years after Felix and Taurus, is all Mommsen can suggest.*)

This precious farrago, I may say in advance, is the sole authority on which Mr. Anscombe and Mr. Wade-Evans would have us throw back Vortigern's dealing with the Saxons to 428. And it is from this, and this only, that Mr. Wade-Evans creates an 'era of Stilicho,' from which he says 'two military events are distinctly computed. . . . These are the words . . . "From Stilicho to Valentinianus and Vortigern's reign are 28 years; and from Vortigern's reign to the battle between Guitolinus and Ambrosius are 12 years."'

He is trying to make out that his so-called 'era' of Stilicho was an era in which military events were computed. Therefore he translates *dis-cordiam* 'battle' (!) and calls Vortigern's accession a military event.

Establishing a military era by these simple means, he tells us that in the first 110 years of the *Annales* three military events are recorded:—

Annus LXXII—Victory of 'Badon' won by Arthur.

Annus XCIII—Arthur's death at Camlan.

Annus CIII—Death of Maelgwn Gwynedd.

—*where the death of Maelgwn during a pestilence is tortured into a military event in order to justify the shifting of its date into a supposed military era.*

Of course the other two events follow suit—Arthur's death being thrown back from 537-8 to 492, while a 471 date for the Badon victory 'is corro-borated by the famous interpolation in the *Excidium Britanniæ*, which computes 'Badon' as the Annus XLIV with one month gone [from Vorti-gern's Invitation], *i.e.* 428+43=471.'

The 'famous interpolation' is in every MS. of the *Excidium*, and has been disputed by no one, so far as I know, except Mr. Wade-Evans and Mr. Anscombe, *to whose attack on the date of the* Excidium *it is fatal!*

Next as to the computation from 428. C. 25 of the *Excidium* ends with

---

[1] *Historia Brittonum*, § 49. Doubtless the Guethelinus abp. of London men-tioned by Geoffrey as obtaining help from Brittany and educating Aurelius Ambrosius (vi. 4, 5).

[2] *See* Prof. Rhŷs in Y *Cymmrodor*, xviii. 73. The name is Vitalinus Kymricised (Prof. Rhŷs).

the victory of Ambrosius Aurelianus; its actual closing words are 'quis' (=quibus) 'victoria domino annuente cessit.' The next chapter begins :—

'Ex eo tempore nunc cives, nunc hostes, vincebant, ut in ista gente experiretur dominus solito more praesentem Israelem, utrum diligat eum an non ; usque ad annum obsessionis Badonici montis, novissimaeque ferme de furciferis non minimae stragis, quique quadragesimus quartus ut novi orditur annus mense iam uno emenso, qui et meae nativitatis est.'

Here 'quique—est' is 'the famous interpolation,' in which there is not a word about 428 or Vortigern's invitation, while the context leaves it to the last degree doubtful whether the 44 years are not counted 'ex eo tempore,' *i.e.* from Ambrosius's victory, and not from Vortigern's invitation at all.

'Again,' says Mr. Wade-Evans, 'as the annalistic year in the fifth century commenced on September 1 with the indiction, 'Badon' was won in October 470 of our reckoning, which is the fact underlying Geoffrey of Monmouth's absurd statement that Arthur slew with his own hand 470 men.'

Now it seems easy to conceive an (imaginary) entry 'an. CCCCLXX Saxones prostravit Arturus in bello Badonis' being so misinterpreted. Yet it is all but impossible that any one reading such entries in a chronicle should be ignorant that the number following 'annus' or 'an.' was the number of the year. Moreover, we do not know the date of Geoffrey's Breton book, but we do know that he did not write before about 1130. Now Arthur's feat is also related by two earlier chronicles (1) the *Historia Brittonum*, not later than the eighth century, and (2) its redactor, Nennius, c. 796—though we *may* not have any *MSS.* of these earlier than Geoffrey's own time. Well, the *Historia Brittonum* and the Latin Nennius do *not* give the number as 470, and the various readings in Mommsen's text are as follows :—

una die	ccccxl	(=440)	N
una	„ dccccxl	(=940)	M
in uno	„ dcccxl	(=840)	CDGLPQ and the Irish version of Nennius.
„	„ dcccclx	(=960)	HK

Here there cannot be much doubt that the original was 840, 940, or 960. The 470[1] of the printed Geoffrey probably arises out of *dcccclx, d* being accidentally dropped (as in N), and *x* accidentally added.

Next Mr. Wade-Evans proceeds to prove that the *invective* of Gildas was written before 502. The proof is a single sentence :—

'Now, as Maelgwn was alive when St. Gildas wrote his rebuke, the *Epistola Gildæ* was written before Maelgwn's death in Annus CIII a Stilichione consule, *i.e.* A.D. 502.'

As, however, we have seen, there is not a shadow of evidence that Maelgwn died before 547, and consequently none for shifting the date of Gildas's invective.

---

[1] The very important twelfth century (Bodleian) MS. Rawlinson, C. 152 reads 460.

We now come to the date of Vortigern's invitation to the Saxons. Mr. Wade-Evans quotes from the precious farrago I have above referred to the passage relating to it, supplying in square brackets '[vicesimo octavo]' after 'quadringentesimo,' and translating 'in the year of the Incarnation 428.' He then asks, 'How then is it that Bede places this event in 449 ?'

'In 532,' he says, 'Dionysius invented his system of Christian Chronology which we use to this day. After a while this system was criticised as follows :—If (it was argued) our Lord was born in A.D. 1, then the day of the Crucifixion must be Nisan 15 and March 25, and a Friday, and the moon fifteen days old, and all in the year A.D. 34. But as a matter of fact it is not so, whereas these conditions are found in A.D. 12. Therefore, argued the critics, A.D. 12 according to Dionysius must be A.D. 34 according to the truth of the Gospel. Consequently they introduced a new system of chronology, which they called that of Gospel Verity, against the system of Dionysius. Now we find that in Northumbria, in the middle of the seventh century, Vortigern's Invitation was fixed at 450, and this computation is quite right *if we only remember that it is according to Gospel Verity.* In other words, the date 450 is based on the date 428, because 428 according to Dionysius = 450 according to Gospel Verity.'

Now this system of dating according to Gospel Verity is first known to have been used by the eleventh century writer, Marianus Scotus, and I have never seen a rag of evidence that it was used before him. In 1901 Mr. Anscombe promised to produce such evidence, but we still wait for the fulfilment of that promise.

The same undemonstrated assumption leads Mr. Wade-Evans to date the *Excidium* after 597. Here is his argument :—

'. . . the system of Dionysius was not introduced into Britain until St. Augustine brought it in 597, and therefore a criticism of it would be meaningless in Britain till after that date. In other words, the computation, according to Gospel Verity, was not possible in Britain till after 597. But the *Excidium Britanniæ* (said to have been written by St. Gildas who died in 554) computes the date of the Invitation, according to Gospel Verity, and therefore it could not have been written by Gildas nor before 597. For the *Excidium* places the Invitation after the third consulship of Aetius in 446 [and in 450].'

This is an incomplete and misleading statement. The *Excidium* does not simply place the invitation after a consulship of 446 ; it places it after a letter, which it quotes, addressed to 'Agitius' as thrice consul. There is no case of *computation*, but of the correctness of sequence of an ordinary historical narrative, fatal, if that sequence is correct, to the 428 date.

Mr. Wade-Evans next passes from mere chronology to history in a larger sense. Let us compare what he tells us with what our Keltic ancestors thought they knew.

According to the *Historia Brittonum* (§§ 31, 36-7), Vortigern's Saxons, who had been expelled from their own country, had landed from three ships, had offered themselves as mercenaries, had first received from him the isle of Thanet, and afterwards had had Kent ceded to them, without the consent or knowledge of its own king, Virangonus.

The essential parts of this account agree with the *De excidio* which Gildas wrote about 548, and which even Mr. Wade-Evans does not try to put later than about 700. Therein Gildas (§ 23) tells us that a 'tyrannus' of the Britons and his counsellors, in order to repel the northern nations,[1] invited the Saxons, who came in three ships, and at his bidding first fixed their claws in the eastern part of the isle.

According, however, to Mr. Wade-Evans, all this is not even worth confuting. In Vortigern's time 'Brittania' merely meant 'Wales + Cornish Peninsula,' having for eastward boundaries the Dorset, Bristol, and Tewkesbury[2] Avons! 'Picts from Scotland, that is the Cymry under Cunedda' (!) 'and Scots from Ireland were pressing on his little patria beyond Builth. . . . Driven by necessity, he invited to his assistance the Saxon kindreds who dwelt beyond the Avons on either side of the lower Thames' (!).

Mr. Wade-Evans proceeds to give reasons why Gildas cannot have written the *De excidio*.

'Inasmuch as the author of the *Excidium* is a Roman Britannus, whose patriotism is kindled by the memory of Ambrosius; and inasmuch as he refers familiarly to the topography of S.E. Wales (not to mention his reference to the Britanni of Armorica in a manner impossible to a Cymro or a Scottus, or a follower of Vortigern), it is clear he is a native either of S.E. Wales or of the Britannic territory between the Severn Sea and Poole Harbour. *In other words, he is not St. Gildas ap Caw o Priten*, who was neither a Roman Britannus nor a native of Romania at all. St. Gildas was the son of Caw o Priten, *i.e.* Caw of Pictland or Southern Scotland, a regulus "beyond the mountain Bannawc" in Arecluta, which means "on or opposite Clyde."'

Now I find no reference whatever to S.E. Wales except in the words 'Aaron et Iulium Legionum urbis cives' (§ 10), where Caerleon is meant, nor any to the Britanni of Armorica unless in 'alii transmarinas petebant regiones,' etc. (§ 25). As Gildas died in the latter half of the sixth century, he was obviously not 'a follower of Vortigern.'

Mr. Wade-Evans says that Gildas could not have written as he has done about the Picts and Scots because he was himself 'the son of the Pictish raider' Caw. This information he extracts from an 'extraordinary story' in the *Vita S. Cadoci*, § 22, of which he transfers the scene from Albania (*i.e.* Scotland north of the Forth) to Anglesey, and which does *not* say that Caw was a Pict. He does *not* mention the following facts:—

> (*a*) That in the life of Gildas by the monk of Ruys (his own monastery) Gildas's father is described as a catholic king in Alclyde;

---

[1] *i.e.* the 'tetri Scottorum Pictorumque greges' (§ 19).

[2] The one point to lay stress on now is this, that the three rivers called Avon (Tewkesbury, Bristol, and Dorset) almost certainly represent Britannic boundaries of the fifth and sixth centuries, Avon being the Britannic word for 'river.' There is no Dorset Avon; be·means the Avon of Wilts and Hants. Perhaps he also regards as boundaries the Avons which disembogue at or near Thurlestone, Aberavon, Avonmouth, Berkeley, Hamilton, Grangemouth, and Ballindalloch.

(*b*) That in the Iolo MSS. (pp. 101 (496), 109 (508), 136 (540)) Gildas's father is said to have been driven out of his country by the Gwyddelian Picts, and to have been the son of Geraint, the son of Erbin, the son of Custenin Gorneu, the son of Cynfar, the son of Tudwal Mynwaur, the son of Cadan, the son of Cynan, the son of Eudaf, the son of Bran, the son of Llyr Llediaith. There is nothing Pictish *there*.

He says that, 'if the author . . . had been Gildas ab Caw writing before 502, he could not possibly have made such a mistake as that in which he tells us that the Walls of Antonine and Hadrian were built after 388, and also the nine forts of the Saxon shore' and that the statement that Hadrian's Wall was built '*between cities which perhaps had been located there through fear of enemies* . . . in itself betrays the late date of the work.'

The answer is (1) that Gildas wrote nearly half a century later, (2) that his tradition doubtless confused repairs with construction, (3) that Hadrian's Wall *was* built along a line of previous Keltic settlements, as is shown by almost every station on it bearing a Keltic and not a Roman name, and (4) that there is no proof that the 'turres per intervalla ad prospectum maris' were 'the nine forts' or anything more than conning-towers.

'Nor could St. Gildas before 502 have made the suggestion which the *Excidium* does in chapters 11 and 12, where it is assumed that the *merthyr* place-names of South Wales are so called after supposed Diocletian martyrs.'

To this and the subsequent remarks of his first paper it is enough to say :—

    (*a*) that the chapters in question do not mention S. Wales at all, and that the only allusion to it which I find in the *De excidio* is the statement that Aaron and Iulius were citizens of Caerleon.

    (*b*) that 'merthyrs (martyria)' are nowhere mentioned in the work, that the word *martyrium* is only used in it of actual martyrdom, and that the statement that the Christians of the early fourth century built 'basilicas sanctorum martyrum' is made of Britain at large, and not of S. Wales.

I now come to Mr. Wade-Evans's second paper, on the date of cc. 1-26 of Gildas.

The work of Gildas consists of a denunciation preceded (cc. 3-26) by a historical narrative. The latter in turn has a preface in which the author states his denunciatory purpose (c. 1.), but announces (c. 2) that before fulfilling his promise ('ante promissum') he will give a historical outline. No work could more clearly proclaim its own unity, and this unity is confirmed by the extraordinarily pretentious and involved style of the whole.

Mr. Wade-Evans ignores the testimony of the work to itself, ignores the evidence of style, and attributes everything before c. 27 to a later writer of about 700. By so doing he gives to the part which he *does* allow to Gildas an inconceivably abrupt beginning, while he leaves the *other* part with the promise of its preface unfulfilled.

He has also failed to notice (or else ignores) two striking correspondences of phraseology between c. 1 of the narrative which he rejects as Gildas's and the denunciation which he accepts. The first of these[1] is 'merito . . . dicebam . . . Stephanum gloriosum ob martyrii palmam, sed Nicholaum miserum propter immundae haereseos notam' compared with c. 67, 'Nicolaum in loco Stephani martyris statuunt immundae haereseos adinventorem': in each passage there is also an antithesis between Peter and Judas. The second is 'Habet Britannia rectores, habet speculatores,' to be compared with c. 27, 'Reges habet Britannia, sed tyrannos; iudices habet, sed impios' and c. 66, 'Sacerdotes habet Britannia, sed insipientes,' etc.

The author of the part which Mr. Wade-Evans rejects has fortunately given us excellent clues to his date. Speaking of the victory of Ambrosius Aurelianus, he adds 'cuius nunc temporibus nostris suboles magnopere avita bonitate degeneravit,' which suggests that he was contemporary with Ambrosius's grandchildren. This would be true of Gildas (whose death is placed by the *Annales* at a year corresponding to 570) but not of an author writing about 700. I grant that 'avita' *may* mean simply 'ancestral,' but if Ambrosius's family had lasted in the male line down to 700, it would be singular that his name is not in the Old Welsh Genealogies—that no Welsh family of note at the time when those genealogies were compiled could claim descent from him in the male line.

The decisive evidence, however, is furnished by the next paragraph,[2] which says that, 'From that time' [*i.e.* Ambrosius's victory] 'now the citizens, now the enemies, were conquering . . . until the year of the blockade of the Badon mount, and of almost the latest slaughter, of any importance, of the scoundrels, and which begins as the forty-fourth year, as I am aware, one month having already been measured out, which is also that of my birth.' It is not certain whether he means that he was born in that particular month, or in that particular year, or whether the forty-four years are from Vortigern's invitation[3] or from Ambrosius's victory, but in either case the author may have been Gildas, who died in 570, and cannot possibly have been a man who wrote about 700. *This* evidence Mr. Wade-Evans cannot ignore—how does he deal with it?

The *Annales* mention two battles of Badon (*i.e.* Bath). The first, at a point corresponding to A.D. 516, is described as (I translate) 'battle of Badon in which Arthur carried a cross of our Lord Jesus Christ in 3 days and in 3 nights on his shoulders, and the Brittons were victors': this is

---

[1] I owe my knowledge of it to Prof. Hugh Williams's edition. He cites Jerome, *Ep.* xiv. 8: 'Attendis Petrum sed et Iudam considera; Stephanum suspicis, sed et Nicolaum respice.'

[2] For the Latin, see above, p. 365.

[3] So Bede takes it, but the other view is supported by the *Annales*, which place the Badon affair at a point corresponding to 516.

obviously the battle referred to by Gildas. The other is at a point corresponding to A.D. 665, and is described as 'battle of Badon a second time' (*secundo*).

We have already seen that Mr. Wade-Evans has tried to push back the first battle from 516 to 470. He now says :—

(i) That the battle of 470 (*i.e.* 516) was not a battle of Badon at all, but of the Mons Agned !

(ii) That there was only one battle of Badon, that of 665 !

(iii) That this was really the battle of '*Bedan-* or *Biedan- heafod*,'[1] not fought by the Britons at all, but by one set of the 'scoundrels' against another (Mercians against West-Saxons), and according to the A.-S. Chronicle in 675.

To maintain (i) and (ii) he has to suppose that the entry of the *first* battle in the *Annales* is due to an erroneous identification of the battle of Mons Agned with that of Mons Badonicus, and that the entry of the latter among Arthur's battles in the *Historia Brittonum* (at least as early as the eighth century) is also due to the influence of the narrative attributed to Gildas.

To maintain (iii) he has to ignore the difference of vowels between '*Bedan-* or *Biedan-*' and *Badonici.* *Biedan-* is the correct form, but it is, I imagine, certain that neither in Welsh, nor Cornish, nor yet Breton, would Bied- or Bed- become Bad-, and that in Anglo-Saxon an original Badon or Badan could not become Biedan or Bedan.

Having thus transferred his author from the middle of the sixth to the end of the seventh century, Mr. Wade-Evans has still to explain what is meant by the forty-fourth year, in which the battle took place and the author was born. He says these words are an insertion by some one who confused the battle of Biedan heafod in 675 with the battle of the Mons Agned of 470 (really 516)! The person in question did so because he knew that the year of that battle 'was also the year of St. Gildas's birth'!

From what source a man of the end of the seventh or beginning of the eighth century is likely to have known the year of Gildas's birth at all, he does not tell us : *we* only know it from this very passage. But the explanation assumes that, when it was made, this historical narrative was already attributed to Gildas. Now Bede, in his *Ecclesiastical History*, which was *finished* in 731, quotes freely from this very narrative at the *beginning* of his work. Moreover, he quotes the very words about the blockade of the Badon mount, and says it happened about the forty-fourth year of the arrival of the Germans in Britain (i. 16). Finally, after a long quotation from this narrative (i. 22) about the Britons, he says that their historian, Gildas, had not exhausted the tale of their wickedness. So that—although the narrative was not, according to Mr. Wade-Evans, written till Bede's own lifetime (indeed not before he was a full-grown man)—yet it had come

---

[1] Mr. Phillimore had already proposed to identify this and the battle of 665.

to be accepted as the composition of a sixth century author, and interpolated accordingly, before Bede began to write his *History* ! [1]

'Badon Hill is described . . . as an *auxilium insperatum*. . . . A victory
of Arthur . . . could not possibly be called an unexpected help.' If Mr.
Wade-Evans had not totally disregarded the Breton tradition delivered by
Geoffrey of Monmouth (according to which the Bretons had a contingent
fighting with Arthur in that very year) he would have known the contrary.
Arthur was at or near Alclyde, and a body of Saxons, who had surrendered
to him on condition of being allowed to sail back to Germany, sailed round
to Totnes instead and marched on Bath : if its relief by a march from
Dumbarton was not an *auxilium insperatum* Mr. Wade-Evans's definition of
the unhoped-for must be a little exacting. Yet, when one turns to the
Latin, one finds that the words 'insperati . . . auxilii' are *not* attached to
the blockade of the Badon hill, and that so far as can be guessed from
their context they more probably refer to the victory of Ambrosius
Aurelianus !

Finally, in attempting to connect the author's theological strictures with
the adoption of the Roman Easter by Britons of Wessex at the end of
the seventh or beginning of the eighth century, Mr. Wade-Evans has
omitted all reference to the letter in *The Academy* of November 2, 1895,
in which I pointed out the striking applicability of the language of the
Excidium to the very time when Gildas (judged by his attack on Maglo-
cunus) was writing. That letter was written in reply to Mr. Anscombe—
but of *replies* to Mr. Anscombe we never hear anything from Mr. Wade-
Evans. He only mentions the 'minute researches,' 'great conquests,' and
'masterly articles' of his friend, to one of whose articles, that on 'The
date of the first settlement of the Saxons in Britain,' in the *Zeitschrift fur
celtische Philologie*, iii. pp. 492-514, I am about to send a reply elsewhere.
In it I shall show what the *Annales Cambriæ* and c. 66 of the *Historia
Brittonum* really are.   E. W. B. NICHOLSON.

BOOK REVIEWS

James Macpherson : *An Episode in Literature*. By J. S. SMART. London
David Nutt, 1905. 3s. 6d. *net*.

'Macpherson,' says Mr. Smart, 'produced spurious Highland poetry from
the first day of his appearance as a translator' (p. 92), and in remarking that
'he is not the only man of mystery,' Mr. Smart draws attention to the
fabrications of Chatterton, of William Ireland, and of Robert Surtees. A
remarkable letter is quoted (p. 193) wherein Macpherson, in 1793, writes

---

[1] Mr. Wade-Evans himself says, 'Bede had the *Excidium* in his hands by the year
725.' In that year he borrowed from it largely in his *De temporum ratione*.

regarding the suggestion of one Davidson, a friend of Ferguson, that the ancient manuscripts should be followed: 'Mr. Davidson writes rationally, but he seems not to know that there is scarce any manuscript to be followed, except, indeed, a very few mutilated ones in a kind of Saxon character, which is as utterly unknown to the Highlanders as either the Greek or Hebrew letters.' Macpherson ends this letter by exhorting his correspondent not to communicate it to Davidson and Dr. Blair—'You will easily perceive this letter is meant only for your own eye; for few men wish to know that they have been so long deceived on a point which the smallest attention might at once ascertain.' Mr. Smart holds that, 'in using the ballads as a basis for his own compositions, Macpherson was within his rights as an eighteenth century poet. But the exhibition of his works as genuine antiques fifteen centuries old, and the unreal pretensions which he wrapped about them, are a different matter. Perhaps nothing else is so likely to harden one's heart against him as a careful study of his own prefaces and notes. The poor Ossianic ballads, and indeed all Highland poetry but his own, are rarely mentioned without a sneer. They are "those trivial compositions which the Irish bards forged under the name of Ossian,"—"puerile and despicable fictions,"—"trivial and dull to the last degree." Such as they are, they were his own original materials. Yet this intrepid man seizes every occasion to laud the works of the real Ossian—himself.' Mr. Smart's book, while it appeals not so much to the Celtic scholar as to the student of English letters, shows a well-balanced mind, an informed judgment, and withal a refined taste—altogether a sound introduction, within its limits, to the study of its subject, embracing the necessary references to the relevant literature, as one expects in a work on a Celtic literary subject published by Mr. Nutt. It but corroborates the verdict of Sir Walter Scott.
G. H.

Religious Songs of Connacht. By DOUGLAS HYDE, LL.D. In eight parts. Dublin: Gill and Son, Ltd. Vols. I.-V. 1s. *per part.*

These volumes are the valuable result of many years' toilsome gleaning in the province of Connacht by the President of the Gaelic League. The work does no small credit alike to the patience, zeal, and tact of the collector, whose sympathy is only equalled by his shrewdness and insight, and to the wonderful people among whom it was possible to find such a great mass of literary material enshrined in the memories and living on the lips of the unlearned, in remote country places, from generation to generation. Dr. Hyde says a true word when he remarks in his interesting notes that a knowledge of these poems is 'almost necessary to any one who would understand the soul of Connacht.' It has been said that 'the soul of a nation never finds such native and intimate expression in the work of its great poets as in the artless folk-songs that have their roots in a people's heart; that grow into articulate melody one scarcely knows how, that wander unclaimed and houseless through the centuries, long after their original makers and singers are forgotten.'

This is equally true of religious songs and stories such as we have in these volumes. The hymns and prayers are full of passionate devotion and earnest piety. The verse is generally sweet and pleasing with a noble simplicity. The thought is not vigorously intellectual as a rule, but devotional and practical. One of these books might, indeed, be mistaken for a church manual. But we miss the *imprimatur* on the title-page! For there are things here that will please neither Rome nor Canterbury. Dr. Hyde, the humanist, includes all that came his way, curses as well as blessings and prayers, satires on the clergy, Protestant and Catholic, heretical opinions, spells and charms, and weird and grotesque prose stories of saints and common men.

The guiding principle of the collector seems to be *nihil humanum alienum puto*. The result is comprehensiveness, and an impression of the true inwardness of the Connacht mind.

It is interesting to compare these books with *Carmina Gadelica*. The number of pieces that are identical or evidently variants of the same original are not so numerous as one might have expected. The one collection supplements the other, and both combined form a noble common heritage for the Gaelic race.

Dr. Hyde's translations are uniformly well done. He succeeds in Englishing the originals without Anglicising them. On the whole the work has been carried through with rare literary skill and judgment. Our readers will look with interest for the concluding volumes of the series. The cheap form in which the parts are issued will doubtless help to a wide circulation and obtain for Dr. Hyde's work the success it merits.

Once or twice the author trenches on the dangerous ground of religious controversy. Criticism might be offered, but we refrain. In a note he says that the phrase, '"Righ na Domhnaigh" has not found its way into English.' But what about St. Luke vi. 5 in the authorised version?   M. N. M.

Manuel pour servir à l'étude de l'Antiquité Celtique. Par GEORGES DOTTIN, professeur à l'Université de Rennes. Paris: Champion, 1906. 5 *fr.*

In 358 pages Prof. Dottin has 'vulgarised,' as his compatriots say, the Antiquity of the Celts. Want of space makes us keep to the linguistic and philological side of the manual, which bears signs of being written hurriedly. Witness, notably, the treatment of such words as 'maw,' Welsh, as he calls it (p. 91). The truth is that 'maw,' or 'meol,' is Cornish. It occurs, according to W. Stokes, as 'mau,' and (in composition) as 'meudaw.' 'Mevel' is Breton. Again, 'cwrf' is given as the Welsh for *beer* (p. 54; in index, wrongly given as p. 55), whereas Pugh's *Dictionary* gives 'cwrw' (as all Welsh now pronounce it) and 'cwryf,' and whereas *the Welsh Laws* seem to have called it 'corraf.' It is right to say that Prof. Dottin quoted from the

Dictionary of Spurrel, and that, preferably, he gives the old Welsh forms. M. Dottin assures us we were never called Celts in these Islands in the earliest times, and lashes the temerity of J. Rhŷs and B. Jones (*Welsh People*) and of E. W. B. Nicholson *re* the Picts. The Fir Bolg are only once touched on, happily! As Irish is his forte, the author gives us relatively more of it. Lyon is called after a god Lug, or after a crow, or else is Endlicher's 'delectable mountain' (presumably, the Fourvières, which the writer did not find agreeable to climb). A. Holder, in the *Revue Celtique* for April 1905, wishes to make the crow an owl! If '*hûs*' (ῦς) meant a kind of *oak* among the Galatians (p. 68), and if *hob* means a pig, as ῦς does, have we here any explanation of 'hob y dery dan do'? On the same page, we find Boudicca's goddess of Victory, Andraste or Adraste, mentioned. M. Dottin finds in it a possible Greek word, translating an unknown Celtic name. But, for maledictions, Adras is familiar still. The Irish *birur*, 'cress,' might have had compared with it, besides Breton and French, the W. *berwr*, *berw* (N. Wales), *berwy* (S. Wales). On p. 92, for 'quatre' read 'appartenant à quatre,' for W. 'petry-.' The Celtomaniacs are well trounced, p. 107. *Paris* from 'par-*Is*' (the submerged town of Brittany) is particularly fine. [An Aberystwyth correspondent sends, for the Celtomaniacs, the following equations: 'Tena Koe'='dyna chwi,' 'tena Koutu'='dyna chwithau.' Here the first half, in each case, is Maori, the second Welsh!] P. 126, 'rotten barley fetid juice' (*jus fétide d'orge pourrie*) is inexact as a translation of Dionysius *Hal.* (xiii. 16), who speaks of *barley* MACERATED *in water*, κριθῆς σαπείσης ἐν ὕδατι,—a very different thing. The voluptuary, for instance, in Athenæus (xii. p. 549), using the same verb, says he is himself *lean* from pleasure, and *macerations* of the flesh were, or are, known in religion. The possible root of 'brogues' from 'suf-*frago*,' 'calf of leg,' possibly opens up the whole question of whence came 'frock,' 'froc' (F.),—from the ninth century down. [A question not discussed, however, here, p. 129.] Naturally the *gæsati* (p. 128) were armed with *gwaywffyn*, 'javelins'; and plaid is due to the Gauls, if Pliny's 'scutulis dividere Gallia [instituit]' bears that translation (p. 131),—for another meaning is, not 'plaid' but, 'knitted.' Philologically, *uxoribus* (pl.) is too weak a proof of polygamy in Gaul, and M. d'A. de Jubainville has practically proved Celtic monogany,—tempered, as he describes it. H. H. JOHNSON.

Faclair Gaidhlig : Lyminge : Kent. Ardmór: E. Macdonald & Co. at the Celtic Press. *6d. per part.*

Nine parts (280 pp.) of this new Gaelic Dictionary have now appeared, bringing it down to *crùbag*. The work aims at presenting an approximately complete vocabulary, and to this end it is evident that no pains have been spared in the way of overhauling previous dictionaries, as also printed books such as Mr. A. Carmichael's *Carmina Gadelica*, Nicolson's *Gaelic Proverbs*, and Cameron's *Names of Plants*. In addition local and dialectic forms have been obtained from Gaelic scholars all over the Highlands. But the work is more than a vocabulary : it is a thesaurus of phrases and expressions illustrative of the word under discussion. Another most praiseworthy feature is the collection under their respective heads of the names of the different · parts of composite structures, and of terms and phrases used in connection with specific operations. Under *bàta*, for instance, there are no less than eight columns—apart from illustrations—containing names of parts and fittings of boats and ships. Under *coinneamh* come six columns of terms and expressions used, or capable of being used, in connection with meetings. Under *caor* we have lug-marks. All this was well worth doing, and for the result we are grateful to the laborious compiler and his helpers. We have observed some, not many, misprints. The type used is small and trying to the eyes. In spite of the diligence exercised there are omissions, of which a few may be noted : *àban* occurs in place-names in the sense, we think, of 'backwater'; sometimes it seems to mean a disused or silted up channel. There is *Abban* Street in Inverness; *Clach an àbain* in Petty Bay ; and *an àban* near Dochfour landing-stage on the Caledonian Canal. Under *àr* might come *tigh-àir*, house of death, used in the sense of 'lyke-wake.' *Breamhain* is a Sutherland and Easter-Ross word for 'barrow.' A compound of *cabar* is *cabar-naisg*, the post to which cattle are tied in a byre. *Càrn*, a cart, is omitted, as also the compound *càrn-fianaidh*, a 'peat-phaeton'—modern representative of the Caledonian *co-vinnus*—and *càrn-lòbain*, a low-set truck-like cart of wickerwork. *Ceapair-taobhaidh* is used in the Reay country to denote a 'love-piece,' *i.e.* a *ceapaire*, or bannock, given by a lady to a man to conciliate his affections. We cannot give the receipt ! *Cobh* is used of a slanting water-worn channel in a rock face. *Coileag* has been given us as a Skye term for a goal at shinty. The word for 'a fence,' obsolete except in place-names, is *airbhe*, not *àirbhe*. We fail to differentiate the sound of *coire*, cauldron, from that of *coire*, corry : the latter meaning is merely an extension of the former, though when standing as the first part of a compound, it is pronounced without emphasis, being unaccented.

We heartily wish the Dictionary success ; it will be found invaluable by all interested in Gaelic. W. J. W.

Celtae and Galli. By PRINCIPAL RHŶS. From the *Proceedings of the British Academy*, vol. ii. London : Henry Frowde, Oxford University Press, 1905.

In this brochure of sixty-four pages Principal Rhŷs has managed quite to startle the world of Celtic scholarship by running counter to a main canon of Celtic philology. For the last thirty years at least it has been held an established rule that initial Indo-European *p* was lost in the Celtic languages. Thus, Gaelic *athair*, father, Old Irish *athir*, corresponds to Latin *pater*. He does not flaunt his apostasy before our eyes ; without a remark he follows Mr. Nicholson, Bodley's librarian, in assuming that Indo-European *p* was preserved in the Celtic language of Mid-Gaul (from east to west), a territory known in ancient times as Celtica, as opposed to Belgica in the north and Aquitania and the Province in the south. The reason for the

Principal's defection is simple. He maintains that the language of Celtica belonged to the Gadelic branch of the Celtic, not, as hitherto held, to the Brittonic. Gadelic changes the Indo-European velar guttural q labialised (i.e. qu) into c, while Brittonic changes it into p, as does Greek. Gadelic is closer to Latin (Latin qui, Gaelic cia). Gadelic, save in late developments of sv, sp, never had p as a letter. But in Celtica some important inscriptions lately brought to light present p in several cases. If Celtica was a Gadelic tongue, then this p referred to must be Indo-European p still preserved. Mr. Nicholson and Principal Rhŷs hold that these p's are Indo-European. The proof that Celtican was a Gadelic language depends on the fact that it presents many words containing the letter qu, the labialised guttural, the Latin symbol of which is qu. Strictly arguing, we should expect in this Gaulish Gadelic not qu, but plain c; but the Ogam inscriptions, under Latin influence, give us this qu for c.

Principal Rhŷs, in the present case, depends mainly on two documents—the Calendar of Coligny (not far from Lyons), discovered in 1897, and the lead tablet found at Rôm, in the midst of old Pictavia (Poitiers). The Calendar belongs to the first century, and the tablet to the third or fourth. Apart altogether from linguistic theories, the Calendar is an exceedingly important document in Celtic history and philology. Any one that can *really* throw light on its contents is a benefactor to Celtic philology. Principal Rhŷs has undoubtedly done this in the present work; he has been so long working at inscriptions, and has come to such brilliant results so often, that indeed we should have expected him to read more of the riddles of the Calendar. The Calendar covers some five years, and shows that the Celtic year was lunar, of twelve months, alternating in 30 and 29 days, giving only 355 days for the year. Intercalary months of 30 days were included every 2½ years, which made the Celtic year average 367 days. The old month-names are interesting, and may be given thus :—

THE WINTER HALF

First Quarter :   Cutios, 30 days = November.
                    Giamonios, 29 days = December.
                    Simivionnios, 30 days = January.
Second Quarter : Equos, 30 days = February.
                    Elembivios, 29 days = March.
                    Edrinios, 30 days = April.

THE SUMMER HALF

Third Quarter :   Cantlos, 29 days = May.
                    Samonios, 30 days = June.
                    Dumannios, 29 days = July.
Fourth Quarter : Rivros, 30 days = August.
                    Anacantios, 29 days = September.
                    Ogronios, 30 days = October.

Some of the etymologies of these are quite easy:—Giamon contains the early Brittonic stem *giamo*, winter, Latin *hiems*, Gaelic *geamhradh*, from a stem *gimo*, be it observed—Gadelic shows no *giamo*. Equos, of course, means 'horse,' Gaelic *each*; for meaning, compare Gaelic *gearran*, gelding, the four weeks from mid-March to mid-April. Elembiv, the deer month, Gaelic *eilid*, Welsh *elain*, but especially for stem the Greek *elaphos* for *elmbhos*. Edrin is probably from the root *aidh*, as in Old Gaelic *aed*, fire (it is spelled also Aedrin). Mac-Aoidh, Latin *aestas*, summer. Cantlos is referred by every writer to Old Irish *cétal*, singing, *cantol, root *can*; but the Gaelic shows here *Céitean* for May, Irish *Céad-shamh*, gen. *Céadshaman*, 'first of summer,' by derivation. It is also the same in Old Irish. Samon, of course, is from *sam*, as in Gaelic *samhradh*. Ogron (October) has been well referred to the root *ogr* in *uar*, *fuar*, cold. The month was divided into two parts, the first containing fifteen days, the second, called *atenoux*-tion (after-nights?) having fifteen or fourteen days. The last half was doubtless the wane of the moon. Pliny says the Celts began their year and month on the sixth day of the moon. It is certain that due regard was had to the solstices and equinoxes, for the Helvetii started on their fatal emigration on the day of the spring equinox in 58 B.C.

The Calendar shows three words containing *qu*, and three having *p*. The former are Equos, Qutios, beside Cutios and Quirnon. They may be from some Gadelic dialect. The three *p* words are, first, *petiux*, which Principal Rhŷs allows to be from Brittonic *pett*, Pictish *pet*, whence English *piece*. But Mr. Nicholson must have his Indo-European *p*, and he refers it to *pitu*, food, Gaelic *ith*, eat! Second, *prinnos*, which seems to mean 'market.' Principal Rhŷs refers this to Indo-European *perna*, Irish *renim*, I sell. Now there is another root of like meaning—Indo-European *qrin*, which appears in Welsh as *prynnu*, buy, Old Irish *crenim*. Surely this is the root. The third *p* word is *pogdedortonin*, where possibly *po* is the prep. *cos*, *co* of Old Gaelic, *pw* of Old Welsh. Principal Rhŷs speaks of a *po*, away, with Indo-European *p*, but he is obscure on this point.

The Rôm tablet found in the land of the Gaulish Picts, and deciphered with great difficulty in 1898, shows several *p*'s, one or two of which are simply borrowed (*pia*, *pura*); but the only one that seems to hold an Indo-European *p* is *com*-*priato*, where *pri* is claimed as Indo-European *pri*, love (English *fri*-end). This foundation is too small to build a theory of preserved Celtic *p* upon. The word *ciallos*, which appears in the Calendar and on the Rôm tablet, is referred to Old Irish *ciall*, gathering, sense; but surely this is extremely rash phoneticising. Old Irish *ia* is broken *ei*, if not due to some contraction. The phonetics of Giamon show that our authors have lost the 'sense of perspective in language.' Two other inscriptions quoted by Principal Rhŷs 'prove naething,' as the Scotsman said about *Paradise Lost*. But one is really astonished to find Marcellus of Bordeaux (400 A.D.) and his medical charms seriously brought forward again. No doubt the *prosag* of *prosaggeri* has been too tempting. It *does* look like a compound of Indo-European *pro* and *sag*, Irish *sagim*, go to ; but the Celtic should be *ro-sag* in that case.   Marcellus's work contains numerous charms —various gibberish—and why pick out one here and there and call such Celtic ?   It is not business.   As in Italy we find various *p* dialects which gave words to the Latin vocabulary and names to its heroes, and likewise dialects in Greece showing *k* for *p* (as at Sparta), so in Celtica and in Spain there may have been remnants of Gadelic dialects surviving until and after the Roman conquest of Gaul.   This was Principal Rhŷs's position at one time, and I agreed with him ; indeed, as he says (p. 56), I have been the only one to accept this idea.   We must, however, draw the line at admitting that Indo-European initial *p* appears in Celtic.   Apart from this heresy, this work is very valuable, and shows no decay in the author's brilliancy of philologic imagination.   ALEXANDER MACBAIN.

The Scottish Historical Review.   Glasgow : Maclehose & Sons.   Quarterly, 2*s.* 6*d. net.*

The October number of this learned magazine contains several articles interesting to Gaels.   One such is that on ' The First Highland Regiment, the Argyllshire Highlanders,' by Robert Mackenzie Holden.   Even more interesting perhaps from our point of Gaelic view is the account of the battle of Killiecrankie, ' by an eye-witness.'   This ' eye-witness ' was Iain Lom, and while we admit his descriptions of the battle are given as if he had been a witness, we are not prepared to accept them as proof of his presence there.   Iain Lom was notoriously lacking in physical courage, and the fact of a poet describing a battle as if witnessing it, when in reality he has never been even on the ground, is a simple literary device which proves nothing except the poet's dramatic power.   It is not commonly accepted in the Highland traditions that Iain Lom was present at Killiecrankie, and there is really no *proof* either way.

Red Hugh.   A Drama in Three Acts.   By T. O. RUSSELL.   Dublin : Gill & Son.   6*d. net.*

An important part of the literary output of Ireland at present is in the form of drama, and this is not Mr. Russell's first play.   The subject is in itself dramatic, dealing as it does with the stirring and pathetic life of Red Hugh O'Donnell, who, if we remember rightly, began his experiences of Dublin Castle as a prison at the age of sixteen.   How he escaped, his suffering on the hills in winter, ill-clad, his rescue, his life of adventure and battle, of victory, of defeat at Kinsale, his death far from the land he loved, all these are incidents of dramatic power in themselves, and Mr. Russell has given them connected and dramatic form in a manner which tends to increase their interest.   That Red Hugh's mother was a Highland Macdonald will not tend to lessen interest in the play on this side of the Boyne.

Epochs of Irish History: Early Christian Ireland.   By ELEANOR HULL.
London: D. Nutt.   Dublin: Gill & Son.   2s. 6d. *net.*

This is the second volume of Miss Hull's series of Irish history books.
It deals with Ireland under her native rulers, Ireland as the 'Island of
Saints,' and with Irish Art, Architecture, Learning, etc.

The authoress aims at being that most ideal of historians, one who lets
the old records tell their own story, and avoids comment.   She has not only
striven for this, but she has in a great degree attained it, and her little
books are unbiassed accounts of the state and position of Ireland in former
days.   Miss Hull has given us no mere record of fights, which is too often
the historian's conception of his duty; but she tells us of the social life and
of the arts as they were followed by the people she would make us know.
After all a nation's life is not in its battles, but in the quiet of the unrecorded achievements along the paths of peace.   Miss Hull also avoids
discussion of the doctrines and discipline of the Irish church, and, wisely,
gives us instead an account of 'the remarkable developments in the national
character and conditions consequent on their teaching and system of things.'

In the first section of the present volume Miss Hull gives us the political
history of the time from King Laegaire, son of Niall of the Nine Hostages,
to Finnachta the 'Festive,' and the close of the early Christian period, while
in the second section she gives us the ecclesiastical history of that time.
The ecclesiastical history is no less important than the political, for it was a
time of great activity in the Irish church, the time of St. Patrick and
St. Bridgit, of St. Columba, St. Columbanus, and of Adamnan.   It was
during this time that Ireland earned the name of 'Insula Sanctorum et
Doctorum'—the Island of Saints and Scholars, for learning flourished
exceedingly within her shores, and from her went out very many missionaries, so that, as one great writer has said, the Celtic missionaries were like a
flood over the continent of Europe.   Even yet one may hear traditions of
them and learn of the love with which they were regarded.

The third section deals with Art, Architecture, Books, Illumination,
Learning, and with some of the Irish scholars who, in the ninth and tenth
centuries, kept alive the torch of learning, and passed it on to continental
Europe.   Such men were Sedulius, Abbot of Kildare, John Scotus Erigena,
Virgilius, Dicuil, Dungal and many others.

Altogether these little books of Irish history will be found to contain as
much interest and information as could well be put into the space, and they
are written in an easy and attractive manner. So little is known, except by
specialists, of the condition and position of the ancient Celts, that Miss
Hull's books must find a large welcome, which they well deserve.

Woman of Seven Sorrows.   By SEUMAS MACMANUS.   Dublin: Gill & Son.   7d.

This is an allegorical drama by an author who has already shown us his
dramatic powers in several moods.   The woman of the title is Ireland, and

her sorrows are told and not exaggerated. In the end she gets happiness, and the children rally round her, the young men and maidens also. There is sorrow but not bitterness, and while the play is propagandist in its nature, it is not rabid. It is well and clearly told, and is pleasing in diction and expression. We can imagine that it would act well; indeed, it has been acted very successfully, and the acting rights are free.   E. O'G.

Heroic Romances of Ireland. Translated into English Prose and Verse, with Preface, special Introduction, and Notes, by A. H. LEAHY. Vol. ii. D. NUTT. 3s. 6d. *net.*

This volume, handsomely printed and bound, contains translations of five of the lesser *Táin bó*, or Cattle-raids,—Táin bó Fraich, Dartada, Regamoin, Flidais, and Regamna. All are preludes to the great Táin bó Cualnge, the Cattle-spoil of Cooley, and, with the exception of the first, have appeared with German translations in Windisch's series of Irish Texts. Readers of the *Celtic Review* will find Táin bó Flidais specially interesting, in that a much fuller and quite different version of it is now being given from the Glenmasan Manuscript by Professor Mackinnon. Mr. Leahy gives the literal prose rendering with expanded metrical version on the opposite page, the latter serving largely as a commentary on the other, which is often laconic to obscurity. Both are well done in their respective styles. The prose version will be found useful by students of Middle Irish, and if in the verse translation occasional liberties are taken, these are largely a matter of taste, and can readily be checked by reference to the left-hand page. Mr. Leahy's method of dealing with Irish proper names is apt to mislead the purely English reader. In the prose version he very properly keeps, as a rule, the Irish form. In the other he is not consistent, sometimes giving Irish forms in the text with so-called pronunciations in footnotes, sometimes *vice versâ*. It should have been made clear that the suggested 'pronunciations' are far from being phonetic; *e.g.* mac Fiachna was not sounded mac Feena, Firbolg is not adequately represented by Feer-bol, nor Loegaire by Leary, though the latter is the modern Anglicised form. Neither is it correct to say that *mag* was pronounced *maw*, though this may come near *magh* in modern Irish. A little care under this head would have saved English readers from amazement. Mr. Leahy has done well in adding a specimen of Irish text with exact interlinear translation. The volume should do much to popularise the study of Irish.

Contribution à la Lexicographie et l'Étymologie celtiques. By J. LOTH. Macon Prolat, 1906.

Professor Loth in this is less impersonal than usual, less Homeric. He indulges in light badinage at the expense of Professors Anwyl and Zimmer, with a side glance at Mr. Wh. Stokes and Professor d'A. de Jubainville occasionally *re* 'Préceltisme,' Celts' lip-courage, the word 'glas' in Erse, and 'Ligurianism,' respectively. Professor Morris Jones is not forgotten (has the 'Appendix' been continued to the world of letters in the Rhŷs-Jones *Welsh People* ?). 'Eullyn' (p. 11) last year exercised the *Western Mail* readers: here it is scientifically explained in the driest of 'dry light.' 'Cromlech' (p. 15) is ill-understood by Bretons; p. 21 has the Rennes altar inscription; 'reinyat' is a dog in Welsh (as *llawr* was, before, *a mare* in Cymric),—the Jaffrennou 'druids' or 'ovates' (pp. 22 and 35, respectively) must look to their laurels.   H. H. J.

NOTE

Notes on the Study of Gaelic :—*continued*—Third Year's Course

The work of the third year will be directed (*a*) to filling in gaps in the departments of grammar and syntax; (*b*) to reading, prose and verse; (*c*) to exercise in continuous composition.

With regard to the first, it may be repeated that grammar and composition are not ends in themselves, but means towards securing correctness of expression. They are subservient to composition, and what is not strictly necessary for that purpose may safely be omitted. This will exclude, except by way of side reference, the philology and history of the language, and the philosophy of its syntax. At this stage we are concerned mainly with the facts; the explanation of them, where it is not absolutely required for intelligent appreciation, belongs to a more advanced stage. It will, however, include a careful comparison of the usage of English and Gaelic, an exercise which should prove a valuable training in observation and judgment.

Special attention should be given to the usage of the Gaelic article, to the treatment of nouns in apposition, and to the construction typified by such a phrase as *piuthar bean a' ghobhainn*, the smith's wife's sister, where *bean a' ghobhainn* is treated as a composite indeclinable noun. These and other points will be found adequately and succinctly treated in Dr. H. C. Gillies's chapter on syntax, which deserves careful study on the part of teachers.

As illustrating the connection which it is important to bring out as between grammar and syntax on the one hand and composition on the other, two points may be dwelt on here. Gaelic has no present or perfect participle, its only participle being the passive in *-te*, *-ta*. The want of this is to some extent supplied by *ag* and *air* with the verbal noun; e.g. *tha e ag iarraidh*, he is asking; *air dha éirigh*, he having risen. But in many cases the English present participle is better turned by means of a clause, *e.g.* he, answering, said to them, *fhreagair e agus thubhairt e riu*. Here the construction with *ag* would be inadmissable. Allowance must also be made, as in Latin, for the ambiguity of the English present participle, which is more often a perfect than a true present; in other words, its time is often prior to the time of the principal verb. The second point worth noting is the treatment in Gaelic of the absolute case. In Gaelic this construction is used in the case of 'attendant circumstance'; *e.g.* I went, my heart almost breaking, *dh' fhalbh mi, mo chridhe an impis sgàineadh.* Very often this absolute construction is introduced by *is*, a thoroughly Gaelic idiom : *mo chridhe òg 's e briste*, my young heart *and it broken.* This Gaelic idiom appears in two classic poems. Burns has :—

> 'How can ye chant, ye little birds,
> *And I* sae weary, fu' o' care.'

And in the 'Burial of Sir John Moore' we have :—

> 'The foe and the stranger will tread o'er his head,
> *And we* far away on the billow.'

But elsewhere it must be rendered by a clause, *e.g.* this said, they separated, *air dhoibh so a radh, sgaoil iad.* The points of contrast between English and Gaelic methods of expression are of course practically endless ; the above will suffice to indicate the lines that may be followed.

(*b*) Reading may be made to serve three purposes. It should serve as an exercise in idiomatic English expression, through translation ; it will serve to enlarge the Gaelic vocabulary, and it will form the most practical means of illustrating grammar and syntax. At this stage it should be as a rule no longer necessary to read aloud and translate the whole of a passage in detail. It should suffice to note and write down new words, and to read, translate, and comment on parts presenting any difficulty or unusual feature. Finally, a paragraph should be written out in English, special care being taken that the English translation is exact, adequate, and idiomatic. On such a plan it will be possible to combine breadth of reading with exactness, while no time is wasted on unnecessary mechanical work.

(*c*) Composition will require much attention. I have already tried to indicate the way in which syntax and grammar may be made to help. Composition should be closely correlated with the reading and largely based on it. This may be done in several ways. In the earlier stages of continuous composition, nothing can be better than a re-translation into Gaelic of the piece that has been done from Gaelic into English, the method practised by Roger Ascham in the case of Latin. Later on the teacher can make up exercises based on the reader, or he can select passages similar in type. Occasionally it will be well to vary this by setting easy pieces quite unconnected with the reading, *e.g.* from J. F. Campbell's translations or Dr. Macleod's *Reminiscences of a Highland Parish.* Teachers who use the *Uirsgeulan Gaidhealach* may utilise the *Butterfly's Wedding*, as translated in the sixth number of the *Celtic Review.* From time to time there may be essays or letters prescribed as exercises in free composition. In order to ensure familiarity with the Gaelic calendar, each exercise should bear the date in Gaelic, including day of week. Bealltainn, Lùnasdainn, Samhain should be known, also Iuchar, Faoilteach, Gearran.

The process of turning English into Gaelic resembles translation into Latin in that it requires a considerable power of dealing with the material, of getting behind the words to the thought. In this respect it is probably a better discipline than translating English into French or German. Like Latin, Gaelic is concrete rather than abstract; but unlike Latin it does not lead itself to long or involved sentences.

Something may be said on the possibility of correlating the Gaelic lesson with other work. In doing the geography of Scotland, for instance, it would be easy to give the Gaelic names of such places as the teacher knows, a process which would at the same time drive home a valuable lesson in Scottish history. Why is Edinburgh known to us as Dun-éideann, Arbroath as Obair-bhrothaig? Gaelic names of foreign countries, too, should be known. In English, again, a useful alternative to the weary paraphrase would be translation from Gaelic prose or poetry into English, unseen. There is no reason why even Latin should not be translated into Gaelic, while for English into Latin Gaelic is often useful in deciding doubtful points. It has been found infallible, for instance, in differentiating the so-called dependent question from the ordinary relative clause, which beginners find so hard to distinguish, *e.g.* I asked him what he had been told, *dh' fhoighnich mi dheth* ciod e *a chaidh radh ris; ex eo quaesivi quid ei dictum esset;* he did what he had been told, *rinn e na chaidh iarraidh air; id fecit quod facere iussus est.* There are many other similar ways in which Gaelic will help. It has been already hinted that boys reading Caesar should be brought to know and understand that those Gauls were their own kinsmen in race, language, and customs, and that their names are still significant to us now.

W. J. WATSON.

QUERY

Sanct Gormoo

In Dr. D. Hay Fleming's *St. Andrews Kirk-Session Register* (p. 227), (The Scottish History Society), occurs this extract:—'The quhilk day (25th October 1564), Schyr Ihon Stephyn delated, and summond be the Superintendentis letteres to this day and session to underly disciplyn, for dayly ministracion of the sacramentis and solemnizacion of mariageis on the Papisticall fasson in the chapell of Sanct Gormoo.' Who was St. Gormoo? In the above extract his name evidently appears in a corrupted form. In the list given in Forbes's *Kalendars of Scottish Saints* there is none resembling it.   J. M. MACKINLAY.

Will 'Northern Celt' kindly send his name and address?

Lightning Source UK Ltd.
Milton Keynes UK
UKHW012342281118
333023UK00012B/1191/P